THE ULTIMATE
AVENGERS

THE ULTIMATE
AVENGERS

Dave Rogers

BOXTREE

in association with

and Channel Four Television Corporation

First published in Great Britain in 1995 by Boxtree Limited

1 2 3 4 5 6 7 8 9 10

Designed by Anita Ruddell and Jervis Tuttell

Printed and bound in Great Britain by Redwood Books for

Boxtree Limited
Broadwall House
21 Broadwall
London   SE1 9PL

A CIP catalogue entry for this book is available from the
British Library.

ISBN 0 7522 1010 6

CONTENTS

ACKNOWLEDGEMENTS

THIS BOOK WOULD NOT have been possible without contributions from the following individuals and organisations. I thank them all for their cordial help during the preparation of this, and the original volumes.

John Herron, Charlie Baker and the guys and gals of the Lumiere Picture Library, Pinewood. Martin Bigham, Tim Hammond, Gareth Watson and Teresa O'Hehir of Lumiere Pictures. Peter Noble for his PR expertise. Ron Saunders of Pathe for being just along the corridor. In France: Huitième Art Editions, Charles Benloulou and his secretary, Florence. David Fakrikian and Alain Carrazé.

Carl Brookes and Colin Bayley for their friendship and loyalty. Friends: Joy and Stephen Curry, Graham P Williams, Dan Recchia, Geoff and Pauline Barlow. The boys and girls of *Kaleidoscope* (in particular Chris Perry for getting to grips with the episode synopses), the *Cult TV* team, for having the presence of mind to include *The Avengers* in their programme, Chris Robinson and Rowan G Thomas.

Special thanks are due to Cyd Child, Bob Fuest, Johnny Hough, Ambren Garland, Jan Rowell and Patrick Downing for sharing their memories, and Marie Cameron for sharing her work.

The following companies for allowing me to use extracts from their publications: The London Express News and Features Service, Mirror Group Newpapers, World International Publishers Ltd, and Harmsworth Publishers Ltd.

This book wouldn't have been possible without the friendship of Paul Madden of Screen First, who allowed me to use transcripts of interviews he conducted for the *Without Walls: The Avengers* TV programme.

Sincere thanks to Honor Blackman, Linda Thorson, Joanna Lumley, Gareth Hunt and the late Patrick Newell, for taking the time to reply to my (original and latter-day) requests for interviews. Patrick Macnee (there is only one) for his continued support and friendship; and, last but not least, to Brian Clemens and Laurie Johnson, for always being there (whatever the time of day).

Though mentioned last, thanks first and foremost to my wife Celia, who never doubted that the task was worthwhile.

This book is respectfully dedicated to the memory of the quiet man of *The Avengers*, Albert Fennell and in particular, Bud Payton (God bless him) without whom *Avengers* fans everywhere would be that much the poorer.

Dave Rogers

FOREWORD

by Patrick Macnee

IT WAS NOT UNTIL I began working on *The Avengers* in the early 1960s, as a man in his forties, that I began to learn about women. Paradoxically, the women from whom I learned so much were platonic friends with whom I still remain on excellent terms. Their names are Honor Blackman, Diana Rigg, Linda Thorson and Joanna Lumley.

As is well-known, the series began as something of a male dominated show with the late Ian Hendry and I swaggering around London in grubby, Gestapo-style, tightly-belted raincoats, the ubiquitous cigarette drooping from our lips. When Ian left, and yes, how I miss that innovative genius, a woman was chosen surprisingly to take his place. The history of Honor's selection and debut is also well-known, but as the series progressed, and without my realising it, I was for what was possibly the first time in my life, gaining a genuine female friend, and not consciously aware of it.

All of *The Avengers* leading ladies became female extensions of Ian Hendry who'd been one of my greatest male friends. Ian, like the girls, had an extraordinary questing intellect, and in his attempts to improve the show and place it in the opposite direction to the average cops and robbers routine, he continually searched for the new and the unusual. Ian was the blueprint for what the show came to be – a national institution. The girls were quite marvellous in that they followed and expanded upon the pattern that he'd laid down. As for me, I have always considered myself to be nothing more than a small shrub in a garden of magnificent blossoms. John Steed/Patrick Macnee was not the master. He was the willing and very happy participant. For those few, happy, golden years, I was just lucky enough to be part of something which in television, at least, was unique.

I made a disgraceful attempt to seduce Honor Blackman, then began to take stock of this beautiful, brisk and frankly, bossy lady who'd rejected my advances outright. The fact that she, as with her successors, was even chosen for the part at all, gives substance to the fact that she was a woman of extraordinary character and originality. Honor was not one of the boys. Her femininity was too innate. But from this friendship, I realised how much easier it is for a man to confide in a woman instead of another man. I could rely on Honor, and it was all so devoid of complication on account of our platonic association. She still tells me what to do, and we enjoy a friendship that has endured until this day.

Honor hung up her black leather boots, and it seemed that whoever took her place, no one could replace her. Even her eventual successor, Diana Rigg, was greeted with some hostility by the die-hard fans. I had never even heard of Diana, but I felt an immediate affinity with her based on the truth. I took her to dinner at the Connaught Hotel in London. I didn't quite know how to react when this highly intelligent woman announced, 'Patrick, I cannot possibly go out with anyone who has an inferior intellect.' I wondered whether I should leave! Instead I was hypnotised into staying to hear more from this extraordinarily perceptive and brilliantly witty woman.

Diana still works and is the mother of a teenage daughter. Honoured with a CBE and more recently made a Dame, she continues to send me deliciously amusing letters, perceptive and hilarious letters, filled with emotion. I was so lucky with Diana. After that first dinner, the two of us had the courage, in a comic way, to be devastatingly honest with each other, something that aided us through so many trials and tribulations. Looking back though, I should have given even more time to Diana, something that I deeply regret. If only I had paid attention to her, when she, the real star of the show, was earning less than the make-up man. Eventually, she left The Avengers because of the rampant male chauvinism, something of which I was still guilty at that time.

Unknowingly, Diana continued to be, through her portrayal of Emma Peel, as magnetic a character as Honor had been with Cathy Gale. Compassionate, desirable and deeply attractive to men, particularly on the American continent. One shake of those beautiful auburn locks demolished and devastated thousands of fans alone, with a few well placed kicks and karate chops. As Emma Peel, Diana gave feminism a more warm and attractive appeal. She has, after thirty years, remained a lovely woman of great distinction.

I've always had a sense of fun and dislike of pomposity, but I learned so much from Diana's abilty to reduce the pretentious to the ridiculous with such ease. She is an actress who can capture all in a single sentence, as she did in the very last line of her Avengers' appearance. When Diana said 'Good-bye' I cried, as I always do when watching that episode. She's a girl who says 'Good-bye' with her heart.

Linda Thorson's sense of humour and emotional outlook was quite different to that of Diana's, but she was nevertheless an extraordinary girl and gave to me a taste of youth during my middle forties. It is often said: 'Oh, to be eighteen and to know what I now know.' Linda all but put me in that position. A warm and sensual Canadian girl of only twenty-one, she was considerably sophisticated for one so young. Originally, I found myself quite surprised when she suggested that we go out dancing, and spluttered innumerable excuses as to the absurdity of a man of my age being seen in discos. Saying nothing, Linda simply twirled her black, feather boa around my neck and led me, like a dog on a feathered leash, off to one of London's night spots.

'Love,' I complained, scampering around the dance floor, 'Aren't I a bit old for this?' Linda's reply was to kick her legs higher, encouraging me to do the same. Linda proved to be immense fun, and did so much to bring out the physical in me, but again, as with my previous Avengers' ladies, I had absolutely no desire to make love to them. Linda was more a woman of raw instinct and sexuality, but through getting to know this young woman, I came to know and understand my teenage daughter.

Joanna Lumley was arguably the most acutely intelligent of all my leading ladies. Possessing the brain of a laser, she was incisive, pointed and witty in comment. She also had a considerable understanding of matters corporate, political, industrial and social. Almost unfair in a woman so stunningly lovely! And yet, she appeared to regard her beauty with such disdain. In her own right she became a personality, wit and writer. She was also remarkable in that she was devoid of brittleness, and being a woman of enormous generosity, she too was always ready to listen to and laugh with me. I readily confess to lusting for Joanna, but true to his tradition, Steed did not molest his ladies! Though by now, I was also conscious of the ever-growing age gap!

INTRODUCTION

ANOTHER BOOK based upon *The Avengers*! Hasn't it all been done before? Indeed, didn't I say in the introduction for *The Complete Avengers* that I had left no stone unturned to deliver what I believed would be accepted as *the* definitive work on the subject. Yes, I did. And I meant every word and believed that the earlier book would be my very last word on the subject. Fate has dealt me a winning hand. I must gamble all on one last throw of the die. *Que Sera Sera*.

No one was more surprised than myself when Boxtree asked for more. They envisaged a revised edition, with such additional information that I could offer. Whilst my contract dictated that I had no option but to run with this, I suggested a compromise: let's consider a 'new' version. Material was no problem. During the years since the publication of the earlier book I had unearthed a wealth of new production documentation and photographic material, had access to much more and, probably the greatest asset of all, had interviewed many of the people who had worked on the programme and were not available to pass comment the last time around. Boxtree agreed.

So what's new? For a start, the overall format – a determined move to give the volume a new identity and allow me to log as much information into the book as is possible (hence the margin notes). The production history of each series has been greatly expanded with comments from the people who were there from day one, when ABC-TV made the decision to mount the programme. The original text has been cross-referenced for 'errors' in both the production detail and the incorrect (quite unintentionally) opinions of the people I've spoken to. No one issued me with untruths, it is simply that memories get confused with the passing of time and one begins to accept that what one has been (mistakenly) saying across the years is the way things happened.

Yes, of course some of the text remains unchanged. I cannot present my case in a different way. The chronology must remain constant, as must the episode synopses which are this time listed in the correct order of production. If, for example, the episode *The Master Minds* is numbered as 80, which it is, this denotes (conclusively) that it was the eightieth episode in the production chronology. Each episode is accorded two sets of dates, relating (where verified) the actual date when the recording or filming was completed, and date of transmission (*The Avengers* transmission dates refer to the Midlands/North ITV regions, *The New Avengers* transmission dates to LWT – these too are listed in their correct order of production). The two-line post-title credit teasers have been revised to match their on-screen identity. Though none of the fifty-two Blackman

The Avengers ladies
always looked their
best – courtesy of
some last-minute
grooming from the
make-up girls.

episodes carried these, Brian Clemens was playing around with
the idea of using them as early as the Second Season Blackman
shows. All twenty-six are included here.

Printed in the last edition were photographs from *The Strange
Case of the Missing Corpse*, the tagged-on colour sequence filmed
to alert the Americans that Steed and Emma would return to
their screens, this time in colour. Courtesy of Laurie Johnson,
the script now accompanies the pictures. There is also a script
for an 'alternative' version of the Rigg/Macnee colour episode
title sequence, censorship guidelines issued by Brian Clemens,
additional 'working' titles (the scriptwriter's original story title as

it appeared on the script before the episode was filmed), some surprises about the fashion side of things (putting an entirely different slant on what myself – and others – have said previously) and a lot more besides.

New photographs are in abundance (those repeated from *The Complete Avengers* being selected by myself as too good to miss).

As I've stated previously, for sheer unabashed style there has never been another programme like *The Avengers*. One hopes that this volume achieves the same pinnacle of success.

Dave Rogers, March 1995

IN CONTENTION

Some friendly observations by Brian Clemens

SEVERAL DAYS after I received confirmation that this book was going ahead, I telephoned Brian to ask his permission to use several items directly attributable to him in this book. Also, provided he could find the time, he might like to peruse my previous book and pick up on any errors in the production chronology (some of which, I explained, had now been clarified after talking to several of his colleagues). Any 'insider' comments might be useful too. His reply arrived that evening. I am delighted to print his comments exactly as he typed them. Here's what he had to say, and please bear in mind that his page numbers refer to *The Complete Avengers*:

'Further to the new *Avengers* book. Apart from the untrue statements attributed to the artistes about how 'they' revised and rewrote the scripts (we never let actors rewrite anything, but we were always alert to the situation where they felt unhappy with the lines – or, perhaps the final set did not complement the action. In that case – on average, about three times a day I would be summoned to the set to rewrite, on the spot. This was time consuming, ate into my writing time on the new episodes, and became something of a joke amongst the crew: "Send for the Guv'nor," was the clarion cry. To, years later, attribute all this hard work to the actors often makes me wonder what I was doing there at all!) ...There are a few other items that come under the 'untrue' banner. They are:

Page 127: *The Forget-Me-Knot* was not an old Rigg episode – it was specifically written by me to encompass the change-over, and was the first creative act on my return to the series, after having been fired. I had to 'block' the episode in thirty-six hours so that the sets could be built *from my story idea* – while I then worked to produce a script within three days. Dennis Spooner did not collaborate on the script.

The dialogue exchange on the stairs was in the script from day one: I have the first draft here to prove it. Although *The Avengers* often looked casual – made up on the spot – spontaneous every word and incident was carefully thought through and sweated over before crew or actors ever saw the first draft of the script.

Page 158: I doubt that Diana Rigg provided the champagne for her final exit. I do know that, at the end of her series, we threw – at some expense – a very unusual party for cast, crew, family and friends. This was planned by myself and Albert – and took place on an

Avengers set, specially set up for a huge party. *Avengers* music played throughout – champagne flowed. Surviving crew members remember it as one of the best 'end of shooting' parties ever – and typically *Avengers*.

Same page: Di's comment that within a week of leaving the show she was not recognized is, of course, complete nonsense; even now, nearly thirty years later, after she has achieved enormous success in the theatre and has been made a Dame, she is still mentioned as being '*The Avengers* girl' in most publicity.

Page 163: Mother's 'strap-hanging' set was not broken up – had we wanted to retain it, we could have done so very easily. It was our idea to move Mother around into a series of bizarre sets/situations – that, after all, was the *Avengers* style.

Page: 164: Not to sully dear Patrick Newell's good name – but Rhonda was not a happy accident – she was planned and written into the scripts from day one. I think I was influenced by an old Arthur Askey comedy series in which a busty young lady named Sabrina became a national star – but never said a word!

The fireman's pole was my idea. I had always wanted to use one in the series.

Brian Clemens, 16 November 1994

Barely two hours later, Brian faxed me several pages of 'inside info'. Too good to miss, I've used the material in the margin notes marked * and in *The New Avengers* notes where designated.

A further two pages flowed from my fax machine the following morning, this time concerning *The New Avengers* vehicles and the trials and tribulations that beset the producers when, determined to remain relentlessly British, they decided to approach British Leyland to supply them with the cars used in the show. This is reprinted (under Brian's name) in *The New Avengers* chronology.

SEASON ONE

Twenty-six monochrome live and videotaped episodes

Starring IAN HENDRY and PATRICK MACNEE   **1961**

PRODUCTION HISTORY

How did it all start, the series that swept the world, made the adventures of that imperturbable cloak-and-dagger man, John Steed, and his succession of glamorous but highly lethal, leather-clad partners, into weekly 'not to be missed' television fare for millions of fans, and established star Patrick Macnee as a household name and face?

The history of *The Avengers* goes back three decades to the day in 1960 when Howard Thomas, then Managing Director of ABC, suggested to Canadian-born Sydney Newman, Head of Drama and originator of Armchair Theatre for the company, that he should balance ABC-TV's drama schedules with a more light-hearted drama series, along the lines of the thrillers that were being popularized by film directors like Alfred Hitchcock and novelists like Ian Fleming in his James Bond books. These were tough and exciting, but also sophisticated and tongue-in-cheek. Audiences were being invited to laugh as well as gasp, and they showed every sign of enjoying the experience.

It was Newman's daring idea to adapt this format into an off-beat formula for television – but to expand it to include the buc-caneering spirit of the day by having the main characters outwit murderers, kidnappers and assassins in an outrageous yet imag-inative fashion.

Newman decided to accomplish this by redeveloping anoth-er ABC series, *Police Surgeon*, a standard cops-and-robbers show, then nearing the end of its run. Although the series had failed to make too much impression on viewers, Newman noted that their letters indicated they liked the brash appeal of its young star, Ian Hendry. If Hendry's talent could be combined with this new formula, Sydney Newman was sure they'd have a success. With this in mind, Newman, together with Police Surgeon's co-producer, Leonard White, came up with the idea of teaming Hendry with another actor: Hendry again playing a doctor, who would set out to avenge the death of his fiancée, shot in a London street by thugs during a drugs investigation. The doc-tor's crusading zeal against these plug-uglies would lead to his being co-opted to assist the British Secret Service by shadowy undercover agent John Steed.

But first they had to find an actor to play Steed. It was then that Newman remembered Patrick Macnee, an actor he'd

The original Avengers, Steed and Dr Keel, take to the London streets in pursuit of villainy.

The title of the programme was one of several under consideration at the time, The Avengers *being selected because of its sinister connotations.*

* *Denotes information supplied by Brian Clemens*

worked with in Canada, and invited him to lunch. There was a role he wanted to discuss. 'Patrick, I would like you to do this show on television,' said Newman, 'a sort of George Sanders type. You'd be perfect for the part. You ought to wear a moustache, though.' Macnee flatly refused to wear a moustache. 'Okay. But will you take the part?' asked Newman, confirming that he had already signed a well-known actor to share the co-star role. 'We're calling it *The Avengers.* I don't know what it means, but it's a hell of a good title!'

Any actor would have been interested, but Macnee was not sure that he wanted to remain an actor. He'd just completed producing a television documentary series based on Sir Winston Churchill's memoirs, *The Valiant Years,* and saw this as the beginning of a new career in television production. On the other hand, the creature described by Newman did sound appealing. Unsure what to do, Macnee demanded a ridiculously high fee and decided to let fate take its course. 'At that time I'd had no success,' Macnee told me. 'I'd done a lot of work but I wasn't successful as an actor. So consequently I was ready for anything. I asked Newman for £250 an episode. He misunderstood me and thought I meant per week.' To his astonishment, the following week Newman rang to accept the terms, and Macnee signed to play John Steed.

The rest is history. Twenty years later Patrick Macnee was still playing the key figure in a series that had become cult viewing all over the world.

On 21 November 1960, Leonard White issued an interdepartmental memo to his *Police Surgeon* production staff, confirming that Hendry and Macnee had been engaged to play the leads. 'A new name is being found for Hendry's character and I will inform you of this as soon as possible. *The Avengers* will now have absolutely nothing to do with *Police Surgeon.* The Hendry character will, however, be a doctor (GP). Macnee will play a

Ian Hendry as Dr David Keel was the mainstay of the first Avengers season.

The three scripts mentioned by Leonard White were Hot Snow, Brought to Book *and* The Square Root of Evil. *In preparation were* Nightmare *(which was heavily rewritten before being accepted),* The Radioactive Man, *and* Kidnapping by Consent *(known later as* Crescent Moon*). Waiting on the sidelines was* The Man on the Trapeze *(transmitted as* The Girl on the Trapeze*) by Dennis Spooner – one of Ian Hendry's favourite episodes.*

character known as John Steed. If you don't know Macnee, I suggest you let me know so that I can arrange for him to come to the studio for a preliminary chat to break the ice and discuss characterization. Scripts for the first three episodes are in hand and a further three are in active preparation.'

Leonard White himself would be investigating the possibility of engaging top composer Johnny Dankworth to arrange the theme music and incidental scores for the new series.

Ian Hendry was enthusiastic about the new series. On the face of it Dr David Keel was rather similar to Dr Brent in *Police Surgeon*, but this time the doctor would have a private practice and would no longer be directly assisting the police. 'Keel is a most attractive character,' Hendry said at the time. 'He combines toughness with compassion, and serves as the conscience of the team. The role will be a kind of extended version of the police surgeon, because Keel will be more directly involved with fighting crime. And as he tangles with villains himself, he'll have more of the action. The accent is on authenticity, with vigorous, fast-moving action and well-researched stories.'

Like Hendry, Macnee was captivated by the role he was asked to play. In the first few stories Steed claimed to be a Secret Service agent, but for whom or for what he was working nobody

Hendry's enthusiasm for the new series was no doubt increased by the fact that he had received a post-Christmas present from his employer. This was a cheque for £428 in settlement for his contractual obligations for the cancelled Police Surgeon series.

Bob Fuest on the First Season episodes: 'Ian Hendry was magic. He was a great actor. Pat Macnee was wonderful, too. Together they quickly developed into a kind of Morcambe and Wise situation because they played off each other so beautifully... . They had this wonderful chemistry.'

Filming live fights had its amusing aspects, as Patrick Macnee reveals. 'You cannot stop the action so if things go wrong, the mistakes are seen. For instance, I'd be having a fight in a hotel bedroom, twenty-five floors up and suddenly the balcony gives way and I'd fall to my death. The very next thing I had to be playing a scene with Ian. So the viewers thought: "Oh, I thought he was dead." The script didn't always explain how Steed escaped. But the viewers didn't mind because the show had a marvellous madness about it.'

knew. 'He is a wolf with the women and revels in trouble,' said Macnee. 'He doesn't think so much about saving hoodlums as just getting them out of the way. By the same token, he doesn't follow the Queensberry rules, and though he works indirectly with the police, he is not too popular with them.' When I spoke to him, Macnee added: 'The character of John Steed was created purely as a name, as an opposite type to the rather steady doctor. At first you never quite knew if he was good or evil. He was a shadowy sort of character who emerged through windows with a pistol and impeccable brolly.' Prompted, he recalled that he did visit the studio before the series went into production. He chatted with the production team and was introduced to Don Leaver, who advised him to read the James Bond books. Macnee did so – and didn't like them. Fleming's attitude to casual violence, Bond's extreme male chauvinism and the author's cynical approach to human life were, in Macnee's words 'extremely unpleasant'. He certainly didn't fancy making Bond a role model. 'Consequently, I took the veneer of Bond for Steed, without using the core. What I left out were the words 'licence to kill'. Steed had no licence to kill. All I really had as Steed was this iron will to bring the enemy to book. I liked to feel that I could go out without a gun and use whatever was to hand as a weapon. The umbrella as a symbol, not of authority or the mighty power of the tragedy of a gun, but to house my gadgets – which again, of course, was pure Bond.'

Interviewed by Paul Madden of *Screen First*, Patrick Macnee said: 'We started in 1960, so we were in at the very early days of Independent Television. I think they cribbed it from New York, where they had *New York Confidential*. Everything was rugged clothes, two men in dirty macs going around looking macho and being buddies. I know we were going before the Bond films, but we were just striking out at different areas. We had a wonderful design and writing team. We didn't realise at the time that we were doing anything special. We just knew that we were doing it the way we wanted to do it.'

Macnee recalls that after they had completed one of the early shows, Sydney Newman came up to him and said that he wasn't impressed. 'Patrick, you're terribly dull. And your clothes. You might be anybody. Can't you brighten the character up a bit? Make him more lively.' Macnee was upset. He was wearing one of his own suits. Faced with the overpowering need to retain his job, he decided to satirize his own class. 'I decided to base him on various people: my father, a wiry old Scot; the foppish, witty Scarlet Pimpernel, daringly snatching prisoners from the guillotine; Ralph Richardson in *Q Planes*; and my commanding officer in the Royal Navy, who was an incredibly brave man. I thought of the Regency days – the most flamboyant, sartorially, for men – and I imagined Steed in waisted jackets and embroidered waistcoats. Steed I was stuck with as a name and it stayed. Underneath he was steel. Outwardly he was charming and vain and representative, I suppose, of the kind of Englishman who is more valued abroad. The point about Steed was that he led a fantasy life – a hero dressed like a junior cabinet minister. An Old Etonian whose most lethal weapon was the hallmark of the English gentleman – a furled umbrella.'

Macnee remembers Ian Hendry with great affection. 'Ian had this extraordinary mind. He would have been extremely good as the admiral of the fleet. He could have been anything, he just happened to be an actor. He would infuse a great deal more into this very ordinary little show than was really there. It all came from him. He conceived it every time we went on. That's how it started. We had this great feeling of alertness and it came mainly from Ian's mind. The show was based entirely on the inherent skills of Sydney Newman, Leonard White, Peter Hammond, Don Leaver and Ian Hendry, but most of all, Ian Hendry, because he wasn't just an actor, he was a writer, an innovator, a wonderful artistic influence – a great and talented man.'

Director Don Leaver remembers Ian Hendry with equal affection. 'Ian was exciting, really, really, exciting. He was just one hundred percent actor. He was inventive. He'd try anything and was always keen to up-end situations. He never wanted to

Patrick Macnee recalls that the original team dressed in dirty macs and ran around looking macho.

do it the obvious, immediate way; he wanted to explore the whole time.' Leaver also recalls that when Macnee was due to visit the studio Ian Hendry took him to one side and told him: 'Listen, kid. We've got this great guy coming over from the States. They tell me that he's marvellous.' Leaver was unimpressed – until, a couple of days after working with Macnee in the studio, he changed his mind. 'He was wonderful to work with, Patrick. He was a joy. Constantly delightful and almost impossible to ruffle.'

Don remembers director Peter Hammond assembling everybody in the studio for a read-through. 'Ian would arrive, pick up the script, look at it, and say: "We're not going to do that, are we!" He would then drop it into the waste-paper basket and start to evolve a new idea during the first week of rehearsal. That was one of Ian Hendry's great contributions to *The Avengers*.'

The series started modestly enough, with a budget of £3,500 (rising to £4,500 mid-way through the first season). The biggest portion of this was allocated to the creation of the studio sets. Set designer, Patrick Downing, told me that the first *Avengers* episodes coincided with the beginnings of Teddington Studios. 'Up until then everything produced by ABC was done from our studios in Didsbury, on the outskirts of Manchester. We had London offices littered all over the place. The Design Department was in Carnaby Street. The first programmes were live, so the first five sets or so were designed together to retain continuity on the set. Many of the early credits for design are approximate, the continuity sets often being drawn up by one designer and looked after by another. I think I designed Dr Keel's surgery for Episode One. Bob Fuest designed the second episode, and later became a director on the series.'

Patrick Downing recalls that he and Bob Fuest were 'freelance' at the time. Patrick tells of an amusing incident when Tim O'Brien, Head of ABC-TV's Design Department, discovered that Patrick was being paid a separate fee for each production. 'Tim called me into his office and told me that I had to come on staff. I was earning more than he was! I was originally down to design the first three episodes, with Mark James as my assistant, but we had problems finishing off a French Resistance series, *Sword in the Web*.'

Bob Fuest well remembers how the design team were always complaining about the financial restrictions placed upon them by ABC. 'They used to count the nails, you know. What happened was this. We would all attend the rehearsals and they would mark out in chalk on the floor where each artiste was supposed to be, where and what was required on the set. Then we would build the set. Well, the sets were actually built by a company called Watts and Corrie, in Manchester. These would then be transported by road to the studio and put together like a Lego set.' Not every set was made in Manchester. 'Some of the sets would be made locally, in the scene dock at Teddington. For example, if they required a set with, say, a set of steps coming down with a handrail, we could do that. But you knew that you had to put this up in two hours, make it sturdy enough to support the artistes, then take it down again for a programme like *This Is Your Life*, the next day. The problem was, of course, that you could not possibly make the steps and handrail as solid as required. So we had to tell everyone "For God's sake, *don't lean on the handrail!*" But in the heat of the action you knew that they were going to lean on the handrail anyway!'

The niggardly budget allowance stretched all the way down to Wardrobe, the team of people who had the difficult task of dressing everyone in the cast – sometimes up to sixteen people in one story. A glance at the programme budget sheet for year one indicates in startling detail the cavalier attitude of the executive minds who ran ABC-TV towards the Wardrobe Department, which was expected to provide creative costumes for the show, week after week.

Approximately half of the total budget was spent on set design and paying actors' wages, the remainder being set aside for all the remaining elements of getting the show on the road. As unlikely as this sounds, Wardrobe had to make do with an average budget of £60 per episode! As we will learn later, things would improve – slightly – during the Blackman era, but most certainly not enough to make life simpler for the girls in Wardrobe, who would continue to find their resourcefulness stretched to the limit.

In keeping with other videotaped programmes of the period ('filmed' inserts to pep up the studio action were well established by this time), the first ever filmed material for *The Avengers* – the sequence in which Peggy, Dr Keel's fiancée, was gunned down outside Vinsons the Jewellers – was completed on 20 December 1960 at a location in Chelsea. Meanwhile the actors due to appear in the first two stories began rehearsals at Teddington Studios.

New productions never run smoothly. *The Avengers* was not exempt from Murphy's Law. Things started to go wrong from the first day of Programme Production No: 3365. On 29 December 1961, during day one of rehearsals for *Hot Snow*, at Teddington's Number Two studios, Floor Manager Patrick Kennedy raised the alarm when he discovered that several of the prop items (a cigarette lighter, a torch and a whisky decanter), listed on the props sheet as being required throughout each stage of the production, had been overlooked. This held up rehearsal time by several hours and left director Don Leaver foaming at the mouth. As far as Patrick Kennedy was concerned, 'getting the show on the road was proving difficult enough without the need to chase around for props that should have been made available in the first place. With a thirteen-week, one-hour series to produce, a little co-operation between the various departments would be beneficial to the production

Designer Patrick Downing tells me that the script for Please Don't Feed the Animals called for a swimming pool. 'It took two weeks to build, in Teddington Number One studio – and I overspent the budget enormously!' To get more money from the producers, Patrick and director Don Leaver staged a mock fight which ended with Leaver throwing Downing (who had borrowed a spare set of clothes from Wardrobe) into the water. They got the extra money.

*The girl whose death started the Avengers avenging (in Episode One) was played by Catherine Woodville, who later became Mrs Patrick Macnee. ***

*Brian Clemens recalls
that, in the first few
Hendry stories,
Macnee used to lurk
in the French win-
dows wearing 'not a
bowler hat, but a
raincoat, sort of
Colombo-ish'.*

as a whole.' Perhaps Leonard White would ensure that this kind of thing never happened again? Things continued to go wrong, with monotonous regularity.

Before joining *The Avengers*, Bob Fuest had been working as a designer on lots of ABC shows, such as *Sunday Break, Oh Boy, Boy Meets Girl*. (In those days a designer would be working on several shows at one time.) Fuest remembers director Peter Hammond turning up to direct the second episode, *Brought To Book*, and virtually turning everything around. Fuest described it. 'Hammond said: ''Forget the locations, let's go ape and do something completely different. We can still keep the thrust of the story, but we'll make it more abstract, more way out and I'll shoot the shit out of it. I'll put everything up on a rostrum. We'll shoot through holes in this, openings in that...'', all the things that are archetypal of Peter. It took about three episodes before Peter was actually holding forth and Leonard White, bless him, hadn't really got the nuts to understand quite what was going on. But, suddenly, this series, which was really a very run-of-the-mill format, kind of took off.

'Peter was absolutely obsessed with shadows and lights and images – and not particularly the best friend of the artistes. He would be perfectly happy to shoot a meaningful scene with a wine bottle very much in the foreground and the principal artiste miles away! He didn't really give a toss and some of the artistes would sometimes get a bit uppity about this. But it really didn't matter because he had this visual flair and somehow he dragged them along. They were seduced by his imagery.'

Keel and Steed were formally introduced to the British public on 7 January 1961 and the partnership would last for twenty-six episodes before Steed was introduced to Mrs Catherine Gale, the first (some say the best?) of his world-famous female partners. That, however, was still some time away and the programmes' format would undergo several changes of direction before *The Avengers*' format as we know it was firmly established.

Barely six weeks into production, Leonard White, dissatisfied with the way the series was heading, drew up the following production directive.

THE AVENGERS:

At this time it is well that we remind ourselves of certain fundamentals concerning the series:

1) Keel and Steed are essentially undercover. They are not private or public detectives and any story which follows the usual 'private eye' pattern is not right for us.

They do not work with the police and usually cannot call upon more police aid than would normally be available to ordinary citizens.

2) Keel, being a doctor, is the amateur. This does not mean that

he is less good at the 'job' but simply txhat his motives for concerning himself with a mission are quite different from Steed's. Without being at all goody-goody he will, usually, be fired by a sense of public service, kindled by his humanitarian instincts. He is an excellent doctor and this proficiency is a specific help in the joint missions.

He is a mature man. Any tendency to make him like a 'little boy' tagging along behind Steed, asking all the questions, and making silly mistakes must be eradicated.

Women find him attractive. Usually, however, he will keep them at a distance. His sincerity does not allow him to flirt and he still has deep feelings for the fiancée he lost.

He is tough, but not hard. Can be very gentle: loves children. Likes sport (would be a keen rugby player if he had the time). Product of a redbrick university. A wry sense of humour. Quite serious normally, but when he smiles – it's wonderful!

Being a good doctor he is well trained to think out a problem and resolve it by positive action. His practice (Chelsea-Victoria district) includes an interesting area comprising city, river, village communities of all social classes.

He has a partner in Dr Tredding – a much older man – whom we rarely see, but who allows Keel to be absent from time to time on his missions (Tredding never knows the nature of Keel's escapades, however).

Another, more active link with the surgery and Keel's professional background is:

3) Carol. As his Nurse/Receptionist, she must be used to keep alive the duality of Keel's life. She does not know of his undercover work – but she may have her suspicions.

Her integrity and great admiration (it might be more) for the doctor prevent her from stepping outside the bounds of her professional status. She is not beyond looking after him in the most innocent (but telling) ways, however. She will mother him but never allow it to be come unpleasant or possessive.

She is attractive, very efficient, with great commonsense. She is not part of the undercover team, but can be used obliquely to assist either Keel or Steed or both where justifiable. Essentially this means that whatever she does will

Ingrid Hafner (pictured centre) played Carole Wilson, Keel's receptionist/nurse. Not part of the undercover team, she did assist The Avengers on their missions.

In *The Springers*, Steed asks Keel to impersonate a convict who is going to escape from prison.

be quite attractive or natural, irrespective of any undercover uses which may be made of her participation.

4) Steed is the professional undercover man. He is suave, debonair, a man-about-town. A sophisticate but not lacking in virility. His sports are probably horse-racing, dog-racing, beauty competitions, etc.

He has an eye for the beautiful and unusual – be it objets d'art or women. He will never be serious with one woman, however. He is very experienced.

He is an expert at his job (but not perfect). He handles the tools of his trade with great proficiency. Probably, gun-handling, ju-jitsu and Turkish baths are part of the ritual for him.

His flat is an indication of his special tastes. Some might think these slightly decadent – but they would be wrong. He has owned a Great Dane (now dead) – but will have another unusual hound. He has a manservant. He has a Rolls-Royce. He dresses superbly – but not altogether conventionally. His motives are not necessarily as moral as Keel's. To him the success of the mission is the only important thing and therefore his means may sometimes be questionable. The success of the mission, however, is a wrong put right, and therefore sometimes necessitates these means being used to this end.

He is very highly paid for his work. It is very, very dangerous. He has no organizational ties whatsoever. He has no one working for him except such as may be paid or persuaded (by him) to do a specific job. He certainly has no plain-clothes types waiting to assist him at the right moment.

His only organizational contact is to One-Ten who feeds him assignments and information. Once on assignment, however, Steed (or Keel) are essentially relied upon to work out their own salvation.

Steed has a quick wit. A very persuasive tongue. Lots of old-world charm. He is not a lounge lizard; he is active.

5) One-Ten is our only link with apparent officialdom. His establishment is necessarily very obscure. He contracts the undercover work, but he will always keep the arrangements on a personal basis. He knows of Keel's activity but doesn't recognise him as anything more than an extension of Steed's work. Very useful of course, but not a professional.

One-Ten is very intelligent. He might be an Oxford don who has been assigned to highly specialized work in big crime detection where normal police activity has to be augmented.

He is usually on a phone – but the phone always seems to be in interesting places.

AVENGERS' INGREDIENTS should always be:

a) Glamour: Beautiful, attractive, unusual women.

b) Unusual and exciting locales: Good visual value and enjoyment to the audience.

c) An important mission: Much more than a usual police story and one that provides the correct motives for Keel's inclusion in the mission. The problem should be a big one (Steed's work) and have relation to individual humans (Keel's interest).

d) Story Balance:
  1. A predominance of attractive, recognisably human characters
  2. Something to intrigue the intelligence, however lightly
  3. Some wit, humour and grace in the dialogue
  4. A constant awareness of the viewers' capacity for friendly affection for our characters
  5. In such a context – violence sinks into place.

e) Action: As much as is compatible with live studio production – plus a little more?

NOTE

The Avengers is a series, not a serial. Therefore nothing should be included in the scripting, performance or direction, in the nature of running gags (character-building or visual treatment) which are not perfectly acceptable to an audience which has not seen other episodes.

A few days later, White added the following comments:

1) Because we are new and will face fierce competition from other productions, our episodes must get better and not slip away as we become established.

2) The series' title must be remembered and each episode must be firmly motivated by this.

3) It appears that the Keel stories seem to be the most difficult to write. Without unbalancing our format, we should therefore try to find opportunities for Keel to get closer to the character than is perhaps necessary in Steed's case.

4) Generally a Keel story should not be one that could be transferred to a Steed story and vice versa.

5) The locale of each episode should be exotic, exciting and unusual. Perhaps a good story could be found in the horse-racing world to take advantage of Macnee's background – and also one in which we could use Hendry's ability as a stunt motorcyclist.

***

Neither idea was used, but it is interesting to reflect if the second suggestion, combined with Honor Blackman's prowess at handling a two-wheeled machine, influenced the decision to make Cathy Gale a dab hand with a high-powered motorcycle.

The series progressed through six more episodes before Leonard White was compelled to put pen to paper again, this time to reply to a memo from head office that the series was in danger of sliding down the slippery slope.

***

The initial script for Hot Snow differs from that of the script as transmitted. In the draft version, the episode opens with the 'Intruder' actually handing the drugs package to Peggy. And in the final sequence Steed watches from the shadows as Inspector Wilson warns 'Dent' to leave police work to the authorities.

1) Far too much drink (in the form of hard liquor) is being consumed in these episodes and especially by our Dr Keel. At first, when used with subtlety, it had some value, but now it has become an excuse to pad and is giving an unsympathetic and nauseating slant to the characters. We should all use our ingenuity to overcome this immediately.

2) At present an under-run on transmission is a great embarrassment to our presentation. Will you therefore make make certain that timings are accurate at dry rehearsal. Also, in general, as we badly need all the pace we can get out of these episodes, I suggest all scripts (and rehearsals) are better conceived as over length, rather than under. In our series, speed will generally help us, but a slow, short episode will kill us.

3) It is inevitable at the present that some rewriting – particularly to suit the respective characters of the lead – will be done at rehearsal. However, I must remind you that the system already established, of a master script being kept in the script department, must be continued. All alterations should be transferred daily from rehearsal scripts to the master script.

4 Whilst I realise the value of red herrings and side issues in our stories, I cannot over-emphasize the importance of clarity in our presentations. Will you please pay particular attention to the clarity of the storyline.

***

On 19 May, five months into the series, Leonard White gave the green light for composer Johnny Dankworth to go back into the studio to record a revised version of *The Avengers*' theme. In addition to this, White was looking for a new set of longer music stingers (the short bridges of music played on the soundtrack to heighten the suspense during the action sequences), some macabre music and something restrained, but with an air of menace in it. White confirmed that this was necessary because ABC were considering extending the show to thirty-nine episodes.

With a few other minor changes (Ingrid Hafner's role was beefed-up to give Carol a bigger slice of the action), the series progressed comfortably to nationwide acclaim. It was the beginning of *The Avengers*' format which was destined to make its stars famous – a wacky but sophisticated, comedy thriller, with a sideline in topsy-turvy, but thoroughly entertaining, madcap antics.

It is interesting to note that though Patrick Macnee's portrayal of the unconventional Steed gathered momentum and swiftly became the viewers' firm favourite – with Hendry's character placed a comfortable second – the latter continued to receive star billing above the title credits, while Macnee's name was credited second.

On 10 February 1961, Leonard White reminded his production staff those ITV regions that hadn't taken the show from day one would broadcast Episodes One and Two beginning 18 March. The rest of the regions would continue with Episodes Ten and Eleven. On 7 March White issued a memo requesting that the timings of Episodes Ten and Eleven conform with those of Episodes One and Two to ensure that network programming coincided smoothly. From Episode Twelve they would revert to a timing of 53.30 as a uniform length for the show.

SEASON ONE CHRONOLOGY

Episode	Title
1	Hot Snow
2	Brought To Book
3	Square Root of Evil
4	Nightmare
5	Crescent Moon (aka Kidnapping by Consent)
6	Girl on the Trapeze (aka The Man on the Trapeze)
7	Diamond Cut Diamond
8	The Radioactive Man
9	Ashes of Roses
10	Hunt the Man Down
11	Please Don't Feed the Animals
12	Dance with Death
13	One for the Mortuary
14	The Springers
15	The Frighteners
16	The Yellow Needle (aka Plague)
17	Death on the Slipway
18	Double Danger (aka Confession From a Dead Man)
19	Toy Trap
20	Tunnel of Fear
21	The Far-Distant Dead
22	Kill the King
23	Dead of Winter (aka The Case of the Happy Camper)
24	The Deadly Air
25	A Change of Bait
26	Dragonsfield (aka The Un-Dead)

Series produced by: Leonard White

The Avengers Theme composed and played by: Johnny Dankworth

Story Editors: Patrick Brawn (Episodes One to Twenty-One)
John Bryce (All episodes)
Reed de Rouen (Episodes Twenty-Two to Twenty-Six)

SEASON ONE EPISODES

1 HOT SNOW *

by Ray Rigby
based on a story by Patrick Brawn

Dr Tredding (Philip Stone) Peggy (Catherine Woodville) Dr David Keel (Ian Hendry) Spicer (Godfrey Quigley) Charlie (Murray Melvin) Johnson (Charles Wade) Det-Supt Wilson (Alister Williamson) Stella (Moira Redmond) Sgt Rogers (Astor Sklair) John Steed (Patrick Macnee) Mrs Simpson (June Monkhouse) Ronnie Vance (Robert James)

Designed by Alpho O'Reilly
Directed by Don Leaver

Dr Keel and Peggy have just announced their engagement, but their plans for the future come to a savage end when Peggy is gunned down. Determined to avenge her death, Keel finds an ally in John Steed who helps him to track down her killers. They are drug peddlers who mistakenly delivered a package to Peggy, instead of to the receptionist of another doctor. However, Vance, the ring leader, eludes capture...

Recorded; 30 December 1960   TX: 7 January 1961

2 BROUGHT TO BOOK *

by Brian Clemens

Prentice (Lionel Burns) Lale (Redmond Bailey) Pretty Boy (Clifford Elkin) Bart (Neil McCarthy) Nick Mason (Charles Morgan) Spicer (Godfrey Quigley) Dr David Keel (Ian Hendry) Dr Tredding (Philip Stone) Carol Wilson (Ingrid Hafner) Lila (Joyce Wong Chong) John Steed (Patrick Macnee) Ronnie Vance (Robert James) Det-Supt Wilson (Alister Williamson) Det-Sgt (Michael Collins) Jackie (Carol White)

Designed by Robert Fuest
Directed by Peter Hammond

Dr Keel and Steed seek again to bring Vance into custody. With the help of the police, Keel infiltrates Vance's gang, while Steed manipulates the leader of a rival gang. Both gangs realise too late that they have been deceived, and Keel extracts a confession which, overheard by the police, leads to the villains' arrest. Having accomplished his mission of avenging Peggy's death, Steed enlists Keel's help in his fight against crime.

Recorded: 12 January 1961   TX: 14 January 1961

Hot Snow *and* Kill the King: *Moira Redmond was one of the actresses shortlisted for the role of Emma Peel.*

In the draft script for Episode One, Hot Snow *(22 November 1960), Hendry's character was called David Dent. The name was changed during week one of rehearsals, as was the name of Keel's senior partner in the practice; Dr Reeding becoming Dr Tredding.*

3 SQUARE ROOT OF EVIL

by Richard Harris

John Steed (Patrick Macnee) Five (Heron Cavic) Secretary (Cynthia Bizeray) Bloom (Michael Robbins) Hooper (George Murcell) Warren (Vic Wise) The Cardinal (Alex Scott) Lisa (Delphi Lawrence) Carol Wilson (Ingrid Hafner) Dr David Keel (Ian Hendry)

Designed by Patrick Downing
Directed by Don Leaver

Steed impersonates a counterfeiter, Riordan, gaining him entrance to a crime syndicate that prints forged banknotes. Having uncovered their plans, he finds his every move being watched by The Cardinal, the second-in-command. Only the pretence of an injury eventually allows Steed to visit Dr Keel's surgery and pass on his information. On the pretext of attending to his patient, Keel arrives at the gang's headquarters in time to intervene when the Cardinal attacks Steed with a knife. Steed telephones the police and The Cardinal and his superiors, Bloom and Hooper are arrested.

Transmitted Live   **TX: 21 January 1961**

4 NIGHTMARE

by Terence Feely

Williams (Gordon Boyd) Dr David Keel (Ian Hendry) Carol Wilson (Ingrid Hafner) Faith Braintree (Helen Lindsay) Commander Reece (Michael Logan) John Steed (Patrick Macnee) Dr Brown (Robert Bruce) Dr Jones (Redmond Bailey) Dr Miller (Robert Sansom)

Designed by Robert Fuest
Directed by Peter Hammond

When Professor Braintree disappears, his wife calls on Dr Keel for advice. During the consultation there is an attempt on Keel's life – somebody has mistaken him for the Professor. Steed's plan to use Keel as bait brings the doctor close to death for a second time, threatened by the scalpel of a shady medico. Carol is caught and tied up by the would-be assassin before she can contact Steed. Steed finds out what has happened in time to save Keel's life and release Carol. The Professor, unaware of all the fuss, returns home. He's been suffering from temporary amnesia.

Transmitted Live   **TX: 28 January 1961**

5 CRESCENT MOON

by Geoffrey Bellman and John Whitney

Senora Mendoza (Patience Collier) John Steed (Patrick Macnee) Bartello (Harold Kasket) Carmelite Mendoza (Bandana Das Gupta) Luis Alvarez (Nicholas Amer) Paul (Eric Thompson) Fernandez (Jack Rodney) Vasco (Roger Delgado) PC Carlos (George Roderick) Dr David Keel (Ian Hendry)

Designed by Alpho O'Reilly
Directed by John Knight

Suspicious that his wife and his family retainer are scheming to seize his money, General Mendoza fakes his own death and arranges for his daughter to be kidnapped and taken to safety. Believing that the girl has fallen into enemy hands, Steed rescues her from the clutches of Senor Paul, who admits to the kidnapping but says that he was working for General Mendoza and only wanted to take her to her father. Back in London, Keel tells Steed that he has been attending on the ailing General Mendoza, who confirms Paul's story.

Transmitted Live   **TX: 4 February 1961**

6 GIRL ON THE TRAPEZE

by Dennis Spooner

Vera (Delena Kidd) Anna Danilov (Nadja Regin) Dr David Keel (Ian Hendry) Carol Wilson (Ingrid Hafner) Policeman (Ian Gardiner) Zibbo (Kenneth J.Warren) Supt Lewis (Howard Goorney) Stefan (Edwin Richfield)

Designed by Paul Bernard
Directed by Don Leaver

A young girl dragged drowning from the Thames murmurs the name Danilov. This clue sets Dr Keel and Carol on the trail to the Radeck State Circus. There he discovers a girl swathed in bandages held captive by Zibbo the clown. She is Anna Danilov, who would replace the drowning girl (a trapeze artiste) when the circus returns to Radeck. Once in her home country, Anna's father will be forced to return after his recent defection. Taken prisoner by Zibbo, Keel and Carol eventually make good their escape. Police surround the circus, Zibbo and his motley crew are taken into custody and Anna is led to safety.

Transmitted Live   **TX: 11 February 1961**

On 21 February, White advised his staff that 'a new surgery is being designed for Dr Keel'. It is impossible to verify this – the episodes no longer exist – but I'm told that neither Keel or Steed were ever seen in permanent living quarters throughout the entire series (the cost of erecting a freestanding set was thought to be prohibitive). Nor was there ever any mention of each character's private life!

Season One had The Avengers outwitting murderers, kidnappers and assassins in tongue-in-cheek style.

7 DIAMOND CUT DIAMOND

by Max Marquis

John Steed (Patrick Macnee) One-Ten (Douglas Muir) Fiona Charles (Sandra Dorne) Dr Collard (Hamlyn Benson) Carol Wilson (Ingrid Hafner) Dr David Keel (Ian Hendry) Stella Creighton (Joy Webster)

Designed by Robert Fuest
Directed by Peter Hammond

Steed poses as an airline steward, in the hope that he will be invited to join a diamond-smuggling gang. After a wild party he awakes to find himself accused of a hit-and-run death. Keel confirms Steed's innocence, but Steed plays along with the gang and allows himself to be blackmailed into smuggling a package to New York. Returning home, he finds the gang leader waiting for him, gun at the ready. Steed's usefulness is over: the gang are clever enough to use a courier only once. Like others before him, Steed is to 'take his own life'. At the eleventh hour the gang leader's plans are foiled by the arrival of Dr Keel.

Transmitted Live   TX: 18 February 1961

8 THE RADIOACTIVE MAN

by Fred Edge

Marko Ogrin (George Pravda) Mary Somers(Christine Pollen) Carol Wilson (Ingrid Hafner) Dr David Keel (Ian Hendry) John Steed (Patrick Macnee) Dr Graham (Gerald Sim)

Designed by Alpho O'Reilly
Directed by Robert Tronson

Marko, an illegal immigrant, believes that if the police find him they will deport him. In reality, the police are searching for him urgently, because he is carrying a radioactive isotope capable of killing anyone in close proximity. With help from Marko's girlfriend Mary, Keel, using a Geiger counter, traces Marko and discovers the crook who smuggles immigrants out of the country for money. With the arrival of Keel, Mary and Dr Graham, Marko hands over the deadly isotope. Relieved, he is then taken to hospital for treatment, after which Marko and his cohorts are arrested and charged by the police.

Transmitted Live   TX: 25 February 1961

9 ASHES OF ROSES

by Peter Ling and Sheilagh Ward

John Steed (Patrick Macnee) Olive Beronne (Olga Lowe) Jacques Beronne (Mark Eden) Johnny Mendelssohn (Peter Zander) Dr David Keel (Ian Hendry) Carol Wilson (Ingrid Hafner) Denise (Hedi Erich)

Designed by Patrick Downing
Directed by Don Leaver

Mendelssohn, a known arsonist, has been hired by the Beronnes to burn down their hairdressing salon for the insurance. Using Carol to gather evidence, Steed discovers that the hairdressers will stop at nothing (including several murders) to achieve their aim. Steed intercepts the Beronnes as they are about to leave the country and Jacques confesses that the salon is about to go up in flames. Meanwhile, Carol, in the company of Denise, one of the hairdresser's assistants, has reached the same conclusion and they have driven to the salon to pour cold water on Mendelssohn's fire-raising. The women are saved from being burned alive by the intervention of Steed, who knocks the arsonist cold as he is about to light the fuse on an incendiary device.

Transmitted Live   TX: 4 March 1961

10 HUNT THE MAN DOWN *

by Richard Harris

John Steed (Patrick Macnee) Paul Stacey (Maurice Good) Dr David Keel (Ian Hendry) Carol Wilson (Ingrid Hafner) Stella Preston (Melissa Stribling) Nurse Wyatt (Susan Castle) Frank Preston (unknown)

Designed by Robet Fuest
Directed by Peter Hammond

Frank Preston leaves jail to collect his stashed robbery money, but thugs are waiting to beat him up to discover the location of the loot. Steed intervenes and takes Preston to Keel. The gang now believe that Keel knows the location and they kidnap Carol to make the doctor spill the beans. Realising that the thugs are in league with Stella, his wife, Preston forces Keel to attend to his injuries and then enlists his help to find the money. However, before Preston can enjoy it or the thugs can seize it, Steed arrives with the police to arrest them all.

Recorded: 12 March 1961   TX: 18 March 1961

11 PLEASE DON'T FEED THE ANIMALS *

by Dennis Spooner

John Steed (Patrick Macnee) Felgate (Tenniel Evans) Carol Wilson (Ingrid Hafner) Dr David Keel (Ian Hendry) Christine (Carole Boyer) Kollakis (Harry Ross) Renton-Stephens (Alastair Hunter) Yvonne (Catherine Ellison) Sarah (Genevieve Lyons) Barman (Mark Baker)

Designed by Patrick Downing
Directed by Dennis Vance

Compromised government officials are leaking secets to appease a sinister blackmailer. Felgate, a junior civil servant, is being watched by Steed, who has been planted in the same office. Steed and Keel tag along when Felgate delivers a package to a private zoo. Though Steed keeps a close watch on the package, it mysteriously disappears from the reptile pit. Someone is making a monkey out of Steed, who (intentionally) becomes the next blackmail victim. This time Keel follows the package and sees a small monkey retrieve the information. The trail leads to Renton-Stephens, owner of the zoo, whose ambitions are thwarted by Steed and the police.

Recorded: 30 March 1961   TX: 1 April 1961

12 DANCE WITH DEATH *

by Peter Ling and Sheilagh Ward

Dr David Keel (Ian Hendry) Carol Wilson (Ingrid Hafner) Elaine Bateman (Caroline Blakiston) Trevor Price (Dudley Sutton) Beth Wilkinson (Angela Douglas) Major Caswell (Ewan Roberts) Valerie Marne (Pauline Shepherd) Mrs Marne (Diana King) Philip Anthony (Geoffrey Palmer) John Steed (Patrick Macnee) Porter (Norman Chappell)

Designed by James Goddard
Directed by Don Leaver

While trying to help one of his patients, Elaine Bateman, Dr Keel is framed for her murder. Steed investigates and suspicion falls on Anthony, a pianist at Elaine's dancing school – a man who was tried, but acquitted of killing his wife. He is still suspected of other murders. Believing that Anthony is guilty, Steed tells Keel that the man was suspected of electrocuting his victims in the bath. Yet the Avengers could be too late, since Anthony has eloped with Valerie Marne and her mother's diamonds. With the bath taps already running, Steed and Keel rescue Valerie from certain death.

Recorded: 13 April 1961   TX: 15 April 1961

13 ONE FOR THE MORTUARY *

by Brian Clemens

Benson (Peter Madden) John Steed (Patrick Macnee) Dr David Keel (Ian Hendry) Carol Wilson (Ingrid Hafner) Scott (Ronald Wilson) Pallaine (Dennis Edwards) Yvette Declair (Malou Pantera) Dubois (Frank Gatliff) Maid (Irene Bradshaw) Bernard Bourg (Toke Townley)

Designed by Robert Fuest
Directed by Peter Hammond

Steed has concealed a new medical formula in microdots in an invitation card that Keel will carry unwittingly to Geneva. Keel hands the card to a young lady he meets and a pursuit ensues to retrieve the card and its valuable contents. Having relocated the girl, Steed finds that his 'safe' contact arrives with two heavies and has plans to sell the formula to the highest bidder. The villains' plans are foiled by the arrival of the police. Steed takes possession of the formula until a new, safe, contact can be made.

Recorded: 26 April 1961   TX: 29 April 1961

Dance With Death, Toy Trap, Kill the King and Dead of Winter: *Actresses Angela Douglas, Sally Smith, Carole Shelley and Zorenah Osborne attended the auditions for the role of Venus Smith.*

While recording The Yellow Needle *one of the leading guest stars dried up. So they started again. The actor forgot his lines. One more time, and the same result, with the added complication that when the episode was transmitted it was obvious to the viewers (and producer Leonard White) that the false starts had thrown the other performers off their stride. White was quick to hammer home the message that 'in the future directors must organise their time so that there will be not less than one non-stop run-through and a dress rehearsal.'*

A typical production schedule on the Hendry series (and, later, the Blackman series), Season One and Two:

Monday/Tuesda/ Wednesday:
Script rehearsal

Thursday
Camera Rehearsal
10.30am-12.30pm
1.30pm -6pm
7pm-9pm
One hour
Lunch/Supper breaks

Friday
Camera Rehearsal
10am-12.30pm
1.30pm-3.15pm
Line-Up, Scan and Make-Up
3.15pm-4pm
Dress Rehearsal
4pm-5.30pm
Line-Up
5.30pm-6pm
Ampex Recording
6pm-7pm
Lunch/Supper breaks in rotation

All Hendry/ Blackman episodes were produced at Teddington Number Two Studio. Whereas all fifty-two Blackman shows were videotaped, only nineteen Hendry episodes were given this treatment, seven being transmitted live from the studio (indicated by * in the episode synopses).

14 THE SPRINGERS *

by John Whitney and Geoffrey Bellman

John Steed (Patrick Macnee) Dr David Keel (Ian Hendry) One-Ten (Douglas Muir) Pheeney (David Webb) Straker (Charles Farrell) Haslam (Brian Murphy) Mr Groves (Arthur Howard) Caroline Evans (Margo Andrew) Neame (Donald Morley)

Designed by Alpho O'Reilly
Directed by Don Leaver

If you have the money, escape from prison is easy. Steed wants to know how, so he sends Dr Keel inside. Keel's information leads Steed and a young female agent to a finishing-school, but Steed's cover is blown and he is captured. His partner informs One-Ten, who is loathe to mount a rescue attempt in case this jeopardizes the mission. Keel arrives after a successful escape, but he too is exposed as an impostor. Investigating the escape route nearly spells the end for the Avengers, but Steed's quick thinking leads to them outwitting gang-leader Neame and his associates.

Recorded: 11 May 1961   TX: 13 May 1961

15 THE FRIGHTENERS *

by Berkeley Mather

Moxon (Philip Locke) Deacon (Willoughby Goddard) John Steed (Patrick Macnee) Carol Wilson (Ingrid Hafner) Dr David Keel (Ian Hendry) Jeremy de Willoughby (Philip Gilbert) Nigel (David Andrews) Sir Thomas Weller (Stratford Johns) Marilin Weller (Dawn Beret) Miss Doris Courtenay/Mrs Briggs (Doris Hare) Nature Boy (Godfrey James) Beppi (Neil Wilson) Butler (Eric Elliot) Secretary (Ann Taylor) Waiter (Ralph Tovey) Inspector Foster (Ben Simons) with Eleanor Darling, Benny Nightingale, Victor Charrington, Frank Peters, Charles Wood

Designed by Robert Fuest
Directed by Peter Hammond

While trying to put the frighteners on Jeremy de Willoughby, it is the bad guys who get their noses bloodied when Steed and Dr Keel intervene and ensure that Deacon – the gang leader – has arranged his final thuggery. It seems that Weller has failed to prevent de Willoughby from marrying his rich daughter Marilin, but a neat piece of deception arranged by Steed ensures that de Willoughby is exposed as a 'professional marrier'. Another case is closed by the Avengers.

Recorded: 25 May 1961   TX: 27 May1961

16 THE YELLOW NEEDLE *

by Patrick Campbell

Sir Wilberforce Lungi (Andre Dakar) Dr David Keel (Ian Hendry) Carol Wilson (Ingrid Hafner) Inspector Anthony (Eric Dodson) Jacquetta Brown (Margaret Whiting) John Steed (Patrick Macnee) Chief Bai Shebro (Bari Johnson) Ali (Wolfe Morris)

Designed by Alpho O'Reilly
Directed by Don Leaver

Sir Wilberforce Lungi is in London to negotiate independence for his country, Tenebra, when an attempt is made on his life. His old friend Dr Keel agrees to help unmask the culprit and suspicion falls upon Lungi's secretary Jacquetta Brown. Steed, meanwhile, investigates the opposition leader in Tenebra, Chief Bai Shebro. Befriended by Ali, a servant, and Judith, one of Shebro's wives, Steed finds that all clues lead back to Jacquetta Brown. In London, the woman has substituted a dose of yellow fever bacterium for Lungi's insulin. She is prevented from carrying out her plan by Keel, who in turn is drugged by Brown. Steed's arrival the following morning prevents the woman from administering a second dose of the drug to Keel.

Recorded: 8 June 1961   TX: 10 June 1961

17 DEATH ON THE SLIPWAY *

by James Mitchell

Kolchek (Peter Arne) Dr David Keel (Ian Hendry) John Steed (Patrick Macnee) Sir William Bonner (Frank Thornton) Liz Wells (Nyree Dawn Porter) Sam Pearson (Paul Dawkins) Fleming (Sean Sullivan) Geordie Wilson (Redmond Bailey) Jack (Robert G.Bahey) Inspector Georgeson (Barry Keegan) PC Butterworth (Tom Adams) One-Ten (Douglas Muir) Pardoe (Gary Watson) PC Geary (Patrick Conner) Sergeant Brodie (Hamilton Dyce) Chandler (Billy Milton)

Designed by Robert Fuest
Directed by Peter Hammond

Steed meets an old enemy – Kolchek – when he investigates a murder in a dockyard. The spy wants the plans for a new nuclear submarine. Knowing that Steed will attempt to prevent him, Kolchek blackmails Fleming, the foreman at the dockyard, into planting a time-bomb in his briefcase and leaving it on board the submarine. Steed locates the bomb, throws it into the water to explode harmlessly and rounds up the villains.

Recorded: 22 June 1961   TX: 24 June 1961

Don Leaver believes that Sydney Newman's talent was the greatest contributor to the success of The Avengers. *'He bestrode the industry like a Colossus. I think it was a question of the right man at the right time. He was just a fantastic influence, his hands-on approach was tremendous.'*

Brian Clemens: 'Overall, the series is Hitchcockian. Alfred Hitchcock knew that it's always better to have a fiendish, amiable looking dentist than a psychopathic hood. The dentist would always be more interesting.'

Death on the Slipway: *Actress Nyree Dawn Porter, was Sydney Newman's choice for Cathy Gale.*

18 DOUBLE DANGER *

by Gerald Verner

Mark Crawford (Charles Hodgson) Harry Dew (Robert Mill) Al Brady (Peter Reynolds) Bert Mills (Ronald Pember) Dr David Keel (Ian Hendry) Carol Wilson (Ingrid Hafner) Lola Carrington (Vanda Hudson) John Steed (Patrick Macnee) Bruton (Kevin Brennan) Bartholomew (Gordon Phillott)

Designed by James Goddard
Directed by Roger Jenkins

Two thieves steal valuable diamonds, but one is shot as he escapes. Steed has no clues, until Carol deciphers a call for help from Dr Keel, who is being forced to treat the wounded man. The jewel thief dies, but gives Keel 'Bartholomew's Plot' as a clue to the location of the hidden diamonds. Keel is now forced to reveal what he knows to the dead man's colleagues. If he doesn't, they will kill Carol. But Steed already has the diamonds by the time the crooks arrive at Bartholomew's cottage. Steed leaves the police to wrap up the case as he takes his fellow Avengers to dinner.

Recorded: 6 July 1961   TX: 8 July 1961

19 TOY TRAP *

by Bill Strutton

John Steed (Patrick Macnee) Dr David Keel (Ian Hendry) Mary Muton (Hazel Graeme) Henry Burge (Tony Van Bridge) Alice (Nina Marriott) Bunty Seton (Sally Smith) Mrs McCabe (Ann Tirard) Freddie (Brandon Brady) Johnnie (Brian Jackson) Photographer (Lionel Burns) Lennie Taylor (Tex Fuller) Ann (Mitzi Rogers)

Designed by Douglas James
Directed by Don Leaver

Dr Keel is puzzled by the disappearance of girls who work at a large department store. Someone is pressurizing the young ladies into prostitution. Bunty, Keel's friend, agrees to help trap the culprit, so that her friend May can come out of hiding. Steed agrees to help. He visits the department store and learns from the supervisor, Hearn, that one of the store's assistants, Lennie, has a criminal record. It is Lennie who has been hiding May from the boss of the call-girl organization. Using Bunty as bait, Steed exposes the ring leader – Mrs McCabe, the girls' landlady. Steed wastes no time in closing down the house of ill repute.

Recorded: 20 July 1961   TX: 22 July 1961

20 TUNNEL OF FEAR *

by John Kruse

Maxie Lardner (Stanley Platts) Jack Wickram (John Salew) Dr David Keel (Ian Hendry) Carol Wilson (Ingrid Hafner) Harry Black (Murray Mayne) John Steed (Patrick Macnee) One-Ten (Douglas Muir) Mrs Black (Doris Rogers) Madame Zenobia (Nancy Roberts) Claire (Miranda Connell) Billy (Douglas Rye) Sergeant (Morris Perry)

Designed by James Goddard
Directed by Guy Verney

Leaks of top secret information to Europe seem to come from somewhere in Southend. Is it a coincidence that Harry Black, a recent escapee from prison, works in the local funfair? Closer examination by Keel reveals that the Ghost Train ride is more scary than it looks and a man named Wickram is arranging the leaks. Steed gets a job at the funfair but his identity is exposed and Wickram sets a trap. Hypnotized by the fairground hypnotist, Steed refuses to reveal anything and is bound and gagged. Together with Claire, Black's girlfriend, he is placed in the tunnel of the Ghost Train to await execution. Trick cigarettes allow Steed to bluff the enemy into submission and Black is proved innocent: he was hypnotized and framed.

Recorded: 3 August 1961   TX: 5 August 1961

Juno, a Great Dane trained by Barbara Woodhouse, appeared in the first season. Steed called him 'Puppy'.

The Far-Distant Dead:
Actor Reed de Rouen took over the script editor's chair from Patrick Brawn at this point – Episode Twenty-one. He continued in that capacity through the first six Blackman episodes.

21 THE FAR-DISTANT DEAD *

by John Lucarotti

Zun Garcia (Reed de Rouen) Dr David Keel (Ian Hendry) Dr Ampara Alverez Sandoval (Katherine Blake) Hercule Zeebrugge (Francis de Wolff) Rayner (Tom Adams) Godoy (Andreas Malandrinos) Mateos (Michael Mellinger) Inspector Gauvreau (Guy Deghby)

Designed by Robert Fuest
Directed by Peter Hammond

As a cyclone ravages Mexico City, Dr Keel and Dr Sandoval struggle to help the victims. The suffering is intensified because the cooking oil they are using is revealed to be hydraulic fuel. Someone is playing a dangerous game: people are dying. The two doctors track down the history of the oil cans and discover that a financier named Zeebrugge was responsible for the deal. Dr Sandoval, has heard the name before. Making an excuse to Keel, she leaves – and attempts to kill the financier in revenge for the deaths of the villagers. Keel stops her. Sympathetic to her cause, however, he allows her to make her getaway before he telephones the police.

Recorded: 14 August 1961   TX: 19 August 1961

Hot Snow *and* Kill the King:
Moira Redmond was one of the actresses shortlisted for the role of Emma Peel.

22 KILL THE KING *

by James Mitchell

King Tenuphon (Burt Kwouk) Prince Serrakit (James Goei) General Tuke (Patrick Allen) Mei Li (Lisa Peake) John Steed (Patrick Macnee) Crichton-Bull (Peter Barkworth) Dr David Keel (Ian Hendry) Carol Wilson (Ingrid Hafner) Mrs Zoe Carter (Moira Redmond) Major Harrington (Ian Collin) Ingrid Storm (Carole Shelley) U Meng (Andy Ho) Suchong (Eric Young)

Designed by Paul Bernard
Directed by Roger Jenkins

Steed is assigned to prevent the assassination of King Tenuphon after an attempt on his life on the plane flying him to London. Harrington is already arranging a second attempt – the King will die from a sniper's bullet as he walks on the balcony of his hotel. Major Harrington has installed himself in a flat opposite the King's hotel suite. Steed has checked for this eventuality but flat-owner Mrs Carter did not arouse his suspicions. It is Steed's sixth sense and a helicopter passing overhead that ensures that King Tenuphon remains safe and the royal bodyguard disposes of Major Harrington – but not before the King's son, Prince Serrakit, takes the sniper's bullet.

Recorded: 30 August 1961   TX: 2 September 1961

23 DEAD OF WINTER *

by Eric Paice

Harry (John Woodvine) Syd (Blaise Wyndham) Gerhardt Schneider (Carl Duering) John Steed (Patrick Macnee) Dr David Keel (Ian Hendry) Dr Brennan (David Hart) Inez (Sheila Robins) Carol Wilson (Ingrid Hafner) Willi (Michael Sarne) Margarita (Zorenah Osborne) Weber (Neil Hallett) Ted (Norman Chappell) Dr Kreuzer (Arnold Marle)

Designed by Robert Fuest
Directed by Don Leaver

Dr Kreuzer has developed the means to suspend life by deep-freezing. This new discovery could help the neo-fascist Phoenix Party sieze power. Keel discovers that the ex-Nazi Schneider was the first guinea pig. Steed and Keel visit the mortuary and find its attendant, Dr Brennan, dead. Schneider's body has disappeared. To get to the bottom of things, Steed arranges for Keel to join Phoenix as a replacement for a doctor they are expecting. Dr Kreuzer shows him Schneider's body – which sits up and winks! Dr Kreuzer knows Keel to be a fraud, however, and only Steed's timely intervention prevents his colleague from becoming the next victim of Schneider's chilling plot.

Recorded: 7 September 1961   TX: 9 December 1961

24 THE DEADLY AIR *

by Lester Powell

Barbara Anthony (Ann Bell) Dr Philip Karswood (Michael Hawkins) Henegar (Keith Anderson) John Steed (Patrick Macnee) Herbert Truscott (Richard Butler) Dr David Keel (Ian Hendry) Dr Hugh Chalk (Allan Cuthbertson) Dr Owen Craxton (John Stratton) One-Ten (Douglas Muir) Carol Wilson (Ingrid Hafner) Dr Harvey (Cyril Renison) Keo Armstrong (Anthony Cundell) Professor Kilbride (Geoffrey Bayldon)

Designed by Robert Macgowan
Directed by John Knight

When several experiments with a new vaccine go wrong, Steed and Dr Keel volunteer for the next test. One of the scientists, Dr Henegar, appears to be sabotaging the project and a potent airborne virus nearly kills the Avengers. As Keel interrogates Dr Henegar for the truth, Steed is discovering that Dr Craxton is the real mastermind. He wants to discredit the vaccine so that he can sell it, suitably disguised, elsewhere. Craxton, meanwhile, has trapped Steed in the test room, taped a phial of the deadly virus to the intake fan, and set in it motion. Rescued by Keel, Steed is convinced that Craxton has fatally poisoned

Bob Fuest on working with Peter Hammond: 'Peter had this marvellous idea for a fight in a laboratory. The villain fires his gun and the other guy ducks. As the actor ducks, the prop man fires a marble with a catapult and a test tube explodes. We practised this and it worked like a dream in rehearsals. On the live show, the prop man is nervous, shit-scared, because he knows that it's the longest trajectory in the world. He's nervous and he blows it. He fires the marble and a glass tank shatters into smithereens.'

One person, who would rather not be named, told me that mid-way through the Season One Blackman shows, Howard Thomas and the management team of ABC, viewed the nineteen Ian Hendry episodes to see which, if any, should be kept or re-used as 'source' material for the Blackman episodes. Due to the prohibitive cost of videotape, television companies often taped over an existing product. I am unable to verify whether or not the Hendry videotapes were wiped, but this might well explain why just the one Season One story (The Frighteners) *is the only Hendry/Macnee episode to have survived the purge.*

him, until it is revealed that the lethal vaccine had been replaced by tap water as a security measure.

Recorded: 20 September 1961   TX: 16 December 1961

25 A CHANGE OF BAIT *

by Lewis Davidson

Archie Duncan (Victor Platt) Lemuel Potts (John Bailey) Peter Sampson (Henry Soskin) Carol Wilson (Ingrid Hafner) John Steed (Patrick Macnee) Herb Thompson (Robert Desmond) Nat Fletcher (Graham Rigby) Dr David Keel (Ian Hendry) Barker (Gary Hope) Andre (Arthur Barrett) Bryan Stubbs (Norman Pitt) Ivy (Gillian McCutcheon) Charlie (Harry Shacklock) Steed's helper (Michael Hunt)

Designed by James Goddard
Directed by Don Leaver

Lemuel Potts finds himself outwitted at every turn by Steed. When Potts attempts to defraud Keel's patient, Archie Duncan, he finds himself pocketing the bill for Archie's cargo of rotten bananas. His other scheme to burn down an antiques shop and claim the insurance money is again sabotaged by Steed, who extinguishes the flames. Even when placed under arrest for attempting to start the fire a second time, Steed tricks the hapless Potts – this time into revealing the names of his accomplices.

Recorded: 27 September 1961. TX: 23 December 1961

26 DRAGONSFIELD *

by Terence Feely

John Steed (Patrick Macnee) Lisa Strauss (Sylvia Langova) Saunders (Alfred Burke) Reddington (Ronald Leigh-Hunt) Susan Summers (Barbara Shelley) Jack Alford (Thomas Kyffin) Technician (Keith Barron) Secretary (Amanda Reeves) One-Fifteen (Eric Dodson) Boris (Steven Scott) Landlord (Michael Robbins) Peters (Herbert Nelson) Second Technician (Morris Perry)

Designed by Voytek
Directed by Peter Hammond

Work on a new material to shield astronauts from radiation is nearing completion at a government research centre. But there are saboteurs about and complicated relationships in the research team suggest a traitor in their midst. Saunders, from Security, decides to uncover the gang. Steed, meanwhile, having volunteered to act as guinea pig in the radiation experiment, and having got wind of Saunder's activities, saves him from being killed. With the saboteurs placed in custody, the traitor is unmasked as Susan Summers, assistant to Dr Alford, one of the research team. Steed neutralises Summers' final fling by rescuing two members of the team from certain death

Recorded: 18 October 1961   TX: 30 December 1961

Studio records show that, contrary to what has been said before, the producers were toying with the idea of giving Steed a pet as early as August 1961. 'What about this for Steed's dog?' asked Leonard White, sending a press cutting and photograph to the series' story editor, John Bryce and director, Don Leaver. The pic showed Milady of Hornsgreen, a two-year-old Great Dane being exercised by his handler, Diana Hewlett – wife of actor/ scriptwriter Donald Hewlett, of It Ain't Half Hot, Mum *fame. The idea wasn't used until dog trainer, Barbara Woodhouse, entered the picture with Juno.*

SEASON TWO

Twenty-six monochrome videotaped episodes

starring PATRICK MACNEE and HONOR BLACKMAN   1962/1963

PRODUCTION HISTORY

Jonathan Alwyn comments on directing the videotaped episodes: 'It was a very complicated series to do. The whole idea of The Avengers, in production terms, was in trying to be original. It had a strange, unique character in studio terms. I will never forget the first day I arrived at ABC Television. Peter Hammond was directing an episode in the studio and I was taken down to the set to see. They were shooting a scene where this guy was sitting behind a desk and on the desk was a rolled-up map. Peter was lining up the shot to the man sitting behind the other side of the desk through the end of the roll! I looked at this and thought to myself, never in a million years would it have occurred to me to take a shot like that.'

THE DECISION TO EXTEND the Hendry series to thirty-nine episodes was taken on 14 December 1961 and plans were made to introduce a new female partner to the team. However, as one might expect, this was not to be Catherine Gale. The new girl was to be a young nightclub singer named Venus Smith, who would be introduced in Episode Twenty-seven and then alternate with Keel as Steed's partner on a fortnightly basis.

As history shows, this never happened. Seven months after its first successful series was closed down by an actors' dispute (Equity, the actors' union, forbade any of its members to appear in film work), the show returned, but without Ian Hendry, who had left the production to pursue a career in the cinema. This time around Steed had three new helpers, all unofficial, all much more concerned than he was with man's behaviour towards his fellow man.

First of these was Mrs Catherine Gale, a character created by producer Leonard White. Finding that he had a half-dozen or so unused scripts commissioned for the previous series, White decided to change the Keel role to that of a woman, 'a 1960s version of Shaw's emancipated young woman, providing the Conscience in Combat with Patrick Macnee's contemporary Chocolate Soldier. The character was based (or so the story goes) on two famous women: Margaret Mead, the anthropologist, and Margaret Bourne-Smith, the photographer for *Life* magazine.

Cathy was to be a cool blonde with a PhD in anthropology, who had married a farmer in Kenya and become adept with a gun during the Mau Mau troubles in which her husband was killed. When Cuba's Fidel Castro was leading a democratic rebellion against dictatorship, she fought in the hills with him. But as soon as Dr Castro achieved power, he deported her because of her opposition to certain aspects of his regime and she returned to Britain to take up a position at the British Museum. Unlike Steed, she was not a professional undercover agent, but her existence was known and accepted by Steed's superiors. A judo expert and three times runner-up at the Bisley rifle shooting competition, her resourcefulness and scientific knowledge were often in demand by Steed, but her attitude to any mission was totally different. A woman of unshakable moral principle, the end, to her, could never justify the means, and she disliked Steed's cavalier treatment of people. Nevertheless, she assisted him as a crusading amateur with a genuine desire to help the victims of crime.

Plans to introduce nightclub singer Venus Smith were placed on hold while White and his team began their search for an actress with the right qualities to become John Steed's first ever female colleague. After ABC had spent six months considering the right actress for the part, Honor Blackman was chosen to join Patrick Macnee in his fight against crime, but not before Leonard White had whittled down his shortlist of hopefuls to six names.

Among these were Honor Blackman and, favourite to get the part, Nyree Dawn Porter. Convinced that the latter stood head and shoulders over the former, producer Sydney Newman told White to 'get Nyree Dawn Porter, but not Honor Blackman', who he believed was too saccharine and genteel for the role. Director Jonathan Alwyn takes up the story. 'There was a very long strike by Equity, as a result of which Ian Hendry disappeared and we had to cast somebody else. We ran round and

Honor Blackman wears her famous leather combat suit designed by Audrey Liddle, Head of ABC TV's Wardrobe Department.

round in circles and eventually we came upon Honor Blackman. Myself and Leonard White were the people who cast Honor and I actually directed the first episode she was in. I thought, in my innocence, that Honor was an extremely handsome lady, which of course she is, but I assumed if we cast Honor Blackman, then we kind of had to exploit what everyone expected Honor Blackman to be – a girl hanging around in a bikini and looking, in a Rank-starlet way, very glamorous.

'Anyway, Sydney Newman was away on holiday. When he came back and saw our handiwork, he just sat there in shock. His face got longer and longer and eventually he said: "Jeez. She looks

Honor Blackman remembers working with Peter Hammond. 'It was marvellous. He was so imaginative. He used to drive you out of your skull though, because he wanted to have shots that were coming through a keyhole or something. So it was absolutely vital that whenever he was shooting, you didn't lift your head. You had to keep it in a certain place so that he could line up the right shot. There was no chance of redoing it, so you had to get it right first time. You'd go out of your mind during the camera rehearsal trying to be in exactly the right place and memorize exactly what you were supposed to be doing. But he got the most fantastic shots. That was Peter's speciality. He directed my first ever Avengers.' (Note: I think not. The honour went to Jonathan Alwyn.)

like Honor Blackman." I said "It is Honor Blackman." He said, "My God, what are we going to do with her? She's too straight." Leonard and myself thought that she looked okay. "No, no," said Sydney, "I tell you what we do. We'll give her a withered arm!" I said, "Sydney, she's got to be quick on the draw, and you want to give her a withered arm...?" And so it went on. We played around with various ideas until the script editor, John Bryce, said, "Let's dress her in leather from head to foot and make her a toughie." Sydney was all for that.' It transpired that Nyree Dawn Porter was unable to accept the role anyway, due to prior commitments. The actress would enter the picture again some time in the future. Honor Blackman signed in June 1962, her original contract being for six episodes only, but the studio retained the option, allowing them to pick up her services for further episodes between that date and January 1963.

Patrick Macnee recalls how Honor came to the series. 'We had lost Ian Hendry and they thought, "What the devil are we going to do now?" By sheer chance it coincided with the beginning of what is commonly referred to as "women's lib". Sydney Newman and Leonard White thought "We'll have a woman in the part" and they got Honor Blackman, who was a beautiful blonde with a bosom to take your breath away and the hips of a boy scout and long, Jesse Owen legs. They brought her in and didn't alter the scripts at all, which was pure genius. Then we got the idea of having her fight like a man, dressed her in something that was exciting and this gorgeous woman was what started the whole *Avengers* off. That's what made it so special, so different. We never fraternized. We never sexualized. We were just together. I was the man and she was the woman and it just coincided with women saying that that's the way it should be.'

Honor Blackman told Paul Madden how she came to get the role. 'I went to see Leonard White, who told me that Sydney Newman had this idea that a woman should take over in *The Avengers*. We talked about it and he told me that the lady might have to do judo. I said, "In that case you'll have to teach me because I don't know anything about it". So off I went to learn judo technique from Douglas Robinson and his actor-brother Joe, in the gymnasium they ran in a street off London's Leicester Square.' Given barely five weeks to teach the actress the basic judo moves, the instructor achieved the impossible. Within the time allotted, Honor had mastered enough of the technique to make her on-screen fights convincing. Within months her technique blossomed and, slowly, her judo expertise was worked into the part. 'It's facinating,' she said at the time. 'It makes you feel quite splendid. Anyway, I couldn't go on stopping villains by producing a gun. I'm not a killer and at the same time I couldn't pretend to heave men over my shoulder. It had to be the real thing.'

Indeed it was. As Honor confirmed to Paul Madden, she

used to plead with the actors she was fighting with to really *fight* her. 'Judo only works if somebody retaliates because you have to use their impetus against them. It doesn't help at all if they fold up and collapse like a sack. Unless you have something to pull on you can't pull it off successfully. So I used to plead with them, "Fight me. Please fight me – *hit me*!"'

Director Don Leaver enjoyed working with Honor. 'It was terribly exciting, the idea of having a woman in the role and its development into judo. It was marvellous. Some of the things that Honor did, when she threw herself about, were quite wonderful. The arrival of Honor Blackman unleashed all sorts of new ideas and new thinking. And the black leather, which of course was built upon, lifted it away from reality into a kind of genre of its own.'

Originally, Cathy Gale was to have carried an assortment of miniature pistols in her handbag. But after two or three weeks of Cathy reaching for her .25 calibre Derringer, or her powder compact which concealed a miniature gold pistol, they got bored with the gun's limitations and decided to change the format.

When I visited her home recently, Ambren Garland, costume designer on the series, told me a delightful story about this. 'Honor and Audrey Liddle, Head of ABC's Wardrobe/Costume Department, were wrestling with the problem of where to conceal this weapon because Cathy had to have both hands free. Audrey finally suggested that there was only one place: between Honor's legs. It was a small, leather thigh holster. It had a belt that ran around Honor's waist and tightened around her thigh. They tried it. Honor liked it. 'Audrey, it's wonderful,' she said, 'but there's no way I'm going to wear it. The holster keeps slipping and the barrel is pointing upwards!' It was a good idea, but it didn't work because carrying this thing meant that Honor had to raise her skirts all the time.' Next they tried concealing the firearm about her person. Underarm holsters are fine for men, but men don't have breasts or tight-fitting sweaters. Miniature swords, daggers and a Kongo-stick (a small club) were the next idea, but they also proved no good: too many cut or broken bra straps. So they were left with purely the physical means of attack. Honor and Patrick were sent to see René Burdet, former head of the Resistance in Marseilles, who taught them how to throw people. (He also taught Honor the 'dirty' tricks used by his women operatives. These were far too rough and explicit to use on the programme.)

Macnee's role was also revamped. Although he had been wearing his Edwardian-style clothes for the final episodes of the Hendry series (the last Hendry episode being produced after Ian Hendry had announced that he wouldn't be staying with the series), the producers asked him to dandify the role more than ever. A return visit to his tailor, Bailey and Weatherhill, brought him embroidered waistcoats, and a visit to a well-

Patrick Macnee and Douglas Robinson practice a judo sequence.

known London hatter brought him a variety of bowlers and trilbys – at least that's the story Patrick told me when I was writing the previous book. As we will learn, he was wide of the mark.

'I design all my own Avenger suits,' Patrick said at the time. 'I like the idea of velvet for the collars; it helps mould and complement the suits. There are no breast pockets and only one button to give the best moulding to the chest. Plus a deliberately low waist, to give the effect of simplicity, but with an individual style.' Expensive shirts, many of them striped, expensive cuff links and tie pins, plus handmade Chelsea boots, completed the wardrobe. 'I visualized Steed as a modern-day Beau Brummell with an iron exterior.'

That's what Patrick Macnee told me several years ago. In a departure from what he said then, the *Avengers* star has asked me to set the record straight. 'About the clothing which I always take the credit for having invented, which I probably did: I certainly said that the style should be this, that and the other. It was in fact created by the lady who was the head of ABC's Wardrobe Department at the time. She put my ideas into practice and turned it into a success. I've never, ever, given her credit. I do so now.' The 'ladies' are the previously mentioned Audrey Liddle and Ambren Garland who, as we will learn shortly, played an even bigger and, until now, uncredited, role in shaping the entire Avengers' wardrobe, including Honor Blackman's leather fighting suits!

About his partnership with Honor Blackman, Patrick told me: 'Honor Blackman was by far and away the most suitable lady for the part. It was a choice between her and another very fine actress. Honor won the part and then, with her incredible beauty, energy, attack and originality, she created Cathy Gale, who was *the* first English television lady. The part she played was virtually that of a man and in her own inimitable way she turned it into a truly female character who had strong tendencies which were met by my own, seemingly disarming, outward casualness. We trod a very, very gentle, narrow line. We had a nice submerged sense of humour and a deep respect for each other.'

Honor Blackman told me that the producers were unsure how a woman would work in a toughie role. 'It was the first women's lib part I suppose... certainly the first woman who was an intellectual equal to the man, and by far and away the very first woman to ever defend herself physically.' She confirmed that they had enormous problems with rewrites at the beginning. 'My part had been written for a man and when they started writing it for me, my problem was that they continued to write it as they'd always written women's parts until then. She waited for the man to make the decision; she had no mind of her own and was incapable of any logical thought process. I was going mad at the time. In fact I was going mad just learning it. Then my husband at the time, Maurice Kauffmann, said, "Why don't you pretend that you're a man and play it that way?" So I did, then gradually we changed the scripts as we went along and the writers soon got used to writing for me, once they'd seen on screen just what sort of character I was producing.'

This is borne out by story editor Richard Bates, who confirms that he was directed to brief the writers to see Cathy's role as though she was another man. 'That gave her exactly the hard edge that we needed to balance the scripts. Indeed, the characters of Steed and Cathy were so interchangable that I often took scenes which were written for Macnee and simply changed "Steed" to "Gale". These were played by Honor and we never had to change a word.'

Meanwhile, the search continued to find an actress to play Venus Smith. In August 1962, ten days after fifty-one actresses had decended upon Teddington Studios to audition for the role, five were requested to return for the producers. Among these was Angela Douglas, a young actress suggested by Leonard White as being an ideal choice for Steed's partner. The actress had previously played Beth Wilkinson, a dance instructress in the Hendry episode *Dance with Death*. Noting that she had a very good sense of comedy and played off the stars with consumate ease, White dictated a memo saying that 'she would make a perfect foil for Macnee'. Angela Douglas, Julie Stevens and song-smith-actress Vera Day were shortlisted. It was decided that they would go ahead and engage Miss Douglas. She was unable to rearrange her work schedule to fit in with *The Avengers'* timetable. Three weeks later Julie Stevens was signed for the role.

As with the earlier series, in order that the writers could familiarize themselves with the new character concept, Leonard White presented them with a new, updated directive.

THE AVENGERS

Name: Catherine Gale (Cathy)   Age 28/30

A widow. she is very attractive, intelligent and has a vital personality.

Her backgound includes a good education. She has been to university and gained an honours degree – BA/Anthroplogy. Her intention was to continue research for her PhD but she met, and fell in love with, a young farmer on holiday in London from his home in Africa. The idea of sharing his life abroad appealed to her lively spirit of adventure. She married him.

Her experiences, during several years on their isolated homestead in Africa, toughened her and she came to accept and thrive in their new environment. Carrying firearms was second nature to her and she became expert in their use. She learned to cope with the practicalities of isolated living as well as any man. She could equally well deal with the mechanics of a car engine as with the delivery of a baby.

After several years her husband was killed on their farm. Cathy returned to this country and resumed her studies to pick up the threads of her original career. She gained a PhD in Anthropology.

She has become a first class photographer. She has presented a paper to the Royal Geographic Society on her recent photographic expedition to the Amazon. During this expedition she was separated from the party and attacked by natives: she escaped only after shooting three of them.

She is essentially a strong, lively personality. She is an individualist. She doesn't make friends too easily, but such as she may have are friends for life. Her experiences may have made her a little withdrawn: she may even appear to be a somewhat lonely person. She may repress the sensual side of her nature, but nevertheless all these characteristics only enhance our desire to get to know her better.

She is sophisticated but not upper class. She has a strong sense of humour.

Her flat reflects her personality and interests. There are some special firearms; some prizes of her expeditions; some of her African treasures and examples of her photography and equipment. There is nothing flamboyant and the effect is not of luxury. It is obviously a woman's flat and strong touches of femininity are seen. In all good taste is evident.

In her undercover activities she is fired by the desire to fight against evil and essentially help those who are victims of crime. During her joint missions with Steed she will, more often than not, provide the moral attitude. She may not always approve of Steed's methods. His is the attitude of the ruthless professional and hers may be that of the crusading 'amateur', who cares deeply for the people involved.

We will care deeply about her.

Name: Venus Smith   Age: 20-ish

She is a vivacious nightclub singer. Her father was a barge owner and her early years were spent with her family on a barge travelling the canals of England. She is the youngest of three children. Her two brothers, much older than she, both emigrated when she was twelve. Her formal education was rather sporadic, but her lack of academic prowess is compensated for by her alert commonsense.

At seventeen she decided to leave home. In London she found ways of developing her natural talent to entertain. At first with amateur and semi-pro jazz groups and then, recently, club work.

The nature of her formative years has created a resilient character quite able and eager to cope with the rough and tumble of her career in show business. Her character is not that of a corny 'sex bombshell' type of entertainer. She is well able to put over a sexy number if necessary, but essentially she is a warm-hearted, lovable, gay girl. She may be earthy, but never coarse or jaded.

Others feel they would like to take care of her. She makes friends easily. She accepts people as she finds them. This does not mean that she is lacking in perception, but that she prefers to think well of people. She hates gossip.

She is by no means a 'goody goody', but she is a good person. She has a special radiant quality which is her great attraction both on stage and off.

She does not know anything of the true nature of Steed's work. She is not an undercover agent. She is involved in Steed's 'escapades' for several reasons. She does it for the excitement; for the opportunity to go places and do things otherwise not possible to her.

She likes Steed, and the aura of mystery surrounding him is an intriguing attaction for her. There is no suggestion of any 'affair' between them. If anything she probably regards Steed as a 'special' elder brother. This attitude he finds rather flattering and he may feel that she needs 'looking after'. Very often, in fact, on her adventures she may indeed need Steed's timely aid

Roger Marshall on the character John Steed: 'Everybody was very vague about Macnee or Steed's background. We knew that he was something to do with the Ministry, that he wore a bowler hat and carried an umbrella and liked Great Danes. Beyond that nobody bothered.'

to get her out of trouble.

Steed usually calls her 'Smith', but to her friends and associates at the club she is known as 'Vee'. 'Vee' for vitality!

Name: One-Ten   Age:55/60

He is our only link with apparent officialdom. His 'establishment' is necessarily very obscure. He contracts the undercover work, but he will always keep the arrangements on a personal basis.

He may know that Steed and Cathy use other people, but they are not 'recognized' by him (and neither are they his responsibility).

One-Ten is very intelligent. He might be an Oxford don who has been assigned to his highly specialized work in big crime detection where it is necessary to use undercover agents.

He is often on the telephone – but the phone always seems to be in an interesting place. If and when he has to make physical contact with Steed or Cathy, it will probably be in the most unlikely places – say a launderette, a barber's shop, an auction, etc.

His use in the stories should be kept to the absolute minimum, and it is not necessary that he should be involved in every episode.

GENERAL

We will woo our audience in the first minute of each story. Whatever happens later, *the first minute* must establish excitement and provocation.

Our heroes are people we (the audience) will like and admire. We should like them because of the virtues they display: we will admire them for the dexterity and intelligence with which they win their battles.

The causes our heroes defend are good causes, and the people they help and protect are people like ourselves.

The stories will be set in environments which are exciting and different (scenes set in offices, drawing rooms, flats, are very dull visually). We need some special quality to make them acceptable. One main exciting and unusual locale (atomic energy plant, zoo, brewery, mass-production factory) gives more value than an endless number of small box sets of dull rooms.

Our leading characters are essentially undercover. They are *not* private or public detectives. Any story which follows this pattern is not right for us.

On their missions they do not work with the police. If the police are involved at all (and this should be very rare) then it is most likely that they believe our undercover characters are on the wrong side!

Steed and Cathy will generally work jointly on their mis-

sions, but occasional episodes using them individually will be used. When working together, the means they use their individ-ualism and the differing attitudes they adopt will often give rise to some sort of conflict. Development of character is of great importance. On occasion Cathy may do even better than Steed. Nevertheless they retain a deep respect for each other. They are not in conflict over either the importance of their mission or the need to bring it to a successful conclusion.

Only fools would dare to tangle with The Avengers.

Jonathan Alwyn on the tribulations of working on a 'live' programme: 'They did what is laughingly known as a dress rehearsal in the afternoon. We then recorded Act One, drew a deep breath and went on to Act Two. I remember one classic occasion when we got as far as the end of Act Two and someone in the control booth said: "We are now over-running by three minutes", and I had to race down to the studio, edit out the first three scenes of Act Three, and go on from there! There was no other way round it in those days. There was a delightful actor called Jack May in one episode (The Secret's Broker, *Blackman Season Two), who was suddenly found up to his neck in malmsey, with no explanation given as to how he got there. But this being* The Avengers, *no one queried it. There was no editing, you see. We grew up with this. We were all a lot younger in those days and such things didn't strike terror into your soul.'*

Venus must only be used as an extension of Steed. She will of course have her own separate private life and career, but as she cannot be 'in the know' her use is oblique to the main issue. Normally she will only appear in stories with Steed.

***

You will note that the directive made no mention of Dr Martin King, the character who shared three adventures with Steed in the Season Two Blackman stories. Jon Rollason, the actor who played Dr King, was contracted solely to bridge the gap between the introduction of Mrs Gale and Venus Smith (the former unable to join the series until five weeks after the production began). This also enabled the use of three scripts originally intended for the Hendry series which had featured a character called Dr Keel.

The new direction planned for the series wasn't without its citics. Before the first Blackman episode went into production, the Controller of Programmes for ABC voiced his concern that several high-ranking company executives had commented that 'the replacement of Ian Hendry by a woman would a) alienate female viewers; b) lose viewers who had obviously enjoyed the bantering camaraderie between Hendry and Macnee; c) tend to introduce elements of sex and sexual violence into the series'. Alarmed that this might be the case, the producers were directed to ensure that item c) in particular was given 'careful attention' and that the scripts avoided this 'unsavoury element'.

Commenting on Cathy Gale's relationship with John Steed, Honor Blackman told me: 'Leonard White particularly wanted Cathy to be pure. As a contrast really, because first of all, Steed's character was wicked, devilish and saucy, so Cathy had to be a contrast. This made her so much more entertaining – and certainly more acceptable. She did all the fighting and therefore it was important that she remained a woman who defended herself for only good reasons and went after the baddies because she cared very much about right and justice. What was so lovely was the sense of humour that was retained throughout, the sort of sexual sparring that went on between them, particularly from Steed, which she warded off, but with humour. That made it much more entertaining. Let's face it, you could hardly have a series with a man and a woman who were both perfectly normal, without having that sort of relationship. Some *sexual* relationship *had* to be brought into it because it would have been rather bizarre without it over such a long period.' In fact there was just enough innuendo and enough fade-outs over popping champagne corks at the end of each story to leave the viewer wondering "do they or don't they?" (go to bed, that is).'

It was an intriguing question. 'I remember that there was one episode where Steed has been taken prisoner and I had to go and visit him,' recalled Honor. 'Steed says that his sister is coming to see him, which gives him the opportunity to kiss me. So we had world press coming down to the studio to photograph us kissing. It was extraordinary. It was so popular. What was so wonderful about that thing was that we knew that it would crash if we actually did get together at some point. But what would would have been the point? There were millions of relationships like that. One of the excitements of it was will he win her? How close will the relationship develop? Will she succumb? That was all part of the fun. We used to know all the answers and the public never did.'

In fact Cathy was a creature of fantasy, commented Honor, 'a girl who could toss minions all over the room and manhandle even the toughest villains wih nonchalant disdain. No one could be so brainy and remote and physical and sexy and untouchable and wear leather and high boots and be perfectly normal as well.'

Perfection in clothes was to play an important part of Cathy's character. Leonard White, still with his finger on the pulse (and setting a precedent that would influence all future Avengers series), circulated a memo to his staff stressing the importance of taking full advantage of the publicity surrounding the introduction of Honor Blackman. It should be used to make her character a leader of fashion. 'It is,' he said, 'the programme makers' declared intention to set fashion, not to follow it!'

This was absolutely in line with Cathy's character and her job as the undercover agent with a passion for high fashion and derring-do and Derringers. Her entire wardrobe was planned with an eye to these trends, but her leather fighting gear came about by accident.

Honor Blackman told the press at the time: 'The leather thing was extraordinary. The fact that I happened to choose leather for my fighting kit was a pure accident. Cathy led a very active life and I soon realised that I needed something that wouldn't rip. Skirts were out of the question. When your legs are flying over your head, the last thing you want to worry about is whether your stocking-tops are showing. It happened that right at the beginning of the series, I split my trousers in close-up, with my rear in full view of the camera. So it became obvious that I had to find some tougher gear. Somebody suggested suede, but we found that suede didn't "light" on television. Then someone, Patrick I think, suggested leather and after trying it, the producers said "great", so I wore it throughout the rest of the show. The only thing you can wear with leather trousers are boots, so they kitted me out with calf-length black boots, and the leather thing was born.'

It was, but perhaps not exactly as Honor remembers it. There are two sides to every story. When I visited Ambren Garland at her home recently and raised the subject of the leather gear, she gave me her interpretation. 'The initial idea to put Honor into leather came from producer/script editor, John Bryce, and, possibly, Francis Hancock, who was very much involved in the early days of the series. Bryce was very much

Steed and Cathy pose for press photographers, circa 1963.

into leather. He had a motorbike and an open-top sports car and wore leather all the time. He was mad about leather. He started the leather thing. Prior to that time nobody had worn leather, from the Twenties right through to the Fifties, and nobody ever wore boots. It simply wasn't fashionable to do so.'

Ambren explained that it was impossible to buy things for Honor from the shops. 'Everything was made for her, or bought from an outside supplier and altered to fit her. Honor had a very handsome bust, a very slim waist and slim hips, so it was essential that her clothes fitted her at the waist and hugged her hips. Otherwise she would have looked like a Two-Ton Tessie.'

Adding that Honor was a very rewarding character to dress because she always looked so good, Ambren confirmed that her original leather outfit was black. 'It was designed by Audrey Liddle, who found out about the leather thing from a shop in London's Soho district, who supplied clothes for transvestites. There were only ever *two* leather fighting suits, but we did design a couple of pairs of leather trousers for her.'

It was a few months into production before Audrey Liddle suggested to Ambren that they really ought to have a second leather outfit; the first one was looking rather shabby. Ambren proposed the idea that instead of having black leather, why didn't they make this a dark colour. The outfit was made in green leather. 'From then on, with perhaps a few exceptions, Honor always wore the green outfit.' As she explained, Honor was wearing the leather week after week and was required to get into (and out of) the costume in a tearing hurry and race back onto the set, so the leather suit got very worn. Ambren suggested using a green outfit because of filming considerations. 'If something was dense black it was useless, really. You never, ever, dressed anyone in dense black. Certain colours photograph in different shades of grey and the clothes had to have really good line. Black blurred the outline and the person wearing it didn't look good at all.'

Once the style of the fashions was set, Michael Whittaker used leather for many of Cathy's clothes. He took on the job as a special favour to Honor Blackman, for whom he had designed many film wardrobes. Whittaker designed everything to fit skin-tight and every outfit accentuated Honor's slim waist – leading one critic to comment, 'Steed's Girl Friday has more curves that a runaway bus!'

Ambren was delighted to hear that Patrick Macnee had (finally) credited the wardrobe team as having played a major part in the creation of Steed's attire. 'Audrey Liddle designed the turned-back cuffs of the suits and jackets. The suits themselves were made rather more waisted than they would have been in Edwardian times, the idea being to make Steed slightly dandy-ish.' As far as she remembers, in those early days Macnee had only one jacket, several waistcoats, lots of shirts and just the one suit. 'These were cleaned and pressed and cleaned and pressed and that was that. The budget wouldn't allow for anything else. He wore stiff collars initially, which we had to dye 'tech white' (in a solution of weak tea!) so that they had a slightly Edwardian look, because no one ever wore white... ideally we 'dipped' everything because of the studio lighting. If you had white right up to your face, the lighting crew had great difficulty in doing anything with the actor's face, particularly when shooting on videotape.'

Hitting your mark on the set at precisely the right time, in the right clothes, was essential in a 'live' programme. Unlike film, there was no chance to re-shoot the scene if someone missed their cue and entered the scene from camera left, instead of camera right. Patrick Macnee recalls racing from set to set pursued by Frank Evans, one of the property men, who was handing him props while his dresser, Bob Johnson, stood by with his changes of clothes. 'It needed a lot of skill to make it work. They had worked it out very, very carefully, but we just raced from one scene to another while changing our clothes, and hoped for the best.'

Honor, meanwhile, was hoping to spare the production crews blushes. As Ambren Garland told me: 'Despite the fact that the leather suit was designed to enable Honor to make

Anythng could happen in those days, as Honor Blackman told Paul Madden: 'On the day of the recording, we used to start at seven or seven-thirty and go right through. We had some hysterical moments. I remember that we had this wonderful props man called Frank Evans. I think the scene had Patrick and I sitting on a sofa talking to each other. The camera had to come right up close, so this coffee table had to diappear from the shot, to allow the cameraman to get us in close-up. There was Frank and this other guy on their knees crawling backwards with this coffee table, and their heads were in shot. So far as I remember it, when the viewers saw it they saw the two prop men moving out with this table! We thought it was funny. We had these ridiculous things happening all the time.'

quick-fire changes of costume, because she was required to get into the leather suit in every episode, she had to change on set, because the action was going out live [the programme was being recorded in real time, with the entire episode being taped in one session]. There was no question whatever that Honor, or Patrick, could get back to their dressing rooms, so Honor changed behind a corner of the scenery, sometimes in full view of the crew. Honor worked under tremendous pressure every-time she wore the leather outfit. She was terribly hot, of course. It was very, very exhausting for her, never having to miss her cue when faced with tearing into the leather gear and racing across the studio floor.' Ambren recalled that whenever Honor and Patrick were required to appear in the next scene, they would under-dress, as actors do in the theatre. 'This sometimes meant that Patrick would be wearing a vest (for a shaving scene), a thin pullover beneath his shirt (ready to strip off and look casual in the next scene) and a top coat and scarf over his suit. The artistes suffered for their trade.'

As did the people on the floor: the cameraman, the set designers, the recording engineer et al. Bob Fuest told me: 'It was a baptism by fire. It was a very complicated show. The final rehearsing and taping was just a fantastic jigsaw puzzle that required guts and and good fortune to get right. The camera crew were absolutely magnificent. As you know, *The Avengers* was in three acts and we had vinyl records for the music. I can remember the floor manager counting down the seconds – 10, 9, 8, 7... 3, 2, 1 – and seeing the needle come down on the record and hearing the theme music. Then they'd cut to camera one, who was trained on the caption 'The Avengers', then another on a different caption and so on. The camera crew were in shorts and singlets, with sneakers on. As were the cable men. Everyone was absolutely stripped down for action. And, after the first commercial break, it was absolute hell because everything had to be reassembled and the cameras had to be moved and this had to be ready for that.

'Can you imagine it? The music was done manually, by a studio man dropping the stylus down onto a record... sometimes too late to accompany the action! And the telephones... a telephone is supposed to ring, but doesn't; and it rings when the actor picks it up! You can understand why, at the end of the first twenty minutes or so, I was running around talking to the prop men to ask them if everything was all right. They'd say: "Sure, Bob. Everything is okay." I'd ask about the cigarette lighter. I'd ask who had got the gun? Then we'd get the countdown. They'd swing into the second act and "action", we're off again. The director would be up in the control box. I'd be on the floor, ducking and diving under the cameras and miles of cables... we were skating on thin ice, and it worked, the energy came through. If the phone didn't ring, if the gun didn't go off, we for-got it in a sense because there was so much energy and passion

Patrick Macnee and Alan Curtis run through a fight sequence during the camera rehearsals for '*Mission To Montreal*'.

and it carried us through – it was all part of the experience.'

Don Leaver, speaking to Paul Madden, recalled that the videotaped episodes were studio-bound out of necessity. 'On the live ones of course, you had the constraint of having to finish a scene on the character who wasn't opening the next scene. You always had to spin out of the scene to allow the chaps who had been standing off-camera to go rushing to the new set, in order to start up there. There were lots of constraints, which made it really exciting. The thing I remember is the fact that the cameras were inextricably intertwined with the actors. You would have a camera shooting sometimes no more than 18 inches from an actor's nose; it must have been awfully distracting for them.'

Leaver paid tribute to the design team who, in his opinion (and that of everyone I have spoken to), were the very best design team in television at that time. 'Tim O'Brien had assembled the most amazing team of designers: Voytek, Jimmy Goddard, Patrick Downing, Terry Green, Bob Fuest... they were tremendous. You would pick up a script and see that Steed is up on an oil rig. There would be a moment of silence and someone would say: "Well, an oil rig is just a collection of girders", and we'd work from that. You'd take a low-angled shot and there would be some oil canisters and some scaffolding around and someone would be spraying blasts of oil at Patrick – and he was on an oil rig. Nothing was impossible.'

Whereas the formula remained the same – a series of wildly over-animated adventures treated as an enjoyable dramatization of, say, a *Boy's Own* paperback yarn, laced with plenty of action and worldly dialogue, this time Steed had a new canine sidekick, Freckles, a two-year-old Dalmatian puppy, who was brought in to replace Juno, the Great Dane. It was Steed's regular companion in the Hendry series, until he lost his life in an accident on London's underground en route to film an *Avengers* story.

On the 12 September 1962, several weeks after taping the first Venus Smith episode, Leonard White confirmed that Julie Stevens had done very well on her first showing. 'Having been thrown in at the deep end, she behaved like a trouper and deserves to succeed. Anything, therefore, that we can do to get her away from the "sophisticated" in her presentation will help.'

His comments were echoed by a memo from Brian Tesler, then Programme Controller at ABC: 'I wanted to say how splendidly I think the new series is going. You have weathered the absence of Hendry, and we are turning out at least as exciting a series as the last with this new format. Macnee and Blackman are excellent, and Julie Stevens is a gamble which has paid off.' Tesler confirmed that White and his team could plan ahead with *The Avengers* for at least as long as the end of 1963.

Near the end of the first Blackman season Tesler contacted the producers, saying he believed that the time was right to re-record the theme music. 'The music sounds terribly "wowy" and distorted these days. Can we not get out the original sound tapes and have a new dubbing made?' Producer John Bryce responded saying that he had already arranged that a re-recording should be made as the master record was now to worn to yield a satisfactory dub. Johnny Dankworth went back into the studio (for the third time) and revamped his original score by adding extra percussion and a xylophone middle phrase.

The series got off to a cracking start with a thrill-packed story, *Mr Teddy Bear*. However, this was not intended to be the first Cathy Gale episode. That distinction was held by the script called *Warlock*. Penned by scriptwriter Doreen Montgomery, this contained passages in which Steed and Cathy meet for the first time. This took place when Steed was ordered by his superior to seek expert advice from anthropologist Cathy, then working at the British Museum, on a Black Magic grimoire he'd found at the scene of a crime. It also had several other 'character establishing' scenes. However, because several other Cathy Gale episodes had already been transmitted prior to this story, the 'introductory' scenes were trimmed before transmission.

SEASON TWO CHRONOLOGY

Episode	Title
1	Dead On Course (aka The Plane Wreckers)
2	Mission To Montreal (aka Gale Force)
3	The Sell Out (aka Traitor)
4	Death Dispatch *1
5	Warlock (aka Zodiac)
6	Propellant 23
7	Mr Teddy Bear
8	The Decapod
9	Bullseye (aka Dead on Target)
10	The Removal Men (aka The Most Expensive Commodity)
11	The Mauritius Penny
12	Death of a Great Dane *2
13	Death on the Rocks (aka Pillar of Salt)
14	Traitor in Zebra
15	The Big Thinker
16	Intercrime
17	Immortal Clay
18	Box of Tricks * 3
19	The Golden Eggs
20	School for Traitors
21	The White Dwarf
22	Man in the Mirror
23	Conspiracy of Silence
24	A Chorus of Frogs
25	Six Hands Across a Table
26	Killerwhale

*1 This was the first televised episode starring Honor Blackman
*2 This story (with slight changes to the script) was later remade as The £50,000 Breakfast (Rigg colour series, episode 124)
*3 This story was scripted as a vehicle for Steed, Cathy and Venus Smith

Series produced by: Leonard White (Episodes One to Fourteen)
John Bryce (Episodes Fifteen to Twenty-Six)

The Avengers Theme composed and played by Johnny Dankworth

Story editors
John Bryce (Episodes One to Fourteen)
Richard Bates (Episodes Fifteen to Twenty-Six)

Dead On Course:
Script supervisor, Anthony John, suggested that there was little to worry about in this episode. 'The "operators", who bring planes in on false beams, work from a convent on (presumably) the west coast of Ireland. This necessitates two of them masquerading as nuns, one of whom impersonates the Mother Superior! All of which sounds rather silly, but I think the sum total will add up to a "whodunit?" type of melodrama with the least obvious character turning out to be the culprit. I would describe the writing as rather hack but, nevertheless, the ratings should be high. There is little violence: that of a "nun" garroting an air hostess with her waistcord. This has already been discussed and will be played down before the actual strangling takes place.'
Howard Thomas, Managing Director of ABC, went further. 'You will have seen Anthony John's note concerning the violence in this episode. Perhaps you will see to it that particular care is taken to ensure that the violence factor is carefully supervised.'

SEASON TWO EPISODES

27 DEAD ON COURSE

by Eric Paice

Pilot (Trevor Reid) Bob Slade (Bruce Boa) Margot (Margo Jenkins) Freedman (John McLaren) John Steed (Patrick Macnee) Deidre O'Connor (Elisabeth Murray) Dr Martin King (Jon Rollason) Sister Isobel (Janet Hargreaves) Mother Superior (Peggy Marshall) Hughes (Nigel Arkwright) Michael Joyce (Liam Gaffney) Vincent O'Brien (Donal Donnelly) Gerry (Edward Kelsey) and Mollie Maureen, Denis Cleary, Wilfred Grove

Designed by Robert Fuest
Directed by Richmond Harding

When a plane mysteriously crashes on the Irish coast, Steed goes to investigate because there had been some currency on board. While Dr King attends to the wounded, Steed pursues the sinister Sisters of the Convent and their ring leader, Vincent, who is not as simple as he seems. Another crash is successfully averted and the Mother Superior is brought down to earth.

Recorded: 9 May 1962   TX: 29 December 1962

28 MISSION TO MONTREAL

by Lester Powell

Carla Berotti (Patricia English) Film Director (Harold Berens) Peggy (Pamela Ann Davy) AG Brand (Alan Curtis) Receptionist (Angela Thorne) Pearson (Eric McCaine) Alec Nicholson (Mark Eden) Stewards (Peter Mackriel and William Swan) Budge (Gerald Sim) Guido Marson (John Bennett) Reporters (Terence Woodfield, Malcolm Taylor and Leslie Pitt) Photographer (William Buck) Sheila Dowson (Iris Russell) Dr Martin King (Jon Rollason) Judy (Gillian Muir) John Steed (Patrick Macnee) Passenger (John Frawley) Barman (Allan Casley)

Designed by Terry Green
Directed by Don Leaver

A relaxing cruise back to Montreal seems an ideal holiday for Dr King and his patient, the famous star Carla Berotti, who seems neurotic but healthy. Conned by her husband into smuggling a secret microfilm of the Dew Line (the early-warning system for North America), her trust in Dr King and his employer, Steed, is well-placed. But tangled loyalties mean that a double agent nearly sinks the Avengers, before the ship safely reaches port.

Recorded: 15 May 1962   TX: 27 October 1962

29 THE SELL-OUT

by Anthony Terpiloff and Brandon Brady

Dr Martin King (Jon Rollason) John Steed (Patrick Macnee) Monsieur Roland (Carleton Hobbs) Policeman (Anthony Blackshaw) Gunman (Storm Durr) One-Twelve (Arthur Hewlett) Fraser (Michael Mellinger) Mark Harvey (Frank Gatliff) Lilian Harvey (Anne Godley) Judy (Gillian Muir) Workman (Richard Klee) Reporter (Henry Rayner) Customer (Cyril Renison) Price (Ray Browne)

Designed by Terry Green
Directed by Don Leaver

Steed finds that his assignment to protect Roland, a UN official attending an international conference, is threatened by a traitor within One-Twelve's department. Faced with terminal illness, Harvey, who is responsible for security at the talks, has sold out, and implicated Steed. At the next session of talks, an enemy gunman nearly brings the press conference to an abrupt end, allowing Steed to redeem himself. For Dr King, it is his final case. He turns his back on espionage and returns to a life of medicine.

Recorded: 9 June 1962 TX: 24 November 1962

30 DEATH DISPATCH

by Leonard Fincham

Baxter (Hedger Wallace) Pasco (Alan Mason) John Steed (Patrick Macnee) One-Ten (Douglas Muir) Catherine Gale (Honor Blackman) Thugs (Geoff L'Cise and Arthur Griffiths) Miguel Rosas (Richard Warner) Anna Rosas (Valerie Sarruf) Monroe (David Cargill) Chambermaid (Bernice Rassin) Rico (Michael Forest) Singer (Maria Andipa) Customer (Jerry Jardin) Travers (Gerald Harper)

Designed by Anne Spavin
Directed by Jonathan Alwyn

Mission To Montreal, Bullseye, Intercrime, Killerwhale: *Actresses Pamela Ann Davy, Laurie Leigh, Angela Browne and Julie Paulle all attended the auditions for the role of Venus Smith.*

Mission To Montreal: *Actress Iris Russell would return to programme as 'Father', in the Thorson story* Stay Tuned.

The Avengers find themselves threatened by Rosas and Monroe in *Death Dispatch*. This was Honor Blackman's first appearance as Cathy Gale.

Warlock:
The storyline attracted this comment from Howard Thomas: 'The black magic item last weekend much in common with a black magic item which Julian Wintle *is proposing to make in* The Human Jungle *series. Could you have the scripts checked and perhaps also see whether there is any adverse reaction to the horrific edition of* The Avengers? *It would not surprise me to learn that* Doreen Montgomery *had written* The Human Jungle *episode under another name.'*
Brian Tesler re-ran the episode and also read the Wintle script Powers of Darkness. *'I'm satisfied that, apart from the basic coincidence of the black magic subject material, there is no similarity between the two stories.* John Kruse, *who wrote the Wintle script, is the originator and story editor of* The Human Jungle. *It is unlikely that he and Doreen Montgomery are one and the same. There has been no adverse reaction to the* Avengers *episode.'*

When a courier is murdered on a routine run to Buenos Aires and some papers stolen, Steed takes the man's place while Mrs Gale follows him. The stolen papers contain the itinerary of a visiting American envoy. His death will spark a revolution in Argentina, placing Miguel Rosas in power. Steed and Cathy follow his henchmen, Monroe, back to Rosas' villa where arrests are made. Their investigation complete, the Avengers attend the reception for the visiting envoy.

Recorded: 23 June 1962 TX: 22 December 1962

31 WARLOCK

by Doreen Montgomery

Cosmo Gallion (Peter Arne) Peter Neville (Allan Blakelock) Mrs Dunning (Olive Milbourne) John Steed (Patrick Macnee) Markel (John Hollis) Julia (Pat Spencer) Mogom (Philip Mosca) Catherine Gale (Honor Blackman) Doctor (Brian Vaughan) Pathologist (Gordon Gardner) Miss Timson (Christine Ferdinando) One-Ten (Douglas Muir) Barmaid (Susan Franklin) Pasco (Herbert Nelson) and Bill Haydn, Anna Sharkey, Roy Gunson, Maggie Lee, Fred Evans, Gillian Bowden

Designed by Terry Green
Directed by Peter Hammond

Cosmo Gallion uses black magic to sell state secrets to the highest bidder. Steed and Mrs Gale investigate the bewitchment of a scientist, Neville, who belongs to Gallion's magic circle. Cathy's life is put in grave danger when, introduced to Gallion, the warlock realises that her birthday, 5 October 1930, at midnight, is pefect for his next experiment. Cathy is kidnapped and taken before the warlock and his coven. Steed enters the scene and breaks Gallion's power over her. His plans frustrated, Gallion collapses and dies.

Recorded: 7 July 1962 TX: 26 January 1963

32 PROPELLANT 23

by Jon Manchip White

Jules Meyer (Frederick Schiller) Jeanette (Justine Lord) Captain Legros (Nicholas Courtney) Co-pilot (Michael Beint) Paul Manning (Geoffrey Palmer) Catherine Gale (Honor Blackman) John Steed (Patrick Macnee) Laure (Catherine Woodville) Jacques Tissot (Trader Faulkner) Lieutenant 'Curly' Leclerc (John Crocker) Siebel (John Dearth) Roland (Ralph Nossek) Pierre (Barry Wilsher) Gendarme (Graham Ashley) Shop Assistant (Deanna Shendy) Baker (John Gill)

Designed by Paul Bernard
Directed by Jonathan Alwyn

Steed and Cathy search frantically for Propellant 23, a new rocket fuel, before it falls into the hands of the opposition. When the courier carrying the fuel sample arrives dead at Marseilles, the sample is mistaken for alcohol and stolen by a hotel worker. The enemy reach Jacques, the hotel tout who has acquired the flask, before Steed and Cathy can. But it is the Avengers who retrieve the contents of the flask, after shots from Mrs Gale's garter-gun!

Recorded: 21 July 1962 TX: 6 October 1962

33 MR TEDDY BEAR

by Martin Woodhouse

Interviewer (Tim Brinton) Colonel Wayne-Gilley (Kenneth Keeling) John Steed (Patrick Macnee) Dr Gilmore (John Horsley) One-Ten (Douglas Muir) Catherine Gale (Honor Blackman) Henry (Michael Robbins) Mr Teddy Bear (Bernard Goldman) Cafe Girl (Sarah Maxwell) Dr James Howell (John Ruddock) Technician (Michael Collins)

Designed by Terry Green
Directed by Richmond Harding

Anyone who can pay enough can hire Mr Teddy Bear for a contract killing. After the public murder of Wayne-Gilley, Mrs Gale does just that – she employs the killer to assassinate John Steed. However, the trap misfires and Mr Teddy Bear lures Cathy into his clutches instead. Enter Steed, whom the killer believed to be disposed of, to ruffle Mr Teddy Bear's fur. Faced with certain capture, the professional assassin chooses suicide.

Recorded: 4 August 1962   TX: 29 September 1962

34 THE DECAPOD

by Eric Paice

Girl in Shower (Pamela Conway) Yakob Borb (Paul Stassino) Stepan (Philip Madoc) John Steed (Patrick Macnee) Bodyguards (Douglas Robinson and Valentine Musetti) Venus Smith (Julie Stevens) Cigarette Girl (Valerie Stanton) Edna Ramsden (Lynne Furlong) Ito (Wolfe Morris) Harry Ramsden (Raymond Adamson) Guards Officer (Harvey Ashby) with Stanley M Ayers and the Dave Lee Trio

Designed by Terry Green
Directed by Don Leaver

President Yakob Borb is on the verge of negotiating a huge loan for his country when an unknown assailant tries to unsettle things by killing

Propellant 23:
'This should be quite an exciting episode,' said Anthony John. 'It has been agreed with producer Leonard White, that flick knives and broken bottles, for which the script called, will not be used.' Catherine Woodville plays Laure in this episode, but had been seen as Peggy, Dr Keel's fiancée in Hot Snow. *Catherine later married Patrick Macnee.*

The Decapod:
Brian Tesler spotted a 'dry' in the playback of the episode 'It wasn't too horrific. Couldn't Presentation cut in a couple of stills of the head they are discussing at the time? It would probably be a sufficient distraction for the viewers not to notice the flounder.' The actor playing Yakob Borb ad-libbed a line to Julie Stevens, who is wearing a tight dress: 'It's obvious that you are not concealing a gun!'

Steed and Cathy turn the tables on professional assassin 'Mr Teddy Bear'.

his bodyguard. Steed investigates the identity of the murderer who hides behind the mask of a wrestler, The Decapod. Venus Smith keeps an eye on the President, who becomes infatuated with her. He reveals that he will steal the loan and live in luxurious exile. When Stepan, from the Balkan Embassy, learns that Borb has been wrestling as The Decapod as a ploy to distract attention from his plan, he kills Borb in revenge.

Recorded: 12 August 1962   TX: 13 October 1962

35 BULLSEYE

by Eric Paice

Jean (Mitzi Rogers) Miss Ellis (Judy Parfitt) Brigadier Williamson (Charles Carson) Foreman (Robin Wentworth) Catherine Gale (Honor Blackman) Henry Cade (Ronald Radd) Young (Felix Deebank) Reynolds (John Frawley) Shareholder (Graeme Bruce) Karl (Bernard Kay) John Steed (Patrick Macnee) Dorothy Young (Laurie Leigh) Inspector (Fred Ferris)

Designed by Robert Macgowan
Directed by Peter Hammond

Henry Cade plans to take-over Anderson's Small Arms Ltd., but before the directors can sell their shares, somebody kills them. The culprit is also responsible for gun-running, so Steed and Mrs Gale investigate. Cathy joins the company's board and teams up with Cade to call for a stock check. This panics the two guilty directors – Young and Miss Ellis – into trying to escape, but Steed is waiting for them.

Recorded: 20 September 1962 TX: 20 October 1962

36 THE REMOVAL MEN

by Roger Marshall and Jeremy Scott

Jack Dragna (Reed de Rouen) Bug Siegal (Edwin Richfield) Godard (Donald Tandy) John Steed (Patrick Macnee) Cecile Dragna (Patricia Denys) Binaggio (George Roderick) Venus Smith (Julie Stevens) One-Ten (Douglas Muir) Waiter (George Little) Jailer (Hugo de Vernier) Nicole Cauvin (Edina Ronay) Charlie (Hira Talfrey) Harbour Officer (Ivor Dean) and the Dave Lee Trio

Designed by Patrick Downing
Directed by Don Leaver

Dragna's firm specializes in professional murder, so Steed is assigned to infiltrate and disband the removal men. Venus, meanwhile, has found employment at Dragna's nightclub. Steed's first job is to kill a film actress, but he puts her in hiding instead. Siegal, the club manager, suspicious that Steed hasn't carried out his orders, finds the actress and exposes Steed as a sham. Using Venus' singing as accompaniment, Steed outwits the gang and shoots his way to freedom.

Recorded: 4 October 1962 TX: 3 November 1962

Bullseye:
Actor Ronald Radd was promoted to Steed's boss in the Season Two Blackman episode, The Outside-In Man.

Death of a Great Dane:

This was Barbara Woodhouse's first 'hands-on' episode. She was there throughout the entire production. Honor Blackman recalls that she came into the studio wih this huge Great Dane. 'There were lots of dog trainers who would say that the dog could do this and can do that, and come the filming it doesn't do it. But with Barbara it was facinating: the dog just went ahead and did whatever she told it to.'

Patrick Downing: 'Apart from a couple of small sets, and I think, some location filming, the whole episode was written to take place in a millionaire's London house. I devised a plan to make this a circular penthouse on top of an hotel, with all curved walls. When I met Peter Hammond and showed him my sketches, he took a small envelope from his pocket, and handed it to me. He had drawn a collection of circles and half-circles inside each other, with a bedroom at the centre.'

37 THE MAURITIUS PENNY

by Malcolm Hulke and Terrance Dicks

Goodchild (Philip Guard) Percy Peckham (Harry Shacklock) John Steed (Patrick Macnee) Catherine Gale (Honor Blackman) Boy (Anthony Rogers) Gerald Shelley (David Langton) Maitland (Edward Jewesbury) Brown (Alfred Burke) Lord Matterley (Richard Vernon) Porter (Raymond Hodge) Inspector Burke (Alan Rolfe) P.C.Andrews (Edward Higgins) Elsie (Grace Arnold) Lorry Driver (Edwin Brown) Lorry Driver's Mate (Anthony Blackshaw) Miss Power (Delia Corrie) Sheila Gray (Sylvia Langova) Foreign Delegate (Theodore Wilhelm)

Designed by Philip Harrison
Directed by Richmond Harding

Steed is intrigued by the death of a stamp dealer and he places Mrs Gale undercover in the stamp shop. Between them they discover that the dealers' lists are a code being used by New Rule to plan an uprising in Europe. In preparation, arms are being stashed, in places such as dentists' surgeries and stamp dealers' shops. When Cathy's cover is blown, she is taken to a New Rule rally to meet Lord Matterley, the new Fuhrer. But Steed has a gun trained on him, so the would-be dictator has no option but to to postpone New Rule indefinitely.

Recorded: 18 October 1962   TX: 10 November 1962

38 DEATH OF A GREAT DANE

by Roger Marshall and Jeremy Scott

Minister (Billy Minton) Gravedigger (Herbert Nelson) Gregory (Leslie French) Catherine Gale (Honor Blackman) John Steed (Patrick Macnee) Mrs Miller (Clare Kelly) First Assistant (Dennis Edwards) Second Assistant (Anthony Baird) Getz (Frederick Jaeger) George Miller (Frank Peters) Policeman (Michael Moyer) Sir James Mann (John Laurie) First Winetaster (Eric Elliott) Second Winetaster (Roger Maxwell) Man from Kennels (Kevin Barry) Dancer (Junia) Bellhound (Heidi)

Designed by Patrick Downing
Directed by Peter Hammond

Steed is convinced that a recent coffin buried at a cemetery for pets actually contains the body of Alex Litoff, a rich recluse. Litoff's butler and his friends are laundering Litoff's money by converting it into diamonds which are smuggled out of the country. Cathy discovers that the Great Dane that should have been buried is alive; it is with the widow of a man who died smuggling diamonds in his stomach. This spurs

Getz, the ring leader of the canine fraud, to attempt to rub out the Avengers, but they turn the tables on him.

Recorded: 1 November 1962   TX: 17 November 1962

39 DEATH ON THE ROCKS

by Eric Paice

Mrs Ross (Annette Kerr) Liza Denham (Ellen McIntosh) Diamond Dealers (Jack Grossman and Vincent Charles) John Steed (Patrick Macnee) Max Daniels (Hamilton Dyce) Van Berg (Richard Clarke) Catherine Gale (Honor Blackman) Painter (Haydn Ward) Fenton (Gerald Cross) Nicky (David Sumner) Samuel Ross (Meier Tzelniker) Jackie Ross (Toni Gilpin) Sid (Douglas Robinson) Mrs Daniels (Naomi Chance)

Designed by James Goddard
Directed by Jonathan Alwyn

Diamonds are flooding Hatton Garden, so Steed goes into partnership with Ross, a diamond merchant, to trace the source of the illicit gems. Fenton, one of the diamond smuggling gang, plans to drive the Diamond Federation out of business and he has both Mrs Ross and Mrs Daniels, wife of another diamond merchant, killed to force their husbands into dealing with him. Cathy, meanwhile, has traced the smuggling method – they enter the country in rock salt containers. With their plans exposed, the ring leader, Mr Daniels and his murderous accomplice, Liza, receive their come-uppance.

Recorded: 15 November 1962   TX: 1 December 1962

40 TRAITOR IN ZEBRA

by John Gilbert

Escorting Officer (Richard Pescud) Captain Nash (Noel Coleman) Crane (Danvers Walker) Maggie (June Murphy) Catherine Gale (Honor Blackman) John Steed (Patrick Macnee) Lieutenant Mellors (Ian Shand) Wardrobe Steward (Michael Browning) Sub-Lieutenant Graham (William Gaunt) Franks (Richard Leech) Rankin (John Sharp) Linda (Katy Wild) Thorne (Jack Stewart)

Designed by Terry Green
Directed by Richmond Harding

There has been a leak of defence secrets and from HMS Zebra. Mrs Gale and Steed try to find out who is responsible, while Crane faces court martial for the crime. The real traitor, Mellors, becomes alarmed and informs his contact Rankin, a local artist, who in turn

Death of a Great Dane *might well have been the nucleus of the first filmed Avengers' episodes. Weighing up the pros and cons of producing the series on film, Howard Thomas asked the Iris Productions team to send along a sample of their work. Don Leaver and Patrick Downing were selected to give the ABC management team the hard sell. 'This episode was the one that Don Leaver and I took to ABPC [ABC's parent company at the time] at Elstree.' Downing told me: 'Originally Don was to direct the first one and I was to design. Thomas liked what he saw, but this all fell through. I think they thought that we were not experienced enough in filming, although later Don directed some of the filmed Avengers.'*

informs Franks, an enemy agent. Franks has Mellors and Graham, a friend of the accused, killed to give him more time. Steed pursues him to Rankin's office, where Franks has planted a booby-trap. Steed narrowly escapes death and follows Franks to the naval base, where the foreigner has planted a second bomb. Faced with being destroyed by his own device, Franks defuses it and Steed saves the day.

Recorded: 29 November 1962   TX: 8 December 1962

41 THE BIG THINKER

by Martin Woodhouse

Dr Clemens (Walter Hudd) Catherine Gale (Honor Blackman) Dr Farrow (David Garth) Dr Hurst (Tenniel Evans) Janet Lingfield (Marina Martin) Dr Kearns (Anthony Booth) John Steed (Patrick Macnee) Broster (Allan McClelland) Clarissa (Penelope Lee) Blakelock (Ray Browne) Nino (Clive Baxter)

Designed by James Goddard
Directed by Kim Mills

The final test on Plato, the most advanced computer ever built, is being sabotaged and someone seems determined to kill the scientists involved. Dr Kearns, a brilliant mathematician, is thought to be susceptible to blackmail because of his gambling problem and Mrs Gale is assigned to help him. Meanwhile, Dr Clemens, who discovered the identity of the saboteur, has been murdered, and the truth now lies within Plato. Kearns and Cathy are forced to send Steed an SOS when they become trapped inside the computer after more sabotage. Dr Farrow is caught red-handed when he attempts to stop Plato from revealing its secret, but he is electrocuted before he can be arrested.

Recorded: 13 December 1962   TX: 15 December 1962

42 INTERCRIME

by Terrance Dicks and Malcolm Hulke

Palmer (Donald Webster) Sewell (Rory MacDermot) Moss (Alan Browning) John Steed (Patrick Macnee) Catherine Gale (Honor Blackman) Hilda Stern (Julia Arnall) Trustees (Charlotte Selwyn and Jean Gregory) Prison Officer Sharpe (Bettine Milne) Felder (Kenneth J.Warren) Lobb (Jerome Willis) Manning (Patrick Holt) Pamela Johnson (Angela Browne) Kressler (Paul Hansard)

Designed by Richard Harrison
Directed by Jonathan Alwyn

Steed arranges for Mrs Gale to replace Hilda Stern when she arrives in Britain, so Cathy can learn the plans of Intercrime, an criminal organization. Stern is their professional assassin. Felder, the British organizer of Intercrime, orders Cathy to kill Palmer and Steed, but she is unable to do so. Then the real Hilda Stern escapes from custody and accuses Cathy of being an impostor. Cathy is put to the test when she is ordered to kill to prove she is the real Hilda. But Cathy cannot and her cover is blown. While Manning, one of Felder's business associates struggles for control of Intercrime, Steed steps in to rescue Mrs Gale and force the company into liquidation.

Recorded: 29 December 1962   TX: 5 January 1963

43 IMMORTAL CLAY

by James Mitchell

Catherine Gale (Honor Blackman) Allan Marling (Gary Watson) Mara Little (Didi Sullivan) Richard Marling (Paul Eddington) John Steed (Patrick Macnee) One-Ten (Douglas Muir) Miller (James Bree) Anne (Rowena Gregory) John Machen (Bert Palmer) De Groot (Steve Plytas) Blomberg (Frank Olegario)

Designed by James Goddard
Directed by Richmond Harding

Has Allan Marling created an unbreakable ceramic cup? De Groot thinks so and bribes Miller to steal it – then kills him when the stolen cup breaks! Lander also wanted the cup and de Groot now tries to blackmail Marling into giving him the secret or the agent will reveal that Allan killed Lander while protecting his brother's wife. No one realizes that Steed has the cup – the night watchman at the Marling factory gave it to him to prevent it being stolen. Steed ensures that de Groot is arrested and the Marling factory is saved from closure.

Immortal Clay:
Jonathan Alwyn was to have directed this episode. Anthony John said the 'story is complicated, even for The Avengers, but provided director Richmond Harding drives it along at a good pace, it should have an intriguing hold on its audience'. Cuts for 'bad taste' had been made to the script and an 'unnatural' break remedied.

Recorded: 10 January 1963   TX: 12 January 1963

44 BOX OF TRICKS

by Peter Ling and Edward Rhodes

Garry Weston (Ian Curry) Venus Smith (Julie Stevens) John Steed (Patrick Macnee) Henriette (Jacqueline Jones) Manager (Dallas Cavell) Denise (April Olrich) General Sutherland (Maurice Hedley) Kathleen Sutherland (Jane Barrett) Dr Gallam (Edgar Wreford) with Robert Hartley, Royston Tickner, Gail Starforth, Lynn Taylor, Gregory Scott and the Dave Lee Trio

Designd by Anne Spavin
Directed by Kim Mills

Julie Stevens played vivacious nightclub singer Venus Smith. She was on song in six Seasons episodes.

A faith healer and a magician conspire to steal NATO secrets: the magician secretes tape-recorders within the healing boxes supplied by Dr Gallam and conveys the information back to the doctor. A vanishing cabinet trick, used to dispose of any unwelcome snoopers, is uncovered by Steed and Venus, and The Avengers are nearly killed by a concealed trip-wire hidden in the device. The deadly duo try their healing scam one more time before Steed plugs the security leak and exposes the pair as phonies.

Recorded: 17 January 1963   TX: 19 January 1963

45 THE GOLDEN EGGS

by Martin Woodhouse

Dr Ashe (Donald Eccles) Elizabeth Bayle (Pauline Delaney) De Leon (Gordon Whiting) John Steed (Patrick Macnee) Catherine Gale (Honor

Blackman) Diana (Irene Bradshaw) Hillier (Robert Bernal) Redfern (Peter Arne) Campbell (Louis Haslar) Hall (Charles Bird)

Designed by Douglas James
Directed by Peter Hammond

Two gold-plated eggs are stolen from Dr Ashe. They contain a deadly virus which then kills the burglar, De Leon, shortly after he has hidden them. His ex-employer Redfern uses Mrs Gale to find the eggs, but before he can kill her she threatens to break them unless he surrenders. Fearing for his life Redfern agrees, allowing Steed and Mrs Gale to return the eggs to their ower. To their amazement Ashe reveals that they are dummies, the real eggs were too dangerous to keep.

Recorded: 31 January 1963   TX: 2 February 1963

46 SCHOOL FOR TRAITORS

by James Mitchell

Ted East (John Standing) Venus Smith (Julie Stevens) Claire Summers (Melissa Stribling) Roberts (Richard Thorp) Higby (Reginald Marsh) John Steed (Patrick Macnee) One-Seven (Frederick Farley) Dr Shanklin (Anthony Nicholls) Professor Aubyn (Frank Shelley) Green (Terence Woodfield) Proctor (Ronald Mayer) Sally (Janet Butlin) and the Kenny Powell Trio

Designed by Maurice Pelling
Directed by Jonathan Alwyn

Venus is performing at university Rag Week while Steed probes the alleged suicide of Richard Davis. He pretends that Venus received a suicide note frightening the gang behind the killing into trying to recover it. Professor Shanklin, the mastermind of the scheme and Claire Summers know the truth; they try to disfigure Venus with beauty cream spiced with acid. Summers then tries to blackmail East, a graduate, to kill Steed but the plan misfires and the killers are exposed.

Recorded: 7 February 1963   TX: 9 February 1963

47 THE WHITE DWARF

by Malcolm Hulke

Professor Richter (Keith Pyott) John Steed (Patrick Macnee) Cathrine Gale (Honor Blackman) Minister (Daniel Thorndike) Henry Barker (Peter Copley) Cartright (Philip Latham) Elizabeth Fuller (Vivienne Drummond) Rahim (Paul Anil) Luke (George Roubicek) Maxwell Barker (George A.Cooper) Johnson (Bill Nagy) Miss Tregarth (Constance Chapman) Butler (John Falconer)

Designed by Terry Green
Directed by Richmond Harding

Barker and Johnson conspire to defraud the Stock Market by convincing the government that The White Dwarf, a star, will collide with the Earth. At the observatory, astronomer Professor Richter and Rahim, an Indian observer, are killed by Cartright, to prevent them from learning the truth. However, when Cartright views The White Dwarf, he is amazed to see the star on a collision course with the planet. It appears that Richter was right and the world will end. Convinced that Barker double-crossed him, Cartright exposes the plan to Steed who sees that the shady financiers are brought to book. Mrs Gale then reveals that the plates in the telescope were rigged by her. The White Dwarf has not changed orbit at all.

Recorded: 14 February 1963   TX: 16 February 1963

48 MAN IN THE MIRROR

by Geoffrey Orme and Anthony Terpiloff

Betty (Daphne Anderson) Strong (Ray Barrett) Brown (Julian Somers) John Steed (Patrick Macnee) Venus Smith (Julie Stevens) Jean (Rhoda Lewis) Victor Trevelyan (Haydn Jones) Iris (Frieda Knorr) One-Six (Michael Gover) Producer (David Graham) and the Kenny Powell Trio

Designed by Anne Spavin
Directed by Kim Mills

Venus is in a Hall of Mirrors at a funfair and accidentally photographs a man's reflection in the glass – a man who is meant to be dead. Brown, who owns the funfair, tries to retrieve the film and Steed discovers that Trevelyan, the cypher clerk presumed dead, was apparently kidnapped by Strong, who runs the cafe at the park. Converging on the funfair, Steed and Venus are taken prisoner by Strong who leaves them wired to a timed bomb. Betty, a worker at the sideshow, sets them free after stabbing Strong, but the real traitors – Mr and Mrs Trevelyan – have already made good their escape.

Recorded: 22 February 1963   TX: 23 February 1963

49 CONSPIRACY OF SILENCE

by Roger Marshall

James (Artro Morris) Sica (Alec Mango) Carlo (Robert Rietty) John Steed (Patrick Macnee) Rickie (Sandra Dorne) Catherine Gale (Honor Blackman) Gutman (Roy Purcell) Leggo (Himself) Terry (John Church) Arturo (Tommy Godfrey) Professor (Willie Shearer) Rant (Ian Wilson) and Elizabeth and Collins

Opposite: A rare behind-the-scenes shot showing the tricks of the trade used by the studio technicians.

Designed by Stephen Doncaster
Directed by Peter Hammond

When Carlo, the circus clown, fails to kill Steed he goes into hiding and Mrs Gale is soon hot on his trail, in the guise of a photographer/journalist. Carlo takes refuge amongst the clowns in a circus, but the Mafia catch up with him and insist that he completes their mission and another attempt is made on Steed's life. Again, Carlo cannot commit the crime and turns his gun on Terry, his Mafia colleague, instead. On the same side now, Carlo breaks his vow of silence and Sica, the Mafia representative who wanted Steed killed, is arrested.

Recorded: 1 March 1963   TX: 2 March 1963

50 A CHORUS OF FROGS

by Martin Woodhouse

Stephanopoulus (Makki Marseilles) One-Six (Michael Gover) Mason (Eric Pohlmann) Anna (Yvonne Shima) Venus Smith (Julie Stevens) Ariston (John Carson) Dr Pitt-Norton (Frank Gatliff) Helena (Colette Wilde) Jackson (Alan Haywood) John Steed (Patrick Macnee) Ship's Officer (Norman Johns) Steward (Steve Cory) Man (Colin Fry) and the Kenny Powell Trio

A Chorus of Frogs: *Author of this episode (and others) Martin Woodhouse, later wrote a bestseller novel,* Tree Frog. *Martin, a computer wizard, probably had the highest IQ of anyone associated with the show. He was consultant on Ergonomics with Farnborough Institute of Aviation Medicine.* * *Raymond Menmuir, who directed this episode, later became producer of Brian Clemens' and Albert Fennell's* The Professionals. *

Designed by James Goddard
Directed by Raymond Menmuir

Beneath Mason's luxury yacht, The Archipelago, Pitt-Norton experiments with a new type of bathyscape. Venus is booked to sing on board, so Steed becomes a stowaway in her cabin to investigate whether there is a connection with the death of a deep-sea diver. The diver belonged to the Frogs and their attempts to find out the truth lead to another of the group being killed. Anna, a foreign agent, and Pitt-Norton plan to use the bathyscape for military purposes. Steed puts paid to their attempts to make Venus the guinea pig in one final test of the bathyscape.

Recorded: 8 March 1963   TX: 9 March 1963

Six Hands Across
a Table:
*It was in this episode,
says Honor
Blackman, that the
scriptwriters started
writing for the
strengths of the Cathy
Gale character. 'I
think I said, "Does
this woman have no
man in her life apart
from Steed?" So they
introduced one where I
had a lover or some-
thing and at some
point in the story he
had to say "I love
you, Cathy," but he
got nervous and called
me by another name...
this didn't endear him
to me at all.'*

51 SIX HANDS ACROSS A TABLE

by Reed R de Rouen

Julian Seabrook (Philip Madoc) Charles Reniston (John Wentworth) George Stanley (Campbell Singer) Oliver Waldner (Guy Doleman) Butler (Ian Cunningham) Brian Collier (Edward de Souza) Lady Reniston (Freda Bamford) Catherine Gale (Honor Blackman) Rosalind Waldner (Sylvia Bidmead) Miss Francis (Gillian Barclay) Draughtsman (Stephen Hancock) Bert Barnes (Frank Siemen) John Steed (Patrick Macne) Receptionist (Illona Rodgers)

Designed by Paul Bernard
Directed by Richmond Harding

There is an important contract going to build a nuclear-powered liner: Brian Collier and the Reniston Group (which opposes any foreign partners) are both bidding for the contract. But somebody seems determined to stop Brian Collier from winning. Rosalind Waldner invites Cathy Gale, who is an old friend, to make enquiries since she is in love with Brian. After a board meeting with Rosalind's father Oliver, Sir Charles Reniston and George Stanley, someone makes an attempt on the lives of Cathy and Brian. Oliver Waldner is the mastermind. Together with Stanley he is planning to stop Collier's bid at any cost. With assistance from Steed, Cathy reluctantly places the two businessmen under arrest.

Recorded: 15 March 1963   TX: 16 March 1963

52 KILLER WHALE

by John Lucarotti

John Steed (Patrick Macnee) 'Pancho' Driver (Patrick Magee) Harry (Morris Perry) Catherine Gale (Honor Blackman) Joey Frazer (Kenneth Farrington) Willie (John Tate) Sailor (Fredrick Abbott) Fernand (John Bailey) Angela (Julie Paulle) Receptionist (Lyndall Goodman) Laboratory Assistant (Christopher Coll) Brown (Robert Mill) Tiger (Brian Mason) Models from the Kenneth Sweet Collection

Designed by Douglas James
Directed by Kim Mills

Mrs Gale decides to manage a promising new boxer, Joey Frazer. Steed suggests the gym run by 'Pancho' Driver. When Joey accidentally borrows another fighter's soap it is discovered that it is ambergris, a valuable element used in perfume. This is the break that Steed has been waiting for. He now traces the destination of the 'soap' to couturiers owned by Fernand, who is using the gym run by Driver as a cover for his illicit trade. Realizing that their smuggling operation has been tumbled, Driver and Fernand try to escape: a quick bout of fisticuffs with Steed and Cathy turn their would-be sweet-smelling operation sour.

Recorded: 22 March 1963   TX: 23 March 1963

SEASON THREE

Twenty-six monochrome videotaped episodes

starring PATRICK MACNEE and HONOR BLACKMAN   1963/1964

PRODUCTION HISTORY

IT USUALLY TAKES SEVERAL MONTHS for a TV series to have an impact on the viewers and for its particular personality to be abosrbed into folklore. Because Saturday night shows received less attention from the press than those screened when journalists were on duty, it was some time before The Avengers team became aware – through growing press interest, viewers' letters, requests for personal appearances and their own contact with the public – that their programme had become the rage. They were told, for instance, that The Avengers was 'the darling of the Primrose Hill set'… It keeps the Bright Young Things of Belgravia and Chelsea at home on Saturday nights.' It has started a new fashion in pin-ups – the photographers of a leading Fleet Street tabloid have taken down their pictures of unclad ladies and substituted the elegantly dressed Honor Blackman' (*Sunday Times*). 'It's trivial and I love it without reservation because it's shrewdly calculated and played with great style' (*The Spectator*). When it was screened for the first time in Scotland it immediately scored the highest viewing figures of any television contractor for the time of day. The Avengers, it appeared, had made it and now bore the accolade of television's most 'with it' drama show.

But not everyone applauded the programme. As plans were being prepared for a new 26-week run, a financial director of Iris Productions, the subsidiary company set up to produce the show for ABC, decided to examine the overall production cost of each episode produced. Only two episodes came in under or broke even with the projected production budget. Script, design, music and wardrobe costs had been rising steadily but, as we'll learn, not by much. The executive sent a memo to ABC; his main cause for concern was the proposed increases of salary for Honor Blackman and Patrick Macnee, both of whom were waiting to learn if their contracts were going to be renewed. Intimating that the company should face up to the fact that they simply could not afford Blackman *and* Macnee, he asked for a decision on which star *should be dropped*. If neither was to go, he asked whether the company would approve a substantially higher budget. Within seven days the series was allocated an extra £1,500 budget per episode and the stars' contracts were renewed.

* Denotes information supplied by Brian Clemens

Meanwhile, an ABC producer put forward the idea that the series could well use the addition of another male lead, to 'prevent the show from becoming *hag*-ridden', and the company's managing director, Howard Thomas, suggested that should they ever decide to give Steed a new second in command, the producers should keep in mind actor John Standing, who had played the role of East in the story *School for Traitors*, and who would prove a perfect foil for Macnee.

These views were in the minority. Most people enjoyed the show's originality. The Cathy Gale character, as one of the screen's earliest liberated women, was a revelation. At the time Honor said: 'I'd been used to playing women of the sweet, fair-

An (unconfirmed) rumour has it that, after a night on the town, one of the crew working on the video-taped Blackman shows, suffering a hangover from a heavy night's drinking, arrived on the set in such a state of lethargy that the director asked him to 'stand in' (i.e. lie down and go to sleep) for the corpse of a murdered man!

Many of the actors and production crew took their lunch break in The Anglers pub, next door to the Teddington Studios, whose gardens ran down to the River Thames.

The Outside-In Man:

Director Jonathan Alwyn had his own ideas on the design for this set. 'It was originally a very straightforward set – on paper. We said: "This is boring, Steed having to go to see this guy's secretary, whatever, and be ushered into the back room." So we decided to change all that. I said "Why don't we call the secretary, Miss Brisket, and instead of him going through to his superior's office, we have him shown into the meat-hanging area."' (Alwyn didn't say who the other person was. It was most likely set designer David Marshall). Incidentally, according to an ABC press handout, the book that Steed is seen reading in the gentlemen's club, was one from his favourite reading: the Tin-Tin stories. The title? The Secret of the Unicorn.

haired English rose variety. So when the opportunity of playing a character like Cathy Gale came along, it was like a breath of fresh air. The first few weeks were extremely difficult and for a time I wondered if I'd bitten off more than I could chew. But then I began to cope with the task of licking Cathy into the beginnings of what she is now. Everybody had ideas of what she was going to be like.' She told Paul Madden that Patrick Macnee had a lot to do with this. 'He would say, "She'd never do that, she'd put her foot down and do this, that or the other." We all pitched in. It was really very much a team effort. We wanted her to be somebody who had some punch. It was great, really great. Sydney Newman's original idea was that there should be this woman who had a wall-eye, or a withered arm or something. We knew right at the beginning what kind of character we were going after. After the first few episodes we used to have a Dos and Don'ts list for the writers: Steed would or wouldn't do this; Cathy would never do this and would always do that. I was always honourable and straight and direct and honest and fearless and had all the virtues. Patrick was always a bit wicked and devilish and michievous and not quite straight.'

Leonard White, who shaped the first two series, had transferred to ABC's *Armchair Theatre* (at his own request), and the series' former story editor, John Bryce, was now heading up the production team. Gone also was Venus Smith. Julie Stevens had left the show to have a baby – and Dr King, One-Ten, Freckles and company were quietly forgotten.

Roger Marshall holds the view that Julie Stevens probably wouldn't have stayed around anyway. 'Honor was such a terrific success that everybody wanted to write for her and that was unfortunate. Julie was perfectly acceptable in her episodes but was elbowed aside by this great tyro that turned out to be Cathy Gale.'

Newcomers in the third season were Paul Whitsun-Jones as Charles, Steed's superior in the stories *Man With Two Shadows* and *The Wringer*, and Ronald Radd, as Quilpie, Steed's chief in the episode *The Outside-In Man*. A distinctive character, Quilpie worked from an office hidden behind a butcher's shop where he passed out prime cuts of meat between briefing his agents as head of PANSAC (Permanent Agency for National Security and Counter-Intelligence). The agents gained entry through the cold store. Quilpie was given the opportunity of uttering a typical *Avengers* line: 'Come into the fridge, there's something that needs to be done.' A third new 'character' was Junia, an 18-month-old Great Dane. Sister of Juno, the canine who shared Steed's adventures in the previous series, Junia had actually made her debut as a replacement for her brother in the story *Death of a Great Dane*. Referred to as 'Puppy' by Steed, both dogs were owned and trained by top dog-breeder/trainer, Barbara 'Walkies' Woodhouse.

One reason for the programme's success was the friendly co-operation between the writers and the production team. *The Avengers* was a show where everyone collaborated in altering or embellishing the scripts to improve the show. Bryce and story editor Richard Bates had gathered together the finest writing talent available. Writers of the calibre of Brian Clemens, Roger Marshall and Malcolm Hulke were asked to devise new and exciting stories that were scripted for tension, lacked solemnity, embodied a broad streak of leg-pulling, and would allow the viewer to be carried along with the action and not be dismayed when something outrageously illogical happened to Steed and Cathy.

Richard Bates, who had joined the team for a 'probationary' period on 10 October 1963, comments on the leg-pulling element. 'Quite where the tongue-in-cheek came from, I don't know. I think that it was probably a series of accidents. Patrick Macnee had and still has a very strong sense of humour and a very good turn of dialogue. Once we'd become attuned to that, the writers and I were able to write very successfully for the Steed character in particular. This happens of course on a series where you have a very large number of episodes. Fifty-two is now a very rare number to see in a one hour drama series. We would make twenty-six in a year and fifty-two in two years. Things grew very quickly in those days.'

However, illogical situations were noted by viewers. *The Grandeur that was Rome* came in for for heavy criticism from John Bryce. He had missed the episode on television and asked for a special playback of the VTR. He wrote:

Three talented guys, left to right: script editor Richard Bates, and scriptwriters Malcolm Hulke and Brian Clemens.

Roger Marshall attributes the show's success to the quality of production. 'I think its quality is best explained when you compare it with the other very flat-footed shows that were being done at the same time. If you compare The Avengers, *say, with* No Hiding Place, *which was then in its swing, then you'll see how far ahead of its time* The Avengers *was. It was tremendous fun to work on.'*

'I understand that there were a considerable number of telephone calls from dissatisfied viewers. Although I thought that the first forty minutes of the programme were magnificent, full of characteristic style and wit, I must confess that the last ten minutes seemed to justify every complaint.

I can't blame viewers being indignant when after leaving Steed in the hands of the enemy at the point of a sword, we suddenly find him in the next scene in time to rescue Cathy and defeat the baddies with no explanation as to how he escaped! Similarly, it was ludicrous to see Cathy and Steed, with only one dagger between them, put to rout a room full of villains, some of whom were armed. And the ending was perfunctory to an extreme: with Bruno dead, was that the end? What about the rest of the crooks?

It isn't good enough to say that logic and reason form no part of the programme's appeal, or that you don't have to understand everything as long as the programme is consistent to itself, if the programme suddenly ceases to be consistent. We have got to see Steed get out of his predicament, or explain, convincingly, how he does so. We have got to be helped to suspend our disbelief in the routing of a whole gang of villains. We have got to be at the very least supplied with, if not utterly convinced by, a denouement. Disappointed or frustrated viewers mean, in the long run, lower ratings.

You will have to get a tighter hold of credibility than this.'

Richard Bates remembers being encouraged to go off and work with the writers on the increasingly exotic storylines. 'Already the thing was beginning to blossom in an extraordinary way. The Avengers was rather like Topsy, it just grew. I worked largely on my own and so I just let my imagination run riot and encouraged the writers to do the same. We had arrived at a small team of writers who were the ones who did have the imagination to come up with the right sort of storyline. The greatest difficulty was always the stories. In those days you had to devise a story which you could tell in sets in the studio. A 51-minute show would be shot in *51 minutes*, so it was a question of devising something in a very tight physical situation, with a restricted number of sets and, possibly, a small amount of location filming. We had a small cast because we had a small budget, so there was a restriction as to how many characters you could have in any one episode.

'Finding writers to turn out the right sort of script was the hardest part of my work. Out of 80 writers that I interviewed, we ended employing only five or six. Of the stories we devised, Brian Clemens and I always worked together very quickly, as did Roger Marshall. Clemens and Marshall were extremely adept and capable of writing a script – an excellent script – in a matter of days. We would sometimes devise a story in a matter of hours. Sometimes it took days, other stories literally took weeks. We were always under enormous pressure to sustain the right balance of story level.

'We tried to keep the basic story firmly with its feet on the ground, so that there was reality behind the exotica of the story. Once we had worked this out, we allowed it to flourish and nothing ordinary was allowed to be in the script. This gave all sorts of opportunities in design – whatever the story was about, it had to be something that would challenge the designer.'

Don Leaver confirmed that team-spirit was the order of the day. '*The Avengers* was very design orientated, very much so. You had these fertile people who weren't just building scenery, but were into saying: "Hey. Why don't we shoot this from here?" One's reaction was: "Oh, don't be silly. That's going to look terrible." They would nevertheless keep coming up with the most way-out ideas – and often, they worked!'

Brian Clemens acknowledges that this always happened, on both the videotaped series, and afterwards, when they went to film. 'Absolutely! We would go along with that completely. We would get suggestions from clapper boys, to riggers to gaffers. If they were good suggestions we would use them. And, because they were used, not only did the person who had put forward the suggestion feel very much a part of the team, he would keep thinking and maybe make another suggestion. I was like a sponge in a way. I would draw it in and then immediately afterwards claim it as my own!'

Urged to attend readings, rehearsals and recordings, and encouraged to regard themselves as key figures in the shaping of the final production, the writing team were relentlessly critical of themselves, constantly conducting their own audience research and welcoming each tuppenny-worth of free advice. They saw their show as a pastiche of the thriller formula which had delighted highbrow and lowbrow audiences ever since it was first devised. If some of the fun the writing team had in putting the show together rubbed off on their audience, they were well satisfied. They relished its bizarre, tongue-in-cheek quality, and they refused to treat it seriously – except in their own terms, which was as an hour of slick, sophisticated and highly-entertaining television. As a result, the scripts became slicker. Week after week the crime-busting duo proved to be remarkable. When confronted with all kinds of mysterious and intriguing situations the twosome would somehow or other always overcome the opposition – usually with the wink of an eye or a smile. One special gimmick was to give the viewer only about half the facts necessary for a reasonable understanding of the plot, then shuffle these into a pattern that took 50 minutes to unravel – leaving the onlooker with a kind of guessing game, which was invariably good fun.

However, when a national newspaper called Steed 'a marsh-mallow Scarlet Pimpernel', and further research indicated that he was becoming too much of a humorous 'feed' to Cathy Gale, steps were immediately taken to toughen up his character and restore the cultivated callousness that had first endeared him to his fans. An example of this appears in *Man with Two Shadows*, in which Steed, during his interrogation of a prisoner suspected of having been brainwashed by the 'opposition' into becoming a 'double agent', angrily snatches away the chair from beneath the prisoner, then kicks him in the ribs as he lies prostrate on the cell floor!

Similarly, Cathy's role was changed to allow her more opportunity to show the feminine and fallible side of her nature. Throughout the earlier series, Cathy's instinct for self-preservation had never faltered – even when her partner was threatened by villains, no hint of female submission had ever cracked her icy cool. She had come to represent women everywhere who wanted to prove their equality with the opposite sex; a woman who fought like a man, used her wits like a man, yet firmly retained her femininity. Patrick Macnee told me that this was the only time he felt uncomfortable with the series. Believing that Cathy Gale was becoming increasingly 'butch' and doing things that Steed should have done, he relayed his opinion to the producers. (Things were changed.)

Once again, a new production directive was called for. John Bryce issued his technicians with his own ideas for the new format.

THE AVENGERS
A Reappraisal

JOHN STEED

Steed is a thoroughly professional and efficient undercover man. His cover is that of a man-about-town with a private income. He is suave, witty, debonair, foppish even. These qualities are consciously cultivated to disarm his opponents and lull them into a vulnerable position for the kill.

Steed is an expert: dedicated, ruthless, unscrupulous. His mission is all-important to him and its success is the justification of whatever methods he has used. He has been thoroughly trained in arson, burglary, forgery, explosives, codes, poisons and murder... to name but a few. He is trained to withstand torture and brainwashing.

Other than Catherine Gale there is no one working for Steed or with him, except such as may be persuaded (by any means from bribery to blackmail) to help him in a specific situation.

Steed's tastes are gentlemanly and slightly self-indulgent. He frequents the best tailor, best bootmaker, best wine merchant, visits the best clubs, best restaurants, reads the Royal Edition of *The Times*, plays bridge, bezique, polo, croquet, etc.

Steed's flat reflects the family tradition and heritage: the Hyderabad All India Polo Cup; a tiger skin; hunting trophies; a portrait of his great-grandfather Steed, etc. Most of Steed's possessions have a history – or at least an anecdotal background to them.

Unlike Cathy, he carries no obvious symbol of his vocation, such as a holster (he uses a gun infrequently). But when necessary he can produce a fund of firearms, poison capsules, time bombs, microscopic transmitters, etc.

When tackling criminals he fights like a cad and uses every dirty trick in the book to knock them out with the least inconvenience to himself.

At all times (whether being menaced or menacing) Steed displays grace and charm.

MRS CATHERINE GALE

A widow. She is trained as an anthropologist. She is now a professional undercover agent. (The two jobs sometimes get in the way of each other.)

Cathy is essentially humanitarian. She is loyal, honest and compassionate. She is as much a professional as Steed, but her attitude to the mission is totally different. The end can never justify the means for her. She cares about people and cannot use them like Steed. (She clashes frequently with Steed over the callousness of his methods.)

Steed deceives people fluently, Cathy deceives people with the greatest difficulty and only when her role makes it inevitable. She will never deceive people simply in order to discover information: her enquiries are more likely to be straightforward.

Cathy prefers plain speaking: Steed says 'assassination', Cathy calls it 'murder'. Cathy carries a gun. She is expert with all firearms and at photography and judo. She drives a car fast and well.

Cathy's flat is modern and functional, predominantly press-button controlled: sliding doors, concealed drinks cabinet, etc. Cathy is avant garde in all her tastes. Her clothes are designed to suit her own individual style of cool, uncluttered elegance, masculine in the manner that emphasises femininity and always practical for the life she leads.

Her possessions: photographic equipment, etc, will be the most modern. Steed is slightly ill at ease among Cathy's gadgetry.

THE TWO CHARACTERS

Steed and Cathy's moral attitudes conflict and this difference is

Extracts from The Avengers, *illustrating Cathy Gale's judo prowess, were shown in the BBC TV programme* On the Braden Beat, *on 30 March 1963. And* The Avengers *was given a plug in January of that year, when Benny Hill, trapped in a tricky situation in* The Benny Hill Show *found himself in a situation where he asked himself 'I wonder what the* Avengers *would do here?'*

Until recently, Ambren still had Honor's original leather boots, bought by her in an ABC-TV wardrobe sale for her daughter, Melanie. She meant to throw them away many times. She didn't. The boots lay in a spare bedroom for twenty-odd years. Then she had them valued by Christies – and hit the jackpot. Expected to reach the reserve price of £800, the boots were sold in October 1993, for £1,870! Asked at the time if she would be bidding for her boots when they went under the hammer, Honor Blackman replied: 'I don't know whose boots they are, but they are certainly not mine. I have got my fighting boots. I shall never part with them.' As Ambren Garland assured me: the boots were indeed Cathy Gale's original kinky boots (Honor having more than one pair of course). Christies contacted Ambren again. Did she have any further Avengers' items? Ambren said no – but she knew of someone who did. Fellow wardrobe girl Margaret Morris had purchased Honor's original brocade waistcoat in the same sale. She hasn't sold it – yet!

emphasised when they are on a mission. (Each character's point of view, although opposed, is of course equally valid).

Now matter how they conflict, the two characters retain a trust in each other. Cathy, for example, will always leave that important anthropology meeting to help Steed... But, of course, each will always be able to surprise the other with some character revelation.

Steed and Cathy do not and could never function as police, private eyes, etc. They are undercover agents, and consequently conceal this identity at all times: they have no badge to show or card to flash, nor does the announcement of their names bring automatic recognition or respect.

Steed and Cathy thrive on audience curiosity and speculation.

FIGHTS/ACTION

There will be at least one fight, and some physical conflict, in every episode.

Cathy is the professional, disciplined judo expert. Steed fights like a cad – with little apparent exertion (and without having to remove his bowler). Cathy throws her opponents. Steed trips his. Cathy's aim is to close with her opponent in order to use judo. Steed stays at a distance by use of props (his bowler hat, his umbrella, etc.)

Stuntmen should always be used as opponents and the scripts will be written to make such casting practicable.

FILM

We will make use of film, but never in the conventional way (establishing shots, as a link between scenes, etc.)

We will only use film when we have a self-contained sequence (including Cathy and/or Steed) which typifies the series: Cathy giving chase on a motorbike; a gunfight during a Steed golf match; Cathy tied to a railway track while the 7.10 thunders closer and closer, etc.

The Avengers is a series with an established popularity. I want to take advantage of this privileged situation and make it an opportunity for direction, design, effects, casting, scripting, etc. All experiments will be contained within the terms of our existing successful format, but there is plenty of scope, so let us take our opportunities to enhance further the style and prestige of *The Avengers*.

Drinking scenes should be kept to a minimum. Smoking scenes should be kept to the minimum. Blasphemy is out!

***

Steed and Cathy's wardrobes were changed for the new series. However, my previous assertion that Frederick Starke, former chairman of the London Fashion House was totally responsible

Honor Blackman
and Patrick Macnee,
pictured during a
publicity session in
London's Oxford
Street, circa 1963.

for the design and manufacture of Cathy's new outfits was
slightly off target, as Ambren Garland explained: 'Neither
Starke, nor Michael Whittaker before him, created *any* of the
outfits worn by Cathy Gale – although they did have an influence on the look. The outfits were bought. The truth of the
matter is that we were furious when the producers started to
give Starke the credit: "Honor Blackman's clothes, designed by
Frederick Starke".

'This happened totally against my and Audrey Liddle's wishes. It was arranged by a woman who at that time was doing the
publicity for the show, Marie Donaldson. She was always trying
to fix up publicity angles to promote Honor's clothes. She was
only doing her job, of course, but we were furious when this
happeed. We created costumes for every single episode – usually at less than seven days notice. Furthermore, the outfits which
were supplied to us by outside sources were not at all suitable. As
I've told you, Honor didn't have an ordinary shaped figure, so all
her clothes had to be specially made. Audrey and myself knew

Then there were the fights...
a) Honor Blackman: 'We always used blanks, of course... but there was an instance when I actually shot someone. We had blanks up the spout and this poor actor had to reach for something, a gun or whatever it was, and I fired – and got him in the hand. He got sprayed with the cartridge packing and I peppered his hand...'
b) Jonathan Alwyn remembers an occasion when anything that could go wrong did. 'Patrick was down to fight this (so-called) judo expert, and Honor was supposed to take over and tackle the guy until Patrick clubbed him down with the brolly. It was a mess. Despite the fact that Steed was supposed to be this debonair Englishman, whose flick of the brolly could save any situation, back then Patrick was hopeless at feigning fight movements.'

what was going to look best on screen – Starke didn't, and he kept on producing things that for many reasons were no good at all. His clothes were sometimes manufactured in checks and would consequently create strobes on camera, or they were in the wrong colours, which made life difficult for the cameramen.'

Ambren Garland says that the leather outfits continued to be used as a sort of symbol. 'Honor's other clothes veered from being high fashion, to being gimmicky.' She remembers one instance when director Peter Hammond suggested that he wanted Cathy to look completely different. 'Honor had been wearing these fairly butch clothes and Peter wanted her to be "floating in chiffon".' The budget really wouldn't run to this, but I nevertheless bought yards and yards of grey chiffon, which were then knocked up by wardrobe into trousers and a floating top. Honor thought that this was splendid. She lay down on the set and burst out with a chorus of "Fry's Turkish Delight". One was always coming up against this with different directors who didn't want her to appear in the clothes she already had.

'One of the things about working in television, is that you have to please so many people. First of all as a designer, you want the artiste to be happy in what you have created for them. But then you are told by the producer that he wants this sort of look for the whole series. Then each individual director tells you that he wants her to look like this and these are the clothes that she should wear for a particular scene, or episode. And all the time you're working to an incredibly small budget. So you couldn't do necessarilly what you wanted to do. You had to please several masters.'

Despite the fact that the wardrobe allowance had been increased, from an average £60 to £100 (the figure frequently dipped well below the century mark), the ABC Wardrobe Department continued to work miracles.

Patrick Macnee's clothes became more Edwardian-influenced than ever, with braided pinstripe suits, elegantly embroidered waistcoats, cummerbunds, drainpipe trousers and curly bowlers. Cathy's leather, though not entirely forgotten, gave way to garments that had either a military or Chinese influence. Suits, hats and boots took their flavour from the officers' uniforms of the Napoleonic period, with fobs, waistcoats and cravats. Dresses and jackets had the simplicity of the Chinese line.

Ambren Garland confirmed that Cathy's original leather boots (previously credited as being manufactured by Frederick Starke), were in fact made by Annello and Davide, of London. Margaret Morris, another member of the wardrobe team, designed and made the longer, thigh boots. The creations were previewed on 29 October 1963 at The Garrison, Les Ambassadeurs Club, in London's Park Lane.

When asked if wearing the leather ensembles influenced her choice of everday dress, Honor Blackman told me, 'I had the most fearful time during *The Avengers*, because some men felt threatened by Cathy Gale – the *image* of Cathy Gale. I would go to parties and they would try to lure me outside for a fight. It was pretty jokey, really, because usually they were sufficiently stoned that one slight push in their stomach and they'd have soon been over. To have worn leather would have been to invite trouble, and in any case, everybody else was wearing leather then. I simply set the fashion. So it certainly affected my choice inasmuch as I didn't wear leather outside the show.'

It appears that Cathy Gale's image problem didn't end there. When pressed, Honor continued, 'I had this extraordinary fan mail. Some of it quite funny, some of it very sick. We used to have this wonderful publicity woman called Marie Donaldson, who admitted quite frankly that a lot of the letters were kept from me. But some I saw and I suppose that around eighty percent were answered. It created some rather strange invitations – some *very* strange invitations. Some people actually imagined that with all the leather and boots I wore, I also carried a whip! I was frequently asked to attend strange parties – provided I carried my whip. I never went, of course!'

Of course, if called upon to do so, Honor Blackman could handle herself in any situation, as this anecdote proves. Just before a live television appearance in the Midlands to promote the show, Honor asked the interviewer what type of questions he would be putting to her during the programme, a request intended to ensure that she could give adequate answers. 'Oh, I never discuss the questions with a guest,' came the reply – leaving an edge to the relationship as they faced the camera. The interview moved along until out of the blue the pompous questioner said: 'Tell me, Miss Blackman, how does it feel to be half man and half woman?' Without batting an eyelid, the *Avengers* star, dressed in a low-cut dress which fully displayed her natural contours to the best advantage, leaned across the table and replied: 'Which half are you referring to?' Cue for a red-faced interviewer to fluff his remaining lines.

Even in those early days, there was no shortage of actors waiting to appear on the programme. Don Leaver puts this down to the popularity that enveloped the show. 'Everybody wanted to be in *The Avengers*. If you offered an actor a role very rarely would they turn you down. It soon developed a kind of cult status and massive viewing figures. I don't think incoming actors were ever given a specific brief, to play it this way or that way. We would work on it like anything else and we would try to find a 'kooky' angle to come at it. That was all part of the added dimension that came with Honor. We all felt that we could be a little more way-out because after all, if you have an attractive lady like Honor Blackman twirling herself across the screen in black leather, then anything's possible!'

Yes it was, but only after producer John Bryce took a look at the first dozen episodes (of Season Two) and decided that it was time to take stock and remind his team of certain fundamentals.

c) *Honor Blackman once had to turn the tables on an actor during rehearsal. Having read the script, the actor knew what he was supposed to do, but decided to play macho. 'He knew that I was going to fight him, and he knew that I was going to win. It was a scene in a storage room stacked with filing cabinets. He was supposed to pop out from behind one of them and we'd start fighting. During rehearsals, in this room with a parquet floor, he said: "Oh, this is where old clever clogs comes out and this is what the toughie does to him." My temper was rising and the director was looking at me as if to say, "Please don't rise to it", and I thought okay. I turned to this man and asked him to show me what he was going to do. He came at me – and I threw him. He landed with a bump and went bang. He was the only one who ever did it!'*

THE AVENGERS

The problem now is to maintain the standard and to *improve it* still more. I therefore make the following points:-

Scripting

I still think the opening and closing contain the main difficulties. I mean the scene(s) where we set the mission and involve Cathy, and then the 'pay-off' scene(s).

Cathy must be correctly motivated. We must involve or refer to her work at some stage. She must have something special to contribute to the mission. So special that Steed needs her help. She must, above all, have the humanitarian and moral attitude to the story. She wants to help those who are in peril or distress. She cares about them. This must of itself give rise to some conflict with Steed. His strictly professional and ruthless attitude will often enrage her.

The 'pay-off' must be clearly understood. We must know why and how Steed and Cathy succeed. They should not succeed too easily. The opposition should be tough; should indeed be worthy opponents for Steed and Cathy.

The fights are still a continual problem in 'live' production. Sometimes they are exciting and excellent: sometimes they are very poor. With care they can succeed.

Further, although the final decision must be left with the individual directors, I urge consideration of the possibility of making the fight sequences the subject of VTR-inserts.

a) We must be ever careful concerning violence. Our leads must fight because there is no other way out and they are in extreme peril themselves. The fighting must *never* be sadistic.

b) Some episodes are still lacking in 'glamour'. All episodes should have their quota of attractive women characters.

c) Casting should be done to ensure that the women characters are glamorous. We must cast as interestingly as possible all round. Let us pioneer the new young actors and actresses (not get an idea or two from *Z Cars* or *Maigret!*)

d) Quite often recently the opening bar(s) of the theme music have been lost on the opening of acts 2 and 3. Therefore, in future, let us make it a rule to 'fade up vision' first and then hit the theme music.

e) The use of music has improved. With due care we can maintain and improve this. I suggest that where music (for mood, effects, etc.) is required beyond that already recorded for the series by Dankworth, we should use the excellent drum recordings which are now available in the library.

***

Richard Bates recalls that the producers placed added emphasis of the fight sequences during Season Three. One of the main reqirements of the script was that there should be at least one fight, possibly two, in every story. 'So we had to devise a different sort of fight and a different location for the fight. In the Blackman series you won't see anything as mundane as the front room of a semi-detached. We always had to come up with settings that were a challenge: exteriors of churchyards, warehouses, a zoo.'

Speaking to Paul Madden, Honor Blackman acknowledged that the fight scenes were not really that well rehearsed. 'We never had the set to work in, so we didn't really know what it was going to look like; what distance I had to work in; how much room I had for movement. I used to work it out with Doug or Joe Robinson, in the gym. We used to practice the moves on a mat, which is very different from actually doing it on the set. What was different about the second series was that in the first year we did all the fights live – we shot the whole show in one sequence. There was one camera waiting for the next scene, there was another camera for the caption credits and we may have had two cameras covering the fights. But that was useless, really, because you really want a camera doing the long shot, you want one for the face and another for the hands and feet. When the fights became so popular, in the second year they decided to shoot the fights the night before we did the show. It was crazy really, 'cause if I had killed myself or the other actor then there wasn't going to be a show the next day!'

Honor Blackman recalls some of the Season Two fights: 'I think that the producers tried to find me bigger and better men every week. I mean, I finished up with somebody who was 18-stone or something. It was ridiculous to try to throw someone like that with a stomach throw. A stomach throw is when you grab them by the lapels, put your foot in their chest and drop-kick to your bottom. Then you roll over and kick. But you can't kick too early, otherwise he lands on your face. I used to get terribly excited doing it though. Then they started to arrange it that there was this great big, heavy man!'

Unlike the filmed *Avengers*, where any loss of production time cost a great deal of money, one of the freedoms of the videotaped series was the fact that the actors had the opportunity to ad-lib their lines if they stumbled. According to Honor Blackman, this became second nature to herself and Patrick Macnee because they knew exactly how Cathy and Steed would react to certain circumstances, although they never deliberately played around with the script. 'Patrick was very good at it. He sometimes used to wing it like mad. If there was a line of dialogue that he wasn't sure of, or wasn't entirely happy with, he'd suddenly wing it, but he'd always come back to the cue, he'd never drop you in it. I never quite reached his air of perfection, though. My hair used to stand on end sometimes because I'm a

'Not guilty, M'lud.' Steed is aquitted of murdering Cathy Gale in *Brief for Murder*.

rock steady kind of performer; I like to know what I'm going to say and what I'm going to do. But Patrick was a great winger, and sometimes when he winged it, it was better than the original script.'

Brian Clemens' script for the season's opening episode, *Brief for Murder*, contained some interesting 'facts' about Steed's background. Once again these were cut from the script before the episode was videotaped. Nevertheless, as they give one writer's view of Steed's formative years, I'll include them here. (Clemens continued to do this, particularly in *The New Avengers*. Watch *House of Cards* and *Dead Men are Dangerous*, and you'll see what I mean.) Clemens' account suggested that Steed was the younger son of a younger son, a scion of a noble family, but he was the black sheep of the family. He was sent to Eton, but spent most of his time in amateur theatricals. He left Eton shortly before war broke out and had a fine war record, which was distinguished when, as a lieutenant in the Royal Navy, he commanded a motor torpedo boat. After 1945 he ran an ex-naval launch in and around the Mediterranean ports at a time when cigarette trafficking was in full swing. Later, he turned up in London and, to some extent, re-established himself with his family by taking a respectable job with the civil service. Shortly afterwards, he appeared in the Middle East as economic adviser to Sheikh Akbar Ben Sidi Ben Becula, ruler of an oil-rich state. While he was there the Sheikh became involved in a quarrel between two neighbouring states. Some say this row nearly started the Third

World War, but others say it averted it. However, the Sheikh became richer through oil royalties and Steed returned to England with an award from him, the Order of the Golden Ram (Second Class), and life royalties from two of the oil wells. From this income he lived in the style to which he had become accustomed. At about this time he is said to have done some work for the State, but no official record exists of such work.

To give an added dimension to the characters of Steed and Cathy, they now had resident addresses, and many of the stories closed with Steed and Cathy at home – something that would be continued in the Rigg/Thorson colour episodes. Steed's flat, at 5 Westminster Mews, was furnished with Victoriana collected during his frequent trips up and down the country. Polo cups and hunting trophies adorned the shelves, complemented by Steed's collection of military paintings. The hearth had a tiger-skin rug and over the fireplace hung a magnificent portrait of his great-grandfather, RKJJ de V Steed (known in his day as 'Stallion'). The flat had red upholstery. Concealed behind a row of books was a secret radio receiver. The spacious window over-

The Avengers pose for a publicity shot in the gardens of Twickenham Town Hall, during the location shoot for *The Undertakers*.

looking Parliament Square was built of bullet-proof glass.

Cathy's flat, 14 Primrose Hill (not too far away from the apartment occupied by Tara King, some years later), was modern and functional, predominantly press-button controlled. Her kitchen was superbly equipped and all the rooms had sliding doors. There was a concealed cocktail cabinet in the sitting-room, which was furnished with uncomfortable-looking backless chairs and a sofa. To make life that much easier, a television monitor screen showed her who was at the door, and her photographic studio contained the most modern equipment. One unusual feature was a magnetic chessboard which, when reversed, concealed a telephone.

As the series went before the camera, no one was more pleased than Honor Blackman and Patrick Macnee when regular scriptwriter Malcolm Hulke went on record as saying: 'The dedication and enthusiasm of the two artistes is one of the most important factors in the development of the series. Despite working a six and seven day week for months on end (and often rehearsing two shows at once), both stars have sacrificed much of their all-too-brief leisure time to activities that would help build up the show: judo and gymnastic sessions to equip them for their fights, endless costume fittings to extend their wardrobes, and of course the personal appearances and press interviews that their popularity has earned them.'

The year ended on a high note, with Honor and Patrick being voted *Independent Television's Personalities of 1963*, in the Variety Club of Great Britain Annual Awards ceremony held at London's Dorchester Hotel.

But dark clouds were gathering on the horizon...

SEASON THREE CHRONOLOGY

Episode	Title
1	Concerto
2	Brief For Murder
3	The Nutshell
4	The Golden Fleece
5	Death a la Carte (aka Fricassee of Death)
6	Man With Two Shadows
7	Don't Look Behind You (aka The Old Dark House)
8	The Grandeur That Was Rome (aka The Glory that was Rome)
9	The Undertakers
10	Death of a Batman
11	Build a Better Mousetrap
12	November Five
13	Second Sight
14	The Secret's Broker
15	The Gilded Cage
16	The Medicine Men
17	The White Elephant
18	Dressed To Kill
19	The Wringer
20	The Little Wonders
21	Mandrake
22	The Trojan Horse
23	The Outside-In Man (aka The Twice Elected)
24	The Charmers
25	Esprit de Corps
26	Lobster Quadrille

Series Produced by: John Bryce

The Avengers Theme composed and played by Johnny Dankworth

Story Editor: Richard Bates

Concerto:
Apart from toning down the killing of a girl (as suggested in the script for this story) and the exclusion of nude pictures pinned up outside a strip club, Anthony John suggested that it should go through unscathed.

Brief For Murder:
a) 'The VTR lacks the sound of a telephone ringing,' said a memo from producer John Bryce, 'and I was assured that the sound would be dubbed in for the TX. But on Saturday, the London TX was not dubbed, nor, I understand, was Southern. Nothing can be done now except to record my irritation and protest by this memo.'
b) Honor Blackman, on pre-recording the scene in which she tumbles into the River Thames. 'We did bits of location shooting, occasional, tiny bits. On that one I remember thinking to myself, you won't be catching me falling into the Thames, ever, because I'm not a great swimmer. So somebody else fell in for me. I have this picture at home, where you see me coming out of the water. So I had to go into the water in order to come

SEASON THREE EPISODES

53 CONCERTO

by Terrance Dicks and Malcolm Hulke

In which Steed spars with an old opponent and Cathy protects a young concert pianist

Peterson (Bernard Brown) Catherine Gale (Honor Blackman) Polly White (Valerie Bell) Burns (Geoffrey Colville) John Steed (Patrick Macnee) Zalenko (Nigel Stock) Stefan Veliko (Sandor Eles) Darleen Lomax (Dorinda Stevens) Receptionist (Carole Ward) Robbins (Leslie Glazer) and Junia

Designed by Robert Macgowan
Directed by Kim Mills

Important East-West trade talks are jeopardized by a naive Russian pianist giving his first concert in London. Several compromising incidents are staged and the musician is blackmailed into shooting the Trade Minister. However, Cathy, assigned to protect the Russian, notices that Veliko has a gun and she disarms him. The blackmailer, Peterson, and another aide try to assassinate the minister themselves, but also fail.

Recorded: 24 April 1963   TX: 2 March 1964

54 BRIEF FOR MURDER

by Brian Clemens

In which Steed is tried at the Old Bailey for the murder of Catherine Gale

Ronald Henry Wescott (Alec Ross) Dicey (June Thody) Marsh (Fred Ferris) John Steed (Patrick Macnee) Catherine Gale (Honor Blackman) Wilson (Anthony Baird) Barbara Kingston (Helen Lindsay) Miles Lakin (Harold Scott) Jasper Lakin (John Laurie) Judge (Robert Young) Bart (Michael Goldie) Maisie (Pamela Wardel) Miss Prinn (Alice Fraser) Foreman Of The Jury (Walter Swash)

Designed by James Goddard
Directed by Peter Hammond

Steed uses a ruse to expose legal malpractice. He decides to do away with Cathy, and seeks the advice of lawyers, the Lakin brothers, before doing the deed. Their advice ensures a not guilty verdict is recorded when Steed is put on trial. This is not the first instance where the Lakins have helped ensure a favourable verdict, but nothing can be proved against them. Posing as Miss Patchett, Cathy tricks the two solicitors into winning a guilty verdict, thereby setting up the brothers so that Steed can finally have the crooked pair banned from practising at the bar.

Recorded: 1 May 1963   TX: 29 September 1963

55 THE NUTSHELL

by Philip Chambers

In which Steed hunts a traitor and finds himself fighting Cathy

Elin Strindberg (Edina Ronay) Catherine Gale (Honor Blackman) John Steed (Patrick Macnee) Laura (Patricia Haines) Military Policeman (Edwin Brown) Disco (John Cater) Venner (Charles Tingwell) Susan (Christine Shaw) Anderson (Ian Clark) Jason (Jan Conrad) Alex (Ray Brown)

Designed by Philip Harrison
Directed by Raymond Menmuir

Who stole the file, codenamed Big Ben, from the Nutshell, an underground security centre used by the government? It seems that Steed is the mastermind when he is photographed leaving the real thief's room. Steed gives himself up, but refuses to say anything in his defence and is placed under arrest. His silence is a ploy to encourage Venner, a secret agent, to break his cover and take the microfilm from Steed, whom he believes to be a traitor. Having convinced Cathy and his superior – Disco – that he isn't working for the other side, Steed regains his freedom.

Recorded: 10 May 1963   TX: 19 October 1963

56 THE GOLDEN FLEECE

by Roger Marshall and Phyllis Norman

In which Steed hunts a modern Robin Hood and Cathy joins the Army

Captain George Jason (Warren Mitchell) Major Ruse (Tenniel Evans) Sgt Major Wright (Barry Lineham) Mrs Kwan (Yu Ling) Mr Lo (Robert Lee) John Steed (Patrick Macnee) Catherine Gale (Honor Blackman) Esther (Lisa Peake) Jones (Michael Hawkins) Private Holmes (Ronald Wilson)

Designed by Anne Spavin
Directed by Peter Hammond

out of it.'
c) *Patrick Macnee recalled a nice anecdote. 'I stood in the dock at the Old Bailey, accused of Cathy's murder. The idea, as written in the script, was that I would win a verdict of not guilty. The jury returned from their deliberations. The clerk asked the foreman: "Have you agreed on your verdict?" "We have," came the reply. "Do you find the prisoner guilty or not guilty?" This was the foreman's big moment, the crux of the scene. But the actor playing the part was so worked up he blurted out: "Guilty!" We had to record the scene again, right from the beginning.' (and it was the actor's only line! **
d) *Anthony John said there was a great deal wrong with the script in terms of legal accuracy. So he passed it around and had a long session with the script editor, who put right the author's misconceptions concerning lawyers, solicitors, etc...*
e) *As a result of writing this episode, Brian Clemens was invited to address the Law Society! **

Don't Look
Behind You:
*a) Honor Blackman
was recorded as saying
that for this episode
she had to get her hus-
band, Maurice
Kauffman, to hear her
moves, instead of her
lines!
b) She remembers that
she got terribly worked
up when she came to
record the story, under
Peter Hammond's
direction. 'I would
begin to cry, and Peter
would say "No. I
want you to be a
toughie, tough, tough,
tough!" I told him
that I didn't think that
I could do it that way.
I never quite got a
hold on it, I was just
too vulnerable to the
horror of this man and
his treatment of
human beings, and it
just poured out. I
don't suppose Peter
was very pleased with
me, but we couldn't
shoot it again.'*

Disgruntled army officers are smuggling gold for the Chinese, through Hong Kong, in exchange for money. This money is used for the Golden Fleece Fund which supports deserving ex-soldiers. When, upon leaving a Chinese restaurant, Steed takes the wrong coat and a cheque is found in its pocket, it reveals a connection between the sinister Mr Lo and Captain Jason. Steed asks Cathy to investigate the army officer. When she discovers that the bullets in the ammunition shipments received by Jason are tipped with gold, Steed arrests the smugglers, but promises them that the names of the former comrades they were helping will not be revealed.

Recorded: 25 May 1963   TX: 7 December 1963

57 DEATH A LA CARTE

by John Lucarotti

*In which Steed turns chef
and Cathy tries to prevent a murder*

Catherine Gale (Honor Blackman) Emir Abdulla Akaba (Henry Soskin) Mellor (Robert James) Ali (Valentino Musetti) Umberto (David Nettheim) Lucien (Gordon Rollings) Arbuthnot (Ken Parry) John Steed (Patrick Macnee) Dr Roy Spender (Paul Dawkins) Josie (Coral Atkins)

**Designed by Richard Harrison
Directed by Kim Mills**

Mrs Gale supervises the visit of Emir Akaba for his annual medical check-up in London, while Steed poses as a chef in the kitchen of the hotel in which the Emir is staying. The Avengers' suspicion that someone will attempt to kill the visitor are confirmed when Lucien tries to poison the Emir. Before the plot can succeed, the Emir dies a natural death which panics Mellor, the man behind the assassination attempt, since his forces are not ready to take over. Steed and Cathy prevent him from informing his countrymen, thereby ensuring that the planned coup is defeated.

Recorded: 14 June 1963   TX: 21 December 1963

58 MAN WITH TWO SHADOWS

by James Mitchell

*In which Steed hides from himself
and Cathy is ordered to kill him*

Gordon (Daniel Moynihan) Charles (Paul Whitsun-Jones) John Steed (Patrick Macnee) Borowski (Terence Lodge) Catherine Gale (Honor Blackman) Rudi (Douglas Robinson) Sigi (George Little) Julie (Gwendolyn

Watts) Dr Terence (Geoffrey Palmer) Miss Quist (Anne Godfrey) Cummings (Philip Anthony) Holiday Camp Official (Robert Lankesheer)

Designed by Paul Bernard
Directed by Don Leaver

Alerted by Borowski that 'doubles' of important people are about to infiltrate Britain, Steed keeps a close eye on Gordon, a scientist, when he is at a holiday camp. After a road accident, Steed suspects that a switch has been made, but the body is so badly damaged that he is unable to confirm this. The man whom he believes to have replaced Gordon passes all his medical tests. Steed himself is the next victim, leaving Mrs Gale with the dilemma of which Steed she must kill. The real Steed plays his undercover game for sufficient time to unveil Cummings as the third impostor, before the Avengers finish their assignment. Steed has already ensured that the real Gordon is alive and in future will work as a double agent.

Recorded: 21 June 1963   TX: 12 October 1963

59 DON'T LOOK BEHIND YOU

by Brian Clemens

In which Steed takes a drive in the country and Cathy endures a night of terror

Watched by Honor Blackman, an ABC TV cameraman takes to the floor to capture a low-angle shot in this scene from *Don't Look Behind You*.

The Grandeur That Was Rome: *One week after the episode was transmitted, ABC received a letter from an anonymous viewer. Written entirely in Latin, the ABC heads were at a loss to understand the missive. Patrick Macnee had the answer. He contacted his old Latin teacher at Eton and arranged to have the letter translated. Alas, the letter's content was found to be quite pornographic and highly unsuitable to be read by his female co-star! Incidentally, Colette Wilde, one of the actresses who appeared in this story, was previously ABC-TV's Weather Girl.*

Catherine Gale (Honor Blackman) John Steed (Patrick Macnee) Ola (Janine Gray) Young Man (Kenneth Colley) Man (Maurice Good)

Designed by Terry Green
Directed by Peter Hammond

Cathy visits Sir Cavalier Resagne for the weekend, but finds only a girl named Ola at his Devon home. After dinner, the girl makes her excuses and leaves Cathy alone in the house. However, it soon becomes obvious that Mrs Gale is not alone: somewhere in the house is a crazed killer that she helped to arrest some years earlier. The man terrorizes Cathy, his intention being to lead her to the brink of madness before wreaking revenge by cutting her throat. Unknown to Mrs Gale, Steed has been with her all along. He has waited until now to show himself and overpower the madman.

Recorded: 5 July 1963   TX: 14 December 1963

60 THE GRANDEUR THAT WAS ROME

by Rex Edwards

In which Steed attends a Roman orgy and Cathy is offered as a human sacrifice

Sir Bruno Lucer (Hugh Burden) Marcus Dodds (John Flint) Eastow (Ian Shand) Catherine Gale (Honor Blackman) Octavia (Colette Wilde) John Steed (Patrick Macnee) Appleton (Kenneth Keeling) Lucius (Raymond Adamson) Barnes (Colin Rix)

Designed by Stan Woodward
Directed by Kim Mills

When Mrs Gale finds ergot in grain produced by United Foods and Dressings Ltd., Steed is sure that it has been done deliberately. Lucer, the chairman of UFD, dreams of reinstating the Roman Empire and plans to decimate the world by releasing bubonic plague. Unbeknown to him, his deputy – Dodds – plans to overpower Lucer and put the World Empire Party in office. When the Avengers stumble on the truth, Mrs Gale nearly becomes the first victim of the plague, but Steed breaks into Lucer's villa and saves her life. It is too late for Lucer; Dodds has already claimed his life.

Recorded: 19 July 1963
TX: 30 November 1963

61 THE UNDERTAKERS

by Malcolm Hulke

*In which Steed meets an undertaker
and Cathy joins the millionaires*

Green (Howard Goorney) Madden (Patrick Holt) Catherine Gale (Honor Blackman) John Steed (Patrick Macnee) Mrs Renter (Lally Bowers) Lomax (Lee Patterson) Wilkinson (Ronald Russell) Paula (Jan Holden) Daphne (Mandy Miller) Mrs Lomax (Marcella Makham) Mrs Baker (Helena McCarthy) Reeve (Denis Forsyth)

Designed by David Marshall
Directed by Bill Bain

Adelphi Park is a very reclusive rest home for millionaires. To escape paying large death duties, actors replace the wealthy for five years. When Steed arrives to discuss a new invention with Professor Renter, he finds that the scientist has entered Adelphi Park. Refused entry, Steed has Mrs Gale pose as the new Assistant Matron and find out if Renter really is there, but Marshall and Green, who run the scam, expose her as a fraud and decide to kill her. Steed's arrival forces them to flee and the Avengers soon run them to ground

Recorded: 2 August 1963   TX: 5 October 1963

62 DEATH OF A BATMAN

by Roger Marshall

*In which Steed is named in a will
and Cathy goes into big business*

Edith Wrightson (Kitty Attwood) John Wrightson (David Burke) John Steed (Patrick Macnee) Catherine Gale (Honor Blackman) Lord Basil Teale (Andre Morrell) Eric Van Doren (Philip Madoc) Cooper (Ray Brown) Lady Cynthia (Katy Greenwood) Gibbs (Geoffrey Alexander)

Designed by Paul Bernard
Directed by Kim Mills

Steed is astonished when his former batman, Wrightson, leaves £480,00 in his will to his wife. Wrightson was a draughtsman for Lord Teale and forgery seems a likely possibility. Teale and his partner, Van Doren, have used Wrightson's knowledge of new share certificates to make a killing on the Stock Exchange and are using the profits to support the British electronics industry from external take-

The Undertakers: *The final shoot-out (in the grounds of a rest home) was filmed in the gardens of Twickenham Town Hall, where the stone nymphs splashing in the fountains received an appreciative (and ad-libbed) pat from connoisseur, Patrick Macnee.*

Death of a Batman: *Whenever ABC received a request from an outside source (private or commercial) to view an episode of* The Avengers *which represented everything good about the series, this was the episode selected by producer John Bryce.*

Opposite: This scene from *The Grandeur That Was Rome* came in for some heavy criticism from producer John Bryce.

Build a Better
Mousetrap:
*Location shots, in this
episode, of the top-up
motorcycle gang in full
cry were filmed on
Cobham Common in
Surrey, with Honor
Blackman riding a
500cc Triumph
Twin, and the gang
being represented by
members of the
Riverhill Riders Club.
She learned to ride a
motorbike as a courier
for the emergency
Blood Donor Service.
Before doing the stunt,
she took a refresher
course at Surbiton
Police Station, which
organized the Riverhill
Riders for charity
events.*

over. Though sympathetic to their cause, Steed has no option but to arrest the men.

Recorded: 14 August 1963   TX: 26 October 1963

63 BUILD A BETTER MOUSETRAP

by Brian Clemens

*In which Steed visits two witches
and Cathy rides a motorbike to do the Ton-plus-ten*

Dave (Donald Webster) Catherine Gale (Honor Blackman) Ermyntrude Peck (Nora Nicholson) Cynthia Peck (Athene Seyler) John Steed (Patrick Macnee) Harris (Harold Goodwin) Colonel Wesker (John Tate) Caroline (Alison Seebohm) Stigant (Allan McClelland) Jessy (Marian Diamond) Gordon (David Anderson)

**Designed by Douglas James
Directed by Peter Hammond**

Mrs Gale becomes a biker to investigate what mysterious signal is jamming all mechanical devices in a neighbourhood. Steed believes that Ermyntrude and Cynthia, the daughters of Professor Peck, have perfected his last incomplete invention. Others have reached the same conclusion and one of them, Stigant, is murdered by Wesker, a retired Army man who steals the invention, a long-range jamming device. Enter Steed who brings the villain to heel. In reality, the machine was merely Ermyntrude's attempt to build a better mousetrap!

Recorded: 28 August 1963   TX: 15 February 1964

64 NOVEMBER FIVE

by Eric Paice

*In which Steed buys a firework
and Cathy stands for Parliament*

Returning Officer (John Murray Scott) Michael Dyter (Gary Hope) Mark St John (Ric Hutton) Framer (Frank Maher) John Steed (Patrick Macnee) First Lady (Aimee Delamain) Major Swinburne (David Langton) Arthur Love (David Davies) Catherine Gale (Honor Blackman) Fiona (Iris Russell) Max (Joe Robinson) Mrs Dove (Ruth Dunning)

**Designed by Douglas James
Directed by Bill Bain**

To further his investigation into political corruption and the theft of a nuclear warhead, Steed persuades Mrs Gale to stand in the local by-election, as a replacement candidate for Dyter, a politician who was shot by someone in the crowd. The Avengers discover that Dyter is, in fact, very much alive. He has faked his death to gain time to blackmail the Government into paying £500,000; otherwise he will detonate the warhead and blow up the House of Commons. Exposing the ruse, Steed arrives on the scene in time to prevent Dyter from becoming a latter-day Guy Fawkes.

Recorded: 27 September 1963   TX: 2 November 1963

65 SECOND SIGHT

by Martin Woodhouse

In which Steed fights in the dark
and Cathy exposes a millionaire's precious light

Dr Vilner (Steven Scott) Neil Anstice (Peter Bowles) Dr Eve Hawn (Judy Bruce) John Steed (Patrick Macnee) Catherine Gale (Honor Blackman) Marten Halvarssen (John Carson) Dr Spender (Ronald Adam) Steiner (Terry Brewer)

Designed by Terry Brewer
Directed by Peter Hammond

Steed is suspicious as to why a live donor needs to provide Halvarssen with two corneas, so that the millionaire may regain his sight. Despatched to watch the transplant operation, Cathy's travelling companion is murdered by the supposed donor, Hilda Brauer. But Steed discovers the real Hilda Brauer has died four years earlier. There is neither patient nor operation; the container for the corneas is being used to smuggle diamonds. With Cathy under threat of death, Steed rounds up the mastermind, Anstice, and takes the jewels and the shady medico into custody.

Recorded: 11 October 1963   TX: 16 November 1963

66 THE SECRET'S BROKER

by Ludovic Peters

In which Steed tastes wine
and Cathy attends a seance

Mrs Wilson (Avice Landon) Julia Wilson (Jennifer Wood) Bruno (Valentino Musetti) Frederick Paignton (John Stone) Catherine Gale (Honor

November Five:
There was a great deal wrong with the script for this episode, according to Anthony John, who confirmed to Howard Thomas that he had been through it line by line with story editor, Richard Bates. A great number of alterations and deletions were made, in particular to references that would bring the House of Commons or MP's into disrepute – or at the very least, might prove embarrassing to the company. 'It seems to me to be tinged with political bias,' said John, 'and by implication rakes up the Ward case where security is concerned, and "Keelerism" where the suggested behaviour of certain MP's is concerned.' (Thirty years on little has changed!)

Second Sight:
Patrick Macnee recalls a self-inflicted wound. 'In this episode my script read: "I work for Her Majesty's Government. These containers are absolutely sterile." What I actually said at the rehearsal was: "I work for Her Majesty's Government and I am absolutely sterile." '

Blackman) John Steed (Patrick Macnee) Marion Howard (Patricia English) Jim Carey (Brian Hawkins) Cliff Howard (John Ringham) Allan Paignton (Ronald Allen) Waller (Jack May)

Designed by Anne Spavin
Directed by Jonathan Alwyn

A bogus medium is blackmailing people who confide in her and her latest target is to discover the secrets of Bridlingtons, a research establishment. Cathy joins the Bridlingtons team, while Steed visits Waller and Paignton's Wine Store, another target on medium Mrs Wilson's hit list. After a failed attempt to steal a tracking device, the culprits are traced when the medium's henchman, Waller, attempts to dispose of Steed. The information they gathered, from micro-dots secreted in Waller and Paignton's wine list, will never be used.

Recorded: 19 October 1963   TX: 1 February 1964

67 THE GILDED CAGE

by Roger Marshall

In which Steed masterminds a robbery
and Cathy is framed for murder

John Steed (Patrick Macnee) Catherine Gale (Honer Blackman) Groves (Neil Wilson) JP Spagge (Patrick Magee) Fleming (Norman Chappell) Manley (Frederic Abbott) Westwood (Alan Haywood) Wardress (Margo Cunningham) Abe Benham (Edric Connor) Hammond (Martin Friend) Peterson (Terence Soall) Gruber (Geoff L'Cise) Barker (Douglas Cummings)

Designed by Robert Macgowan
Directed by Bill Bain

Steed plans to entrap Spagge, a millionaire suspected of crooked activities. Mrs Gale is the lure, particularly when she has a plan to steal £1,000,000 worth of gold – bait that Spagge finds difficult to refuse. Having passed the millionaire's initiative test, Cathy heads up the robbery team, unaware that Spagge means to kill her when the gold is in his hands. Meanwhile, an attempt is made on Steed's life. Believing Steed to be out of the way, Spagge turns his gun on Cathy – but the 'dead' man arrives to forestall the millionaire's lethal intentions and arrest the bank raiders.

Recorded: 25 October 1963 TX: 9 November 1963

68 THE MEDICINE MEN

by Malcolm Hulke

*In which Cathy takes a Turkish bath
to help Steed prove the value of good soap*

Catherine Gale (Honor Blackman) John Steed (Patrick Macnee) Geoffrey Willis (Peter Barkworth) John Willis (Newton Blick) Frank Leeson (Harold Innocent) Taylor (John Crocker) Fay (Monica Stevenson) Masseuse (Brenda Cowling) Miss Dowell (Joy Wood) Edwards (Peter Hughes)

Designed by David Marshall
Directed by Kim Mills

Spurious pharmaceutical products are causing Willis Sopworth to lose money, but Cathy, having taken a job at the company as an efficiency expert, is unprepared when murder enters the equation. A new packaging design was being prepared in secret, but the details have been leaked to a group who plan to poison future products and as result destabilize a foreign country. Steed, however, quick to respond, adds his own wording – 'Poison' – to the new batch of products, rendering the cartons useless. Geoffrey Willis is arrested as the ring leader and Cathy takes care of his accomplice, Miss Dowell.

Recorded: 8 November 1963   TX: 23 November 1963

69 THE WHITE ELEPHANT

by John Lucarotti

*In which Steed tracks a white elephant
and Cathy hunts for big game*

George (Martin Friend) Noah Marshall (Geoffrey Quigley) John Steed (Patrick Macnee) Brenda Marshall (Judy Parfitt) Fitch (Bruno Barnabe) Joseph Gourlay (Toke Townley) Madge Jordan (Rowena Gregory) Lawrence (Edwin Richfield) Lew Conniston (Scott Forbes)

Designed by Philip Harrison
Directed by Laurence Bourne

When Lawrence arrives from Africa to reassert his role in an ivory-smuggling racket, only Snowy the elephant can identify the hunter who has been presumed to be dead. But Snowy has disappeared, which leads Mrs Gale to becoming a zoologist at Noah Marshall's zoo, while Steed chases up a clue – a sample of dust from a gun shop run by Fitch which, when analysed, proves to be ivory. Steed and Cathy eventually

The White Elephant:
a) This story found Cathy and Steed investigating a private zoo. Booked to appear as 'extras' were assorted birds, monkeys, a tiger and a leopard. When the script called for a gunshot to be heard, a studio technician fired off a blank (synchronized to the actor's movements). This caused the birds to flutter – and one of them died from shock! The leopard caused a few nervous moments in the studio, when it decided to go 'walkies'.
b) Patrick Macnee remembers the fight that he had with actor Scott Forbes. The latter could wield a knife to dangerous effect, having starred in his own series in the USA as the title character in the western show Jim Bowie. Macnee says the encounter was 'the toughest and best fight I've ever had in The Avengers'. Macnee should know. He badly sprained his ankle during the spectacular fall at the end of the episode.
c) We all know where we were when the news came of President John F Kennedy's death. On the set of The Avengers, shooting this story! *

A rare shot taken on location at Cobham Common showing director Peter Hammond giving Honor Blackman some last minute instructions as she gears up to do the Ton-plus-Ten for episode 63.

find ivory contained in the structure of the cages delivered to Marshall's zoo and they are quick to slam the door on the illicit ivory-smuggling trade.

Recorded: 22 November 1963   TX: 4 January 1964

70 DRESSED TO KILL

by Brian Clemens

In which Steed is quick on the draw and Cathy becomes a highwaywoman

Newman (Leon Eagles) First Officer (Peter Fontaine) John Steed (Patrick Macnee) Catherine Gale (Honor Blackman) Napoleon (Alexander Davion) Pussy Cat (Anneke Wills) Barman (Frank Maher) Highwaywoman (Anthea Wyndam) Policeman (Richard Leech) Sheriff (John Junkin) Robin Hood (Leonard Rossiter)

Designed by David Marshall
Directed by Bill Bain

Festivities at a New Year's party held aboard a train turn sour when one of the guests starts to kill off his companions. All the revellers share an interest in the ownership of land next to defence early-warning stations. One of the guests seems determined to stop them reaching their destination, an important business meeting at which they can take up their options for the plots of land. Before dawn, Steed and Cathy (an uninvited guest) discover that it is unwise to place their trust in a policeman at the OK Corral!

Recorded: 6 December 1963   TX: 28 December 1963

71 THE WRINGER

by Martin Woodhouse

*In which Steed is sentenced as a traitor
and Cathy helps to brainwash him*

Hal Anderson (Peter Sallis) Charles (Paul Whitsun-Jones) John Steed (Patrick Macnee) Catherine Gale (Honor Blackman) Lovell (Gerald Sim) Bethune (Neil Robinson) 'The Wringer' (Terence Lodge) Murdo (Douglas Cummings)

Designed by Philip Harrison
Directed by Don Leaver

Investigating deaths on an escape route between Austria and Hungary, Anderson, an agent, believes that Steed is the cause. Steed is arrested and subjected to brainwashing by The Wringer, head of the interrogating unit. Cathy's intervention stops him from falling victim to interrogator's attempts to sabotage the Service by creating mistrust and suspicion amongst its members. To prove Steed's innocence, Cathy deconditions Anderson by surrounding him with familiar memories and The Wringer is unmasked.

Recorded: 20 December 1963   TX: 18 January 1964

72 THE LITTLE WONDERS

by Eric Paice

*In which Steed joins the clergy
and Cathy follows a headless doll*

Mr Beardmore (Tony Steedman) Sister Johnson (Lois Maxwell) Bishop of Winnipeg (David Bauer) Catherine Gale (Honor Blackman) John Steed (Patrick Macnee) Gerda (Rosemarie Dunham) Hasek (Frank Maher) Porter (Alex Macdonald) Harry (Harry Landis) Big Sid (John Cowley) Fingers (Keneth J.Warren) Coalman (Mark Heath) Thugs (Christopher Robbie and Rick Jones)

The Wringer:
a) Author Martin Woodhouse told the press at the time: 'The brain-washing techniques used in this story are only a very condensed and dramatised version of what we know about the real thing. Long periods of solitude play an important part in any alienation process, and these can be no more than suggested in a TV show. In any case, The Avengers *is a thriller series, not a documentary programme and we aim to entertain rather than harrow our audience.'
b) In the story* Man With Two Shadows, *Steed helped to brainwash Borowski, thought to be a traitor. The character was played by actor, Terence Lodge. By a nice twist of revenge, Terence Lodge was chosen to play The Wringer, the man who is elected to preside over Steed's brainwashing, in the episode of that name.*

Mandrake:
Richard Bates recalls that the idea for the episode came from the autobiography of Sydney Smith, a famous pathologist, who had noted that in a certain Cornish churchyard there was an unusual amount of arsenic in the soil. 'Consequently we devised a sort of murder incorporated, where they were bumping people off and burying them in Cornwall, in the arsenic-impregnated soil, so they couldn't be caught out afterwards. Fairly ridiculous – but it worked.'

The Trojan Horse:
The horse that features in this story was actually a show-jumper named Roy, a 12-year-old grey of sixteen hands, owned by the father and son firm of Dennis and Peter Harman, at Shepperton. Whereas a real racehorse might have become excited when working in the studio, Roy was the ideal choice. A veteran of films and television, he quite happily chewed his way through sugar lumps supplied to him during the two-day shoot.

Designed by Richard Harrison
Directed by Laurence Bourne

Delegates from Bibliotek, a crime syndicate, meet to appoint a new Bishop. Steed is amongst them posing as the Vicar of Salisbury. Suddenly, they are massacred by Sister Johnson and Mr Beadmore, a Harley Street specialist, who launches his own take-over bid for Bibliotek. Cathy, meanwhile, has been investigating the baggage of the clergy and stumbles upon some secret micro-film, which Beardmore wants. Steed's timely rescue prevents her from being killed by Beardmore and his cohorts.

Recorded: 3 January 1964   TX: 11 January 1964

73 MANDRAKE

by Roger Marshall

In which Steed pulls crackers to help Cathy unearth a grisly racket

Rev Adrian Wyper (George Benson) Roy Hopkins (Philip Locke) Benson (Robert Morris) John Steed (Patrick Macnee) Dr Macombie (John Le Mesurier) Catherine Gale (Honor Blackman) Scott Sexton (Jackie Pallo) Mrs Eve Turner (Madge Ryan) Judy (Annette Andre)

Designed by David Marshall
Directed by Bill Bain

The Church of St Albans has no parishioners, but the graveyard is full of new coffins, with the bodies of wealthy people. Dr Macombie and his assistant, Hopkins, specialise in staging murders that look like natural deaths; the bodies are then buried in the St Albans cemetery. The soil in the ground has a very high arsenic content from the mandrake plant growing there, which makes it difficult to do a post-mortem. Steed, who is there to attend the funeral of a friend, calls in Cathy, who discovers that all of the deceased left large fortunes. The Avengers ensure that the next victim remains above ground and an autopsy spells the end for the poisoners.

Recorded: 16 January 1964   TX: 25 January 1964

74 TROJAN HORSE

by Malcolm Hulke

In which Steed goes horseracing and Cathy becomes the favourite for murder

Johnson (Derek Newark) Rt Hon Lucien Ffordsham (Geoffrey Whitehead) Kirby (James Donnelly) George Meadows (Arthur Pentlelow) Major Ronald Pantling (Basil Dignam) John Steed (Patrick Macnee) Ann Meadows (Lucinda Curtis) Tony Heuston (TP McKenna) Lynton Smith (John Lowe) Catherine Gale (Honor Blackman) Tote Girl (Marjorie Key)

Designed by Richard Harrison
Directed by Laurence Bourne

When Steed puts Sebastian the Second, a racehorse, into the stables of famous trainer, George Meadows, he soon finds the cause for so many recent killings. The stables hide a dangerous betting syndicate, who are prepared to win races at any cost, including murder. Heuston, the ringleader, plans to dispose of Steed, but Johnson, his assassin, hesitates and Cathy ensures that it's an odds-on certainty that the betting syndicate lose both their profits and their freedom.

Recorded: 30 January 1964   TX: 8 February 1964

75 THE OUTSIDE-IN MAN

by Philip Chambers

In which Steed plots murder and Cathy tries to stop him

A rare publicity shot of Patrick Macnee taken during the filming of location scenes for *The Undertakers*.

The Charmers:
a) This production almost had to do without Honor Blackman. The strain of all that judo, not to mention the standing about at rehearsals, finally took its toll. She missed two days rehearsal to have a minor operation on her foot, then came back to the studio to begin gamely on her fencing lessons. A footnote to her hospital visit, concerns a certain well-known television doctor. As Honor emerged from the lift in a wheelchair, she was greeted by actor Andrew Cruickshank (Dr Cameron, in Dr Finlay's Casebook.*) 'Very reassuring,' said Honor.*
b) Brian Tesler thought that this was one of the best-ever Avengers *episodes. 'It was marvellous. Beautifully written, played, directed. Thank you for trying out Fenella Fielding in the way that I suggested: it seemed, to me, to work splendidly; certainly there are possibilities here for the future' – a reference to the fact that Tesler saw Miss Fielding as a possible replacement for Honor Blackman.*

John Steed (Patrick Macnee) Catherine Gale (Honor Blackman) Alice Brisket (Virginia Stride) Quilpie (Ronald Radd) Jenkins (Ronald Mansell) Edwards (Anthony Dawes) Ambassador (William Devlin) Major Zulficar (Basil Hoskins) Helen Rayner (Beryl Baxter) Michael Lynden (Arthur Lovegrove) Sharp (Philip Anthony) Guards (Valentino Musetti and Eddie Powell) Butcher (Paul Blomley)

Designed by David Marshall
Directed by Jonathan Alwyn

When Mark Charter is released from custody in Abarain, Steed becomes worried that he will seek revenge and kill Sharp, the man he was ordered to eliminate five years earlier. Sharp is returning to Britain under diplomatic immunity and Mrs Gale is assigned to protect him. Charter's release is no coincidence; the Abarain government wants Sharp to be killed, since he is now no longer of any use to them. Steed knows this and Charter is playing along. He never really intended to kill Sharp. Grateful for Steed's help, Sharp promises better trading links as a reward.

Recorded: 12 February 1964   TX: 22 February 1964

76 THE CHARMERS

by Brian Clemens

In which Steed goes to Charm School and Cathy fences with the opposition

John Steed (Patrick Macnee) Catherine Gale (Honor Blackman) Martin (John Barcroft) Keller (Warren Mitchell) Kim Lawrence (Fenella Fielding) Bety Smythe (Vivian Pickles) Sam (John Greenwood) Harrap (Frank Mills) Horace Cleeves (Malcolm Russell) Mr Edgar (Brian Oulton) George Vinkel (Peter Porteous)

Designed by Richard Harrison
Directed by Bill Bain

A third party is intervening to cause trouble between Steed and the Russian opposition, so an uneasy truce is arranged to discover the culprit. To allay mistrust, agent Keller is loaned to Cathy and Steed is given an actress, Kim Lawrence. Steed and Kim find a clue: it is the corpse of Martin, the agent working with Cathy. This leads them to a charm school and Mr Edgar, who is training opposition agents to be gentlemen. Schoolmaster Keller has changed sides. Enter Cathy to cut through the opposition's defences – but it is Kim who cuts Keller down to size.

Recorded: 27 February 1964   TX: 29 February 1964

77 ESPRIT DE CORPS

by Eric Paice

*In which Steed faces a firing squad
and Cathy becomes Pretender to the Throne*

Captain Trench (John Thaw) Sergeant Marsh (Douglas Robinson) Private Jessop (Roy Kinnear) Brigadier General Sir Ian Stuart-Bollinger (Duncan Macrae) John Steed (Patrick Macnee) Mrs Angela Craig (Pearl Catlin) Catherine Gale (Honor Blackman) Lady Dorothy Stuart-Bollinger (Joyce Heron) Private Asquith (Anthony Blackshaw) Admiral (Hugh Morton) Signaller (James Falkland) Piper (George Alexander) Drummer (Tony Lamdon) Highland Dancer (George Macrae)

**Designed by David Marshall
Directed by Don Leaver**

Obsessed by his belief that he is a direct descendant of the Stuart kings, Bollinger plans to overthrow the monarchy using his regiment, while supposedly on routine defence manoeuvres. Posing as a journalist, Steed probes some unusual court-martials, while Cathy rewrites her family tree. Bollinger attempts to convince her that he believes that she will become the next Queen, but Cathy dethrones the soldier and the General is disgraced. Cathy's noble birth was a sham: Steed forged her family tree!

Recorded: 11 March 1964   TX: 14 March 1964

78 LOBSTER QUADRILLE

by Richard Lucas

*In which Steed goes fishing
and Cathy hunts a knight*

Max Bush (Gary Watson) Quentin Slim (Corin Redgrave) John Steed (Patrick Macnee) Catherine Gale (Honor Blackman) Dr Stannage (Norman Scace) Mason (Burt Kwouk) Captain Slim (Leslie Sands) Katie Miles (Jeannie Linden) Jackson (Valentino Musetti)

**Designed by Patrick Dowling
Directed by Kim Mills**

Jonathan Wilson's charred body leads Steed and Mrs Gale to investigate Captain Slim's lobster-fishing business. An unusual chess piece found in Wilson's pocket leads Cathy to a dealer, who also peddles dope. Meanwhile, Steed finds that Slim's son, Quentin, has not died at

Lobster Quadrille:
*a) Patrick Downing
was responsible for the
set design on this
episode. 'I remember a
chess shop and, I
think, a mortuary
with a chessboard
floor, with the actors'
standing around on
squares like chess
pieces. (I stole the idea
from a Basil
Rathbone* Sherlock
Holmes *film.)'
b) Not even Patrick
Macnee was told
exactly what was
going to happen to
Cathy Gale. A memo
was circulated by
John Bryce to the
effect that 'Cathy will
not be tied to that
railway line. The set
will be closed and no
photographs are to be
taken when the episode
is recorded.' Even the
script by Richard
Lucas was left 'open',
with a short, unscript-
ed scene being added
just before the record-
ing, by Brian
Clemens.
c) The 'Richard
Lucas' who wrote this
story is actually two
people: Brian Clemens
and Richard Bates.
Thereafter, Clemens
wrote the last episode
of every series.* *

sea as believed, but has merely staged his death to evade arrest: Quentin is guilty of smuggling dope. When clues lead Cathy to Quentin's hideaway, he tries to silence her but he becomes trapped in an inferno of his own making and dies. For Cathy this is her final case. She is off to the Bahamas for a well-earned holiday from a life of fighting crime.

Recorded: 20 March 1964   TX: 21 March 1964

SEASON FOUR

Twenty-six monochrome filmed episodes

Starring PATRICK MACNEE and DIANA RIGG   **1965/1966**

PRODUCTION HISTORY

In December 1963, a proposal was the received from the United Artistes Theatre Corporation, who wished to mount a production of *The Avengers* through their subsidiary company, Magna Incorporated. They wanted to put the television series onto the cinema screen. Were ABC interested? Needless to say they were – provided the proposed film's format retained the spirit of the series and, most important of all, if Honor Blackman and Patrick Macnee agreed to take part. Both stated their willingness to do so and within days the company received a summary of the film's format.

The two-hour film would be shot in colour using the newly developed Dimension-150 process – a 70mm, wide-angle, one-lens system which the owners believed to be superior in every way to the new Cinerama technique. The screenplay would be based upon a story outline devised by Howard Thomas and written by Brian Clemens, who in turn would be assisted by John Bryce. Patrick and Honor would star opposite their American counterparts, who would be star names. In the event that the D-150 version fell through, Louis de Rochemont, an American film producer, had expressed his interest in co-producing a 35mm black-and-white version with Magna. It would be a condition of any production financed by Magna that ABC would not licence the transmission on television of *The Avengers* series until a mutually agreed date after the release of the feature film in the United States. ABC agreed and an agreement was drafted between the two parties. Also interested at this time was Leslie Grade, who had expressed his interest in a joint production with ABC. Julian Wintle was interested in an *Avengers* series on film using the same technique as he was employing for the second series of *The Human Jungle*, then in production.

Here is an edited version of the proposed film's storyline, as prepared by Howard Thomas:

THE AVENGERS
The Pursuit of Evil

The location is established: Beirut – the gateway of the East. In the School of Asiatic Languages, a classroom of a dozen young

Programme Coordinator, E Flackfield, thought it wise to advise the ITV stations, Rediffusion and Southern, that the first scene in reel 4 of The Master Minds, and two or three of the scenes that follow, were purposefully upside-down. 'It would be a great pity if some tele-cine opearator stopped the show, being under the impression that 'he had the reel in the wrong way!' he commented.

* Denotes information supplied by Brian Clemens

Englishmen and Americans are listening intently to their Lebanese teacher. These are the cream of the Foreign Office and the State Department; tomorrow's diplomats and other men who work in less respectable government departments – the espionage branch.

Enter two masked men in flowing robes, gripping the most modern of automatic weapons. Calmly, methodically, they fire. We see the students slumping defencelessly over their desks.

The chatter of the guns dissolves into the stutter of newspaper tape machines as the story is tapped out: 'Young Diplomats Slaughtered in Classroom Massacre.'

In Washington, grave-faced men assemble to count their losses and to decide on action. In London, the head of the Secret Service is telephoning Steed, his key man.

Steed is seen in his splendid Belgravia flat. At his side is Mrs Catherine Gale, the tough, judo-trained beauty who has worked with him on so many assignments. 'They've wiped out some of our best men, Steed. Take Mrs Gale with you and you'll be joined by two people from Washington. Your job is to establish our organization in the Middle East.'

'And there's another job, too,' says Steed grimly, as he replaces the receiver. 'We must avenge our colleagues.'

In Washington, Drew Vernon is packing his gun and answering the telephone at the same time. 'You're teaming me up with a woman!'

The four people set out for Beirut to create new espionage links – and to avenge their friends. Four worldly, elegant Londoners and New Yorkers, two sophisticated men and two women trained to kill, face up to unknown hazards in one of the world's most spectacular and sinister settings.

Copyright: ABC Television Ltd, 1964

Brian Tesler thought the scripts to Dial a Deadly Number *and* The Cybernauts *to be excellent. However, he did pass the comment that the 'gratuitous trick (and editing joke?)' at the end of the first one to be unnecessary. 'Shouldn't the watch merely be playing its tune as they come out of the tunnel?'*

Meanwhile, an equally intriguing project landed on the desk of Howard Thomas. Having read about *The Avengers* in a *Sunday Times* supplement, Cheryl Crawford, a well-known American producer of plays, approached ABC about the possibility of producing a musical based upon the series! Though unfamiliar with the show's format (the Blackman series was first transmitted in the USA in 1990, mainly because of the lack of technology at the time to convert successfully a 405-line recording to a 525-line US transmission). After viewing several of the episodes and reading numerous scripts, she believed that the show could be successfully transferred to the stage. Her idea was to open on Broadway, then bring the cast to London's West End. Recognising that the idea had possibilities, ABC gave their blessing to the project – but stuck firmly to their guns that, musical or not, the production would retain the fast-moving, fairytale, Avengers format, told against a tough, sometimes

Sometimes Steed could be a pain in the neck, but Emma fell in with his plans good naturedly enough.

bizarre, contemporary setting.

It was then that Honor Blackman dropped her bombshell. On 19 September 1963, she told ABC that she would not be continuing the Cathy Gale role after the end of the current series (due for completion in March 1964). Honor had signed a five-year film contract with Harry Saltzman and Cubby Broccoli, which took effect from 1 November 1964. Convinced that she was putting out feelers in order to gauge her prospects for the future, ABC wasted little time in discussing the possibility of introducing a new character into the series in case Honor really did intend to get up and go. If the producers had become hysterical at this point no one would have blamed them. Not only did they now have to find a new female lead for Steed, they also had to invent a new character, because Honor Blackman had made the role of Cathy Gale so much her own, it would be almost impossible for another actress to take over. Though several attempts were made to convince Honor that she was making a very unwise move, she had been told that the film industry was in a very precarious state. She felt that all indications were that things would get tougher as the year went on. So Honor refused to change her mind. Her decision was final – Cathy Gale would disappear from *The Avengers* in the final story of the current season.

Within hours of the announcement that Honor was quitting the show, the British newspapers carried the following headlines. 'Cathy Hangs Up Her Boots For Good'; 'Cathy is Quitting *The Avengers*'; 'Exit Cathy of *The Avengers*'.

All editions carried a similar story: 'Cathy Gale, leather-clad heroine of ITV's *The Avengers* is to leave the programme to step into a five-year film contract. Honor said last night: "I've got a lot to thank television for, and my biggest debt is to Cathy." Celebrating at her home, she added, "I'm sorry about having to ·quit the Cathy Gale role. But I felt it was better to do this than wait until she goes out of fashion. My part in the series was a little different from that of John Steed, the eternal Englishman who can go on forever. Cathy Gale was a child of her times and I feel that if I go on too long I will outstay my welcome."

Honor told me: 'By this time the show had become such a wild success that they didn't imagine that I would actually leave at that point, while the series was such a runaway success. So when we finally achieved what had been our ambition – or certainly Patrick's – to go onto film, I'd already arranged to play Pussy Galore in *Goldfinger*. In any case, as far as I was concerned, I was getting out because two years is enough. You can't sustain that kind of show for longer than two years. They were very upset that I didn't stay, because by then the two of us were such national characters that they couldn't imagine replacing me. But that was my decision, so when it came to the final episode and they knew that I was going, Patrick put in a reference to my "pussy-footing around" on some glorious beach in Miami. It was Patrick's "in" joke, because I was going off to play Pussy Galore. It was terribly moving, the last episode, the farewell party and everything.'

Honor recently told Paul Madden that there were cries of traitor when she left. 'But I still think it was the right decision. I'm sorry in lots of ways because it would have been fun to have stuck around. We'd heard that it was going onto film, quite possibly on the cinema screen, but two years was long enough...and the scripts had started leaving the ground a bit. I wanted to get into pastures new. Mind you, the pastures new weren't all that different, were they? Similar format. Slightly different feller...'

In point of fact, the end sequence of *Lobster Quadrille*, was written by Brian Clemens, who went along with Patrick Macnee's suggestion that Steed should make reference to the Bond film. The very last scene, when Cathy has left and Steed is left standing alone in his flat, was written by Clemens barely hours before the scene was filmed separately to the story action. Having caught a brief glimpse of the script, Macnee ad-libbed this in his own inimitable way.

The scene follows.

CATHY: *'I'm not going to be pussy-footing along those shores. I'm going to be lying on them.'*

Though he didn't always visit them, Brian Clemens was always involved in the choice of locations. 'I favoured weird locations. They would bring in photographs and say: "Which do you want, Guv?" If I wanted a castle they'd bring me five and ask which one I liked the look of. It would be an instant decision. I'd say "I like that one, or this one." When you're producing, you really have to have the veto, or otherwise, on everything that happens.'

STEED: *'No pussy-footing? I must have been mis-informed!'*

End of script. Cut to additional filmed scene.

Steed picks up the telephone and dials a seven-digit number. He grins widely as someone (a woman) answers.

STEED: *'Hello, my dear. John Steed...'*

Apologizing that he hasn't kept in touch (he's been very busy) he throws in a line about the inclement weather and suggests a cure.

STEED: *'Look, I think you should get a little sunshine... Beautiful blue skies, sandy beaches... I've got a little job I want you to do for me. Yes, of course we can start this at our own leisure. Why not tonight... Say, 8 o'clock. I know a little place down by the river...'*

Steed grins. Mission achieved.
Fade/Cue End Titles

We never see (or hear) the girl on the other end of the receiver. It might well have been a certain Mrs Emma Peel (it was certainly Brian Clemens' way of leaving the way open for a new girl to enter the picture), but 'beautiful blue skies, sandy beaches...' in Bazeley-by-the-Sea?

The conclusion of the episode and the fact that it was the very last time that Steed would be supported by Cathy Gale, left Patrick Macnee gutted. 'I felt perfectly dreadful, particularly as it came quite suddenly. I completely understood that anyone who is offered a large part in a Bond film would hardly want to go on doing television, but I missed her desperately. The show missed her. She was a unique person and still is,' Macnee told me. Did he think that this was the end of *The Avengers*? 'Oh yes. Each time it came to an end I thought that it was the end. Indeed, I suppose if you take the broader view, I might have left and gone on to bigger and better things. I know that I turned down some very fine plays and other things just to stay with it to the end, which indeed I did.'

With no female lead to offer de Rochemont, Crawford or the other interested parties, ABC were forced to take stock of their position. Two months earlier, the American Broadcasting Company (USA) had indicated their interest in buying a filmed series of *The Avengers* – but not until the autumn of 1965. Talks were then held with the American company about financing the production of a new one-hour hour filmed pilot story – with an option to buy a series with American producers, writers and performers at the helm. The offer was turned down because

Originally, Emma Peel's fights were to have been choreographed to music. Of this experiment only the fight in Death at Bargain Prices *remains. ***

Brian Tesler said the following about Philip Levene's script for Small Game for Big Hunters: '*I think it is far too talky for the first three-quarters of the way,*' *said Tesler,* '*although the final hunt is excellent. It needs more excitement injected into it in the earlier stages.*'

ABC were reluctant to abandon their successful award-winning product and its current 'uncertain' future due to the loss of Honor Blackman. ABC decided to take the show off the air to give them time to mount a 'new improved' twenty-six-episode series, to be made on film. Plans to co-produce the new series in Britain, in partnership with the Associated Rediffusion TV Company came to nothing.

On 25 March 1964, four days after the final Blackman episode was transmitted by ITV, Brian Tesler sent a memo to Howard Thomas seeking authority to go ahead with the 'new' project and requesting confirmation that it had been agreed that ABC were 'prepared to finance and produce the new series, on film, themselves and that Julian Wintle will produce them for us, in association with our own producer, writers, story editor team'. Tesler said that the company was facing 'dangerous deadlines' with both the contracting of Patrick Macnee and the commission of new scripts. Tesler emphasized to his boss that a delay of more than a fortnight was likely to jeopardize the smooth and successful consumation of the product. A reply from Thomas was received a few days later. Confirming that the series was to be made by a new company jointly owned by ABC, and an existing Julian Wintle company. Thomas suggested that while this was being set up scripts should be commissioned and it was 'imperative that Patrick Macnee's contract be negotiated'. Had the Rediffusion tie-up gone ahead, the staff of Iris Productions, the Teddington Studio-based company who had nurtured the programme through the first three seasons, would have crossed over onto the new filmed series.

Indeed, believing that they were odds-on favourites to get the job, publicity girl Marie Donaldson advised producer John Bryce to 'look again' at Nyree Dawn Porter, as a replacement for Honor Blackman. She had been told by a colleague, 'a very useful spy who works in the Drama Department at the BBC', that the Beeb 'are so impressed with Nyree Dawn-Porter's star potential in *Madame Bovary*, that she is likely to feature in an even bigger way in their future plans'. Donaldson suggested that if there was any question of ABC wanting her for *The Avengers*, it might be wise for Bryce to contact Porter's agent under a vow of silence. As things turned out, the Teddington team had already been left out of the equation – although Donaldson would go over to the filmed series (as would Bryce, at a later date).

Wintle assembled a team of experienced tele-film professionals headed by Albert Fennell (hand-picked by Wintle as 'the only man for the job') and Laurie Johnson, neither of whom had worked in television before. (Composer Bob Sharples was also considered. He couldn't work on the show due to contractual commitments.) Laurie Johnson recalls that when Wintle approached him, he wasn't all that keen to join the club. 'I told him that I didn't know much about television and he said, "Oh,

In charge of production, Albert Fennell

Music composer, Laurie Johnson

Associate Producer, scriptwriter, Brian Clemens

The team of experienced telefilm professionals assembled by Julian Wintle to produce the new filmed series.

The woman who dubbed Emma Peel's footsteps on The Avengers, *wore out – on average – a pair of shoes every three weeks!* *

it will be easy. Come and enjoy it". So I joined the team and Albert got down to planning the series with barely a handful of scripts – certainly not as many as we soon realised we needed. No one in their right mind would start making thirteen films today unless they had the scripts thoroughly finished and ready for filming so that you could go out onto the floor with the blueprint and shoot. We soon found that we didn't have that luxury, so we had to go on and do them as well as one could while getting the important things as right as possible within the time allocated. We nevertheless set out to shoot each one as a feature film insofar as the filming, the cutting, the editing, the scoring, etc.'

Brian Clemens came next. I asked Brian why they chose him? 'Because I knew about film. When they went to film they wanted somebody who knew film and knew *The Avengers*. I was uniquely qualified as I had started out not in television, but in film, and of course I had worked on the series before.' Appointed Associate Producer and Story Editor for the new series (the latter being uncredited on the film prints), Clemens immediately commissioned 26 scripts from the best British writers in the field.

Auditions were held to find a partner for Patrick Macnee and more than sixty actresses were tested for the as-yet unnamed part. (Actually Steed's partner had been named. In the first three scripts, the character was known as Samantha, shortened to Mantha in rewrites, but no one, including Brian Clemens, who had originated the name, found the name appealing.) It was then that Marie Donaldson, the production's newly-appointed press officer, had a brainwave. She realised that the new character had to have man appeal, and as she played around with the phrase in her head she couldn't help thinking Man Appeal, M appeal – Emma Peel. She liked the sound of the name and the producers leapt at it.

Emma Peel quickly became the internationally educated daughter of a wealthy shipowner and youthful widow of Peter Peel, a famous test pilot. A woman of independent means, she was the complete one-jump-ahead jet-set female. Emma Peel was a cool, luscious British counterspy with wicked brown eyes and auburn hair who would effortlessly karate chop and knee her opponent into submission; an English rose with the ability to toss a man over her shoulder as if he were a sack of feathers – the pefect partner for Steed in the espionage and counter-espionage game. (The fact that these two activities are covered by separate departments, MI6 and MI5 respectively, didn't deter the producers. They cheerfully explained that Steed was an employee of 'MI5 and a half'.) Outwardly Emma was cast in the same image as Cathy Gale. She lived in a streamlined London penthouse, wore avante-garde clothes, drove a high-speed Lotus Elan and fought free and furious by every known technique from judo and karate to her own brand of balletic 'feinting' and a straight left to the jaw. But the relationship between Emma and Steed became much warmer and more lively than Steed had with Cathy. This despite the fact that, as a ruthless professional agent, Steed continued to use every trick in the book both in dealing with his adversaries and in commandeering help from his amateur assistant. Emma was permanently aware that Steed's charm was a cloak for yet another attempt to involve her in some dangerous mission. She reluctantly accepted his insistence that being innocent of what was going on was her best protection, so she fell in with his plans good-naturedly enough. Yet she lost no opportunity to get even with him for the indignities inflicted on her person.

It was vital, however, to find the right Emma, and after months of searching it began to look as if she didn't exist. It was then that they found a beautiful actress called Elizabeth Shepherd, daughter of a Welsh non-conformist minister. She had been dubbed one of the most beautiful of the current British actresses, and she was signed for the role. Patrick

Patrick Macnee and Elizabeth Shepherd in a scene from the first version of *The Town of No Return*.

Reproduced courtesy of Brian Clemens.

DIANA
RIGG
as
Emma Peel

The main title graphics used on the press preview film prints.

Macnee said at the time, 'She is very, very good looking, She's obviously different from Cathy in many ways, although at first sight they look quite similar.' (The actress bore a striking resemblance to Honor Blackman.)

Miss Shepherd, who was on holiday at the time in Italy, acquiring a last-minute tan, was chosen by Julian Wintle who told the press that he had chosen her for her 'terrific personality and good looks'. However, Miss Shepherd failed to impress the producers, or ruffle the characteristic well-bred charm of Patrick Macnee. After viewing rushes of the first episode, *Town of No Return*, they decided that, although an accomplished actress, she didn't give the character the light comedy touch they were looking for. Having spent over £12,000, they stopped the production half-way through *The Murder Market*, and Elizabeth Shepherd was dropped.

I asked Brian Clemens to shed some light on the reason why Miss Shepherd didn't make it. 'She just wasn't right. She was a very beautiful lady and a very good actress, but she just wasn't right for the part. Julian Wintle contracted her originally – without tests. She looked great, but you never really know if it's going to work until you get your artistes working side by side. She didn't have the humour we were looking for. We were following in the footsteps of Cathy Gale and we didn't really want to disturb that. If Honor Blackman had been available to us she would have played it, but she went on to do the Bond film. So

Diana Rigg poses for photographers at the press reception to 'launch' Emma Peel.

we looked for a new and interesting and exciting artiste and found, after a lot of testing, Diana Rigg.' He told me that Elizabeth Shepherd played it for realism, 'which wasn't right – and she came prepared with these ideas for the character. She kept turning up with whole scenes rewritten! You can't have that on a television series. One could have put up with that if she was delivering on screen – she wasn't. She was quite beautiful, but not right for the part.'

Coincidentally, Miss Shepherd recently explained her side of the story in a letter to the *American Video Watchdog* magazine. Having read the editor's comments regarding her participation in the series, which she felt perpetuated the 'official version' of why she left the role, she provided her own explanation. 'When I was cast, the producers said to me: "We are putting the show on film because we believe it can be ten times better than it was on tape, and we welcome your ideas". I was naive enough to take them at their word, and in my enthusiasm, I inundated them with ideas! However, it was still the days when actresses were valued for being seen, not heard. Emma Peel was to assert herself on screen, but toe the company line when off. That's showbiz for you!'

Clemens certainly had the veto – or otherwise – on the name of Steed's new partner. Reading the script for Town of No Return, Anthony John put a question mark against the name of the heroine, Mantha. Did Brian Tesler like this? Tesler didn't. Neither did Brian Clemens (who had coined the name Samantha). The heroine was given a new name. Tesler's opinion of the script (one of the first to arrive on his desk) was that this was very much on the right lines and made full use of 'film' rather than 'studio'. His only reservation was that there was a great deal of dialogue and development in act one, which tended to lack action and pace.

A spokesman for ABC at the time toed the company line and said: 'ABC and Miss Shepherd have agreed she shall relinquish the role. The interpretation of the role, as played by Miss Shepherd, does not coincide with that visualized by ABC. But the company has the greatest admiration for Miss Shepherd's talent, which has already been seen to effect in two ABC-TV productions.' (A studio memo, written by Marie Donaldson, gave an insight into the character the actress could have produced. Her £600 wardrobe consisted of clothes created by New York designer Bonnie Cashin. The most startling outfit was a red leather fighting suit that had a large cowled neck, which could be pulled up into a hood. Worn with poppy red thigh boots and red leather gloves with which she could administer karate blows, Emma Peel, Shepherd-style, was to be a top-flight swordswoman, an expert with firearms and a dab hand with a longbow.

A further twenty or so actresses were tested before Dodo Watts, the programme's casting director, asked the producers to look at an actress she'd just used in *The Hothouse*, an Armchair Theatre production. After viewing a tape of the play, Brian Clemens and Albert Fennell sensed that this could be the girl they'd been searching for. Diana Rigg was invited to the studio to do tests with eight other actresses who had been shortlisted for the role. Clemens remembers that they had a big showing. 'Howard Thomas was there. Julian Wintle was there, others came along and we ran these eight tests. At the end of it I was leaning towards Moria Redmond, with Diana Rigg second. It was a hung parliament except for Howard Thomas or Julian Wintle, who said that they would go with Diana, because she was a new face. I'd written these little scenes for the tests because we wanted to see how the new girl would work alongside Patrick.' I jogged his memory. Diana Rigg remembers that she had to race about with a gun in her hand, then place a bandage on Steed's head. 'On his head. yes, that's right. That was the scene. He'd been shot and she had to bandage his head. Then they had a typical *Avengers* scene to do where they had to talk about anything but the bandage. I recall that we had her turn to the camera to show that she felt comfortable handling the props.'

The results were first class. Macnee and the young actress seemed to find an immediate rapport. She was signed to a long-term contract, and eighteen months after the last series had ended, *The Avengers* were on their way back. The rest of course, is history.

Patrick Macnee told me: 'The lady before Diana Rigg, Elizabeth Shepherd, was a very beautiful woman and a wonderful actress, but totally miscast. She was far too serene and lovely for anything like *The Avengers*, in which you had to be a bit quick and cocky, the way Diana Rigg was. The woman needs to be a hermaphrodite – a woman, but one who runs like a man.

William Friedkin, later to be director of The Exorcist *and* The French Connection *was a big* Avengers *fan – he shared offices next to the* Avengers *producers and often hinted that he would like to direct an episode. At that time he didn't think he had enough experience or talent!* *

When Diana came into the show she was only 28, but she had this total, complete technical comedic style and sparkle, surety and assurance. In fact she was so good that it sharpened, in a sense, my own comedy style which was there, but dormant. My style changed considerably. We were also doing it on film for the first time, which necessitated a different approach. The scenes that we played together, with the full approval of Brian Clemens, were largely rewritten by Diana and myself [they weren't selfish actors towards each other and they would sometimes interchange their lines if it seemed to work better]. She had a very sharp and lively imagination and understanding of what a woman, a woman like her, would say in any given situation, however outrageous or mad. We, and I say we advisedly, took perfectly straight situations and made them slightly ludicrous. You had to be slightly mad, but you also had to be basically cool. We tilted everything, made it humorous – and it worked.'

If Emma represented the future of Britain, Steed, as before, stood for the best of the past. He still embodied tradition and all that people associated with the British way of life – gracious living; a London home full of family heirlooms and handsome antiques; a cultivated appreciation of food, wine, horseflesh and pretty women; proficiency at gentlemanly sports such as fencing, archery and polo; exquisite tailoring; a high-handed way with underlings and an endearing eccentricity which now manifested itself in such preferences as driving a vintage Bentley convertible and fighting with a swordstick, rolled umbrella or any other handy implement, rather than the most obvious weapons. In the previous series, when he needed to get around, Steed had driven ordinary everyday saloon cars. Only once was he seen behind the wheel of a vintage machine, a Bugatti, in *Don't Look Behind You.*

In the best British stiff-upper-lip tradition, however, this rarified exterior camouflaged a highly efficient operator, who quietly got his man while his opponents were still being distracted by his amusing ways – just as Emma's wit and femininity concealed a cool resourceful woman who was at her best in a crisis.

Consequently there was never a shortage of wisecracks between Steed and Emma. The twosome deliberately echoed the classic partnership of William Powell and Myrna Loy in the famous *Thin Man* films. Their adventures, however, recalled the exploits of early film favourites like Douglas Fairbanks and Pearl White: Steed engaging in spectacular fights on moving trains, and Emma being constantly rescued from appalling hazards, of which being trussed up in a harness, tied to a railway track and clamped into a metal wine press were just a sample. The series embodied the best of the old, with many fresh and more spectacular elements (not least of which were the resources of a big motion picture organization, not available in the earlier videotaped series). It was, of course, the first programme to exploit

The Bentleys were temperamental – and most people, especially Patrick Macnee, hated driving them. *

this formula on television, and it added an element of its own – labelled by the press as 'kinkiness' – which gave a twist to clothes, humour and action that highlighted the flashpoint between comedy, sex appeal and violence.

Emma's mode of fighting was different, too. Cathy had been the judo expert. Emma's fighting technique was judo influenced. Villains were attacked with the edge of the hand (palm and fingers held rigidly flat), the elbow, fingers and thumbs, and the foot, which, in action, became part of a graceful, but deadly, balletic movement. (The short, musical riff which accompanies Emma's, finger-snapping, karate sequence in *Death at Bargain Prices* was composed by Laurie Johnson, who had it in mind to use this in all stories as Mrs Peel's action 'theme'. The concept was not followed up.) A jolting, stiff-legged kick was delivered as high as an adversary's jaw, to great effect. The fight sequences became more ambitious – choreographed mayhem – meticulously planned and arranged by one of Britain's top stuntmen, Ray Austin. The news that Emma would be using her 'bizarre' combat methods to throw a man down a flight of stairs or hurl him through a plate-glass window, led the company's publicity manager to comment: 'I think we must be extremely careful, when arranging fights for this series, to avoid highlighting some of the individual blows. It would be damaging to say the least if, for instance, a teenager were to injure another, having picked up his tuition from one of our episodes. With karate this could happen.'

As things turned out, the rough and tumble scenes were mapped out in minute detail long before the series went before the camera. Interviewed at the time, Ray Austin (who was asked to join the programme by Brian Clemens, who had worked with Ray on *Ghost Squad/G.S.5*) said: 'When Steed meets trouble – and that happens at least once in every story, he does so unarmed. This allows us to show the ruthless streak in his character and stop at nothing in his methods. He uses every trick in the book – and quite a few unwritten ones. His fights are staged extravagantly and always with a sense of humour. His partner, Emma Peel, is a much more conventional fighter. She uses guns, swords, karate, the lot. The vital difference, of course, being that all these arts are employed not by a tough guy, but a delectable and intelligent woman.'

Unlike her predecessor, Honor Blackman, Diana Rigg wasn't given lessons in self-defence. 'I had a crash course,' she said, 'and a group of wonderful stuntmen did it for me. I'd give them a push with my index finger, and they'd exercise a double-somersault and fall to the floor.' But Emma Peel's dangerous rough and tumble action scenes were handled by a man! As director James Hill told Paul Madden, 'For anything that smelled of danger, you used a double. It would have been stupid to have used your principal artist and have them risk breaking an arm or something. What happened was, you would normally have a

*Director Lewis Gilbert's mother was an extra on several episodes! ***

*On one occasion Steed's wardrobe was stolen from his car in Chelsea. At that time a number of the stunt people had other dubious jobs – some had criminal contacts. It was vital to get the clothes back before the next day's shooting. The 'word' went out and the clothes mysteriously returned. A few weeks later it happened again. Again the 'word' was put out – but this time to no avail. 'Sorry, guys,' a stuntman reported.' It must have been an amateur.' ***

Wearing a wig and black leather, stunt double Billy Westley takes the fall in this scene from *The Murder Market*.

couple of days to do rehearsal with the stunt arranger and you'd get the artist to come down and watch it. The stunts and fights were worked out very carefully shot for shot, so that when they came to do it they could come in and do the bit where you could see their faces. Diana had a young man doubling for her, in the catsuit and wearing a wig. When he went sliding and smashing across the floor you'd think: "Oh, Diana. Diana!" Then, when Diana stepped back into the shot, she'd turn around and the viewers' would see that it was her. It was fine. Nobody ever thought that there was a double at all. The edits were very well done. If there was an element of danger we would always use him.' Don Leaver found the whole thing somewhat disconcerting. 'It really was quite curious to see this stuntman hurl himself across a desk and then witness your heroine getting up from the floor as the stuntman lifted off his wig.'

Brian Clemens had more to say on the subject. 'Oh, sure. We'd do that all the time. His name is Billy Westley. He's now an assistant director, you'll see his name on lots of things. He was very slim for a stuntman and he took a lot of stick from the crew because he used to sit around on the set wearing his black leathers and a wig! The stuntmen were always kidding him about this and said things like "How about a date, Billy?" ' Clemens told me that they used a man because, although there were women stuntmen around at the time, most of them had big backsides because they were horseriding doubles. 'Diana was very slim. Her figure was boyish – no bum and small breasts.'

As the previous series had made a breakthrough in setting fashion trends, ABC were determined that the new series would once again lead the way. Marie Donaldson fired the opening shot, after talks with Albert Fennell and Brian Clemens. The new girl would definitely be keeping the Cathy Gale style and her clothes would certainly have the tailored, masculine appeal. So Donaldson suggested that Steed's girl, as the epitome of the jet-age woman, might be given a push-button wardrobe of super separates. 'This wardrobe is stored behind electronically-controlled panels in her elegant penthouse bedroom. Card-indexed by computer, when she wants to go, say, to Morocco, she presses a button for that climate and the appropriate garments shoot out on their hangers. This would give good opportunities for comedy if Steed got at the computer and reset it, so that the Morocco button produced a wardrobe for Alaska!' The idea wasn't used.

Once the decision had been taken to continue Cathy's black leather look into Emma Peel's wardrobe, the film-makers shopped around for a costume designer with the talent to produce the first in a long line of leather catsuits. The lady was already at the studio.

Jan Rowell, a graduate of the Central School of Arts and Crafts, London (Theatre Department) had recently been hired by the Elstree Studio Costume Department. She landed the job of costume designer on the new series with particular responsibility for the appearance of the new leading lady, as then still uncast. She remembers the events quite clearly. 'A succession of young actresses and starlets were auditioned, many of whom made a speedy exit from the casting sessions with only two or three real possibilities emerging during the first weeks.' She recalls speaking with Elizabeth Shepherd, who informed her that she only wished to wear clothes by Bonnie Cashin, who specialised in voluminous cloaks and skirts – which Jan Rowell knew would be hopelessly impractical for speedy movement, and bulky and unappealing on camera, however stylish they were in real life. Then she heard that a new girl was hot favourite to take over the role.

'I was delighted when Diana Rigg was confirmed as the new *Avengers* girl,' she told me. 'Tall, slim and graceful, with long legs, flowing Titian hair and pale-skinned oval face, Diana was a pleasure to dress. Used to the discipline of the RSC, her punctuality and friendly politeness charmed the crew, who were most impressed when she wished them good morning and procured her own cup of coffee.'

She knew instantly that the black leather look was not only practical, but would look stunning on Diana Rigg. After speaking to Albert Fennell, whose only comment was to make it 'kinky', she designed a one-piece catsuit with lots of zips and a wide, low-set belt. Classic knee-length boots from Annello and Davide completed the costume. (This is the ensemble worn by

Chapeau Melon et Bottes De Cuir, the French episodes, were dubbed. The French actor, who dubbed Macnee's voice throughout every filmed episode, was Jean Berger. During the Sixties Emma Peel's voice was dubbed by actress Michele Montel. When a deal was finalized for the new, digitally-restored videotapes to go on sale in France, in 1993, the voices were re-dubbed: Steed once again by Jean Berger, Emma, this time, by Francine Laine, Michele Montel having retired.

Diana in the first eight episodes and more particularly in the series' opening montage titles.) 'Diana was very happy with this and the bosses approved. I made this of soft, black leather skins and the suit was lined throughout with cotton calico, as it had to be very strong to take the strain of all the strenuous movements Emma Peel would use in repelling her assailants. A girl named Doreen Brown constructed the outfit with great skill, and then had to make another one for the young stuntman who would double for Diana in the more dangerous sequences.' She was as surprised as anyone to see how convincing the double appeared on film. 'In his wig and costume, with careful filming and editing so that his face was never glimpsed, the momentary illusion was kept.'

As it was clear that Diana Rigg would need a number of other outfits quickly, as the auditions had eaten into the preparation time, she accompanied Diana on a shopping spree and they selected an assortment of skirts, tops and trousers to mix in with the other costumes she had designed and were being produced. 'This was the customary practice with most productions with a contemporary setting. It is the choice of purchased items combined with original designs which portrays the individuality of the character.'

What, you may ask, of Steed? Jan Rowell acknowledge that Patrick Macnee had by then assumed total control of his impeccable wardrobe. 'This perfectly complemented the more offbeat glamour of his leading lady, so there was no necessity to change his image.'

She recalled that Diana would sensibly arrive with little or no make-up. 'The make-up man had his own ideas on how she should look as Emma Peel, at first applying a dark lipstick and heavy foundation more suitable for the hey-day of Margaret Lockwood than the swinging sixties. But eventually Emma's look evolved successfully, based on a younger, more natural look, which enhanced rather than changed her appearance.'

Jan Rowell left the series after working on the first eight episodes and was replaced by top fashion designer John Bates who, working independently and away from the studio, produced a new and daring wardrobe for Emma. This was the first collection of clothes designed specifically for a television programme that was adapted in its entirety for retail distribution.

The project was inspired by the demand from viewers for the type of clothes worn by Honor Blackman in the earlier series. Some of her clothes were made available for sale, but only on a small scale. For the new series, the Jean Varon fashion house sought the cooperation of several well-known firms to make all the clothes designed by John Bates available in stores throughout Britain and overseas.

'The Avengers Collection' consisted of some three dozen outfits, with all the relevant accessories. The principles on which John Bates designed Diana Rigg's wardrobe were necessarily

The Avengers take a break during filming. Diana Rigg is wearing the leather fighting suit designed for her by costumier Jan Rowell.

different from those which guided any ordinary fashion collection. As the new series was being made on film for world distribution, it could expect a screen life of five years or more, so Emma Peel's clothes had to be as modern as her character and yet timeless enough to remain acceptable for a long time afterwards. As Jan Rowell explained: 'At this time, colour television was still to come, so one had to remember that rich colours, such as peacock and scarlet would translate into a dull iron grey on black-and-white film; the most interesting effect was achieved by translating colour into dark, light and medium tones used in combination. Texture also plays a part. A matt jersey absorbs light, and satin or any other shiny fabrics reflect it.' The costumes had to photograph clearly and simply on the small screen. This meant using uncluttered lines and materials that would not 'strobe' in front of cameras, and that would stand up to the strenuous adventures in which the character became involved. Basically, the collection took as its theme the black and white of the television medium – the 'lines' that make up the TV screen. These lines were seen repeatedly in the use of braid on coats and dresses. The other recurring motif was a target, symbolising the Op Art designs of the space age (seen in Emma's Avenger beret and the dial of her Avenger watch). Since Emma was to be a younger, more carefree and more feminine character than her predecessor, John Bates's designs included a number of day and evening dresses which were by turns both demure and daring, in feminine materials such as lace, silk, lamé and crepe.

Emma's fighting suits now largely discarded the old leather image for a different kind of sex appeal. This was based on form-fitting jersey, or (where leather was used) on an 'animal look' conveyed through snakeskin, or a 'soft-centre' look achieved by wearing leather over a crepe blouse. The new designs were launched in August 1965 at the Courtaulds Fashion Theatre, in London, and ABC commissioned tie-ups with 14 British manufacturers. Soon major stores and boutiques in Britain and overseas were selling what became known as the Jean Varon/*Avengers* pack.

Director James Hill recalls an amusing incident about Diana's clothes for *Town of No Return*). 'One day, Diana appeared on the set in this mini-skirt – quite possibly the first time one had ever been seen in England. Julian Wintle was on set and he couldn't believe it when he saw this long-legged girl in this tiny little skirt. "She can't possibly wear that!" he exclaimed. "Julian," she replied, "These are going to be very popular." She did wear it. I think Diana wore the first ever mini skirt to be seen on screen.'

Brian Clemens introduced certain ground rules. He told me: 'The series had to have unity, and thus enable us to do anything – any kind of story, our way. I laid down the ground rule that no women should be killed, no extras should populate the streets. We admitted to only one class – and that was the upper. As a fantasy, we would not show a uniformed policeman or a coloured man. And you would not see anything so common as blood in *The Avengers*. Had we introduced a coloured man or a policeman, we would have had the yardstick of social reality and that would have made the whole thing quite ridiculous. Alongside a bus queue of ordinary men-in-the-street, Steed would have become a caricature.'

However, treading a fine line between fantasy and reality had its problems, as in the script for *Two's A Crowd*. Reading the script, Anthony John said: 'The story necessitates Steed having a double, a ploy that was used in *Man With Two Shadows*. Provided no-one objects to such duplication, the story is otherwise quite good.'

One aspect did concern him, however: 'We are obviously dealing with Russian spies, the Russian Embassy, the Russian Ambassador, etc, etc. I cannot see how, if we are to take our responsibilities seriously, that these kind of references can possibly help international relations. There are shots of the driveway leading to the Russian Embassy and the hallway thereof. Are the makers going to reproduce the actuals? If so, I would imagine the Russian Embassy would be most displeased and would have something to say to the Foreign Office...' He suggested that the programme-makers gave serious attention to this aspect.

Brian Tesler read the script on 23 February 1965. 'The two central ideas, a double for Steed, and the mysterious Psev who turn out to be a quartet, are very good. However, I do feel that the running theme of model weapons of destruction goes so far over the acceptable fantasy line as to be just plain funny, not to say ludicrous. A toy bomber dropping its message in the Ambassador's soup; a toy battle ship killing Ivenko with a broadside in the park; a toy helicopter with a tiny television camera flying all the way to peep into Steed's apartment; a toy spitfire with machine guns lethal enough to kill, its bomber with a bomb powerful enough to kill all four villains; it's all just too much to accept, and I cannot see us getting away with it.'

Two other things: 'The script seems to cheat us over the Steed double business. How, if Webster is Steed, do we justify the close-up of Steed in scene 22 answering Brodny's phone call when Webster has just finished modelling? It just isn't fair to say that Brodny's call to Steed's flat was transferred behind the fashion room's curtain, and that it was Steed/Webster answering the phone. Since we, the viewers, have been thoroughly deceived too, the ultimate explanation of the deception to Mrs Peel is far too brief and casual (four short lines) a throwaway to carry conviction.' Point two reiterated Anthony John's comments.

Julian Wintle replied that he would safely leave this one to Brian Clemens to get into a shape acceptable to everyone. Clemens revised the script.

Some of Tesler's comments had received attention, but his main criticism (that of the telephone cheat) was still niggling. Tesler was obliged to return the script with the following comments: 'I thought we had all agreed that the one thing we would great care to avoid was just this sort of deliberate, unexplained cheat, for which the taped series used to be so criticised. I cited, you will remember, Steed helpless at swordpoint in one scene [of *The Grandeur That Was Rome*] and bounding in to save Mrs Gale in the next, with no explanation of his escape. When did we agree that the teaser could be a non sequitur cheat, provided it is dramatic? None of the other scripts you have commisioned play unfair in this way. It seems that there is still work to be done on this script which would in no way emasculate it.'

The script was revised several times until Tesler was happy, although he still thought that the teaser was a thoroughly bad idea. 'But I'm prepared to accept the Spitfire and Shackleton – and even, at a pinch, the battleship – if you really think you can pull them off on screen. I have my doubts, and I shudder at the thought of those giant models being bought and rehearsed with at £500 a time.'

Brian Clemens comments: 'Ironic that miniature planes, cars, etc., were later – much later – used in Hollywood movies: *Special FX TWO* and Eastwood's *Dead Pool*, spring to mind. But then, *The Avengers* was always ahead of its time.'

Clemens quickly realised that the only way to break into the American market (and thus ensure a profit) was to create something with which the Americans themseves could not compete. 'I think there are two kinds of things that succeed, which no other country can do. Dickensian television and spy television, the Bulldog Drummond type of show. When the Americans attempt to do it they realise that the only people who can do it are the British. So I've always believed that we shouldn't try to imitate what the Americans can do better than us, but to go for that fairly narrow area where we always succeed. So the formula was to set the stories against a tongue-in-cheek panorama of the picture-postcard Britain illustrated in tourist brochures. Every aspect of British life was incorporated as it was promoted overseas; from atom stations, bio-chemical plants and modern industry on the one hand to fox-hunting, stately homes and the Olde Englishe Inne on the other.' It was all gently sent up as a good-humoured counterpoint to the dangerous adventures of the two secret agents who hid their iron fists beneath the velvet gloves of high-living and sophisticated luxury.

'We became terribly British,' said Clemens. 'A car is a car is a car, and not an automobile. A lift is a lift is a lift, never an elevator. It is this Britishness that fits the fantasy world so appealing to the Americans.'

Once the style of the show was established, it was felt that the new series would require its own distinctive signature tune. Johnny Dankworth was approached, but declined because of work commitments. Julian Wintle asked Laurie Johnson to compose a title theme. Johnson was making an album at the time; he wrote the theme music and recorded it as *The Shake* (on the album *The Big New Sound Strikes Back.*) As Laurie told me: 'It was written for *The Avengers*, but because I didn't want to anticipate the series, which had just started production, I put it out on the album. I wrote it and called it something else so that I could put it out as a single called *The Avengers Theme*. Then I re-recorded it exactly as we did it on the titles.' (Brian Clemens says that Laurie, a former Guardsman, and one-time French horn player, is a close personal friend of the great Bernie Herman, who did most of Hitchcock's best films, plus the original *Cape Fear*. From time to time, Bernie would pop in to offer advice, or to indulge in recrimination, in his inimitable manner!)

The production went before the cameras in mid-November 1964, with the Patrick Macnee and Elizabeth Shepherd episode *Town of No Return*, at a location in Norfolk. Completed on 21 November (minus music, effects, etc. which would be added later in the editing suite), the team moved over to *The Murder*

Market. Elizabeth Shepherd left the programme and shooting resumed on 16 December, on Sound Stage Three, at Elstree Studios. Brian Clemens elaborates: 'We'd only done about two days shooting on that (the second Shepherd episode); very little material had actually been filmed that couldn't actually be re-used. We certainly didn't have to reshoot that episode in its entirety, because little of the material had been shot on Liz Shepherd. When we got Diana Rigg, we simply reshot the episode again. But *Town of No Return* was obviously a whole episode. So we had to pull out all the bits with Elizabeth Shepherd in them and reshoot them with Diana. This was done sometime later of course.' (Seven months later, in July 1965.)

Brian Clemens has an interesting aside about the reshooting. In the original version, Alison Seebohm played Jill Manson. The role in the reshoot was played by Juliet Harmer. However, in her brief time with the company, Alison met stunt director Ray Austin and later became his wife.

Mid-way through the production, ABC received correspondence from a representative of the Australian Broadcasting Commission, indicating that the company would be interested in contributing to the production cost of the new series – provided ABC would agree to three of the twenty-six episodes being shot in Australia. This never happened. The financial aspects of doing so, let alone the cost of flying the stars, the cast and the film unit to Sydney, were prohibitive and the offer was politely refused. As was the suggestion by the ABC Board of Directors that production of the series should be moved from Elstree to either the Beaconsfield or Bray Studios! It appears that Howard Thomas and his team were sitting on the fence regarding a request from the Elstree management to authorize the provision of additional sound stages at the studio, backed by more extensive facilities, such as tele-cine, sets and personnel. Julian Wintle, who was informed of this, had agreed that he might accept a move to Beaconsfield (but not Bray) provided a firm decision was reached and all costs of re-establishing the production would be borne wholly by ABC. After due consideration was given to the request, the ABC management decided that production of *The Avengers* would remain at Elstree. A direct consequence of this was that Albert Fennell became responsible for 'all production matters up to and including completion of the scripts and casting of each episode' and 'Graham Scott would become responsible for supervising the production on the floor. Albert Fennell would also assist with the post-production work'.

The decision to allow the production to remain at Elstree was confirmed to Wintle on 16 March 1965, as was the (alarming) fact that the company was now saving about £150 a week on the salary paid to Diana Rigg, compared with that budgeted for Elizabeth Shepherd! An additional £1,500 was to be added

Patrick hated one particular double wearing his clothes for doubling duty. 'BO!' he would mutter and send them off to be cleaned. *

to the budget and Harry Pottle would replace Bob Jones as Art Director.

Brian Clemens recalls that at Elstree the series had famous neighbours with offices next door: Gregory Peck, William Friedkin, Raquel Welsh, Charlton Heston, Ned Sherrin – not too mention Bob Baker and Monty Berman (*The Saint*, *The Champions*, *Randall & Hopkirk*, etc.), and Gerry Anderson (*Fireball XL5* etc.) Latterly, Harrison Ford and Alec Guinness of *Star Wars*. Lunch tables were shared by Chewbacca and R2 D2 – who, because it took so long to put on, remained in make-up throughout the day!

Whereas most of the Honor Blackman stories had been designed as a one-hour thriller series with a tongue-in-cheek slant to balance the off-beat adventures of Steed's chipper secret service agent and Cathy's sylph-like Amazon, the new *Avengers* series became more science-fiction orientated. Plots focused on the efforts of power-mad scientists hell-bent on ruling the world, using such outrageous devices as a giant man-eating plant; torrential rainstorms; agents being brainwashed in a Manchurian concentration camp – situated in the heart of London's West End – and even a pair of steel robots.

The robots, The Cybernauts, were selected to be the villains to introduce Steed and his colleague, via the American Broadcasting Company (ABC), to American viewers. UK viewers were, of course, well acquainted with the exploits of Steed and his female partners, but the Blackman series, though screened in Canada and Australia, had never been shown in the USA; this only happened recently, courtesy of the Arts and Entertainment channel. The problem, then, was one of familiarizing the American viewers with the characters.

This was solved when Albert Fennell and Brian Clemens decided to film a special 'introductory' teaser sequence which was tagged on to the beginning of the American prints. The sequence began with a man wearing a waiter's jacket, walking into view across a giant chessboard. Suddenly, he falls to the ground and we notice that he has a dagger implanted into a 'target' motif on his back. Enter Emma left and Steed right. They cross to the dead figure and Steed kneels to pick up a bottle of champagne from the dead man's hand. He smiles coyly at his partner as she deftly replaces a small, gold-plated pistol into the top of her black leather boot. Emma returns the smile as, in close-up, Steed fills two glasses.

Proposing a silent toast, they drink the bubbly and, carrying the champagne bottle, walk off into the background – cue *The Avengers* main title.

Throughout this sequence, the music builds to a crescendo of tenor drum rolls, while a voice-over narration tells us that:

Extraordinary crimes against the people and the State have to be avenged by agents extraordinary.

Two such people are John Steed, top professional, and his partner, Emma Peel, talented amateur – otherwise known as The Avengers.

The shooting schedule was long and arduous. (Diana Rigg and Patrick Macnee were required to learn 60 pages of dialogue per week, and work a 14-hour day.) Each episode cost £30,000 to produce and had a ten-day shooting schedule (although most ran over and took an average of 14 days to complete). Because the stories were being filmed for the first time, greater use was made of outdoor locations, with the majority of the episodes being filmed in and around the country lanes of Radlett and

Brian Clemens wanted to give the new girl an entrance. He elected to introduce Emma Peel in the fencing scene from *The Town of No Return*.

Shenley, in Hertfordshire, a short drive from EMI's Elstree Studios (known at the time as Associated British), where the principal shooting took place.

At the beginning of *Town of No Return* (the first episode screened in Britain), Emma and Steed were already known to each other, but Brian Clemens incorporated an 'introductory' scene into the script to introduce Emma to the viewer. As he told me: 'I wanted to give her an entrance and there is no better entrance than to have someone doing this and that with a sword. She does so to Steed, when he calls at her apartment. Then we see her in close-up. It was a theatrical device.' No mention was made of Cathy's disappearance. However, Cathy Gale is mentioned in *Too Many Christmas Trees*. Steed is opening his Christmas cards and, finding one from Cathy, says to Emma: 'A card from Mrs Gale! Whatever can she be doing at Fort Knox?' A reference, of course, to Honor Blackman's *Goldfinger* Pussy Galore character.

The series premiered on the ITV network in Britain on 2 October 1965. Two months later, on 3 December, Laurie Johnson's *The Theme From The Avengers* was released to the record shops.

The Avengers was off and running – but there were (seemingly) insurmountable problems to overcome before the series became an 'instant' success.

The main titles graphics used on the press preview film prints.

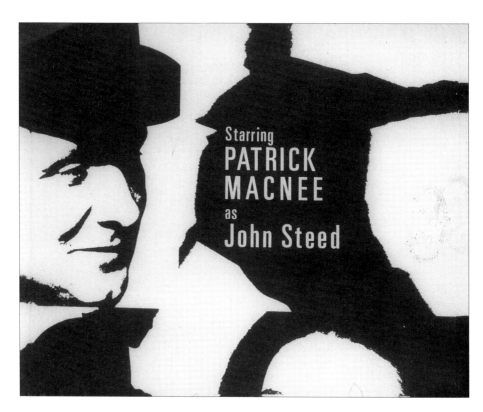

Starring
PATRICK
MACNEE
as
John Steed

SEASON FOUR CHRONOLOGY

Episode	Title
1	The Murder Market
2	The Master Minds
3	Dial a Deadly Number
4	Death at Bargain Prices
5	Too Many Christmas Trees
6	The Cybernauts
7	The Gravediggers
8	Room Without a View
9	A Surfeit of H_2O
10	Two's a Crowd
11	Man-Eater of Surrey Green
12	Silent Dust (aka Strictly for the Worms)
13	The Hour That Never Was (aka An Hour to Spare/Roger and Out)
14	The Town of No Return
15	Castle De'ath
16	The Thirteenth Hole
17	Small Game for Big Hunters
18	The Girl from Auntie
19	Quick, Quick Slow Death
20	The Danger Makers
21	A Touch of Brimstone (aka The Hellfire Club)
22	What the Butler Saw
23	The House That Jack Built
24	A Sense of History
25	How to Succeed... at Murder (aka How to Succeed at Murder...Without Really Trying)
26	Honey for the Prince

There was a two-week break in production between
Episodes Fifteen and Sixteen

Produced by: Julian Wintle
In Charge of Production: Albert Fennell
Associate Producer: Brian Clemens
Production Designer: Harry Pottle
Script Editor: Brian Clemens (Uncredited)
Music by: Laurie Johnson

The Murder Market:

a) Julian Wintle considered this to be one of the best scripts, as did Brian Tesler who commented: 'Excellent; one of the best scripts I can ever remember reading. Two tiny points: i) Won't Togetherness strike a chord (no matter how far separated) with the Togetherness in the script for A Touch of Brimstone? *ii) Lovely idea to have a romantic tune accompanying the fight in scene 47, but will you be sure, of course, that it has no copyright implications for the US sale. Irving Berlin is supposed to be very tough about clearances. b) Wintle wanted to shoot this as Episode Two. Tesler agreed. (It was filmed second, first with Elizabeth Shepherd, then again with Diana Rigg.) Incidentally, documentary evidence shows that director Wolf Rilla filmed the short-lived Shepherd sequences of this story. c) Writer Tony Williamson was a hypnotist. He and writer Dennis Spooner met when in the RAF together. Tony was a dental assistant and pulled one of Dennis's teeth without anaesthetic, under hypnosis!**

SEASON FOUR EPISODES

79 THE MURDER MARKET

by Tony Williamson

Steed takes a wife
Emma gets buried

John Steed (Patrick Macnee) Emma Peel (Diana Rigg) Mr Adrian Lovejoy (Patrick Cargill) Walter Dinsford (Peter Bayliss) Barbara Wakefield (Suzanne Lloyd) Mrs Jessica Stone (Naomi Chance) Robert Stone (John Woodvine) Jonathan Stone (Edward Underdown) Receptionist (Barbara Roscoe) Fred Beale (John Forham) JG Henshaw (unknown) Lyric for *Togetherness* by Herbert Kretzmer

Directed by Peter Graham Scott

Why is Steed, London's most eligible bachelor, visiting the Togetherness Marriage Bureau? The attractions of his beautiful escort, Barbara Wakefield, proved fatal for her previous partners Jonathan Stone, Henshaw and other men before them. Lovejoy and Dinsford, believing Steed to be genuine, offer him their most exclusive service: if he will commit a murder for them they will kill his cousin allowing an inheritance to pass to Steed. His victim will be...Emma Peel. Her investigations have led her to suspect that Robert Stone is in league with Barbara Wakefield. Henshaw's floating corpse in the bath being a very convincing reason. Steed 'kills' Mrs Peel and her burial seems to convince Togetherness that Steed is genuine. He now insists on taking his orders from the real boss – Jessica Stone, wife of the late Jonathan. With Robert Stone exonerated from suspicion, Steed and Emma close down the bureau and exit the scene in a hearse!

Filmed: 18 December 1964/January 1965
TX: 13 November 1965

80 THE MASTER MINDS

by Robert Banks Stewart

Steed becomes a genius
Emma loses her mind

John Steed (Patrick Macnee) Emma Peel (Diana Rigg) Sir Clive Todd (Laurence Hardy) Holly Trent (Patricia Haines) Dr Fergus Campbell (Ian McNaughton) Davinia Todd (Georgina Ward) Desmond Leeming (Bernard Archard) Sir Jeremy (John Wentworth) Major Plessy (Manning Wilson)

Directed by Peter Graham Scott

Serious acts of treason committed by eminent officials lead Steed to deduce that the Ransack Club is the only common denominator in the crimes. Deciding that it's time that he enrolled for the intellectual challenge, he attends a special course at their country hideout. Holly Trent, the local archery instructor, also seems suspicious of Ransack, as does the new school secretary, Mrs Peel. Physical fitness and academic brainstorming by day gives way to mass hypnosis and brainwashing by night, as radio waves induce deep-conditioned sleep. However, Steed's trance is false (he had previously disconnected the sleep-inducer), and Mrs Peel is ordered to dispose of him. She is the better actress, but her trance is exposed as a fake and plans are made to kill her as well. It is Steed to the rescue! The voice behind the screen is Holly Trent and, after destroying the gang's plans, exit the Avengers in a Bentley.

Filmed: December 1964/January 1965
TX: 6 November 1965

81 DIAL A DEADLY NUMBER

by Roger Marshall

Steed plays bulls and bears
Emma has no option

John Steed (Patrick Macnee) Emma Peel (Diana Rigg) Henry Boardman (Clifford Evans) Ruth Boardman (Jan Holden) Ben Jago (Anthony Newlands) Fitch (John Carson) John Harvey (Peter Bowles) Frederick Yuill (Gerald Sim) The General (Michael Trubshawe) Macombie (Norman Chappell) Warner (John Bailey) Waiter (Edward Cast)

Directed by Don Leaver

Henry Boardman's clients may be rich, but death keeps on preventing them from spending their money. Steed's attempt to invest £2,000,000 gains the brokerage services of Yuill, a skilful operator who, along with Jago, has made considerable profit from recent deaths. However, Yuill, too, suffers a terminal dose of the same illness, before Steed can elicit the truth. Yuill, like all the other fatalities, was carrying a bleeper device and Mrs Peel's investigations lead her to Fitch, the mechanic responsible for the high-tech equipment. His latest project is a lethal replica of Steed's watch! Before he can be warned, by a now-captive Mrs Peel, the switch is made and Steed is now only a phone call away from death by injection. Steed, however, spots the watch device and comes to Emma's aid, with fatal consequences for Fitch. With every suspect carrying a harmless bleeper, Steed soon discovers that Ruth Boardman and Jago are the deadly diallers. Exit the Avengers in a taxi-cab, with a bottle of claret to uncork!

Filmed: January 1965   TX: 4 December 1965

The Murder Market, The Master Minds, Dial a Deadly Number, Death At Bargain Prices: *Slightly different versions of these episodes exist. The main titles for these are composed from grainy black and white photographs of Steed and Emma, and the title graphics are different. Produced specifically as press preview copies, the latter contains a different 'tag' sequence to the print generally used for transmission purposes.*

82 DEATH AT BARGAIN PRICES

by Brian Clemens

Steed fights in Ladies Underwear
Emma tries 'feinting'

John Steed (Patrick Macnee) Emma Peel (Diana Rigg) Horatio Kane (Andre Morrell) Wentworth (TP McKenna) Farthingale (Allan Cuthbertson) Massey (George Selway) Tony Marco (Harvey Ashby) Jarvis (John Cater) Professor Popple (Peter Howell) Glynn (Ronnie Stevens) Julie Thompson (Diane Clare) Moran (unknown)

Directed by Charles Crichton

'How ostentatious to be shot six times.' A death in the lift at Pinter's Department Store, leads Steed and Mrs Peel to investigate a store receipt for Department 19, issued on a Sunday. On the top floor, in the department of Discontinued Lines, the new store owner 'King' Kane has no time for Steed, whilst the new lingerie lady – Mrs Peel – finds staff meetings where the staff are not invited! Jarvis, the store detective, nevertheless invites himself along, a terminal move. The receipt for Department 19 is in fact a feed card for the giant atomic bomb that Kane has created around the store. With the work of the drugged Professor Popple finished, the store renovations are complete, the descent of the north lift, temporarily out of order, will act as the detonator. Kane's price is simple – he wants Britain! Whilst Steed and Emma avenge the deaths, Kane attempts to create a 50-mile wide crater with the lift, but its descent mechanism is jammed by Steed. The gang rounded up, exit the Avengers by bicycle.

Filmed: January/February 1965   TX: 23 October 1965

83 TOO MANY CHRISTMAS TREES

by Tony Williamson

Steed hangs up his stocking
Emma asks for more

John Steed (Patrick Macnee) Emma Peel (Diana Rigg) Brandon Storey (Mervyn Johns) Dr Felix Teasel (Edwin Richfield) Janice Crane (Jeanette Sterke) Martin Trasker (Alex Scott) Jenkins (Robert James) Jeremy Wade (Barry Warren)

Directed by Roy Baker

Freddy Marshall is dead, victim of the same heady cocktail of mirth, mistletoe, recurring nightmares, white cardboard Christmas trees and a jolly Santa that Steed is now suffering. Off to a houseparty hosted by Bendan Storey, Steed's mind is being assailed by the telepathic Trasker and Wade. With the arrival of the medium, Janice Crane, the final stage of the Dickensian plan can begin and a mind-reading act at the witching hour seems to be unlocking State secrets from Steed's mind. Witnessing her partner's mental breakdown, Mrs Peel finds that she can trust no-one and Wade is murdered before he can change sides. However, she needn't have worried. Steed has known the score all along – his breakdown is a ruse to reveal Storey as the Santa of his dreams. The nightmare over, Steed sees to it that Trasker's condition mirrors the distorted imagery of the other do-badders. Exit the Avengers in an open-topped Surrey.

Filmed: February/March 1965   TX: 25 December 1965

84 THE CYBERNAUTS

by Philip Levene

Steed receives a deadly gift
Emma pockets it

John Steed (Patrick Macnee) Emma Peel (Diana Rigg) Dr Clement Armstrong (Michael Gough) Benson (Frederick Jaeger) Jephcott (Bernard Horsfall) Tusamo (Bert Kwouk) Sensai (John Hollis) Lambert (Ronald Leigh-Hunt) Hammond (Gordon Whiting)

Directed by Sidney Hayers

Several businessmen have been given the chop in spectacular fashion. Is karate the secret? Every businessman wanted to buy a new Japanese circuit system and soon only United Automation and its chairman, Armstrong, are left alive. He has invented the perfect killing machine: the Cybernaut. Robotic assassins that stalk their victims by homing in on radio pens...like the one that Mrs Peel is carrying. Steed escapes from captivity in time to warn her, but Armstong's advanced prototype kills on sight and the Avengers are surrounded by two mechanical monsters. Clipping the pen to the advanced model, Steed and Emma duck as the two titans clash. Beserk with rage, Armstrong dies trying to stop the two Cybernauts. With the pen crushed, the remaining Cybernaut deactivates – allowing Emma to tilt the odds in her favour and prove that her finger is mightier than the sword. Exit Emma in her Lotus whilst Steed, sitting in his Bentley pondering a crossword clue, declines her offer of a pen.

Filmed: March 1965   TX: 16 October 1965

The Cybernauts:
a) The script came in for some stick from ABC executive, Anthony John: 'The best thing I can say about this one is that it seems all right. I should imagine that it will need tremendous pace in order not to let us see through it and something distinctive to distinguish Cybernaut No 1 from Cybernaut No 2. No 1 is on his way to do Emma. No 2, in a white coat, is sent to repair the heating system. How do we know that it isn't No 1 with a white coat on?' The filmed version was considered by Brian Tesler as 'easily the most effective episode I have seen to date. It can do us nothing but good in terms of audience and critics.'
b) Writer Phil Levene's big start in life was as an actor in the famous stage play Reluctant Heroes. He graduated to writing for radio. Late one night while he was retruning home, Brian Clemens heard one of Levene's short plays for Just After Midnight and realized he might make a terrific Avengers writer. He was right!
*

The Gravediggers:
*a) The transmission print was trimmed by 30 seconds, when Brian Tesler asked Wintle to 'cut the railway train sequence'. Incidentally, the miniature railway sequences were filmed at the home of Lord Gretton, who built the 10.25 gauge miniature track in the grounds of his Stapleford home, in Buckinghamshire.
b) When we went on location in Melton Mowbray, we met Lord Gretton. He quivered visibly when we said that we would be bringing a unit to Stapleford. 'Will there be gels?' he inquired. 'Will Patricia Roc be coming?' (Pat Roc was a sex symbol of Forties films.)
c) Exploitation footage (notably Emma Peel on a white horse) was shot on the beach near Beaulieu, where we were entertained to lunch by Lord and Lady Montagu. *
d) Actor Victor Platt, who appears as Sexton, remembered an amusing incident. During the scene where Emma Peel is tied to the railway track, someone raced into the studio saying that there was an urgent phone call for Miss Rigg. Quick as a flash, the director Quentin*

85 THE GRAVEDIGGERS

by Malcolm Hulke

**Steed drives a train
Emma is tied to the tracks**

John Steed (Patrick Macnee) Emma Peel (Diana Rigg) Sir Horace Winslip (Ronald Fraser) Johnson (Paul Massie) Miss Thirlwell (Caroline Blakiston) Sexton (Victor Platt) Fred (Charles Lamb) Nurse Spray (Wanda Ventham) Baron (Ray Austin) Sager (Steven Berkoff) Miller (Bryan Mosley) Dr Marlow (Lloyd Lamble)

Directed by Quentin Lawrence

Frustrated by lack of funding, Dr Marlowe stages his own death in Pringby and retreats to Winslip Hospital for Retired and Ailing Railwaymen. Steed and Mrs Peel visit Pringby and follow his exhumed coffin back to the hospital. Steed's arrival causes panic. Marlowe has been burying equipment in graveyards around Pringby, so that he can jam the nation's early-warning system. It isn't long before Emma finds herself tied to a railway line, hoping that the train will be delayed, or Steed will rescue her. He does so by running the grave-diggers to earth and shunting their plans into the sideline. Exit The Avengers on Sir Horace Winslip's miniature steam-driven train.

Filmed: March/April 1965   TX: 9 October 1965

86 ROOM WITHOUT A VIEW

by Roger Marshall

**Steed becomes a gourmet
Emma wakes in Manchuria**

John Steed (Patrick Macnee) Emma Peel (Diana Rigg) Max Chessman (Paul Whitsun-Jones) Varnals (Peter Jeffrey) Dr Cullen (Richard Bebb) Carter (Philip Latham) Pascold (Peter Arne) Pushkin (Vernon Dobtcheff) Dr Wadkin (Peter Madden) Anna Wadkin (Jeanne Roland)

Directed by Roy Baker

The service in the Chessman Hotel is quite unlike any other: eminent scientists arrive for a night's sleep and awake in Manchuria! John Wadkin managed to escape, before the Chinese laundry cleaned up their mistake, but now Dr Cullen has booked into Room 621 for the longest overnight stay in history. Pascold, keen for Cullen to work for his firm, finds that the hotel has a lethal room service, whilst the new hotel receptionist, Mrs Peel, finds herself in the same prison camp as Cullen. In exchange for exclusive hotel rights inside the Eastern Bloc, Chessman is offering the kidnapped scientists, all held in a replica concentration camp, to the Chinese. Steed, meanwhile, has discovered the secret of the room without a view: a perfect replica of Room 621. Slamming the door closed on Chessman's plans, the Avengers exit in a rickshaw – pulled by Steed!

Filmed: April 1965   TX: 8 January 1966

Lawrence said: 'Tell them Miss Rigg is tied up at the moment!'
*e) Actor Steven Berkoff got his first film role in this episode. ***

87 A SURFEIT OF H20

by Colin Finbow

Steed plans a boat trip
Emma gets very wet

John Steed (Patrick Macnee) Emma Peel (Diana Rigg) Jonah Barnard (Noel Purcell) Dr Storm (Albert Lieven) Joyce Jason (Sue Lloyd) Eli Barker (Talfryn Thomas) Sr Arnold Kelly (John Kidd) Martin Smythe (Geoffrey Palmer)

Directed by Sidney Hayers

Jonah's ark is nearly finished, which is jolly good news because the rainclouds above Grannie Gregson's wine-making factory just keep on growing. The new business proprietor, Dr Sturm, seems reluctant to show visitors around the factory and all intruders seem to drown in localized storms. Sir Arnold Kelly, the meteorological expert, confirms his theories by drowning in a field, though his compatriot, Mrs Peel, has already reached the same conclusion. Too late. Emma is invited to visit Stum's factory – at gunpoint. Strapped to a wine-press, she faces imminent pulping while Sturm reveals the secret of his rain-making device to his captive audience. But Steed has already decided to close down the factory, determined that his partner won't become their latest vintage. After a heavy downpour of action in comes the clear skies of resolution. Exit the Avengers in a mini-buggy.

Filmed: April/May 1965   TX: 20 November 1965

A Surfeit of H$_2$O, *Brian Tesler felt that Colin Finbow's script for this story lacked the pace and excitement of some of the others and was 'slightly depressing in that it is yet another story with a science-fiction premise'. Writing to Julian Wintle he asked: 'I wonder, Julian, if the scripts aren't on the whole veering too much (and too often) towards fantasy. Aren't we going to get any more, fast straightforward thrillers with action and wit?'* *Little is left of his original script. Colin Finbow is now a director and leading light of the Children's Film Foundation. ***

88 TWO'S A CROWD

by Philip Levene

Steed is single-minded
Emma sees double

John Steed (Patrick Macnee) Emma Peel (Diana Rigg) Brodny (Warren Mitchell) Alicia Elena (Maria Machado) Shevedloff (Alec Mango) Pudeshkin (Wolfe Morris) Vogel (Julian Glover) Ivenko (John Bluthal) Major Carson (Eric Lander)

Directed by Roy Baker

Are there really two Steeds wandering around London? Colonel Psev, the major spymaster, appears to have found the perfect entrance ticket to a top secret defence conference. His four agents have found Webster, a duplicate Steed. Mrs Peel is not fooled though and her abduction is assured. The real Steed, however, has been less lucky: Webster has permanently disposed of him. His spying completed, Webster returns and insists on giving his prize information to Psev himself. Psev is a myth; he is, in fact, the four agents who work for him. The truth unveiled, the spies are in for a surprise; it was Webster who died and they are talking to Steed. The Avengers now make their escape, pursued by Psev's model aeroplanes – kiddies' toys, with adult weapons. Steed turns their own technology against them and Psev's plans go boom! Exit the Avengers on horseback – but Mrs Peel is moved to ask the question: is the man at her side really Steed?

Filmed: April/May 1965 TX: 18 December 1965

89 MAN-EATER OF SURREY GREEN

by Philip Levene

Steed kills a climber
Emma becomes a vegetable

John Steed (Patrick Macnee) Emma Peel (Diana Rigg) Sir Lyle Peterson (Derek Farr) Dr Sheldon (Athene Seyler) Laura Burford (Gillian Lewis) Alan Carter (William Job) Wing Comm. Davies (David Hutcheson) Publican (Joe Ritchie) Bob Pearson (Donald Oliver) Joe Mercer (Joby Blanshard)

Directed by Sidney Hayers

The stangest things fall from the skies and a previous space-shot brought back an intelligent man-eating vegetable! The whereabouts of the plant – and several missing horticulturalists – is unknown, but Sir Lyle Peterson knows more than he tells. Steed and Mrs Peel stumble upon the plant's existence while searching for the missing scientists. They now all appear to be at work cultivating the plant which, according to Dr Sheldon, not only has a brain and the capacity to grow to enormous size, but is man-eating! As the plant reaches germination stage and grows taller than a house, the Avengers race to the scene with weed-killer and the only defence from the plant's hypnotic powers: hearing aids. The enemy resists the invaders and threatens to make

Man-Eater of Surrey Green: *Tesler thought that they could just about get by with Phil Levene's script for this, 'but please let us now firmly eschew science-fiction from these stories. I'm certain that they are damagingly out of place. I would undoubtdly want to schedule this one a long way from the beginning. Incidentally, I think the rewritten denouement of* Town of No Return *is absolutely first class.'*

Mrs Peel dish of the day. But this early lunch has a weedkiller dressing and the plant dies from food poisoning, hiccuping Mrs Peel free from its deadly spell. Exit the Avengers in a haycart.

Filmed: May/June 1965   TX: 11 December 1965

90 SILENT DUST

by Roger Marshall

Steed watches birds
Emma goes hunting

John Steed (Patrick Macnee) Emma Peel (Diana Rigg) Omrod (William Franklyn) Juggins (Jack Watson) Mellors (Conrad Phillips) Croft (Norman Bird) Miss Snow (Joanna Wake) Clare Prendergast (Isobel Black) Sir Manfred Fellows (Charles Lloyd Pack) Quince (Aubrey Morris) Minister (Hilary Wontner) Howard (Robert Dorning)

Directed by Roy Baker

It was supposed to be the greatest discovery in modern agriculture, but the wonder fertilizer, Silent Dust, caused such devastation at Manderley that the area was never inhabited again. Its inventor, Prendergast, was discredited and sacked. The fertilizer killed every-

Silent Dust:
Parts of the script for this needed some further consideration. 'Steed's deus ex machina arrival in Scene 79 is going to need some thought. Alternative (1) is too contrived and unlikely. Alternative (2) is used at the climax of The Master Minds.*'*

Emma is threatened by Juggins in *Silent Dust.*

thing and now it's happening again. Local birdwatcher, Quince, alerts Mrs Peel that the birds are dying on landowner Omrod's estate: is it a coincidence that Prendergast's daughter is supported by this country squire? Unless Omrod's demands are met, Silent Dust will once again wreak havoc on nature, county by county. Steed is shot and Mrs Peel discovers that an apple a day hasn't agreed with Quince. Invited to the local hunt, the Avengers find themselves on the list of prey. Cutting Omrod and his cronies down to size, they exit in a hot-air balloon.

Filmed: June 1965   TX: 1 January 1966

91 THE HOUR THAT NEVER WAS

by Roger Marshall

Steed has to face the music
Emma disappears

John Steed (Patrick Macnee) Emma Peel (Diana Rigg) Geoffrey Ridsdale (Gerald Harper) Philip Leas (Dudley Foster) Hickey (Roy Kinnear) 'Porky' Purser (Roger Booth) Corporal Barman (Daniel Moynihan) Wiggins (David Morrell) Driver (Fred Haggerty)

Directed by Gerry O'Hara

On their way to the closing-down party of RAF Camp 472 – Hamelin, a car accident seems to freeze the Avengers in time. Upon arrival at the camp all the clocks have stopped at 11am and the place is deserted. A thorough examination of these strange circumstances reveals only a dead milkman with a live milk-float, strange high-pitched noises and Hickey, a tramp. Then, after another bump on the head, Steed awakes again to find that Emma has disappeared this time, while the rest of the personnel has returned! Only Hickey's dead body convinces him that the previous incidents did take place. Somebody is abducting officers, using C11 gas to brainwash secrets from them and carrying their bodies away in the milk float. Subduing the new camp dentist, Leas, and his henchmen proves to be the funniest experience of the day. Exit the Avengers on a milk float – at 'high speed'.

Filmed: June 1965   TX: 27 November 1965

92 THE TOWN OF NO RETURN

by Brian Clemens

Steed finds a town full of ghosts
Emma gets into harness

The Hour That Never Was:
a) Roger Marshall confirms that they wanted Vera Lynn singing We'll Meet Again *to be used over the RAF scenes. 'They couldn't clear the rights – or wouldn't pay?'*
b) The 'deserted air-field' idea came about when Roger and Brian Clemens went to recce locations for the first filmed episode. 'We saw this old airfield and thought that it would make the basis of a good script. So we wrote the story in his car on the way back home. Then Gerry O'Hara filmed it, but not at the same air-field. Imagine, a dentist going to conquer the world with a drill!'

John Steed (Patrick Macnee) Emma Peel (Diana Rigg) 'Mark Brandon' (Alan MacNaughton) Smallwood (Patrick Newell) Flying Officer 'Piggy' Warren (Terence Alexander) Rev Jonathan Anesbury (Jeremy Burnham) Saul (Robert Brown) Jill Manson (Juliet Harmer) Mark Brandon (Walter Horsbrugh)

Directed by Roy Baker

On a Norfolk beach, a man steps out of the sea – a plastic bag covering his suit, Cheerfully, the man walks off towards Little Bazeley. After the disappearance of four agents, it is the turn of Steed and Mrs Peel to say at The Inebriated Gremlin in Little Bazeley. Another visitor, Smallwood, has perished by the following morning; his only crime being to visit his brother. However, nobody is who they appear to be any more – the whole village has been infiltrated by enemy agents. A vast arsenal of weapons is being amassed in underground bunkers at a nearby airfield. Only after an unholy row with the agents trapped in their own bunker can the Avengers exit on a moped.

Filmed: July 1965   TX: 2 October 1965

93 CASTLE DE'ATH

by John Lucarotti

Steed becomes a strapping Jock
Emma lays a ghost

John Steed (Patrick Macnee) Emma Peel (Diana Rigg) Ian (Gordon Jackson) Angus (Robert Urquhart) McNab (Jack Lambert) Roberton (James Copeland) Controller (Russell Waters)

Directed by James Hill

The mournful wail of bagpipes dissuades visitors from going to Castle De'ath, but if the ghostly Black Jamie on the battlements doesn't scare people, then the very real torture chamber below probably will. Steed and Mrs Peel go undercover to investigate the death of a diver who was four inches taller when alive than the corpse that is in the morgue. In the lair of the Lairds, they discover an unusual new method of fish farming. Before the night is over, a high body count will have been amassed and a ghost laid to rest, forcing the Chief to seek comfort in the arms of his Iron Maiden. Exit the Avengers in an amphibious vehicle.

Filmed: July/August 1965   TX: 30 October 1965

94 THE THIRTEENTH HOLE

by Tony Williamson

Steed finds a bogey
Emma gets a birdie

John Steed (Patrick Macnee) Emma Peel (Diana Rigg) Reed (Patrick Allen) Colonel Watson (Hugh Manning) Dr Adams (Peter Jones) Jackson (Victor Maddern) Collins (Francis Matthews) Professor Minley (Norman Wynne) Waversham (Donald Hewlett) Man on TV Screen (Richard Marner)

Directed by Roy Baker

The unusual death of Ted Murphy leads Steed and Mrs Peel to the strange events on the greens at Cranleigh Golf Club. Adams and Reed seem prepared to win the club tournament at any cost, whether with a three-iron or a .303 rifle – leaving Steed to ponder why it is par for the course that nobody ever completes Hole Thirteen? Eagle-eyed Steed soon uncovers Colonel Watson's plan to steal Dr Adams' secrets by satellite (the Thirteenth Hole has a bunker without any sand) and swings into action to save Mrs Peel. Tournament to Steed. Exit the Avengers in a golf buggy.

Filmed: September 1965   TX: 29 January 1966

95 SMALL GAME FOR BIG HUNTERS

by Philip Levene

Steed joins the natives
Emma gets the evil eye

John Steed (Patrick Macnee) Emma Peel (Diana Rigg) Colonel Rawlings (Bill Fraser) Simon Trent (James Villiers) Professor Swain (Liam Redmond) Dr Gibson (AJ Brown) Fleming (Peter Burton) Razafi (Paul Danquah) Tropical Outfitter (Tom Gill) Lala (Esther Anderson) Kendrick (Peter Thomas)

Directed by Gerry O'Hara

There is an outbreak of sleeping sickness in the British Isles, so Steed calls in Professor Swain, an expert on tropical matters. He pronounces that Kendrick, the latest victim, is suffering from the Curse of Sleep, induced by the Shirenzai cult in Kalaya. Kendrick was found in full tropical kit: is it a coincidence? He was close to the Kalayan Ex-Servicemen's Headquarters. Steed and Emma find a touch of the tropics amongst the English countryside: Swain and his former colonial colleagues are plotting to reconquer Kalaya by spreading disease in a new strain of tsetse fly. However, their plans are washed away by the Avengers, who exit in a rowing boat.

Filmed: September 1965   TX: 15 January 1966

96 THE GIRL FROM AUNTIE

by Roger Marshall

Steed almost outbids himself
Emma is a bird in a gilded cage

John Steed (Patrick Macnee) Emma Peel (Diana Rigg) Georgie Price-Jones (Liz Fraser) Gregorio Auntie (Alfred Burke) Arkwright (Bernard Cribbins) Ivanov (David Bauer) Aunty Hetty (Sylvia Coleridge) Old Lady (Mary Merrall) Receptionist (Yolande Turner) Taxi Driver (Ray Martine) Russian (Maurice Browning) Fred Jacques (John Rutland)

Directed by Roy Baker

Mrs Peel has been kidnapped – Steed's only clue is a female imper-sonator from a theatrical agency whose contacts seem to share a pas-sion for dying with knitting needles in their backs! Only one clue is forthcoming: 'Auntie did it'. Tracing the needles to the Arkwright Knitting Circle, Steed finds the tenants are less than friendly and are almost certainly involved. It seems that the only way Steed will get his partner back is by bidding for her in an auction arranged by Gregorio Auntie. However, Lot Seventeen proves too wild for her cage and the knit two, kill two murderers are cast off and closed down. Exit the Avengers in a bubble-car – while Georgie steals Steed's Bentley.

Filmed: September/October 1965. TX: 21 January 1966

97 QUICK-QUICK SLOW DEATH

by Robert Banks Stewart

Steed has two left feet
Emma dances with danger

John Steed (Patrick Macnee) Emma Peel (Diana Rigg) Lucille Banks (Eunice Gayson) Ivor Bracewell (Maurice Kaufmann) Chester Read (Larry Cross) Peever (James Belchamber) Bernard (Colin Ellis) Willi Fehr (Michael Peake) Nicki (Carole Gray) Captain Noble (John Woodnutt) Fintry (Alan Gerrard) Piedi (David Kernan) Huggins (Graham Armitage) Syder (Charles Hodgson) Bank Manager (Ronald Govey)

A Touch of Brimstone:

a) Tesler's verdict on the script: 'A good one, but it shows dangerous tendencies towards violence, horror and sordidity, which could preclude the show from being transmitted before 10pm.

'By any criteria, the following items all seem to go a little too far:

Page 21: Bates' electrified body: "jerking and shuddering amid a blaze of sparks...".

Page 31: Not too authentic a replica of an Hogarthian orgy, I hope...

Page 40: Darcy pinned to his seat by the heavy sword which drops on him from above and impales him "up to the hilt!" Ugh!

Page 48: The whole idea of Willie's wooden hand, and the jovial exhibition of it...

Page 60: Willie's wooden hand again: this time, close-up emphasis of it and its spring mechanism...

Page 61: Willie's wooden hand yet again: this time, Steed's sabre lopping it off...

We could not, and should not want to, get away with all this, not even in a gay, tongue-in-cheek series.'

b) Emma Peel was still being depicted as Mantha in this script.

Directed by James Hill

A body in a pram takes Steed and Mrs Peel on a tricky trail to trace a tattoo saying 'Lucille'. Tattoos seem to recur throughout their investigation with a 'rose tattoo on the right wrist' pointing towards the killer. Enrolling at the Terpsichorean Training Techniques dance class, Mrs Peel takes all the right steps to graduate quickly with the truth: lonely dancers are dying – and are being replaced by subversive elements. In a quick-quick slow move, Steed and Emma teach mastermind Read a few dance steps he doesn't know. Exit the Avengers dancing.

Filmed: October/November 1965   TX: 5 February 1966

98 THE DANGER MAKERS

by Roger Marshall

Steed joins a secret society
Emma walks the plank

John Steed (Patrick Macnee) Emma Peel (Diana Rigg) Major Robertson (Nigel Davenport) Dr Harold Lang (Douglas Wilmer) Colonel Adams (Fabia Drake) Peters (Moray Watson) Lieutenant Stanhope (Adrian Ropes) RAF Officer (Richard Coleman) Gordon Lamble (John Gatrell)

Directed by Charles Crichton

If the pace of civvy street is too slow, why not join the Danger Makers? Steed and Mrs Peel are puzzled by the important military officers who are risking their lives unnecessarily and the answer seems to reside in Manton House. Dr Lang, its director, is harnessing the desire of his colleagues to live dangerously, so that he may fulfil Operation Grand Slam and steal the Crown Jewels. Whilst Steed is relieved to discover that it is 'too easy to kill a handcuffed man', Emma springs the trap to ensure that Lang gets the shock of his life. Exit the Avengers in go-carts.

Filmed: November/December 1965 TX: 12 February 1966

99 A TOUCH OF BRIMSTONE

by Brian Clemens

Steed joins the Hellfire Club
Emma becomes the Queen of Sin

John Steed (Patrick Macnee) Emma Peel (Diana Rigg) Hon John Cleverly Cartney (Peter Wyngarde) Lord Darcy (Colin Jeavons) Sara (Carol Cleveland) Horace (Robert Cawdron) Willy Frant (Jeremy Young) Pierre (Art Thomas) Big Man (Alf Joint) Huge Man (Bill Reed) Roger Winthrop (Michael Latimer) Tubby Bunn (Bill Wallis) Kartovski (Steve Plytas)

Directed by James Hill

Several VIPs are finding themselves the butt of practical jokes, much to the amusement of John Cartney. Deciding that murder is not a laughing matter, Steed must intervene. However, membership of the Hellfire Club has far more sinister purposes as Steed discovers when he enrols. The tests to become a 'Superior' member convince him that Cartney's plan to destroy Calverstone House is real enough. Whilst the Hellfire Club engages in debauchery upstairs, it is left to Steed to

c) Jeremy Young was Kate O'Mara's husband – she later played Madame Gerda, the villainess, in the Avengers *stage play – and was suggested for the role by Brian Clemens.* *

Diana Rigg teases director James Hill on the set of A Touch of Brimstone. The whipping scenes in this story were trimmed in the UK and banned by the American network.

What the Butler Saw:
Tesler found the shooting script 'surprisingly dull: hardly any action, and a persuasive feeling of "we've been here before" with the officers and gentleman send-ups.'

The House That Jack Built:
The 'horrific' side of things reared its head again in Tesler's critique of Brian Clemens' script for this episode, which he believed was 'absolutely first class'. His main concern was its horrific impact. He quoted Anthony John's comments on this point: 'I believe that the script could be done and that we could get away with it simply because it is quite fantastical. The abundance of gadgetry is a prime reason for diverting some of our attention from the would-be horror of the situation. Further, and I think that this is important, we are not dealing with a screaming, hysterical, maiden-in-distress-type-of-picture. Emma is a resourceful and brave woman who gives the impression (throughout this script) that she will manage. Now, provided the producer does not get her

foil the gunpowder plotters, with the help of Mrs Peel, Cartney's newly-elected Queen of Sin! Cartney plays his whip hand to dispose of his enemy, but he cannot prevent his own downfall. Exit the Avengers via an 18th-century coach.

Filmed: December 1965   TX: 19 February 1966

---

100 WHAT THE BUTLER SAW

by Brian Clemens

Steed becomes a Gentleman's Gentleman
Emma faces a fate worse than death

John Steed (Patrick Macnee) Emma Peel (Diana Rigg) Hemming (Thorley Walters) Benson (John Le Mesurier) Group Captain Miles (Dennis Quilley) Major General Goddard (Kynaston Reeve) Brigadier Goddard (Howard Marion Crawford) Vice Admiral Willows (Humphrey Lestocq) Sgt Moran (Ewan Hooper) Barber (David Swift) Reeves (Norman Scace) Squadron Leader Hogg (Leon Sinden) Walters (Peter Hughes)

Directed by Bill Bain

Steed has a whole host of eccentric suspects who may be selling defence secrets, but his barber is given a short-back-and-sides before he can tell what he knows. All of the men seem to share a common factor: recent changes in their butlers (all supplied from the Butler's and Gentleman's Association). Now in service, Steed finds that their unique laundry service does more than just wash clothes. Microphones hidden in jackets record the owner's secrets. As Steed suspected, the butler did it! A frontal attack from the army enables Steed and Mrs Peel to quell mutiny in the lower ranks, with a touch of class. Exit the Avengers by helicopter.

Filmed: December 1965/January 1966
TX: 26 February 1966

---

101 THE HOUSE THAT JACK BUILT

by Brian Clemens

Steed takes a wrong turning
Emma holds the key to all

John Steed (Patrick Macnee) Emma Peel (Diana Rigg) Professor Jack Keller (Michael Goodliffe) Burton (Griffith Davies) Withers (Michael Wynne) Pennington (Keith Pyott)

Directed by Don Leaver

When Emma Knight stopped Professor Keller's research work for her father's firm many years before, she could hardly envisage that the automation expert would leave a legacy for her all these years later. Now, Mrs Peel has inherited Uncle Jack's present and her only escape is the special suicide box which he has left. Trapped in the madman's automated fantasy, can Emma discover the key to finding her way out of the vast indestructible machine, or will Keller's laughter still be echoing when she herself is quite mad? After a successful short cut, she finds a worried Steed a-waiting. Exit the Avengers on a tandem.

Filmed: January 1966   TX: 5 March 1966

102 A SENSE OF HISTORY

by Martin Woodhouse

Steed dons a gown
Emma becomes a Don

John Steed (Patrick Macnee) Emma Peel (Diana Rigg) Richard Carlyon (Nigel Stock) Dr Gordon Henge (John Barron) Grindley (John Glyn-Jones) Professor David Acheson (John Ringham) Duboys (Patrick Mower) John Pettit (Robin Phillips) Millerson (Peter Blythe) Allen (Peter Bourne) Marianne (Jacqueline Pearce)

Directed by Peter Graham Scott

The Rag Night Ball at St Bodes is the culmination of a week of jolly japes that began with the murder of James Broom and has led to further deaths. The lynch-pin seems to be the author of a paper on *Economics and a Sense of History*; a deranged academic who wishes to complete Broom's Europa Plan and divert the course of the future. Tonight he will complete the task by dispensing of Carlyon, Broom's assistant. The theme for the evening is Robin Hood. Steed plays the role of Sheriff to Emma's lady in Lincoln green to round up the merry band of university outlaws, including the ring leader, Grindley, who was thought to be dead. Exit the Avengers with motorbike and sidecar.

Filmed: January/February 1966   TX: 12 March 1966

103 HOW TO SUCCEED...AT MURDER

by Brian Clemens

Steed becomes a perfect boss
Emma goes seeking charm

into a state of great feminine distress, I think we will get away with it.'
John touched on several aspects that needed improvement: the 'in' joke was protracted, and, aware that this was to be meant to be an Emma Peel solo effort, he thought the sacrifice of Steed from the overall picture was a hindrance, not a help.
b) This may be the only example of a thriller in which the villain is dead before the action starts! *

Writer/producer Brian Clemens poses with Diana Rigg on the set of *How to Succeed…at Murder*

John Steed (Patrick Macnee) Emma Peel (Diana Rigg) Mary Merryweather (Sarah Lawson) Sara Penny (Angela Browne) Gladys Murkle (Anne Cunningham) Henry Throgbottom (Artro Morris) Joshua Rudge (Jerome Willis) JJ Hooter (Christopher Benjamin) Sir George Morton (Kevin Brennan) Jack Finlay (Robert Dean) Liz (Zeph Gladstone) Barton (David Garth) Annie (Sidonie Bond)

Directed by Don Leaver

'Leap into my fervid arms' is a delicate perfume that business executives just keep on dying for. Keeping-fit is the least of Mrs Peel's worries when she joins Henrietta Throgbottom's aerobics class, particularly since Henrietta died in 1951. Emma is soon joining the advanced class – discovering how to kill her employer and take control of his business. 'Death to all men' is their byword. Steed, meanwhile, finds that his new secretary has designs on changing jobs as well. All avenues of enquiry lead back to Henrietta, a toy doll controlled by her husband Henry through simple ventriloquism. With Henry exposed, Steed and Emma wind-up his business. Exit the Avengers in a high-speed caravan, Steed practising the art of throwing one's voice.

Opposite: Actor Ken Parry (pictured left as Mr B. Bumble in a scene from *Honey For the Prince*) missed out on the opportunity to play Mother in Season Six.

Filmed: February 1966 TX: 19 March 1966

104 HONEY FOR THE PRINCE

by Brian Clemens

Steed becomes a genie
Emma joins a harem

John Steed (Patrick Macnee) Emma Peel (Diana Rigg) Ponsonby-Hopkirk (Ron Moody) Prince Ali (Zia Moyeddin) Arkadi (George Pastell) Vincent (Ronald Curram) Grand Vizier (Bruno Barnabe) B Bumble (Ken Parry) Ronny Wescott (Jon Laurimore) Postman (Reg Pritchard) Bernie (Peter Diamond) Eurasian Girl (Carmen Dene) George Reed (Richard Graydon)

Directed by James Hill

Agents are dying. Steed and Emma must find the link between honey and their fantasies. While Mrs Peel distracts Prince Ali with the Dance of the Six Veils ('She couldn't count' says Steed), her partner struggles to prevent the assassination of the royal figure. A deadly assassin, hidden in a huge jar of B Bumble Honey follows a carefully-planned Quite Fantastic plot. Mrs Peel proves her worth in goats by singlehandedly saving the day, whilst Steed waits outside the harem. Exit the Avengers on a magic carpet – perched on the roof of a van!

Filmed: February/ March 1966   TX: 23 March 1966

Honey For the Prince:
a) Director James Hill told Paul Madden: 'The episode required Diana Rigg to wear an oriental dancing girl costume. She finally realized that we meant her to do the Dance of the Seven Veils. Laurie Johnson had written the music for this short version of the oriental dance, to which she had to dance while pulling off these veils until she is left with a kind of a brassiere top and bikini bottom. She wasn't very keen on this, but being a true professional she agreed to do it. I started turning the camera and the

music came through the speakers and she started to dance, weaving around and looking very good. She pulls off the first veil and continues dancing. Then the second veil and the third – which got stuck. She was pulling and saying "This veil, it's stuck." The music was grinding on and Diana was pulling. She did it right the next time. That was a wonderful moment when veils got stuck and she couldn't get them off!'

b) We had to stick a gem in Di Rigg's navel because navels are not permitted on American TV. *

Several scripts were written, but never filmed.

a) Among the scripts submitted by Julian Wintle, was one by John Kruse, *The Day it Rained Poets* . It was a story about a young, female scientific engineer whose brilliant do-it-yourself inventions (machines that think for themselves) run amok and threaten both herself and her father. Even Wintle had doubts about this one. Brian Tesler advised him to work on the story. 'This is a lot of fun, but so far-fetched that it goes over the line way before the Tom and Jerry finale. Can we at least dispense with the young do-it-yourself female? Can't all the inventions be her father's?'

b) *Rip Van Winkle* by Martin Woodhouse, revolved around the theme of suspended animation. Tesler poured cold water on the idea. 'I don't like this one at all. Like the Admiral Nelson script, this is sci-ence-fiction fantasy, dependent entirely on whether we can believe in Rupert's suspended animation and therefore in Rupert himself. I don't think we do for a moment – especially since the whole business seems at times drummed up merely to provide someone whose accrued share-interest in Seddons, gums up the works for the heavies. I feel we should shelve this one, unless it could be radically reworked.'

c) Tesler's reference to Admiral Nelson was to the main character in a script entitled *The Disappearance of Admiral Nelson* (author unknown, but believed to be Philip Levene). It was intended to be the third black and white story (Emma was still being referred to as Mantha). Anthony John wasn't impressed. 'This is not a new idea by any means – it is almost another *Invisible Man*. However, of its kind, it is good and is bound to be acceptable to a large public. The cost of this film is likely to be very high as the main requirement is a geat deal of trick camera work as you will see from this short storyline.

John summarized the plot: A professor has discovered a ray which will reduce all matter, including humans, to a tenth of its original size. He imagines that only his daughter knows his secret. Unfortunately his weak-minded assistant is a spy and tips off the enemy. A demon-stration is prepared, at which the professor will shrink a new one-man tank, which is then pocketed by his assistant and handed over to the crooks. Alas, poor Steed, reduced by the ray, is trapped inside the tank... Sound familiar? It should be. The idea was dusted off and served as the basic storyline for *Mission, Highly Improbable*.

Note: Brian Clemens has come in for criticism recently re his com-ments about the non-use of black actors in *The Avengers*. I'm delighted to give him a platform to respond. 'I have recently taken some stick over this because I have always been under quoted. We were loath to use black actors partly because of "the intrusion of reality basis", but mainly because it was the nature of the series to send up stereotypes (think of the endless civil servants, German villains, etc.) and I did not think it fair to impose that upon an ethnic, and very sensitive, minori-ty – being black in racist Britain was not to be laughed at. I ducked the issue entirely by excluding them – although, as has always been stated, rules could always be broken in *The Avengers* when the right opportunity presented itself, and indeed we did use black actors in context (*Big Game For Small Hunters, Have Guns – Will Haggle*).' Incidentally, Brian didn't really want to pursue this. It took some arm-bending to get him to do so.

SEASON FIVE

Twenty-four colour filmed episodes

starring **PATRICK MACNEE** and **DIANA RIGG**   1966/1967

PRODUCTION HISTORY

B Y NOW, *The Avengers* had a worldwide audience of over 30 million viewers in 40 countries. However, it had still not sold to the vitally important American market, although two American networks had seen a number of episodes and expressed their interest. One of these, NBC, liked what they had seen, but stated that they were not yet ready for such an extreme series, with its very British flavour. The most serious difficulty, they felt, was the inability of the great American audience to understand and appreciate the light, flippant, throwaway dialogue between Steed and Mrs Peel. They thought, however, that Diana Rigg was 'remarkably good', and perhaps the biggest selling point in the series, both in the conception of her character and the way she was playing it. Another consideration was that *The Avengers* was in monochrome. Partly because Britain and other countries were still transmitting in black and white, and partly to save money, ABC had decided to produce the first filmed series in monochrome and looked set to continue their cavalier ways. In a letter mailed to Julian Wintle on 21 July 1965 - as the team were gearing up for the filming of *The Town of No Return* - Howard Thomas acknowledged that he had given a great deal of thought to Wintle's request that the production should go to colour film, 'but I do not think that we would gain very much by making an episode of *The Avengers* in colour,' said Thomas. He would rather concentrate on making the *Elephant Boy* series in that medium. The American networks, however, were moving rapidly to colour and, as NBC had announced their intention to go entirely to colour, the other networks, ABC and CBS, would clearly have to follow suit.

It was then that ABC Television made the biggest and most far-reaching deal ever made for a single British television series. Concerned that their product would be left out in the cold, with little chance of recovering its production costs, they decided to take over the sales effort themselves, and Howard Thomas, together with another director, Bob Norris, flew to New York for discussions with the two networks which had earlier shown interest. They were offering two things. If a network would buy the first 13 episodes in monochrome, they would immediately order the second 13 to be made in colour; or, if a network would buy the first series, ABC would give them an option on a second, colour, series, which would go into production immediately after the completion of the first 26 episodes.

After meetings in London and New York, Bob Norris secured a deal on the second proposal to the American Broadcasting Company, which would bring four-and-a-half million dollars to Britain over an eighteen-month period and guaranteed *The Avengers* a peak-time US network, coast-to-coast transmission slot starting in January. This meant that the programme would be seen on US television screens continuously for over 18 months. A simultaneous Canadian renewal for *The Avengers* was also arranged by Bob Norris during his trip - ensuring that the whole of North America would see the programme more or less simultaneously with British audiences.

'This is a major breakthrough for British TV. The deal we have made for *The Avengers* represents a British export contribution of far-reaching significance for the future,' Bob Norris told the press. 'The news from America confirms our confidence in the show, and Julian Wintle and his team,' said Howard

Patrick Macnee designed several of his own suits, including this one. Diana Rigg wears ice-blue lame belted hipster pants and matching bra-top, created for her by John Bates.

▲John Steed and
Cathy Gale.

▶Patrick Macnee
and Honor
Blackman fluffed
their lines in this
scene from 'The
Man With
Two Shadows'.

▲ *Emma slips into SNOB unobserved, her intention being to rescue the man in the photograph, in 'The Correct Way To Kill'.*

▶*A rare publicity shot of Diana Rigg.*

The pictures on this page were taken during the first day's shooting on the colour series, at Palace House, Beaulieu.

▲*Linda Thorson, aka Tara King, agent 69.*

▶*Patrick Macnee wearing a self-designed suit, with velvet collar, matching bowler, umbrella and suede boots.*

◄ *Tara finds herself handcuffed to ammunition boxes in the finale of 'Have Guns – Will Haggle'.*

► *Steed, Purdey and Gambit - The New Avengers.*

▼ *Tara pictured in her apartment, No.9 Primrose Crescent.*

▶*Joanna Lumley – absolutely fabulous!*

▼*The captivating Joanna Lumley as Purdey.*

Thomas. 'It gives particular pleasure to us all, because the really significant factor in the success of *The Avengers* is that the series is one hundred percent British in conception, content, casting and style.'

Meanwhile, a subject closer to home required the attention of ABC and associate producer, Brian Clemens. Some weeks earlier, Rediffusion, the company transmitting *The Avengers* in the London area, had requested 'cut' *Avengers* prints – episodes edited to a maximum transmission time of 46.15. (Southern Television, who were responsible for the transmissions to Anglia, televised the same, shorter-length prints two nights later). Rediffusion were now demanding additional cuts in the story *A Touch of Brimstone*. One of the highlights in the story was a scene where Emma Peel, posing as the Queen of Sin, is whipped by the leader of a modern-day Hellfire Club. Deciding that has the programme would be seen by a family audience before 9pm, the whipping scene had to go, Rediffusion called for the scene to be cut. Quite happy with the original version, ABC nevertheless removed the sequence, but flatly refused to make further cuts. Apparently even hardened studio technicians shared Rediffusion's concern over the skimpy costume worn - and designed by - Diana Rigg in the story; it was a tightly-laced, figure-hugging, black Edwardian corset, worn with knee-high leather boots and an iron collar with 3-inch spikes bristling from it! The same scene caused a furore when the story was screened in America. 'The scene where Diana Rigg was attacked four times by a man wielding a whip had to be cut down to one crack of the whip,' said Brian Clemens at the time. Interviewed for the Channel 4 documentary *Without Walls*, Clemens told Paul Madden: 'The interesting thing was, although the American Broadcasting Network banned the episode, their executives used to play it at their conventions - because they liked it!'

With the prospect of further clashes with the American censor, Clemens issued a set of guidelines to his production staff:

CENSORSHIP

American censorship restrictions are more strict, complex, weird and wonderful than we imagined. Frequently, it is a question of interpretation - the American Television Code is to weighty to issue for our benefit.

Below I append certain restrictions that have been brought to our notice in relation to our first half dozen scripts. The ultimate criterion is 'when in doubt check with me please'.

1) Since mental illness is a subject which causes distress, great care must be taken not to play upon this. Reference to the word 'idiot' is not permitted.

2) The word 'damn' is not permitted, but 'darn' is okay.

3) Emma's fights: We must be careful to avoid showing Emma striking or kneeing a man in his peculiarly masculine areas.

Director James Hill recalls working working with Macnee and Rigg: 'We all got on very well together. They were just a joy to work, no matter what the hour. One always knew it would be an enjoyable and instructive experience. She was very constructive. She used to make some very good suggestions from time to time.'

About filming, he said: 'Broadly speaking, on television you were required (supposed) to shoot five minutes a day. The Avengers *was one of those rare series where there was a little latitude. If it went on a little longer – if it improved the thing – they didn't worry too much if it wasn't five minutes. Five minutes of quality screen time is quite difficult to achieve and so you had to have very professional people. In fact we had a very, very good technical crew, including the stunt people – and a super team of producers. Julian Wintle, Albert Fennell and Brian Clemens. I came to* The Avengers *as a director through Julian Wintle. He asked me to direct the episode, which I think was called* The

4)   Cigarette advertisers are very sensitive as to the image of other products – cigarettes must not be ground out under foot. Neither must cigarettes be used to point to stress or strain.

5)   Guns should not be pointed direct at camera, nor at a person's head (suggest guns be aimed somewhere between head and the peculiarly feminine/masculine areas).

6)   Telescopic sights are not used.

7)   The American flag must not be defaced, destroyed or ridiculed in any way.

8)   Beer bottles and other possible commercial items must not be commercially recognisable by shape or label.

These are items of censorship brought to our attention so far. As they arise I will issue further bulletins. Please consult and abide by these rules, or we will be involved in re-shooting the scenes.

Having initiated the use of *The Avengers'* 'teaser' and 'tag' scenes in the monochrome series, Clemens was now being asked to remove these from all completed episodes and edit all references to them from future scripts. The directive came from Brian Tesler, who pointed to the 'speeded-up' milk float tag in The *Hour That Never Was* as a point of reference. Replying to Tesler's comment that the tag scene in this episode was 'irritating' and did not fulfil its purpose, Julian Wintle wrote: 'We all here feel most strongly that the 'tag' scene in *An Hour to Spare* [as the episode was still known, it later became *Roger and Out*] should stay as is.' Wintle had received a letter from Brian Clemens, a copy of which was shipped to Tesler, who was growing increasingly dissatisfied with the 'tag' endings.

Clemens defended the tag scenes on the grounds that they were of vital imortance if the show was to retain its own identity. 'One of the supreme virtues of *The Avengers* is that no two episodes are alike, but in this concept there is a hidden vice. The average viewer, rightly or wrongly, has been conditioned to anticipate the unexpected; to expect the familiar. So, in view of the versatility of our stories, we have to offer the viewer a certain rigidity of form, a story 'shape' that may be relied upon, i.e. a most intriguing teaser; first scene bringing in Steed and Mrs Peel and setting up the plot; high spot endings to the USA and UK breaks; denouement and a big fight sequence in the penultimate scene – and finally a 'tag' scene: always played in some moving vehicle going towards a bright horizon and a new adventure, the accent of lightness and comedy to reiterate that *The Avengers* is fun and not to be taken too seriously. That, then, is the 'shape' – and, like a well-constructed building, to remove one part is to endanger the whole.' Clemens underlined his point still further by explaining that the tag scenes were intended as non sequiturs, rounding off each episode in a uniquely satisfying way; a touch of style that is unique to the series. 'They are in fact *The Avengers* style of "happy ending" demanded by the viewers. The story is over, our hero and heroine are triumphant. They have no need to recapitulate what has gone before – and in any case, why discuss it at all? It should be clearly understood that the "tag" scenes are designed to have a cumulative effect – in much the same way as the Hope and Crosby 'Road' films, where the fact that Crosby always gets the girl in the last shot was expected and indeed looked forward to with some anticipation. Obviously, it will take several episodes to achieve the rhythm we are aiming for – but once this has been achieved, I feel sure that the audience response will be most rewarding. I expect our viewers to remain tuned in until the very end of the show, in order to see just what new vehicle Emma and Steed have found this time.'

According to Clemens, the earlier videotaped episodes of *The Avengers* had been enthusiastically received because they chose to break many of the established rules of television, creating their own unique style in the process. 'It became a big talking point just because it did break the rules. Since then many of the conventions have been imitated in films and television: the Bond films, for instance, have been strongly influenced by *The Avengers*; *Burke's Law* and *The Man from U.N.C.L.E.* are pale imitations in many areas, and of late I have noticed both *The Saint* and *Danger Man* becoming more and more *Avenger*ish. To be imitated is to be highly complimented – and I fancy that our running gag 'tag' scenes will be adopted by other series in the future.'

On the whole, Clemens' arguments were accepted by Tesler. He nevertheless shot a broadside at 'the good-ship Avengers' and voiced his opinion to Julian Wintle in no uncertain terms:

'It seems to me that there is a danger of losing perspective down there at Elstree among – admittedly! – the workers. *The Avengers* is a very good series, but it is by no means sacrosanct; and frankly I am getting rather tired of the repeated implications in Brian Clemens' memos and letters that to criticise any aspect of The Conception is to be frightened or square.

'For programme makers to create a production mystique and insist on perpetuating the bad things in it as well as the good is to do any show a disservice. The worst thing about the new *Avengers*, for example, is that it blithely ignores signposting (Who are the Avengers? What are they avenging? Why?) just as the old series did. If anybody thinks that signposting is demeaning and inartistic let him look at *The Fugitive*.

'But not even to recognize the bad things seems to me to be extraordinary. The 'Uncle' credit is absolutely consistent with the style of the rest of *The Man From U.N.C.L.E.*: it isn't animated or printed in Chinese or stencilled on the behind of an elephant wobbling into the distance. It is straightforward because it's funny enough exactly as it is. And no matter how fantastic that series gets it never uses obvious camera tricks, because it

Marriage Bureau [The Murder Market], *but I'd already been contracted to go to Africa to do* Born Free. *So he released me from my contract with* The Avengers *and I went off to direct the lion film. When I came back, he had this episode waiting for me called* Castle De'ath. *I directed that and got on very well with Brian Clemens, who wrote a great number of incredible scripts. They were excellent,* The Avengers *team.'*

The tag sequence at the end of the The See-Through Man, *showing Emma and Steed climbing into (and out of) vintage motorcars, was filmed on location at Palace House, Beaulieu, home of Lord Montagu, and his famous Motor Museum. Director Roy Rossotti lensed the two-day shoot, day one being spent in the museum grounds filming Patrick Macnee and Diana Rigg driving (or not as the case may be!) the splendid machines in Lord Montagu's collection. A second day was on Lord Montagu's private beach, with Diana Rigg riding a horse across the golden sand. It was the producers' original intention to use the Beaulieu motoring sequences for the colour episode tag scenes. This was abandoned in favour of the tags as featured in the stories. Together with the Diana Rigg horse-riding scenes, the vintage car sequences were edited into a promo reel for the benefit of the American Broadcasting Company. (Note: all filmed sequences –*

knows that they will prick the bubble of its own peculiar fantasy world and reveal the whole as a trick.

'And that's exactly what the speeded-up camera does at the end of *The Avengers* tag I saw. Suddenly, an essentially phoney technical trick that belongs to the world of slapstick fantasy pricks the sophisticated bubble of our fantasy world. Why? The tags are fantastic and funny enough anyway. It looks like a sudden lack of confidence on our part if we superimpose camera tricks on top of them.

'Our audience isn't privy to internal production agreements and attitudes. It's no good Brian saying that we have agreed that our tag scenes should be regarded as a separate entity, as part and parcel of the closing credits, if the audience doesn't agree; and you would need a pretty hefty signpost to ensure that!

'Surely we have enough confidence in the show to think that it will be the talking point – not, for heaven's sake, a bit of speeded-up camera at the end of a tag, which is the only trite thing in the show. Surely we can't want the flavour that is left in the viewers' mouth, the supposedly characteristic *Avengers* flavour, to be that of a speeded-up camera, even if it does get a cheap and easy laugh. And surely we don't in any case think that the speeded-up camera bit is different: it's the only thing that isn't different in the entire show.

'It seems to me that you are all so understandably immersed in the show that you are finding it difficult to accept an objective opinion on this relatively small point. I assure you it does not constitute the rape of the immaculate Conception; merely prophylaxis.'

Clemens reaction was typically forceful:
'This particular episode is an extremely tough and realistic one for *The Avengers* – indeed, for the first two acts, it might easily fit into any of another dozen crime series. It was with this in mind that I injected the laughing gas scene – so that, in the final analysis, the audience might have it reaffirmed that it is *The Avengers* they are watching. To my mind the tag scene only strengthens this cause.

'We have always agreed that our tag scenes should be regarded as a seperate entity – almost another series on their own – a build up joke, designed to keep the viewer tuned in to the very end. I feel that we have succeeded in our intentions. Therefore, if the tag scene is a separate entity, then, no matter how fantastic it is, it cannot possibly intrude upon the episode preceding it – or – dissipate whatever tension or excitement we have generated, since the episode is concluded before the tag scene appears.

'It would help us all a great deal if in our minds we firmly placed the tag scene where it logically belongs, as part and parcel of the closing credits. As the ultimate seal on *The Avengers* style.

'Our tag scenes should be part of our style trademark, and certainly the one in dispute is no more fantastic than *The Man From U.N.C.L.E.* thanking "Uncle" for their co-operation!

'In conclusion, the tag scene in *An Hour To Spare* uses speeded-up action with, I think, flair and humour. I am sure it will get the laugh it deserves – and surely, to leave the customers amused is not such a bad thing? Admittedly this is only the second time we have used this device, but it seems appropriate in context (as does the rickshaw scene), and the very worst that could happen is that it might become a talking point of some controversy. Again, I do not think that this is such a bad thing. At least we are maintaining the tradition of being a show that is different – and these days, with "Uncle" in hot competition, I feel the more different we can be, the better.

'Let's not forget that part and parcel of the "old" *Avengers* popularity was that it became something of a cult. Because it had something no other series had (or has had since). Because it bent (and sometimes broke) the rules. Because it had a unique style. I don't think we should be frightened of extending that style on film.'

Clemens won the argument.

The American deal had by now been signed and delivered, which handed the producers the benefit of being able to alert American viewers that *The Avengers* would be returning to their sitting-rooms, in colour, shortly after the end of the black and white episode transmission run. To fulfil this requirement, Brian Clemens wrote a short vignette which was tagged onto the end of the last episode to be networked in the USA. Called *The Avengers: The Strange Case of the Missing Corpse*, the script for this is reprinted exactly as Clemens composed it:-

PREAMBLE FOR USA.

INT. STUDIO STAGE:

OPEN UP CLOSE ON DIANA RIGG'S AND PATRICK MACNEE'S CHAIRS – facing camera – their names clearly readable on the backs of the chairs.

PAT wears bowler, holds unbrella. DIANA wears fighting outfit – she holds her goldplated gun in one hand – a rose in the other.

PAN AROUND THEM – or CUT TO ANOTHER ANGLE.

REVEALING that they are both studying a script clearly marked THE AVENGERS. Then they become aware of the camera's presence.

and photographs – showing Macnee and Rigg with the vintage vehicles (with Diana Rigg sometimes shown wearing the white kid gloves and Perspex visor designed by Alun Hughes), and the Diana Rigg horse-riding scenes, originate from this shoot.)

PAT
Oh... Good morning ladies and gentlemen of the United States of America

DIANA (flip)
Hi, Yanks!

TOGETHER
Nice to be back with you again. Of course...
They stop – react. PAT gestures.

PAT
After you

DIANA
After you

PAT (at camera)
Of course you remember my devastating partner Mrs... Emma Peel – alias Diana Rigg

DIANA
And my sidekick – dashing, elegant John Steed – alias Patrick Macnee. We want to welcome you to our Studio here in Elstree, England...

PAT (corrects)
Great Britain. Yes, as you can see – we're back at work again – making...

DIANA
By public demand...

PAT
...new episodes of the Avengers – which premieres on ABC

DIANA
In colour. Don't forget the colour

PAT
How could I? Amazing revelation when we saw ourselves in colour!

DIANA
We flipped!

PAT (very confidential)
I never knew her hair was a marvellous russet-red. Anyway – see for yourself – on Friday nights

DIANA
From 10 to 11pm.

PAT (confirms)
From 10 to 11pm. – Friday nights – beginning January 20th

THEY sit back – the commercial is over – but no! The camera still runs on them.

PAT (whispers)
What do we do now?

DIANA (whispers)
Let's show them the missing body

PAT (whispers)
The missing what..?

DIANA (whispers)
Body... you know... body...!

PAT
Ah yes – (at camera again) *Naturally – we were anxious to see how colour cameras worked... and how we looked......*

DIANA
...in all those living shades

PAT
So we devised a little bit of nonsense called 'The Missing Body'..... and it's quite amusing

DIANA
It's a gas! AND – this is the one and only time our view-ers will ever see it..... (gestures) *Maestro!*

PAT (announces)
Ladies and gentlemen – a short, short entitled........'The Missing Body'

DIANA (winks)
See you

She pops the rose into the end of the gun – so that it becomes the *Avengers* symbol.

The monochrome/colour vignette, filmed on the set of *Honey For the Prince* to alert American viewers that *The Avengers*-in-colour would soon return.

HOLD THIS THROUGH TO:

'THE MISSING BODY'

The success of the previous series had shown that the qualities which endeared *The Avengers* to its audience were its essential Englishness (no concession was ever made to mid-Atlantic compromise), its stylized offbeat, way-out humour and its preoccupation with a distorted view of the world. The producers kept these elements in mind when planning the colour series, but this time they added more danger, leaving Steed and Emma exposed to every hazard that ingenuity could devise. New twists were added to allow the implacable spycatcher to react to danger with jocularity, while his partner whammed baddies senseless with a wallop of her delicate little fist and a cascade of chestnut hair. At the time, ABC believed that the spy series was on the wane, so, in the new series, the Avengers fought the private sector of villainy. Dangerous madmen with delusions of power outnumbered agents of a foreign power. The villains became more diabolical and the show continued its unique blend of black humour, imaginative direction and polished bonhomie.

While plans for the new series were being formulated, Diana Rigg was finding that some of the rewards of being a celebrity had actually become penalties: being approached in public by strangers, signing autographs, making personal appearances, coping with fan mail. At one point she enlisted the help of her mother, who eventually took charge of it all. 'Mother was frequently quite startled by what fans wrote in their letters,' she told a magazine interviewer. 'Some letters were horrible, vicious and nasty... every new batch included kinky letters. Men wanting to buy my black leather gear. I received hundreds of invitations to spend the night away from home.'

Publicity sessions worried Diana: she found it difficult to talk about herself or her work unless the interviewer was on her wavelength, or to relax with photographers unless there was a rapport between them. Although a superb film actress, who worked fast and expertly on the studio floor, she was never at her best in the early morning. Understandable really, considering that her working day began at 6am, when a car arrived to take her to the studio, where she'd work until 6pm (or later), and was often so tired when she returned home that she was in bed by 9 o'clock. The monastic life which intensive film work demanded was thus a considerable sacrifice for her. So it's little wonder that, during the summer recess, Diana, who had been earning £150 a week from the show, declared 'I'm worth at least three times that,' and issued an ultimatum to ABC, that unless she received more money, she would not return to the series. Her demands were met and she returned at £450 a week. (In fairness to Diana Rigg, however, it should be pointed out that she did not return simply for the financial benefits, but more from her loyalty to Patrick Macnee, the show and all those who were involved in it. She did make it quite clear, however, that this would be her last series.)

On hearing of her decision, Patrick Macnee said: 'I'm glad that Diana is staying. She is wonderful to work with and we share a mutual obsession for detail. We deliberately set out to contrive new and different ways of playing two-handed scenes for comedy. We put Emma and Steed in routine situations, like having a meal or playing a game of chess. Then, while serving the soup, we would casually discuss some mastermind's ploy to rule the world.'

'It didn't start that way,' Laurie Johnson told me. 'When Diana first came to us, the two were very much individuals – there was no rapport between them. The style – the quirkiness – evolved through the black and white films. It was nothing that was written, it was in the interpretation, the attitude of the artists. We learned how to set this mixture of tongue-in-cheek incredulity against a backdrop of weird situations.'

Viewers of the previous series seemed to prefer the episodes with a science fiction theme, so many of the new stories were slanted in that direction. Brian Clemens was reported as saying: 'When you're dealing with a make-believe world populated by larger-than-life villains, it is difficult not to get into bizarre situatons.' Confirming to Paul Madden that the science-fiction thing wasn't a conscious decision, Clemens added: 'It really came about because of natural evolvement; it just happened that way. No-one said "Let's go into science-fiction". I've always said that it was science fact, because most of the science-fiction

Alan Hume, who was director of photography on many of the episodes, now does the lighting for the Bond movies. *

*All vehicles used in
The Avengers,
including Steed's vin-
tage modes of trans-
port and Emma's
Lotus Elan's, were
hired from either
Kingsbury Cars or
Farncraft Motors.*

we did was only one step away from what has since been achieved. Things we suggested are being investigated at this time.'

I asked Clemens if there were any specifics that had to be adhered to when writing for the show. 'A new plot, or twist – that unique *Avengers* twist – or an old one. We became fond of inverting the cliché... Mother became a man, Father a woman. The Sherlock Holmes character didn't find clues, he planted them. I also required at least three high spots per story – action or an intriguing scene – an up-front teaser, and then I was ready to put the jigsaw together.' He told me recently: 'There was never a brief, a formula. That's the magic of *The Avengers*; the parameters were totally boundless. You could do anything as long as it had a certain style. I always thought that they were like Hope and Crosby. The women played Hope and Crosby was Steed, who was always getting to wrestle the alligator and coming out best. An illustration of this was Emma Peel, who would climb up the outside of a building, across barbed wire, and get into this room to find that Steed was already there – because he'd used the key or found the door wasn't locked! That was the disparity between them and their approaches to the case. They solved it together, but in separate and quite diverse ways.'

A popular feature of the previous series had been the closing sequence, which had shown Steed and Mrs Peel driving away in various forms of transport. This time around Steed would summon Emma to duty with the words 'Mrs Peel – we're needed!' The scenes formed part of the opening credits and usually took place in Emma's apartment, as did the closing tag sequences, in which the story was brought to an end with an appropriate flourish. (Brian Tesler had nothing discordant to say about these. He liked them!) There was still no indication, of course, of who needed the Avengers. Unlike most of the world's favourite thriller heroes and heroines, the duo had no 'M' figures, 'Uncles' or other visible or invisible means of support to control their activities; at least, not until the arrival of 'Mother' in the Thorson series. Steed and Emma fitted into no known category and continued to be a law unto themselves.

As previously, the programme continued to present first-class actors in guest roles, and the audience were kept guessing as to which of them were on the side of the angels. Of these, two actors returned to appear in roles they'd played in the monochrome series: Warren Mitchell as Brodny, the Iron Curtain Ambassador in London *(Two's A Crowd)* and Frederick Jaeger, as Benson, Dr Armstrong's assistant, in *The Cybernauts*.

Laurie Johnson explained that the baddies were never for real. 'The danger was that some of the bad characters would turn up in the script and the actors who played them would take themselves seriously. That wasn't right, of course. It didn't work.' Director James Hill agreed that this was always a hazard, so the guest artists were instructed to play it as written. 'Some actors might be inclined to do anything but play it as written. Indeed, some were at a loss to understand exactly what was going on around them. So we advised them to keep to the script and the plot and then we would see if we could embroider on that. We did anything and everything to attack the cliché.'

Once again, ABC decided to change both the fighting and fashion formats. This time Emma would be using Kung Fu – a 5,000-year-old Chinese art of self-defence, based on relaxation, rather than the brute strength required for karate, or the complicated throws and holds of judo. Diana Rigg was coached by stunt-arranger Ray Austin for the second time. Austin taught her the basics of Tai Chi, a series of balletic-type movements which improved her posture, relaxation and breathing.

The stuntman also coached Diana Rigg's new stunt double, Cyd Child – a novice in the action stakes. Before joining the series, Cyd had never set foot on a studio set and had never done a stunt in her life!

She told me how she came to get the part. At the suggestion of one of her teachers at the Ministry of Aviation (where she was learning photography), she contacted stuntman, Frank Maher (of *Danger Man* and, later *The Prisoner* fame), who passed her name along to Ray Austin. Three months went by before she heard anything. Then her mum received a telephone call while Cyd was at work. The call was from Ray Austin, who wanted to meet her at Elstree Studios the following day. Told by the stunt arranger that the *Avengers* people were looking for a stunt double for Diana Rigg (Billy Westley had left the series to train as an assistant film director), Austin arranged a film test and the young hopeful was introduced to Diana Rigg – to whom she bore a strong resemblance.

'Because I was the same height as Diana and looked vaguely like her, I got the job,' Cyd told me. 'Before this they had had a man doubling for Diana. There were no tall, female stunt

Cyd Child told me that the stunt people jokingly referred to Diana and Patrick as their 'dialogue doubles.'

Cyd Child, who joined the series as Diana Rigg's stunt double, adds the finishing touches to her make-up during the location filming for *Murdersville*.

Reproduced courtesy of Cyd Child.

Murdersville:

a) Cyd Child tells a nice story about the ducking-stool sequence. 'We had this agreement that they wanted the surface of the water to look very still while I was in there – to make it look as though Emma had been in there for a long time. So I agreed to go down on the ducking-stool, stay under for as long as I could – until I'd had enough – then wiggle my toes as a signal for them to bring me up. I went down, and stayed down for quite a while. I knew that I could have stayed down for longer, but they suddenly brought me up. "Why did you bring me up?" I asked. "I didn't ask you to and I could have easily stayed under for longer." The director, Bob Asher, said "I didn't like it. It made me feel sick just watching it. I felt peculiar!"'

b) Besides Cyd, seven stuntmen worked on this episode: Rocky Taylor (doubling Patrick Macnee) Joe Dunne (Colin Blakely and John Ronane) Bill Sawyer (John Ronane) Romo Gorrera (John Ronane) Bill Cummings (John Ronane) Les Crawford

doubles in the business, so there really wasn't anyone else who could double her. We just sort of found each other at the right time.' Austin said that they would give it a shot to see how things worked out. 'He was very pleased that they had actually got a girl, instead of a man,' said Cyd. 'You're very limited when using a man. You can get away with a lot more with a woman because when you dress up a man in drag he doesn't move in the same way and it limits the performance.'

Cyd doubled for Diana throughout the series and stayed around to double for Linda Thorson. Incredible as it sounds, Cyd actually learned how to handle the stunts, from Ray Austin, during the early days of the production. She remembers that it was a bit like being at school again. Austin would explain what was required in this scene or that scene, and then would teach her the rudiments of the stuntman's craft. 'He taught me what I needed to know for each episode. If there was a fall, he would show me how to do it – and what to do to make it work. Then, when the writers saw that we could fulfil what they were putting into the scripts, they started to put more and more in.'

She made mistakes, of course, but day by day Austin's training carried her through. The fights she found easy – well, most of the time. Cyd, who had being doing judo for six years, was a second Dan (two grades higher than a black belt) and took to the fights like a fish to water – but she still had to learn a thing or two about faking the fights. As she told me: 'If you are going to be good at judo, you are going to use the judo technique as well as you can; you will do it as fast as you can; you will go in as hard as you can and try to throw your opponent. You don't do that in the stunt business. You perform the technique to look as good as possible and you allow them, the stunt people, to do the tumble themselves.' She recalled that the first time she did a fight, Ray Austin – whom she believes was trying to let her know that he knew a bit about the judo terminology – said 'Right, you throw this guy with tai-otoshi. Then so-and-so will do this and so-and-so will do that.' So she threw the guy with tai-otoshi – and the hapless soul hit the deck with a resounding thud. As he staggered up off the floor, Ray screamed that she should never do that again. 'So I learned that you didn't do everything quite the way I thought they did. It was faked, otherwise someone would get hurt and you had to do it over again.'

But accidents during filming were the exception rather than the rule. There were, however, times when things did go (comically?) wrong. Brian Clemens recalls one such occasion during the production of *Escape in Time*. 'This motorcyclist had to crash. He crashed spectacularly – and lay still. Somebody who was new to the floor, a rigger or an electrician, rushed onto the set to give him the kiss of life. So we had to do the scene over again.'

Cyd Child recalled another occasion on the same episode. 'There was this motorbike thing with Diana. On that one we had to keep doing these near misses when the bike was chasing me and I had to jump out of the way. They kept saying "It does-n't look close enough, Cyd." It was close enough as far as I was concerned, really close... I could feel the backdraft of the motor bike as it was going by. So we kept on doing it. I spent the whole day running around and I thought that we had finally done it. Then, a few days later, we were called back to the studio back-lot to do yet more run-bys for the bike scene. By now I could actually feel it touching me as it sped by – but the second unit director kept insisting that it still didn't look close enough. So I thought, sod it – and I let the bike hit me! "Is that close enough?" I asked. He nodded. It was fine.'

Cyd Child has happy memories about *The Living Dead* and in particular the scene in which Emma Peel hoists the guard (stuntman Terry Plummer) over her head and escapes. 'I remember that well because he was very heavy. When we did it, they wanted me to whirl him around and then throw him down again, and I staggered under the weight. "Do you think you can do it any quicker?" they asked. "It looks as though Emma Peel *is* in trouble." I shot back "Emma Peel *is* having trouble!" There was a big song and dance about that. Jack Greenwood, the Production Controller, said: "We're in trouble here. We've got the double's face going straight past the camera." That's why they wanted me to do it quicker, because everyone got a good look at my face and they were afraid of people writing in. We didn't have one letter! The only thing I heard about was that someone had written to the *TV Times* asking how it was done.'

It was time to ring the (by now obligatory) changes in the fashion stakes. This time around Emma's wardrobe was in the cabable hands of Alun Hughes. It was Diana herself who sug-gested him to ABC. 'I felt the leather gear had to go,' she told the Press. 'It wasn't me. It belonged to Cathy Gale. Although I don't design Emma Peel's clothes, I do talk them over with the designers, and this time I get to wear the sort of clothes I like. They are based on my physique, which is larger than people imagine from the screen.'

Anne Trehearne, former fashion editor of *The Queen*, was brought in by the producers as consultant for Emma's clothes. The guiding principle of the brief given to her and Mr Hughes was to make Emma elegant and feminine, but dangerous. Alun Hughes interpreted this as Feminine and Feline: his Emma in day or evening clothes looked beguilingly innocent and charm-ing, but was capable of delivering a knockout blow to any unsus-pecting villain. His 'action suits' (which he called 'Emmapeelers') were in stretch Crimplene and jersey, with a recurring motif of buckles, links, thigh watches and braiding, and differed from Emma's previous *Avengers* fighting gear by having bootees of the same material to give an all-in-one effect from throat to toe.

'In her Emmapeelers,' said Hughes, 'Emma is like a cat in the night, prowling silently on her secret assignments, ready to

(Ronald Hines) Dinny Powell (Robert Cawdren)

*c) A retake was nec-essary in this episode because one of the leads – during some vigorous action – fart-ed, and the sound man captured it! ***

Gil Taylor – another lighting director – also lit Polanski's Repulsion – *and went on to win an Oscar. ***

John Birt – now head of the BBC – was an Avengers *fan.*

*Brandy sales rocketed after the showing of the videotaped series... Champagne sales rocketed after the filmed series began. ***

strike at anyone who challenges her.' To enhance the feline effect, Mr Hughes also designed several fur coats, including one with a tiger motif. Emma wore boots only with her trouser suits or, in a blatantly theatrical manner, at highwayman length. She wore very little leather, but lots of glove-soft suede in coats, trouser suits and co-ordinates which alternated with Bermuda shorts.

Albert Fennell and Brian Clemens were the instigators of this. Apart from the fact that the leather catsuits looked great on their heroine, the producers knew that the leather carried with it all sorts of technical problems. It sometimes looked shiny on camera; it 'creaked' on the soundtrack, and Diana Rigg had just got bored with wearing leather all the time. As Clemens told me: 'You could always tell when a fight was coming up because she magically changed into the leather suit. When you're doing a long-running television series, you get ever so bored just getting into and out of the same old clothes – and it starts to show.'

Emma Peel did wear leather again, in *You have Just Been Murdered* but not for long, as Cyd Child explained. 'There was one occasion, after people had been writing in to complain that Diana wasn't wearing leather any more, when they decided that perhaps she should have a new leather outfit. So they had this wonderful leather suit made for Diana, which cost well in excess of £400. It was made of black glove leather and had a silver leather trim with three little chains across the front. It was so expensive that we only had the one, so I didn't have a duplicate outfit. I'm afraid I ruined it! We did this thing on the bridge. The idea was that I would meet this man coming across the bridge who tries to stop me from reaching the other side. We'd worked out a fight sequence, which involved all sorts of hand-to-hand combat holds. We met and I ripped the suit under the armpits. Then I had to zap him under the chin – and that split the costume up the crotch! Then I had to dive forwards and pick up this stick – and the suit was tearing all over the place. I can't remember how much Diana had worn it before I got hold of it, but it was certainly kaput afterwards!'

But the team were looking for a new image – the slim lines and physical elegance of Emma's new wardrobe were echoed by the new Pierre Cardin collection for John Steed. Cardin designed all Patrick Macnee's clothes for the new series, and introduced two new ideas for him – breast pockets with handkerchiefs, and trousers with a parallel line from knee to ankle to give a slightly more flared effect. As on previous occasions, the suits were made by Bailey and Weatherhill, the tailors in Regent Street, London. Macnee, however, found that his usual Chelsea boots didn't complement the trousers, and Alan Hughes designed some new shoes to go with the Cardin suits, the shoe designs being brought to fruition by Annello and Davide, who had manufactured Macnee's shoes from the beginning, not too mention Honor Blackman's 'kinky' foot attire and the boots worn by Diana Rigg in the monochrome series. Steed's familiar bowler and umbrella were also changed. Purchased from one of London's most established hatters, Herbert Johnson, they now came in assorted colours to match the new wardrobe.

The new fashions were launched on 1 May 1967, at Teddington Studios, with fashion icon Twiggy, racing driver Graham Hill, boxer Billy Walker and many more personalities parading in the new *Avengers* gear for photographer Terry O'Neill.

In order to take full advantage of the new colour process, the set designers were briefed to spray the sets to complement Steed and Emma's colourful new attire. It didn't stop there. Art direc-

Patrick Macnee is all tied-up while fashion model Twiggy adopts a dominant pose during the launch of the new *Avengers* fashions at Teddington Studios. circa 1967.

tor, Bob Jones (who had now rejoined the team), is on record as saying that he never worked so hard in his life. 'The Avengers needed a very special mental approach,' he told a reporter for an Australian journal. 'Writers would say this guy's a solicitor. Let's make him a collector of top hats – not one, hundreds of 'em. A train enthusiast might live underground in a disused tube station. A bank manager couldn't be just an ordinary bank manager; we'd have him riding along the corridor to his office on a penny-farthing bicycle. Steed was once reduced to Tom Thumb size, so we made a 72ft-long fibreglass desk, and an enormous phone to scale – that actually worked!'

Steed's apartment at 5 Westminster Mews, near London's Houses of Parliament, had now been given a face lift. Having been able to buy the freehold of the property, he had done it over in pine panelling with buttoned red leather upholstery and a gorgeous, red 18th-century porter's chair by the hall door. (Set designer, Wilfred Shingleton, wanted to move Steed out of London into a luxuriously conveted oak-beamed cottage in the country. The idea wasn't used.)

Emma, too, had moved. She no longer lived in her pent-house apartment in London's Primrose Hill, but had taken up residence in an L-shaped studio nearby, which had an artist's north light window, an antique stove in a tiled alcove, a scarlet baby grand piano in a matching alcove, and an early Victorian sofa and chairs in white and gold.

Integral to the programme's success, was the music of Laurie Johnson, who told me that he treated every episode as a sepa-rate feature film. 'The advantage of working on The Avengers was that each episode had its own indigenous colour – personality. Once the schedule gets under way, the turnaround is pretty rapid. So while you might have two directors working on two separate units, they only had one composer – who is working twice as hard as the film makers. I was writing a score every 10 days. The problem with The Avengers films was time. I would see the fine cut on a Monday and the recording session was fixed for the following Monday, which meant that I had to finish com-posing and scoring the whole episode by Thursday at the latest, so that the copyist could copy out each individual instrumental part. If you leave him short of time, there is always the possibil-ity of copying errors, which meant that, when we went to the recording stage, there would be a hold-up while the notes were corrected. So I always made sure that I was finished well in advance of time in order to allow the copyist to get the score accurate.

I would say that each Avengers score was written in four days, which could be anything up to 35 or 40 minutes of music! I can remember one episode (Silent Dust) which has, I think, nearly 40 minutes of music. Sometimes, when I got stuck, or there was a shortage of time in which to compose new music, I would select various pieces of music I had used before, to allow me breathing time in which to compose new music for an indigenous episode. I remember that on one of them, *The Superlative Seven*, the music couldn't be shot by the time I came to record the rest of the episode's score. So I went through the script with Albert Fennell and we estimated how long the scenes for the cut-aways to the aeroplane and its interiors would be, and I composed and recorded the music to blank spaces on the

Debonair Patrick Macnee, voted by the Press as one of Britain's best-dressed men.

Apart from the leads, which artiste appeared most often in The Avengers? *Use this book to check for yourself!* *

film – and we cut in the action to fit the score afterwards. That was the result of the pressure of time.'

The new format called for new title credits. In place of the stylised animated opener of the previous series was a live-action vignette in which Steed, finding difficulty in opening a bottle of champagne, has the task made that much easier for him by the entrance of Emma who, pistol at the ready, pops the cork with a well-aimed shot. The couple cross to a table, raise their glasses and drink. Cue *The Avengers* main title logo (superimposed over a table bearing Steed's bowler and umbrella, Emma's gold-plated pistol and two empty glasses). Unsheathing his umbrella's swordstick, Steed selects a single red flower from a vase of carnations, then deftly whisks it across to Mrs Peel, who in turn proceeds to place the bloom in her partner's buttonhole. In silhouette, the stars perform a choreographed display of umbrella thrusts and kung-fu moves, and cut to that week's storyline.

Things might have been different. The title sequence described above differs in many respects to the scene-by-scene action written by Brian Clemens on 15 November 1966. This is how the title credits were intended to be played:

OPENING TITLES

Note: This is to be shot on a LIMBO SET (to be composed of French grey flats) – what we are after is a long perspective set.

1) OPENING IN EXTREME CLOSE UP.
A CHAMPAGNE GLASS lying on its side (although at the moment we cannot identify it as a glass) – it is moving slightly from side to side – and through it we see the distorted image of STEED – some way away.

HOLD – THEN PAN UP ABOVE THE GLASS (during this pan we will identify it as a glass) – and SEE AND HOLD ON STEED seen above the rim of the glass in LONG SHOT. He is strolling slowly along our 'limbo land'.

CUT TO:
2) CLOSE SHOT. STEED – we now see that, as he walks towards us, he is starting to remove the cork of the champagne bottle. Suddenly he stops – reacts to something off ahead – off screen.

CUT TO:
3) The classic Western shot.
EMMA'S BOOT slams down into DEEP FG – pearl-handled revolver tucked into the top of it. BEYOND IN LONG SHOT can be seen STEED.

HOLD THIS – then EMMA'S hand slips down to draw the gun (her long hair cascades into DEEP FG as she performs this action). She draws the gun – fires in classic Western style.

The SOUND OF THE GUN SHOT BECOMES ONE WITH THE POPPING OF THE CHAMPAGNE CORK – and:

CUT TO:
4) REVERSE ANGLE.
STEED'S HANDS HOLDING BOTTLE, the cork has been shot out – champagne is starting to spill out of the bottle. EMMA SEEN BEYOND IN LONG SHOT.

CUT TO:
5) STEED – REACTING.

CUT TO:
6) REVERSE SHOT,
EMMA – standing, legs straddled Western style – just putting her gun back into her boot – then she too smiles – and starts to walk towards:
CUT TO:
7) STEED – walking foward.

CUT TO:
8) ANOTHER ANGLE
In the absolute centre of the limbo land corridor is a marvellously elegant and spindly table – bearing two champagne glasses – one upright – and one on its side (the one seen in the opening shot).
STEED and EMMA meet at this point. And as they move to pick up the champagne glasses:

CUT TO:
9) CLOSE UP. TWO CHAMPAGNE GLASSES -
They cheerily bubble with liquid – they are now held in STEED AND EMMA'S hands – as they clink together in a toast:

THROUGH TO:

MAIN TITLE:
THE AVENGERS

THROUGH TO:

10) CLOSE UP. TWO CHAMPAGNE GLASSES.
HOLD THIS – THEN PULL OUT TO REVEAL:

THE GLASSES stand on top of a super marvellous desk top –

on one side lies Emma's pearl-handled revolver – on the other side lies Steed's bowler and umbrella -

PULL OUT WIDER TO REVEAL – propped up on one side of the desk – STEED'S elegantly shod feet. And on the other side – EMMA'S booted feet.

PULL OUT TO A STYLISED SET-UP. ABSOLUTELY DEAD CENTRE TO THE
DESK – with STEED and EMMA'S FEET angled perfectly straight on in, from either side.

HOLD THIS – then:

STARRING

CUT TO:
11) STEED'S FEET – as they withdraw.

CUT TO:
12) ANOTHER ANGLE.
As STEED rises up from the leather, club chair – moves to pick up his bowler and umbrella.

HOLD ON HIM as he dons the bowler – smiles – tilts it at a jaunty angle and taps it firm in characteristic manner.

OVER THIS ACTION:

PATRICK MACNEE.
HOLD HIM – then:

CUT TO:
13) EMMA'S FEET up on desk.

AND.

14) EMMA'S FACE appears around side of club chair. She pushes aside her hair with the pearl-handled revolver -

OVER THIS ACTION:

DIANA RIGG.

EMMA starts to put the gun towards her boot.

CUT TO:

15) Close shot. As gun slams into top of boot.

16) STEED'S UMBRELLA – as the hilt is turned and snapped open to reveal the beginnings of the length of steel blade it conceals.

CUT TO:
17) ANOTHER ANGLE.
STEED – as he draws up the sword from his umbrella – turns and dabs delicately at:

CUT TO:
CLOSE SHOT.
THE BOWL OF WHITE CARNATIONS as the steel blade stabs in and flicks out the solitary RED carnation. It flies into the air – and:

CUT TO:
18) EMMA catches the red carnation – she smiles at STEED (we have PULLED OUT TO REVEAL HIM) as she moves to put the carnation in his buttonhole.

HOLD THIS charming moment – then suddenly a menacing shadow falls over them – they both turn into camera in alarm – then both start to move out of shot.

CUT TO:
19) STEED – going through attacking motions with his umbrella – finally opening it up RIGHT INTO CAMERA BLACKING OUT THE SCREEN FOR:

PRODUCED BY
ALBERT FENNELL
&
BRIAN CLEMENS

CUT TO:

20) EMMA – going through her attacking movements – finally executing a throw – ending up with her long hair falling forward into CAMERA – BLACKING OUT THE SCREEN FOR:

A JULIAN WINTLE PRODUCTION.

FADE OUT.

If you haven't already identified the differences they are:
1) 2 glasses are seen (both identifiable)
2) Steed doesn't walk towards the camera

*Christopher Lee and Peter Cushing both played the same role in The Avengers – Never, Never Say Die and Return of The Cybernauts – both sequels to the original Cybernauts. ***

Diana Rigg, at St. Mary's Bay in Kent, during the first week of shooting on the colour series. Additional beach scenes were filmed on the private beach at Palace House. owned by Lord Montagu of Beaulieu.

3)   There is no boot (for the pearl-handled revolver to be tucked into)

6)   No she doesn't

12) Steed does not rise from the chair (at least we do not see him do so – nor pick up his umbrella and brolly)

13) No feet. Scene cuts to back of club chair

14) (Sub-para) There is no boot in which to holster the gun

17) A bowl containing RED carnations

18) Nice idea, but there is no menacing shadow

19) This is totally different as is...

20) inclusive of the Wintle credit which reads: Julian Wintle Executive Producer. The scenario was changed after Albert Fennell and Brian Clemens had discussed the action with the director, believed to be (but unconfirmed as) Robert Day.

Filming on the colour series began on 5 September 1966 at Lord Montagu's Museum of Vintage Cars, Palace House, Beaulieu, Hampshire, and continued for 28 weeks. After completion of episode 16 *(Who's Who?)* the production team took a 16-day recess and resumed filming in May 1967. The production was completed in September that year.

SEASON FIVE CHRONOLOGY

Episode	Title
1	The Fear Merchants
2	Escape in Time
3	The Bird Who Knew Too Much
4	From Venus With Love (aka The Light Fantastic)
5	The See-Through Man
6	The Winged Avenger
7	The Living Dead
8	The Hidden Tiger
9	The Correct Way to Kill
10	Never, Never Say Die
11	Epic
12	The Superlative Seven
13	A Funny Thing Happened on the Way to the Station
14	Something Nasty in the Nursery
15	The Joker
16	Who's Who???
17	Death's Door
18	Return of the Cybernauts
19	Dead Man's Treasure
20	The £50,000 Breakfast
21	You Have Just Been Murdered
22	The Positive-Negative Man
23	Murdersville
24	Mission... Highly Improbable (aka The Disappearance of Admiral Nelson)
25	The Forget-Me-Knot (See Season Six)

There was a 16 day break in production between Episodes
16 and 17

Produced by: Albert Fennell and Brian Clemens
Executive Producer: Julian Wintle
Production Designer: Wilfred Shingleton (Episodes 1-6)
Robert Jones (Episodes 7-25)
Music by: Laurie Johnson

The Fear
Merchants:
*Actor Jeremy
Burnham asked Brian
Clemens for a chance
to write an* Avengers
*script. He did, and
then wrote several
more – and is now a
distinguished TV
writer. ***

SEASON FIVE EPISODES

105 THE FEAR MERCHANTS

by Philip Levene

**Steed puts out a light
Emma takes fright**

John Steed (Patrick Macnee) Emma Peel (Diana Rigg) Pemberton (Patrick
Cargill) Jeremy Raven (Brian Wilde) Dr Voss (Annette Carell) Gilbert
(Garfield Morgan) Crawley (Andrew Keir) Gordon White (Jeremy
Burnham) Richard Meadows (Edward Burnham) Fox (Bernard Horsfall) Dr
Hill (Ruth Trouncer) Saunders (Declan Mulholland) Hospital Attendant
(Philip Ross)

Designed by Wilfred Shingleton
Directed by Gordon Flemyng

With confectionery and a card, Steed calls upon Emma Peel one more
time. The Business Efficiency Bureau have a motto: 'Our merchandise
is fear'. They uncover people's fears and frighten them to death, so
Steed enrols as a client and Mrs Peel becomes his business rival. Steed
feels the earth move, before he finally closes down the BEB, leaving the
chairman Pemberton in the dark as to what went wrong. Exit Steed,
fearing that Mrs Peel may have run out of champagne.

Filmed: September 1966   TX: 21 January 1967

106 ESCAPE IN TIME

by Philip Levene

**Steed visits the barber
Emma has a close shave**

John Steed (Patrick Macnee) Emma Peel (Diana Rigg) Thyssen (Peter
Bowles) Clapham (Geoffrey Bayldon) Vesta (Judy Parfitt) Anjali (Imogen
Hassall) Sweeney (Howard Caddick) Parker (Nicholas Smith) Tubby
Vincent (Roger Booth) Josino (Richard Montez) Paxton (Clifford Earl)
Mitchell (Rocky Taylor)

Designed by Wilfred Shingleton
Directed by John Krish

Mrs Peel is needed – to attend the Grand Hunt Ball. But first she is on
the trail of Josino – one of many notorious criminals who have disappeared recently. Steed has already taken the path through time to

1790, whereas Emma finds herself in the Tudor era. A leap across time saves Emma from the stocks and exposes Thyssen's spy chain. Exit the Avengers in a vintage taxi.

Filmed: September/October 1966 TX: 28 January 1967

107 THE BIRD WHO KNEW TOO MUCH

by Brian Clemens
Based on a story by Alan Pattillo

Steed fancies pigeons
Emma gets the bird

John Steed (Patrick Macnee) Emma Peel (Diana Rigg) Jordan (Ron Moody) Samantha Slade (Ilona Rodgers) Tom Savage (Kenneth Cope) Verret (Michael Coles) Edgar Twitter (John Wood) George Cunliffe (Anthony Valentine) Robin (Clive Colin-Bowler) Mark Pearson (John Lee) Danvers (unknown) Frank Elrick (unknown)

Designed by Wilfred Shingleton
Directed by Roy Rossotti

Emma gets the point that she is needed and feathers fly as Steed and Mrs Peel avenge the death of two agents, killed by Robin and Verret. The key clue rests in the mind of Captain Crusoe, a prize parrot that has disappeared from Heathcliffe Hall. When the parrot talks, Cunliffe is exposed and his carrier pigeons have their cameras seized, preventing further security breaches at Muswells Back. Exit the Avengers to meet a bird, but in whose car?

Filmed: October 1966 TX: 11 February 1967

108 FROM VENUS WITH LOVE

by Philip Levene

Steed is shot full of holes
Emma sees stars

John Steed (Patrick Macnee) Emma Peel (Diana Rigg) Venus Browne (Barbara Shelley) Dr Henry Primble (Philip Locke) Brigadier Whitehead (Jon Pertwee) Crawford (Derek Newark) Bertram Smith (Jeremy Lloyd) Jennings (Adrian Ropes) Professor Clarke (Arthur Cox) Ernest Cosgrove (Paul Gillard) Sir Frederick Hadley (Michael Lynch) Lord Mansford (Kenneth Benda)

The Bird Who Knew Too Much:
a) Director Roy Rossotti, who only directed this one episode, was a protégé of world famous film director, David Lean. *
b) The swimming pool high dive was done by Peter Elliott. An Olympic gold medallist, Elliott returned to the show several times, He played the waiter aboard the train in A Funny Thing Happened on the Way to The Station, *doubled Diana Rigg's dive from the bridge in* You Have Just Been Murdered *and stunt-doubled Linda Thorson in the over-the-perimeter-fence trampoline jump during the opening sequence of* Have Guns, Will Haggle. *

From Venus With Love:
a) Director Robert Day is married to Dorothy Provine, who was famous in The Roaring Twenties *TV series. He went on to live and direct in Hollywood (*Tarzan, *etc).* *
b) The car used in this episode was a Ford GT40, at that time the fastest road car in the world. *

Steed crouches behind a desk to avoid the deadly beams fired at him from Primble's laser in *From Venus With Love*.

Designed by Wilfred Shingleton
Directed by Robert Day

From the tip of her epee to the tips of her toes, Mrs Peel is needed – to investigate whether the Venusians have invaded the planet. Are aliens killing the rich patrons of the British Venusian Society? Steed is unconvinced and, once he finds that £20,000 is missing from the BVS funds, it is soon clear that Primble has stolen the money to build a deadly laser-gun. Exit the Avengers to 'have dinner on Venus', after reflecting on Primble's downfall.

Filmed: October/November 1966   TX: 14 January 1967

109 THE SEE-THROUGH MAN

by Philip Levene

Steed makes a bomb
Emma is put to sleep

John Steed (Patrick Macnee) Emma Peel (Diana Rigg) Elena (Moira Lister) Brodny (Warren Mitchell) Quilby (Roy Kinnear) Ackroyd (Jonathan Elsom) Sir Andrew Ford (John Nettleton) Ulric (Harvey Hall) Wilton (David Glover)

Designed by Wilfred Shingleton
Directed by Robert Asher

Mrs Peel has been summoned – by a microscopic message – to investigate an invisible man. Ambassador Brodny is convinced that Major Vazin, their top agent, has acquired the secret of invisibility. The Eastern Drug Corporation recently purchased the formula from Quilby. It is all part of a plot to fool Steed, but he sees through the scheme. The Avengers exit to find dinner – but can they catch up with the taxi...?

Filmed: November 1966   TX: 4 February 1967

110 THE WINGED AVENGER

by Richard Harris

Steed goes bird watching
Emma does a comic strip

John Steed (Patrick Macnee) Emma Peel (Diana Rigg) Sir Lexius Cray (Nigel Green) Professor Poole (Jack Macgowran) Arnie Packer (Neil Hallett) Stanton (Colin Jeavons) Julian (Roy Patrick) Tay-Ling (John Garrie) Peter Roberts (Donald Pickering) Simon Roberts (William Fox) Dawson (AJ Brown) Dumayn (Hilary Wontner) Fothers (John Crocker) Gerda (Ann Sydney)

Cartoon drawings by Frank Bellamy
Designed by Wilfred Shingleton
Directed by Gordon Flemyng and Peter Duffell

Mrs Peel finds Steed canvassing for her attention, and her painting is distracted. A comic-strip character steps into real-life and begins to kill ruthless businessmen. The illustrator, Arnie, has turned fiction into fact using the latest technology, and a battle ensues on the ceiling before Emma can bring the Winged Avenger down to earth. Drawn to Steed's apartment with the promise of dinner, the ping of cymbals announces that their feast is ready. Exit the Avengers to eat a good meal.

Filmed: November/December 1966
TX: 18 February 1967

The Winged Avenger:
Director Gordon Flemyng began this story but was pulled off the episode and replaced by Peter Duffell 'not because Gordon was a bad director; he just wasn't an Avengers director,' Brian Clemens explained.

The Living Dead:
*Anthony Marriott,
who wrote the story,
also wrote the long-
running play,* No Sex
Please, We're
British. *

111 THE LIVING DEAD

by Brian Clemens

**Steed finds a mine of information
Emma goes underground**

John Steed (Patrick Macnee) Emma Peel (Diana Rigg) Masgard (Julian Glover) Mandy (Pamela Ann Davy) Geoffrey (Howard Marion Crawford) Kermit (Jack Woolgar) Hooper (Jack Watson) Rupert (Edward Underdown) Olliphant (John Cater) Spencer (Vernon Dobtcheff) Tom (Alister Williamson)

**Designed by Robert Jones
Directed by John Krish**

Steed uses an unorthodox highway code to tell Mrs Peel that he needs her. The ghost of Rupert, 15th Duke of Benedict, has arisen from his coffin and haunts the local church. Actually, the Duke has escaped from a vast underground city that has been built below a local mine-shaft. Steed and Emma's investigations are shrouded in fog and smog before Steed lifts Rupert and his friends to safety, leaving his opponents trapped below, Exit the Avengers to investigate a 'ghost' in the engine of Steed's Bentley.

**Filmed: December 1966/January 1967
TX: 25 February 1967**

112 THE HIDDEN TIGER

by Philip Levene

**Steed hunts a big cat
Emma is badly scratched**

John Steed (Patrick Macnee) Emma Peel (Diana Rigg) Chesire (Ronnie Barker) Dr Manx (Lyndon Brook) Angora (Gabrielle Drake) Nesbitt (John Philips) Peters (Michael Forrest) Erskine (Stanley Meadows) Sir David Harper (Jack Gwillim) Dawson (Frederick Treves) Samuel Jones (Brian Haines) Williams (John Moore) Walter Bellamy (Reg Pritchard)

**Designed by Robert Jones
Directed by Sidney Hayers**

Redecorating is interrupted by Steed's call for help to track down a large, vicious cat on the rampage. The killers are in reality ordinary moggies, fitted with electrophones in their collars. Dr Manx and Angora, from PURRR, plan to unleash every domestic cat on their owners, using radio waves to heighten their killing potential. Tied to a chair, Emma has to tackle the furry felines on her own and to disable the transmitter. Faced with cat-astrophe, Manx panics and dies in a car accident. Mission accomplished, Mrs Peel can return to her house-painting. Steed tries to help, but puts his foot in it once again.

Filmed: January 1967   TX: 4 March 1967

Redecorating her apartment walls, Emma tears off a strip of wallpaper to reveal that Steed requires her help to expose *The Hidden Tiger*.

113 THE CORRECT WAY TO KILL

by Brian Clemens

**Steed changes partners
Emma joins the enemy**

John Steed (Patrick Macnee) Emma Peel (Diana Rigg) Olga (Anna Quayle) Nutski (Michael Gough) Ivan (Philip Madoc) Ponsonby (Terence Alexander) Percy (Peter Barkworth) Algy (Graham Armitage) Merryweather (Timothy Bateson) Hilda (Joanna Jones) Winters (Edwin Apps) Groski (John G Heller)

**Designed by Robert Jones
Directed by Charles Crichton**

Mrs Peel makes headline news by helping Steed as requested. Steed is paired with Olga and Emma joins Ivan to discover the identity of the real murderer of Grotski; the opposition believe that Steed is to blame. Both sides are being double-crossed by Nutski, Olga's employer, until Olga and Steed arrest the gang. Exit the Avengers with Steed wearing Cossack attire.

Filmed: January/February 1967   TX: 11 March 1967

114 NEVER, NEVER SAY DIE

by Philip Levene

**Steed meets a dead man
Emma fights the corpse**

John Steed (Patrick Macnee) Emma Peel (Diana Rigg) Professor Stone (Christopher Lee) Dr Penrose (Jeremy Young) Dr Betty James (Patricia English) Eccles (David Kernan) Whittle (Christopher Benjamin) Sergeant (John Junkin) Private (Peter Dennis) Carter (Geoffrey Reed) Selby (Alan Chuntz) Elderly Gent (Arnold Ridley) Young Man (David Gregory) Nurse (Karen Ford)

**Designed by Robert Jones
Directed by Robert Day**

Steed interrupts Emma's television viewing, because he needs her help – with a corpse that will not die. The body is a computer-controlled clone of Professor Stone and other duplicates are being created as well. Steed and Emma investigate and find themselves trapped within Stone's laboratory. Emma uses radio signals to disable the doppelegangers, and Steed firmly rejects any further schemes of this nature.

With the task complete, the Avengers return to viewing television – an enthralling Party Political Broadcast.

Filming completed 14 February 1967
TX: 18 March 1967

115 EPIC

by Brian Clemens

Steed catches a falling star
Emma makes a movie

John Steed (Patrick Macnee) Emma Peel (Diana Rigg) Stewart Kirby (Peter Wyngarde) Damita Syn (Isa Miranda) Z Z Von Schnerk (Kenneth J Warren) Policeman (David Lodge) Actor (Anthony Dawes)

Designed by Robert Jones
Directed by James Hill

Mrs Peel is needed – to appear in the film *The Destruction of Emma Peel*, a role she would rather do without. Kidnapped and made the principal player in Von Schnerk's technicolor epic, Emma winds up tied to a circular saw, while Von Schnerk and Kirby prepare to film her dying moments..... Steed's belated arrival finishes off Kirby's plans to make the epic of the century. Emma decides to stay at home and avoid visits to the Plaza cinema in the future.

Filming completed: 27 February 1967   TX: 1 April 1967

116 THE SUPERLATIVE SEVEN

by Brian Clemens

Steed flies to nowhere
Emma does her party piece

John Steed (Patrick Macnee) Emma Peel (Diana Rigg) Mrs Hana Wild (Charlotte Rampling) Mark Drayton (Brian Blessed) Jason Wade (James Maxwell) Max Hardy (Hugh Manning) Freddy Richards (Leon Greene) Joe Smith (Gary Hope) Jessel (Donald Sutherland) Kanwitch (John Hollis) Stewardess (Margaret Neale) Toy Sung (Terry Plummer)

Designed by Robert Jones
Directed by Sidney Hayers

Mrs Peel retrieves a plastic duck – to prove that she is always needed. Stranded on an unknown island, Steed finds that one of his colleagues

Epic:
Actress Isa Miranda, hit by a chair during filming, sustained a cut forehead. Diana Rigg did practically all her own stuntwork in this episode.

The Superlative Seven:
a) Doubling for Patrick Macnee, stuntman Rocky Taylor suffered a gashed wrist during the run-through of the fight. A replacement stuntman stepped in. He, too, received a minor cut to his arm!
b) Charlotte Rampling played a character called Hana Wilde in this story. Sound familar? It should. Sue Lloyd, Steed's sidekick in The Avengers *stage show was called Hannah Wild!*

is a killer. The scenario has been staged by Jessel to convince Kanwitch that his agent is unbeatable. Mrs Peel drops in to expose that the two-faced agent is actually a pair of identical twins and Jessel is taken into custody. Exit the Avengers on a duck shoot, looking for teddy bears!

Filming completed: 13 March 1967   TX: 8 April 1967

A Funny Thing
Happened on the
Way to the
Station.
*The Bryan Sheriff
who wrote this is
actually two: Brian
Clemens and Roger
Marshall. ***

117 A FUNNY THING HAPPENED ON THE WAY TO THE STATION

by Bryan Sheriff

**Steed goes off the rails
Emma finds her station in life**

John Steed (Patrick Macnee) Emma Peel (Diana Rigg) Ticket Collector (James Hayter) Crewe (John Laurie) Groom (Drewe Henley) Bride (Isla Blair) Salt (Tim Barrett) Admiral (Richard Caldicot) Warren (Dyson Lovell) Attendant (Peter J Elliott) Lucas (Michael Nightingale) Secretary (Noel Davis)

**Designed by Robert Jones
Directed by John Krish**

Steed and Emma find themselves on the right track when they investigate the Norborough railway line. Dissidents plot to explode a bomb on board one train, whilst the Prime Minister passes close-by on another. As the minutes tick towards 8.57pm, Steed follows a lead to disconnect the device, while Emma tackles the train's unfriendly passengers. The Avengers make a quick exit and avoid the PM's long speech of thanks.

Filming completed: 22 March 1967   TX: 15 April 1967

Something Nasty
in the Nursery:
*Steed's Bentley was
slightly damaged by a
generator when filming
on location. The gen-
erator was swung on a
pulley chain and
clipped the front bon-
net.*

118 SOMETHING NASTY IN THE NURSERY

by Philip Levene

**Steed acquires a nanny
Emma shops for toys**

John Steed (Patrick Macnee) Emma Peel (Diana Rigg) Mr Goat (Dudley Foster) Miss Lister (Yootha Joyce) Lord William Beaumont (Paul Eddington) Viscount Frederick Webster (Paul Hardwick) Sir George Collins (Patrick Newell) General Wilmot (Geoffrey Sumner) Gordon (Trevor Bannister) Martin (Clive Dunn) James (George Merritt) Nanny Roberts (Enid Lorimer) Nanny Smith (Louie Ramsay) Nanny Bown (Penelope Keith) Donson (Dennis Chinnery)

Designed by Robert Jones
Directed by James Hill

The Joker:
a) Brian Clemens on why he did the rewrite. 'Because we were missing a script. We had been promised one, it didn't turn up. Anyway, it was always in my mind that we should re-make Don't Look Behind You *because I thought it was a story that the Americans shouldn't miss out on. I think it worked very well in both formats.' **
b) Stuntman Art Thomas doubled for actress Sally Nesbitt.
c) Sally Nesbitt is the daughter of Sir John Hunt, who headed the team that first climbed Everest. *

Awakened by a toy carousel calling for her assistance, Mrs Peel bounces into action to investigate the Guild of Noble Nannies. Goat, disguised as Nanny Roberts, has been revisiting the children placed in 'her' charge, who are now all senior military men. 'She' then uses a special drug to extract secrets from them. Startled by Steed's intervention, Goat loses his hair and an ex-pupil shoots the fraud. What will the future hold for Steed now? Emma's crystal ball might hold the answer.

Filming completed: 2 April 1967   TX: 22 April 1967

119 THE JOKER

by Brian Clemens

Steed trumps an ace
Emma plays a lone hand

Who's Who?:
a) Philip Levene, who along with Brian Clemens was the most prolific writer on the colour series (between them they supplied 20 of the 24 scripts), appears in this story as Tulip, an agent employed by Major 'B'.

b) The announcer (who appeared after every ad-break to keep us up-to-date with the plight of Steed and Mrs Peel/Basil and Lola) was actor Richard Bebb – who also supplied the unseen voice of Emma's nemesis in The Joker.

c) Cyd Child was kept on her toes in this story. She doubled for Diana Rigg and Patricia Haines. For the scenes in which Lola fights Emma, Cyd played the former and stuntgirl Annabelle Wise doubled for Diana Rigg. Stuntmen Les Crawford and Joe Farrar doubled for Freddie Jones and Peter Reynolds respectively.

d) Director John Moxey directed his own second unit team for this episode.

e) This episode came about because one of

John Steed (Patrick Macnee) Emma Peel (Diana Rigg) Max Prendergast (Peter Jeffrey) Ola Chamberlain (Sally Nesbitt) Strange Young Man (Ronald Lacey) Major George Fancy (John Stone)

Designed by Robert Jones
Directed by Sidney Hayers

Mrs Peel is needed – to care for an invalid Steed, but she has already arranged to spend the weekend in Devonshire playing Bridge. Steed soon realises that his injury was no accident: someone is trying to kill the Avengers. Alone in a country manor, Emma is nearly murdered by Prendergast, but Steed plays his joker finishing the criminal's plans. A trick of cards produces a bottle of bubbly to celebrate.

Filming completed: 11 March 1967   TX: 29 April 1967

120 WHO'S WHO???

by Philip Levene

Steed goes out of his mind
Emma is besides herself

John Steed (Patrick Macnee) Emma Peel (Diana Rigg) Lola (Patricia Haines) Basil (Freddie Jones) Major 'B' (Campbell Singer) Tulip (Peter Reynolds) Krelmar (Arnold Diamond) Daffodil (Philip Levene) Hooper (Malcolm Taylor)

Designed by Robert Jones
Directed by John Moxey

Hoping for reflected glory, Mrs Peel joins Steed when he visits Hi-Limba Products. Once there, Krelmar forces the Avengers to change personalities with Lola and Basil, two assassins, who then proceed to infiltrate Floral – a secret department of British agents. Trapped in Lola and Basil's bodies, Emma and Steed run a gamut of thorny battles before they find Krelmar and force him to reverse the process. To celebrate, Steed plans a surprise weekend in Paris... and finds that Emma has already packed.

Filming completed: 18 April 1967   TX: 6 May 1967

121 DEATH'S DOOR

by Philip Levene

Steed relives a nightmare
Emma sees daylight

John Steed (Patrick Macnee) Emma Peel (Diana Rigg) Sir Andrew Boyd (Clifford Evans) Stapley (William Lucas) Lord Melford (Allan Cuthbertson) Becker (Marne Maitland) Dr Evans (Paul Dawkins) Pavret (Michael Faure) Saunders (Peter Thomas) Dalby (William Lyon Brown) Haynes (Terry Yorke) Jepson (Terry Maidment)

Designed by Robert Jones
Directed by Sidney Hayers

Sinister dreams become reality and government officials predict their own deaths on the eve of an important conference. Becker's plan to wreck the summit nearly works, but the Avengers find the storage area where the delegates have been drugged and brainwashed. With Becker and Stapley exposed as the perpetrators of this act, Steed and Emma tear a strip off Becker and a stray bullet puts out Stapley's light. Exit the Avengers, with Emma predicting a visit to the theatre.

Filming complete: 7 June 1967   TX: 7 October 1967

122 RETURN OF THE CYBERNAUTS

by Philip Levene

Steed pulls some strings
Emma becomes a puppet

John Steed (Patrick Macnee) Emma Peel (Diana Rigg) Paul Beresford (Peter Cushing) Benson (Frederick Jaeger) Dr Neville (Charles Tingwell) Professor Chadwick (Fulton Mackay) Dr Russell (Roger Hammond) Dr J.W.Garnett (Anthony Dutton) Conroy (Noel Coleman) Rosie (Aimi Macdonald) John Hunt (Redmond Phillips) The Cybernaut (Terry Richards)

Designed by Robert Jones
Directed by Robert Day

Paul Beresford resurrects his brothers's most dangerous invention the Cybernaut. Using the robot to kidnap important scientists, he gives them a task: kill the Avengers! The scientists create two watches that contain micro-circuitry to overpower the mind. But Steed is not so easily duped. He puts the watch forced on him by Beresford onto the Cybernaut's wrist, causing it to kill its master. The controlling devices destroyed, the Cybernaut freezes into immobility. It is a pity that Steed cannot handle an electric toaster with the same skill.

Filming completed: 15 June 1967
TX: 30 September 1967

the leads was ill, the other on a much-needed holiday. There were 10 days shooting without either – hence, Brian Clemens and Philip Levene came up with the idea of having them being physically taken-over by two other persons. Director John Moxey later made his mark by helping to create Charlie's Angels. *

Death's Door:
a) Location shooting on this episode was cancelled, so the second unit returned to the studio – and stood around for the best part of the day on the Nightmare *set. They were unable to shoot because the principal artists were working on another episode.*
b) Actor Michael Gough visited the studio during the production of this episode to have a plaster bust made of his head and shoulders for Return of the Cybernauts.

Dead Man's
Treasure:
*a) The white Jaguar
E-type, briefly seen in
the opening, and with
the registration 140
MPH, belonged to
Brian Clemens.
b) Valerie Van Ost
later became a respect-
ed agent. We have no
idea what happened to
Arthur Lowe! ***

Emma is trapped in
the racing car simu-
lator in this exciting
scene from *Dead
Man's Treasure.*

123 DEAD MAN'S TREASURE

by Michael Winder

**Steed rallies around
Emma drives for her life**

John Steed (Patrick Macnee) Emma Peel (Diana Rigg) Mike (Norman
Bowler) Penny (Valerie Van Ost) Alex (Edwin Richfield) Carl (Neil
McCarthy) Sir George Benstead (Arthur Lowe) Bates (Ivor Dean) Bobby
Danvers (Rio Fanning) Miss Peabody (Penny Bird) First Guest (Gerry
Crampton) Second Guest (Peter J.Elliott)

**Designed by Robert Jones
Directed by Sidney Hayers**

Dying from his wounds, Danvers hides his despatch box inside a treasure chest that is the prize in a forthcoming car rally. Steed and Emma
enter the race to retrieve the box, but enemy agents pursue them at
every turn. Emma is shocked to find that her navigator, Mike, also
wants the box, and his attempts to locate its whereabouts drive the
Avenger to distraction. Steed rallies round to put a red light on the villain's plans and Emma discovers that she has been sitting on a secret.
With the box recovered, Mrs Peel determines to have no more close
shaves.

Filming completed: 5 July 1967   TX: 21 October 1967

124 THE £50,000 BREAKFAST

by Roger Marshall

Steed dabbles in tycoonery
Emma in chicanery

John Steed (Patrick Macnee) Emma Peel (Diana Rigg) Glover (Cecil Parker) Miss Pegram (Yolande Turner) Sir James Arnell (David Langton) Mrs Rhodes (Pauline Delaney) Judy (Anneke Wills) Minister (Cardew Robinson) First Assistant (Eric Woolfe) Second Assistant (Philippe Monnet) Rhodes (Richard Curnock) Security Man (Jon Laurimore) Mechanic (Richard Owens) Kennel Man (Michael Rothwell) Jerezina (Yole Marinelli) First Doctor (Christopher Greatorex) Second Doctor (Nigel Lambert)

Designed by Robert Jones
Directed by Robert Day

'High on carat, low in protein.' A stomach full of diamonds alerts Steed to a slick smuggling operation. Alex Litoff died some weeks earlier, but his cohorts have hidden the truth to give them time to liquidate the millionaire's assets. Litoff's body was buried at the Happy Valley Resting Place for pets. Once the authorities learn of Litoff's demise, the scheme is over and they come quietly. This leaves Steed with the dilemma of what to do with the two Borzois Emma has found and the Dalmatian-spotted tie she has presented to him as a gift!

Filming completed: 20 July 1967   TX: 14 October 1967

125 YOU HAVE JUST BEEN MURDERED

by Philip Levene

Steed chases a million
Emma runs off with it

John Steed (Patrick Macnee) Emma Peel (Diana Rigg) George Unwin (Barrie Ingham) Lord Maxted (Robert Flemying) Needle (George Murcell) Rathbone (Leslie French) Gilbert Jarvis (Geoffrey Chater) Skelton (Simon Oates) Chalmers (Clifford Cox) Hallam (John Baker) Morgan (Les Crawford) Nicholls (Frank Maher) Williams (Peter J Elliott)

Designed by Robert Jones
Directed by Robert Asher

Blackmailers intimidate their victims by staging mock attempts at murder. Unwin pretends to agree to their terms and then sends a bomb instead. This move worries Steed because Emma has been kidnapped

You Have Just Been Murdered: a) Diana Rigg and Patrick Macnee were absent from the set for one day due to a 'tummy-bug'. They returned the following morning, then Macnee fell ill again. Returning to the studio while they were filming The £50,000 Breakfast, *he was required to put in extra hours, working until late in the evening to catch up on lost time. It didn't end there. At one point he had to 'triple-up' and do work on this episode,* The £50,000 Breakfast *and scenes for* Dead Man's Treasure – *all on the same day! b) Stuntman Frank Maher (perhaps better known as Patrick McGoohan's double in* The Prisoner*) doubled for actor Barrie Ingham in this story. c) The Borzoi dogs were played by Dancer and Bellhound.*

The Postive-
Negative Man:
*a) Stunt arranger Ray
Austin planned a real
tough set-to for Steed
in this one – and
Patrick Macnee was
glad that the script
confirmed that he was
to turn out the winner.
For the loser went
head-first through a
glass window! Not a
sugar glass mock-up –
the real thing, so it
had to solidly fixed, in
order that it would
shatter properly.
Director Robert Day
decided to film the
sequence with two
hand-held cameras,
operating one of them
himself. With nurses
and helpers standing
by, the sequence went
ahead. The result? A
few minor cuts for
stuntman Dinny
Powell (standing in for
Ray McAnally) and a
remarkable – first time
– shot in the can for
Macnee.
b) Having steered the
crew safely through
this, Robert Day 'dis-
graced' himself by sus-
taining an ankle injury
later that day!*

Opposite: Stunt double
Cyd Child takes a
break during the
filming of the duck-
ing stool sequence
from *Murdersville.*

Reproduced courtesy of
Cyd Child.

by the Needle, the mastermind, and his gang of assassins. Despite the
odds, Steed discovers the Needle in his haystack and Emma is rescued
from destruction. In gratitude, his partner helps Steed to become a
halfpenny millionaire!

Filming completed: 2 August 1967   TX: 28 October 1967

126 THE POSITIVE-NEGATIVE MAN

by Tony Williamson

**Steed makes the sparks fly
Emma gets switched on**

John Steed (Patrick Macnee) Emma Peel (Diana Rigg) Creswell (Ray
McAnally) Haworth (Michael Latimer) Cynthia Wentworth-Howe
(Caroline Blakiston) Mankin (Peter Blythe) Maurice Jubert (Sandor Eles)
Miss Clarke (Joanne Dainton) Charles Grey (Bill Wallis) Receptionist (Ann
Hamilton)

**Designed by Robert Jones
Directed by Robert Day**

Government research at Risley Dale has been halted and Project 90
has been shelved, but someone has perfected the ability to broadcast
electricity. When scientists die in shocking circumstances, Steed traces
the culprit: Creswell, the Project's instigator. Haworth and Creswell are
soon brought down to earth, as Steed wades in to rescue Emma from
her insulated captivity. Free, the Avengers find themselves inseparably
magnetised to Steed's Bentley.

**Filming completed: 31 August 1967
TX: 4 November 1967**

127 MURDERSVILLE

by Brian Clemens

**Emma marries Steed
Steed becomes a father**

John Steed (Patrick Macnee) Emma Peel (Diana Rigg) Mickle (Colin
Blakely) Hubert (John Ronane) Dr Haymes (Ronald Hines) Prewitt (John
Sharp) Jenny Prewitt (Sheila Fearn) Major Paul Croft (Eric Flynn) Forbes
(Norman Chappell) Banks (Roger Cawdron) Miss Avril (Marika Mann)
Maggie (Irene Bradshaw) Higgins (Joseph Greig) Jeremy Purser (Geoffrey
Colville) Chapman (Langton Jones) Miller (Tony Caunter) Morgan (John
Chandos) Frederick Williams (Andrew Laurence)

Designed by Robert Jones
Directed by Robert Asher

If the price is right, anyone can be murdered in Little Storping -in-The-Swuff. When Mrs Peel goes looking for Croft, an old school friend who has disappeared, she stumbles upon the village of murderers. Half-drowned and imprisoned in a chastity belt, Emma is forced to summon her husband, John, who also knows the secret of the village, but Steed is forewarned and craftily pelts the villagers into submission. Mrs Peel has found her knight in shining armour!

Filming complete: 25 August 1967
TX: 11 November 1967

128 MISSION...HIGHLY IMPROBABLE

by Philip Levene

Steed falls into enemy hands
Emma is cut down to size

John Steed (Patrick Macnee) Emma Peel (Diana Rigg) Shaffer (Ronald Radd) Susan (Jane Merrow) Professor LT Rushton (Noel Howlett) Chivers (Francis Matthews) Colonel Drew (Richard Leech) Josef (Stefan Gryff) Gifford (Nicholas Courtney) Sir Gerald Bancroft (Kevin Stoney) Sergeant (Peter Clay) Corporal Johnson (Nigel Rideout) Blonde (Cynthia Bizeray) Brunette (Nicole Shelby) Henrick (Nosher Powell) Karl (Denny Powell)

Mission Highly Improbable:
For whatever reason, Diana Rigg crammed her entire input for this episode into the first five days filming. Her scenes were filmed in this order: Day 1: Interiors. Emma's apartment, with Patrick Macnee. Day 2: Interiors: Rushton's Office. Interior: Skirting board, Shaffer's office. Interior: Giant Desk and Photo. Day 3: Interior: Shaffer's Study. Exterior: Rushton's House. Exterior: Pavilion. Day 4: Interior: Shaffer's Study. Interior: Shaffer's Hallway. Day 5: Interior: Shaffer's Study. Exterior: Pavilion. Her last day of filming was 30 August 1967. She would return to the series on 14 December that year, for four days filming on The Forget-Me-Knot.

Designed by Robert Jones
Directed by Robert Day

Professor Rushton has invented a miniaturizing ray, which Chivers uses to steal the new Saracen FV603 armoured car. However, the buyer – Shaffer – is unaware that Steed has been given the miniaturization treatment and is trapped inside the Saracen. When Shaffer also tries to buy the ray-machine, Steed manages to escape from confinement and telephone Emma. Though cut down to size, she manages to shrink Shaffer's plans and release Steed. The villains safely installed inside Steed's bowler hat, the Avengers depart for a gigantic feast. Rain is expected, so Steed offers Emma his miniaturised umbrella...

Filming completed: 22 September 1967
TX: 18 November 1967

The Forget-Me-Knot

See Episode 131 (page 225)

Other works on this subject assert that the colour episodes were produced in two distinct blocks of sixteen and eight episodes respectively, and list these accordingly as Seasons Five and Six. They qualify their reasoning by suggesting that there was a six-week break in production between *Who's Who?* and *Return of The Cybernauts* – and compound their mistake by stating that *The Forget-Me-Knot* episode was part-filmed in September 1967.

A glance at the production records shows how easily the mistake has been made. Episode One *(The Fear Merchants)* through to episode 16 *(Who's Who???)* were filmed between 5 September 1966 and 18 April 1967. The crew then took a two-week recess (actually 16 days), and filming recommenced on Wednesday 3 May, with the episode *Death's Door*. However, production on the series did not cease during the recess. Several directors were employed to film 'pick-up' shots (to be edited into the episodes sometime later), the film editing continued apace and Laurie Johnson visited the studio to record incidental music. Conclusion? I insist that there is no sixth Emma Peel colour season!

Furthermore, the producers would have been hard pressed to abandon filming on *The Forget-Me-Knot* episode in September. Production on the Rigg/Thorson cross-over story didn't begin until 14 December 1967 – some six or seven weeks after the completion of the Bryce-produced Thorson episodes – placing *The Forget-Me-Knot* third in the Thorson production chronology, which is where it appears in this book.
Sorry about that. Good form, you know.

SEASON SIX

Thirty-three Colour filmed episodes

starring PATRICK MACNEE and LINDA THORSON   **1967/1969**

PRODUCTION HISTORY

THE COLOUR SERIES proved to be a big money earner
worldwide. Foreign sales were in excess of £5,000,000 and
the show was being screened in more than 70 countries. In May
1967, the show was put forward as a candidate for the best foreign dramatic series of the year by ABC in America. Diana
Rigg was nominated for an American Emmy (television's equivalent of the Oscar); – this was eventually won by Barbara Bain
of *Mission Impossible* – and voted Actress of the Year by the 16
European countries screening *The Avengers*.

The success of the show had once again led to discussions
about making a feature-length film of *The Avengers*. Sadly, as with
earlier plans, it never materialized.

After filming of the colour series was completed in
September 1967, Diana Rigg left the show and returned to
Shakespeare, as the female lead in the filmed version of *A
Midsummer Night's Dream*. In true *Avengers* spirit, her departure
from the set was greeted by the clink of champagne glasses, the
bubbly being provided by herself, as she drank one final toast to
her co-star and production staff. Soon afterwards she said,
'Television is so immediate. Within one week of appearing in
my first *Avengers* story, I was recognized by 90 percent of the
viewing public. A week after I'd left, I was unrecognized by 90
percent of the public.'

After screening the colour series, the ITV network repeated
the 26 Rigg monochrome episodes. (Ironically, until Channel 4
began to re-run them at the end of 1982, British viewers had
only seen the Rigg colour episodes once in colour. That was in
1970, only a few months after its introduction, when very few
people had colour sets.)

At the time, ABC (having become Thames Television) felt
that, while the filmed series had been successful and had 'style',
it was getting more extreme. They felt that a move of one or two
notches back towards reality would help prolong the success,
and this needed to be achieved mainly in the writing. It was
decided to appoint John Bryce (formerly story editor and then
producer on the last Blackman series) as producer of the new
series.

Unfortunately, this didn't work out and, as ABC were committed to deliver transmission prints for American and British

telecast dates, ABC had no option left open to them than to go cap in hand to Brian Clemens and Albert Fennell, and ask them to return to the series. They did so, as joint producers with almost total control. Julian Wintle, who had taken a back seat during the Rigg colour series, now had little input beyond acting as 'consultant' for the new series, this being a courtesy credit accorded to him by Fennell and Clemens.

Brian Clemens recalled the sequence of events that led to their dismissal and reinstatement. 'Having made *The Avengers* a magnificent show and sold it to the American network – it is still the only British show to be sold prime time to the American network – ABC said thanks and fired us! I went on a motoring holiday around Wales, and wherever I went I was preceded by phone calls: would I get in touch with so-and-so. Would I please contact this person. I eventually did so and they said would I please come back. They asked me first...it's not generally known but they didn't ask Albert back. They asked me and I said that I wouldn't go back without Albert. By this time they had almost completed three episodes – one of which was virtually unshowable and the other two were pretty awful. The way that they were shot made them totally incomprehensible.'

Johnny Hough, who joined the team as second unit director a few weeks before the completion of the Rigg colour episodes and had crossed over to the new series, described the problems that were inherent from day one: 'No-one was told why Albert, Brian and Laurie were fired. All we heard at the time was that it was a cost-cutting exercise, which everyone knew to be untrue. Albert Fennell was the finest cost control guy they ever had, and he also believed in quality. But the studio had obviously been sold a bill of goods that the new people could turn *The Avengers* around and give the show a new look and new situations. What they had overlooked, of course, was that neither Brian or Albert could tell you the raison d'être for the series. You either knew how to do it or you didn't know how to do it. It was almost like a special talent, a sort of shorthand. And when they were taken off the show it was a total mess.

'*The Avengers* had run smoothly up to then. Despite the fact that it was very difficult to shoot all these episodes at the same time (the directors and principal artists were sometimes working on up to three different episodes in one week), the actual operation that was handed down from the production office was really a very, very slick machine. To have somebody else come in and take this over, and be able to operate something that Brian and Albert had done so well, simply didn't work. So the new series began to run behind from day one. You had to stockpile your screenplays ahead of time and this hadn't happened – so the whole thing became mass confusion. The show had lost its X-factor, the magic that Brian, Albert and Laurie had added to it, which you couldn't define.'

This is borne out by the day-to-day progress report sheets for

Invitation to A Killing, the first Bryce-produced Thorson episode. Four days into filming and the production team had managed to complete the princely sum of just 2.9 minutes of usable footage!

Reflecting the same sentiment as others I have spoken to, Johnny Hough told me: 'That period was, in a word, chaos. There is an awful lot more to producing a show like *The Avengers* than just shooting X number of feet of film. *The Avengers* was not a mechanical thing. It was a very, very inventive series – and it just overwhelmed the new production team. It was too much for them to handle, and the cost began to look as though it was going to spiral totally out of control. It soon reached a point where the whole series was in jeopardy and looked in danger of closing down. To go back to Brian and Albert was the right decision – but a major turnaround by the directors of ABC. That's how bad the confusion was. I have this memory of day-to-day chaos that nobody was able to resolve.'

Laurie Johnson, who had been working on feature films at MGM and rejoined his colleagues when they returned to the programme, told me that the proof of the pudding is in the eating. 'The first Thorson films didn't work. Without that knowledge of the animal, they totally missed the point. I remember seeing some of the footage – it was very strange. We had to come back and get on with making them where we left off.

Tara King raises her hat to the camera.

Although we had several regular scriptwriters, Brian was the main contributor, and it was he who established the balance between drama and humour. He was very inventive...and speedy.'

Speedy indeed. As Brian Clemens told me: 'When we came back they had already made these episodes and I said "Christ! In mid-stream we suddenly had *The Avengers* – a show that was still running on television – and the girl has changed!" So I looked for a way of covering the change-over. There had to be a way. So I insisted on writing *The Forget-Me-Knot*. I came back onto the show on a Thursday, I think. Started writing the script on Friday. Finished it on the Saturday, and we started filming it on the following Monday or Tuesday.' (It was actually Thursday, 14 December 1967.)

They had never done this before, despite Steed having changed partners on several occasions. Why now? 'Because we were in the middle of a run. It was all very well to stop the series and then come back six months later with a new cast; in the middle of a series it would have been ludicrous. They wanted to kill Mrs Peel off. I said that I loathed this because the whole of your audience hates that episode. You know, you're in love with Emma Peel, so the last thing you want to do is switch on the set and see her killed... and they had already cast Linda Thorson. It was a fait accompli.'

Having read Brian Clemens script for *The-Forget-Me-Knot*, Diana Rigg consented to return to the studio to film the episode in which she would tender her resignation and hand the role over to Linda Thorson, making this the only bridged series. Linda Thorson recalls that original producer John Bryce had no idea how to get rid of Emma Peel. 'I think that they wanted her to be killed, but Brian Clemens didn't like the idea. So he dreamed up the idea of having her husband come back – which was really quite witty because the character looked just like Steed. In the hand-over scene, I remember that they had originally just wanted us to pass on the stairs without saying anything beyond Diana giving me a wink. But then they decided we should say something, so Brian whipped up some dialogue about Steed preferring his tea to be stirred anti-clockwise.' The cross-over scene, filmed on 19 January 1968, was restricted to a 30-second encounter on the staircse leading to Steed's flat.

Before this staircase sequence the two actresses had never appeared together. Johnny Hough, who was there during the filming as assistant director to James Hill, confirms that the raison d'être for keeping the two actresses apart was not done deliberately. 'It's the sort of thing one would do when one was handing over. One would schedule it, not for any reason that perhaps the two artistes wouldn't get on; you'd schedule it as a point of courtesy to the outgoing artiste.' Linda Thorson recalls that she was the more nervous of the two.

Shooting on the Bryce-produced episodes got under way on

Hello, my name's Tara. Steed's new partner makes her entrance under the direction of James Hill, in *The Forget-Me-Knot*.

Director James Hill explains how he wants newcomer Tara to react when outgoing Mrs Peel hands over her position in *The Forget-Me-Knot*.

Always keep your bowler on in times of stress – and a watchful eye open for diabolical masterminds. Emma says goodbye in this poignant scene from *The Forget-Me-Knot*.

Dennis Spooner began his show biz career as a fledgling scout in one of Ralph Reader's Gang Shows. He went on to become a stand-up comic, first in the RAF, later, professionally on the road. He was also a postman and a footballer (pro) on the books of Leyton Orient.

*One night, a comic came back stage to tell Dennis: 'You are the worst comic I have ever seen. But who writes your material?' Dennis wrote his own. The comic was Harry Illingworth later known as Harry Worth! He later wrote material for Arthur Haynes and many other top comics. ***

23 October 1967. The original production team were reinstated six weeks later, eight days into the production of the episode, *The Curious Case of the Countless Clues.*

Production on *The Forget-Me-Knot* began just one week later, on 14 December, using Add-a-Vision, a video aid to film production pioneered by ABC at Elstree. This allows the director to see, via a screen with a frame, the limits of the picture that would be received on a home television set, exactly what was in frame during shooting. The process had previously been used on the last 13 colour Rigg episodes. Johnny Hough told me that the system wasn't everything it was cracked up to be, and sometimes brought unwanted problems of its own. 'The producers were able to cable this up to their office, with sound. There was a danger sometimes that if the sound was left on, the producers were able to view and hear what was happening on the sound stage. So eventually, the union boys stopped the use of Add-a-Vision and insisted that the microphone was turned off whilst it was not in use and banned the cabling up of the system to the producers' office. Nowadays it it used by everyone and no one can do anything about it.' He confirmed that neither Albert Fennell or Brian Clemens came onto the set unless there was a drama of some kind. 'They didn't want to see it actually being made; they preferred to see what we had created in the rushes the next day. They never interfered. They never came down to the set once, to say anything – unless there was a crisis. Sometimes you had to reshoot something because one may have interpreted a scene the wrong way. It might not have enough underlying humour or menace in it, or what have you. Then they would ask you to reshoot.'

Linda Thorson had been formally 'launched' as Tara King at a press reception held at Thames Television on 19 October 1967, with a 'meet the new Avengers girl' photo-shoot held three days later on 22 October, at London's Savoy Hotel. Press photographers pulled out all the stops to give 'Steed's new bubbly platinum blonde companion' a launch to rival that of her predecessor. Patrick Macnee and Linda Thorson were pictured on the steps of the British Museum, strolling down the Thames embankment and, as a nod to *The Avengers*, had Macnee pouring a glass of champagne for his new co-star.

It is interesting to note that the producers were aware as early as 16 July 1967 that Diana Rigg would be leaving the show. The auditions to find the (as-yet) un-named new Avengers girl took place over four days between July and October 1967. On 20 July, Gerry O'Hara put the following hopefuls through their paces: Linda Thorson, Penny Riley, Jill Medford, Gabriella Licudi, Barbara Steele, on the set of Emma Peel's apartment, with actor Charles Stapley playing Steed.

On 12 September, Linda Thorson shared the studio with Valerie Van Ost, Anita Morrison, Mary Peach. This time the women tested on the above set with Patrick Macnee, the tests being directed by Patrick Dromgoole. On 19 September, actresses Tracy Reed, Christine Taylor, Jane Merrow and Anne Lawson tested with Macnee, under the direction of Sidney Hayers.

By this time, the choice was between Linda Thorson and Tracy Reed, with Mary Peach a close third. All three women attended the studio, separately, for one final test.

Two weeks later, on 3 October, Linda Thorson was called back to the studio to do a read-through and action test with actor/writer Jeremy Burnham. Filmed on the set of Steed's apartment, Patrick Dromgoole sat in the director's chair.

Twenty days later, Linda Thorson was working on the episode *Invitation to A Killing*. Just before this Linda had appeared in a play, *A Month in The Country*, with Susannah York and Ian McShane (who played an off-camera speaking role in Linda's screen test).

Film director John Huston was partly responsible for Linda getting the role. Having seen the young actress at the Royal Academy of Dramatic Arts (RADA), he had promised her a lead part in his next film *Sinful Davey*. When circumstances forced Huston to change his mind, the director sent Linda to see Robert Lennard, the casting director of ABC, who told her that they were casting the female lead in *The Avengers*. Linda had heard about the series, but never seen it because she did not have a TV set at home! She told me: 'I was one of 200 girls, which soon became a 100, then 50, then 25 and eventually 8. Three of us, Tracey Reed, Mary Peach and myself, were given screen tests and the tapes were sent to Don Boyle, then head of the ABC network in America. He liked what he saw and I was sent to Henlow Grange Beauty Farm to lose weight.' After eight days on hot water and lemon, she received a telegram from ABC telling her that she had the part. She signed for her *Avengers* role in October 1967.

Neither Clemens nor Fennell believed that Linda was the right choice. As Clemens told me: 'She was pulled straight out of drama school, without any experience. She was Canadian, and she lacked the kind of 'acid Chelsea' sense of humour that the other two girls had brought with them. She was also slightly overweight and for some reason they had stuck her in a blonde, bubby wig which made her look a bit like Harpo Marx. In the space of two or three episodes, I had to change her image.'

Cyd Child, retained on the series as Linda's stunt double, revealed the 'secret' as to why both Linda and herself wore wigs for the first ten episodes. 'John Bryce wanted her to be blonde, so they arranged for us to go and have our hairstyles changed. Both Linda and I have a strong dark pigment in our hair, so it had to be bleached over and over again – and it just killed the hair! Then Brian Clemens came back and said he didn't like her blonde. So we had to wear wigs. We had to have our hair cut

On the principals ad-libbing their own lines, Johnny Hough told me: 'What did happen, sometimes, is that Patrick would stop acting because he had a particular problem with a term or phrase or the dialogue of the scene. And Brian would have to come onto the set and instantly make up a new scene. That was always exciting to watch, as Brian convinced Patrick of the new dialogue. As a director you couldn't touch the dialogue. If I do a film, I'm able to change all the lines any time I want. On The Avengers *the words and the lines were sacrosanct – there wasn't any improvization. What Patrick and the girls did do was to discuss how they would play the scene and suggest to Brian that it might be better if so-and-so did this or that. They certainly thought the scene out and certainly improvized action in terms of what they should do, what they should pick up, etc. So they were creative in saying: "Wouldn't it be nice if I had the bowler hat here, or opened up my umbrella there, or played the tuba here," whatever. But the*

very, very short, like a crew-cut, and wait for it to grow again.'

I discussed this with Linda Thorson, who said: 'They were so afraid that I was going to be just like Diana, that everything was done to go against that image: blonde instead of dark; fluffy pink instead of black leather. Being a natural brunette, they decided to give me a day-to-day, weekly treatment of 90-volume peroxide. As a consequence, my hair became brittle – and eventually fell out! I was left with a short stubble of patchy growth on my head. So during the first half-dozen episodes, I camouflaged this by wearing a selection of colourful wigs and hid from the public gaze for about six months until my own hair had regrown and I could show my face in public.'

'That damned silly blonde wig did not help matters,' Clemens told me, confirming that he took an instant dislike to the culottes and kid-leather, thigh-high boots selected by the original producers as Tara's fighting suit (the one worn by Linda Thorson in the cross-over scene with Diana Rigg). 'When I saw all the costumes that they had designed for Linda, that was the best of the bunch. So we had to shoot on that and then run up a whole new wardrobe that did something for her.'

Acknowledging that Linda gained experience very quickly (who wouldn't, filming five or six days a week for so many months?), Clemens confirms that the main problem they had to overcome was the relationship between the characters, because Linda was so young. 'I think, up front, it gave Patrick more confidence and perhaps more of a mentor's role. He was more of an uncle looking after a novice in a sense. That subtly changed their relationship – you know, she was too young and made Steed look like a dirty old man. The main problem was that she never really had a definitely prescribed attitude to Steed. One never quite knew what she was doing there.' Linda agreed. She said: 'The problem arose because the one thing that RADA didn't do – couldn't do – was to teach you camera technique. I'd never been in front of a camera before. So I'm there making episodes of a well-known television series, with no experience whatsoever. I was still learning and there was a lot of tension on the set. I was very sorry when John Bryce had to go, and I toyed with the idea of leaving with him. But Patrick and two of my colleagues, including John himself, said "You can't do it." By then Patrick had become very supportive and was always taking the time to find out if everything was all right. He was marvellous. The directors soon got to trust Patrick and myself as to what we would do as the characters. A lot of the time they would simply say "do what you want to do". Their main concern was to get the action shot, what was needed as far as the action was concerned.' Linda was never concerned about the age gap. 'I don't remember being told a lot about the sexual thing, or anything else other than, you're breathing too hard, or don't point the gun at the camera. Their relation was after all, a relationship of equals. Yet there was this wonderful ying and yang thing, a strong male-female happening as well as the play-fullness of the tongue-in-cheek action. Patrick was brilliant at never taking things too seriously. Whenever danger was involved, he always had this twinkle in his eye. This was the first time that you really saw a woman who was not really an equal. I think that particularly came across very well in Tara's character because she was able to be a femine character and still have a sense of humour. She was quite glamorous too, and also knew how to beat somebody to a pulp and protect her man and the situation, and do whatever was needed for her country. The secret behind the whole thing was in the writing.'

The name Tara was Linda's own choice. 'Because *Gone with the Wind* was my favourite movie at the time and that was the name of the estate. And King for king and country, which I felt was a nice touch.'

Tara was the daughter of a prosperous farmer, and had all the skills associated with the outdoor life. At her expensive fin-ishing school, she had learned how to glide, ski and fly, and had acquired the sophistication of the young international set. She was a warm, feminine and sexy woman, with an exhuberant and jaunty approach to her adventures with Steed.

There was a bond between the two principals not in evi-dence before. Whereas the hallmark of Steed's relationships, both with Cathy Gale and Emma Peel, was haughty, well-hid-den respect, the bond of friendship with Tara was frequently sealed with a kiss and a cuddle. Unlike Steed's earlier partners, Tara was single. 'That was my idea,' Linda told me, 'They sug-gested it might seem indecent for a single girl to be shown in his flat and perhaps having stayed overnight. I thought it was high-ly indecent for a married woman to be staying with him. So I persuaded them that it was much better for Tara to be single. Before my series, you had never really seen a girl making a fuss of Steed. But I saw Tara as being in love with him – absolutely, unquestionably in love. Let's face it. Here was this young girl who had been trained to do this job and tripped around to his "Ra-boom-di-ay" beck and call. No one could have worked that closely with Steed and not been in love with him. Originally she was flying by the seat of her pants quite a lot of the time, so she had this image of Steed looking after her. Patrick would be there and I'd throw my arms around him in a gesture that implied love – but without saying the words. We took the sex relation-ship for granted and Tara, like Emma before her, did sometimes stay overnight – but it was all very civilized.'

Linda told me that she was extremely concerned about how the public would receive her. She got letters that said 'How dare you take over. Who do you think you are? We'll never love you.' Then after the show had been running for about a month, more letters arrived. 'I had letters of apology and some saying,"You're great. You're different and you're fine and we like you." Of course, when you're 20, you've got lots of guts and audacity and

actual dialogue, the actual meat of the tag scene and what it was about, was always Brian's creation. They might improvise some dialogue in this, some little line they had thought of, but nothing that altered the content of the scene.'

Charles Crichton was a distinguished editor. He directed some of the best Ealing Comedies and, in his 80th year, was nomi-nated for an oscar for A Fish Called Wanda. *

Overheard at an air-port as two women watched Patrick Newell passing through customs. 'Is that Mother?' "Yes – and isn't he fat!' Dear Paddy was entrusted with picking up a Spanish Writers Award for The Avengers. *He quaffed too much of the First Class hospitality on the plane – and came off it empty-handed. The award has never been found. **

I thought I'd won the part through enthusiasm – and I wasn't going to be knocked out by anyone else. I was going to go and capture my own audience.'

Patrick told the media at the time: 'As a younger girl, Linda will be more defenceless. I'll be able to put my arms around her; look after her more. I want us to share the same easy, friendly relationship I had with Ian Hendry and then Honor and Diana Rigg. We're going to spend a lot of our working lives together, and I'd like it to be happy for both our sakes.'

Ray Austin, stunt arranger on the two previous Diana Rigg series (and creator of Tai Chi, Emma Peel's fighting technique for the colour episodes), would soon leave the show and the role would pass to fight co-ordinator Joe Dunne, who decided that there was to be no new fighting techniques for Tara. No judo, karate or kung fu. Instead she would rely more on feminine guile than muscular skill. Tara would hit her opponents with a straight right-hander, her handbag, or whatever was at hand that might be used as a weapon. She would even give the occasional scream for help! (This idea slipped away as the series progressed. Tara would soon be throwing baddies over her shoulder in true Cathy Gale style.)

Linda told me that she nevertheless had to get physically fit and learn all the moves. 'I learned the basics of judo and karate. In a television series or a film, what you always do is pull the punch. You learn to just miss, which is the exact opposite of martial arts where you make contact. On television you learn to go through and past the object that you're going to hit. It's a different principle. You have to make it look good and realistic, but just miss.' She had a very good working relationship with Joe Dunne and his team of stuntmen. 'They were my best buddies and I'd spend my lunch hour with them. I used to get memos from head office suggesting that perhaps I should eat lunch in the executive dining room, with the other actors and producers.'

Linda did lots of her own stunt work, but Cyd Child was always around to handle the more complicated and dangerous leaps, falls and no-holds-barred action. Linda did few, if any, of the driving sequences. Having failed her driving test five times, and crashed Tara's sports car into a wall during the second day's shooting (on the Bryce episodes), a double always replaced her behind the wheel.

Indeed, while *The Avengers* has an enviable record for not having sustained any major injuries to either its stars or guest actors, the cars seemed to have a mind of their own. Johnny Hough declares that they were always breaking down – particularly the vintage roadsters driven by Steed. 'We used to roll then down a hill with the engine turned off, or sometimes tow them, or have the studio people shove them onto the set.' Brian Clemens confirms that when this happened they'd get round it. 'The vintage cars were rarely used in chases because they were such a cow to drive.' Patrick Macnee remembers the absurdity of it all. 'The fact that one would drive a 1920-vintage Bentley and think that it could overtake an Aston Martin – which it couldn't, of course – didn't matter to the viewer. If we said it did so, it did.'

Two men were responsible for designing Linda Thorson's Avenger clothes: Harvey Gould and Alun Hughes. Harvey Gould was a successful coat and suit designer. In fact, he was so successful that he only had time to create the clothes for the first six stories. Costumes for the remaining 27 stories were created by Alun Hughes, the man who had designed Diana Rigg's second screen wardrobe. Asked what special considerations there were when designing clothes for a series such as *The Avengers*, Hughes replied: 'The key word is movement. It's basically an active series, so the clothes have to be active, too. Yet for this particular heroine, Tara King, with her essentially feminine character, the clothes must not be harsh. I think a good example of the combination of action and femininity comes with my design for the brown gaberdine poncho-culotte outfit. Of course, the series is shot in colour, so I must think in terms of this at all times. Not just the avoidance of horrible clashes with such flamboyant sets as Tara's flat, but also in the manner in which colour is transmitted on the television set. I have to know how much colour actually comes over on the screen. And sometimes colours can appear differently during interior scenes shot under strong studio lighting than in scenes set outdoors,'

It wasn't only Tara's coat and dresses that Hughes designed. His job was a full-time one, designing hats, scarves, gloves, handbags, shoes – even stockings. 'I must create an outfit as a whole,' he said, 'not a hodge-podge of separate units. Every single colour and shade has to blend pefectly.'

He designed about 24 outfits during the transition stage of the early Tara of, say, *Split,* to the sex-bomb Tara that followed in *My Wildest Dream.* By the summer of 1968, the producers had completely changed the role around. Linda's hair had re-grown, she was slimmer and was beginning to get to grips with her character. Hughes designed outfits that were more in keeping with the dual personality that was emerging: part soft, feminine and vulnerable, yet adventurous, resourceful and assertive when she had to be. When the credit titles were re-filmed to mark the beginning of the new season, although Tara is introduced wearing a long, backless, black crepe evening gown and pearls, she soon changes into a new-style fighting suit of brightly coloured shirt, waistcoat and trousers, to replace her earlier brown gaberdine culotte fighting gear. (Incidentally, the original credits titles, the 'target-alley' motif, followed by Linda appearing in a light tan, figure-hugging, two-piece suit, with gun at the ready, were filmed by director Harry Booth on a free-standing set at Elstree Studios, on 12 January 1968. The second set of titles, showing Tara dressed in her new fighting suit, running to Steed,

A shot from the first Thorson title credits sequence, filmed three months into production by director Harry Booth. Director Bob Fuest filmed the second title credits six months later.

surrounded by armour in a field – were filmed six months later by director Bob Fuest, at Berkhamsted, on 3 July 1968.)

During the summer break, Patrick Macnee gave a press interview in which he said: 'I thought of leaving after Diana went, but as I've always believed that once you start something, you should always see it through to the end, I stayed. I was feeling pretty jaded and beginning to look like Methuselah. I had a double chin and,' indicating his waistline, 'my stomach was out here. Well, I ask you, how could I carry on with the show looking like that? I cut down on smoking and visited my doctor, who gave me some pills to help me cut down on food, and now I'm down from 14 stone to 12.'

The weight loss meant that all Patrick's Avenger suits had to be taken in at the seams to suit his sprightly figure.

Macnee's weight problem was not shared by the second newcomer to the show, Patrick Newell. His vital statistics were 50-50-50. Newell had been signed to play Mother, John Steed's superior. The introduction of Mother to the series was almost by accident.

Patrick Newell turned up at the studio (for what he believed was a one-off cameo spot) on 2 January 1968, on the set of Mother's headquarters, erected on Stage three at Elstree, just five days into the filming of *The Forget-Me-Knot*. The episode was shown in America on 20 March 1968, and the character of Mother was so successful that ABC telephoned Brian Clemens the next day and suggested that Newell be put under contract.

When I interviewed him, Patrick Newell gave me his own

hilarious version of events: 'I was sitting in the home of an actor friend of mine, when this taxi arrived with a script from *The Avengers* people. Having thumbed through its pages, I said to my friend: "Why this is absurd. There's no part in this for me – none at all. There's this woman's part called Mother, but I don't see any other." He suggested that they had perhaps sent along the wrong script. So I telephoned the studio and said: "What's all this then? Where is my part?" That's when they replied: "It's Mother – Mother is a man!" Oh lumme, I thought. So I went along and did the part and when I'd finished they said "Thanks very much, old boy. We may be bringing the character back again, so if you're free..." That was the last I heard of it until, during a party being given by Johnny Mortimer, I bumped into James Hill, the director I'd worked with on *The Avengers*. He said "Congratulations. Isn't it wonderful. You must be very pleased. It will do you a lot of good all over the world." As the evening crept on and other friends passed similar comments, I cornered James Hill to ask him what they were talking about. "*The Avengers*," he said. "Haven't you heard?" So the following morning I rang the studio and they said "Oh, we were going to tell you. It's the Americans. They seem to like your character, so we'd like you to come into the show permanently." So that's how it came about. The Americans picked up the phone and said "Get the fat guy!" Everyone had known apart from me!'

The character might well have been totally different if fate had not intervened. When interviewing actor Ken Parry (for reasons not entirely tied to this book), the subject turned to Ken's two appearances on the show, as Arbuthnot in the Blackman second season story *Death a la Carte*, and B Bumble in *Honey for The Prince*. Ken chatted merrily away for several minutes, then astounded me by saying that he might have been Mother, had he been free to accept the part. 'My agent was contacted to ask if I was available. Five or six times this happened. Quite by accident I had met an old friend of mine who had this friend with him whom I'd been in repertory with, Patrick Johns, who asked me if I'd do a pilot for Thames Television called *Horne A' Plenty*. From that pilot they asked me to do the series. Then my agent received another telephone call from ABC, who said, "We'd like to book Ken Parry." My agent told them that I was contracted to Thames. I later found out that it was for the part of Mother, in *The Avengers*! Apparently, someone at Thames had heard that they were looking for an actor for the role and he had sent a memo to Albert Fennell advising him to "look at the guy who played B Bumble". So I missed the part by a cat's whisker!' Ken isn't bitter about this, just unhappy that that's the way these things sometimes happen in the business. Oddly enough, throughout his entire career, Ken has been affectionately known by his friends and colleagues in the industry as Mother Parry.

Mother was crippled when he was blown up in the prime of

The Avengers *had two Irish barons on the team: Eammon Duffy (a second assistant) was one; Ray Austin became one through marriage. His title: Baron Devere-Austin, Lord of Bradwell!* *

his Secret Service career. Unable to walk without the aid of special straps and ladders suspended from the ceiling, and in constant pain from his injuries, he was not the kindest of men to work for. He often carried a stick, which he used as much to strike his colleagues as to support himself. Patrick Newell added: 'In the first one we did, *The Forget-Me-Knot*, I moved around the room swinging on these straps. But unfortunately, not knowing that it was going to be a permanent set, they'd broken it up and it would have cost too much to rebuild. So they came up with the idea of the wheelchair. It's a pity. I would have liked to have swung around more. That would have made the character more lively.' Mother was forever turning up in the strangest of places. In one story, *False Witness*, Steed boards a London bus and finds the upper level has been transformed into Mother's office. In another, he comes across the huge man and his telephones in the middle of a field of buttercups, and in a later story, Mother and his office equipment are floating in the middle of a swimming pool! (The idea was gradually phased out, due to the technical problems of achieving a good sound balance and the additional cost of post-synching the actors' voices.)

Patrick Newell told me: 'It was probably the best break of my career. I actually had a studio chair with "Mother" written on it – instead of my own name. It didn't bother me – I thought it was wonderful. Like Steed, Mother was terribly British. He spent most of his time drinking champagne out of silver tankards and saying things like "Good show, old boy". In addition, he was irascible, ruthless and had a dislike bordering on hatred for organisations like MI12 and MI15. He was a real character – the best I've ever played.'

Brian Clemens told me that he had originally created the character because he believed that they needed someone for Patrick Macnee to play off, to get some humour into the dialogue. 'Mother was a deliberate thing because at that time, Linda couldn't handle the humour. She would do so later of course, when she became more confident, but I couldn't take the chance at the beginning.'

Another semi-regular character (she didn't arrive until a third of the way through the series), was Rhonda, Mother's statuesque assistant. Her role came about by accident. Twenty-one-year old Rhonda Parker, a 6ft-tall Amazon with a 39-25-37 figure, was booked as an extra for the episode *All Done with Mirrors*. Her role called for her to walk onto the set in the scene where Steed finds his chief sitting in the swimming pool. The scene was set up, and Rhonda (wearing a white swimsuit) walked onto the set. As she arrived, Patrick Macnee and Patrick Newell stopped what they were doing and just gaped at her.

Patrick Newell told me, 'I remember that I was finding it extremly difficult to manipulate the wheelchair. I'd pick up these drinks and telephones and move around on fixed marks, which was proving very difficult – I'm a lousy driver. It was then

that Rhonda arrived on the set, so I said "Mother should have
a servant of sorts, a housekeeper or something. Well there you
are, she's different from the other girls, let's have her," and she
was put under contract that day. So poor Rhonda had to push
me around for the next year or so.'

There were no dialogue problems for Rhonda. She never
spoke. Fashion didn't trouble her. She was mostly seen wearing
white boxer shorts and tight-fitting sweaters!

One other member of the Secret Service department that
Steed worked for was introduced in the episode *Stay Tuned*. This
was Father. (Well, *someone* has got to look after the department
during Mother's absence.) Father was a middle-aged, blind colleague of Mother. She was more gentle than her opposite number, but just as perceptive – she only had to feel the lapel of
Steed's jacket to know he was using the same tailor. Father
appeared only once, and was played by actress Iris Russell

Steed's address in this series was changed to 3 Stable Mews,
but, with slight changes of decor, remained the same. With the
arrival of Tara, however, the production team really went to
town on her flat.

Set designer Kenneth Tait gave her a brand new apartment.
The flat, 9 Primrose Crescent, was a mixture of modern and
antique fashion design. It contained two primitive paintings,
two Chinese pendant lanterns and a collection of shop signs;
giant spectacles from an optician's; a giant boot from a bootmaker's; a padlock from a locksmith's (that hid a spy-hole in her
front door); a bearded bust of a Turk from a snuff and tobacco
shop; a wooden horse's head, from a French meat shop; plus
two giant goldplated letters, TK on one wall, and NO on another. A fireman's pole enabled her to get from her upper landing
to the ground at top speed.

The rooms were furnished with shocking-pink carpets; blue,
grey, mauve and imperial yellow panels; a couch in orange,
green and yellow, with curtains to match; and scatter cushions
in a mass of colours. There were a dozen period telephones –
through which Tara had to search when one of them rang. A
wooden postbox was converted into a drinks cabinet. There was
even a glass-panelled door with a stained-glass bird in it from an
old pub.

Director Robert Fuest explained that the apartment sets
were built in one tiny corner of the studio. 'They measured
about 20ft by 20ft. These were on the stage all the time, permanently, with the lights set to go on at a minute's notice, so that
if the weather was bad on location – and it usually was – the
crew could go back to the studio, Steed and Tara were redressed
and the crew shot a scene from another episode.' (The filming
schedule had always been that of shooting two episodes back-to-
back. On the Thorson series it was not unknown to have three
episodes running side by side in different sound stages or locations.) Brian Clemens said that this was done out of necessity.

The Avengers production crew, pictured on the set of Tara King's apartment, to celebrate the end of production. Seated in the front row are Patrick Macnee, Linda Thorson, Albert Fennell and Brian Clemens.

'You don't have four-walled sets in the studio. You always had to lose a wall to get the camera in and out. We'd try to get as many location shots in the can as was possible, then come into the studio for our interiors. It all comes down to practical things (like production schedule and cost). It's no good writing a beach scene in November. For a start you start to lose daylight at three-o'clock, then you have to get the Brute lamps out.'

Art director Bob Jones crossed over from the Rigg colour series – and sometimes wished that he had stayed at home! Having delivered a variety of intricate set pieces on the previous series, this time his inventiveness was stretched to the limit creating the bizarre – and sometimes seemingly impossible – props conjured up by the scriptwriters. These included giant, 14 foot, milk churns; a computer-controlled death factory to kill agents; a faithful reproduction of the Oval cricket ground at Kennington in 1880, with wickets, nets, pads, the lot. The effect of realism had to be achieved, no matter the cost.

The directors, too, had their creative talents severely stretched. Johnny Hough recalls the episode *All Done with Mirrors* as a case in point. Wanting to get a shot of Tara tumbling to her 'death' from the clifftop, he hired a cherrypicker crane, his intention being to anchor the truck securely to the edge of the cliff, swing the cherrypicker arm out from the cliff-face and photograph the heroin's fall in long-shot. He hadn't considered the weather. Having joined the cameraman in the crane's cradle seat, the two men were swung gently out to sea and Johnny lined up his shot. Then the cradle began to sway from side to side, gently at first, then quite wildly, in sweeping arcs high above the rocks. It didn't take long for them to realize that they were dicing with death. The shot was abandoned in favour of what appears on screen. (Incidentally, at that time the crew didn't have access to articulated dummies, so the 'Tara' who tumbles from the cliff was a dummy filled with straw.)

Once again the title theme music was revamped. It now started with a frentic staccato drumbeat and progressed to a more exuberant version of the familiar *Avengers* theme. Laurie Johnson explained the need for the change: 'We thought the new series ought to reflect the times we live in a bit more. So we generally jazzed it up, adding the sound of gunfire and a lot more percussion and brass. When Tara King came into the series, I decided to superimpose a counter melody over the existing title music at the point at which the face of the new character appeared on the main titles. This counter melody I then used and developed in the incidental score, where appropriate. Unlike many television series, *The Avengers* does not contain the same music throughout. In fact it is doubtful that anyone has even noticed the music that accents the action. If it has been noticed, then I haven't done my job well. Good scoring should be unobtrusive.' He also composed a new tag theme, called, appropriately enough, *Tag Theme*, for the closing segments of each episode, in which Steed and Tara were seen in a short, self-contained vignette.

As Brian Clemens recounts: 'I don't think anyone took a holiday, ever. We were totally involved during the whole run, sometimes working an 18-hour day. Success is a terrible monster because once the networks bought it, they wanted more – and quickly.' He recalls that they once had to cut, dub and music an episode in seven days, 'which sounds a lot, but it is really up against it because Laurie virtually scored every film – every episode – like you do in a movie. He used to pinch tiny little bits, but basically we sat down and pin-pointed where we wanted the music to be and he'd go away, write it, and then have a complete music session with an orchestra of sometimes 30 pieces or more.' Before the original producers returned to the show, John Bryce had planned to have Johnny Dankworth arrange and compose the music for the Thorson series. Dankworth would have revamped his original Blackman theme, and his wife, singer Cleo Laine, would have recorded a vocal version – to be called *Tara's Theme* – together with a special vocal 'stinger' that would have been added to the soundtrack during Tara's fight sequences.

As before, Albert Fennell remained quietly in the background – but continued to play an influential role in the production. Brian Clemens highlighted the fact that Fennell was probably one of the best film editors he has ever worked with – although he wasn't an editor. 'He would drive the editor mad. He would sit by his shoulder in the editing suite and stay there for hours trying to get, say, the sound of the right fly buzzing

The Avengers take a break during the filming of *Noon Doomsday*. Pictured left to right: Patrick Macnee, unknown script continuity girl, and, seated, Linda Thorson and her father.

and so on. I learned more about editing from Albert than I ever learned from an editor. People don't do that any more, not even on big movies. When we made *The Avengers*, we cared about what kind of fly it was and when it appeared – because we used sound effects to create our atmosphere. That was Albert's main thing.'

Laurie Johnson emphasised that Albert was far too busy working to share the limelight. 'He was always bringing in new elements – even during the actual shooting – but this was because the demands of his job didn't allow him to do it at the right time, which was up front, when he first set eyes on the script. In other words, if a script turned up which had to be filmed the very next week and Albert thought it didn't work, he would get in there and make it work, the rationale being that he had the knowledge to do the job. We would work from early morning and would still be at the office at Elstree or Pinewood until the late evening, and even when we went home, we would still be talking about certain sequences at 10 or 11 o'clock at night, on the telephone. This went on day after day, month after month, year after year, until it was second nature to us that whenever we looked at a piece of film, we would know what was wrong with it and didn't have to say what had to be done with it. It was as simple as that! Albert gave it class. He led and we followed his lead. He was a very remarkable man.'

Johnny Hough readily agreed, everyone loved Albert. 'Albert's main input was in not only harnessing, encouraging and maturing the talents of the directors, but the way that he harnessed the meteoric energy and wild ideas from Brian. Brian would come up with 20 different ways to solve something and 20 different ideas to shoot off at tangents with wondrous innovations. Albert would select the ones that were possible, the ones that one was able to knock into shape in a practical way, without losing the sort of ingenuity and innovativeness of Brian's original idea. Brian and Albert had offices side by side, and Brian would continually race into Albert's office and say: "Look. I've just thought of this. This is how it starts; we begin like this." Then, having thought of this marvellous opening, he would come back again with another idea. He might do this four or five times. Albert was the person who made the choice of which idea to go with. He would mould the idea and channel Brian's excellence into practicality. You had to be both innovative and administative to be able to do that. Albert would do this to the directors too. Once you were on board, he would give you every support and talk to you about why you did certain things in a scene after you had done them. He was a very creative person, but at the same time a strong administrator in terms of watching over the cost. There wasn't anything he didn't know about the practical side of film-making. He had good

The only one of Steed's colleagues to be single, Tara had a more open relationship with him.

taste. The whole of *The Avengers* is about Brian's innovation and Albert's good taste. He had good taste for class and quality.

'The other great thing about Albert was that he didn't want it cheap. He didn't even want it quick. So if you were the type of director who could shoot fast and quickly and finish on the floor at 4 o'clock instead of 6 o'clock and save Albert £600, he didn't want that – he wanted something clever, something that was beautifully photographed, something that you took your time over. He drew out the best in you in every way. He didn't want second class, he wanted first class – everytime. That filtered down all the way through the ranks. That was the kind of person he was. Each episode of *The Avengers* was treated as an individual film – and all were treated with loving care.'

Confirming what Brian Clemens had told me about Albert's editorial input, he described how Albert supervised the editorial content and the music on every show. 'Then, after that was finished, he would call Brian in and present his version of it. Brian would inject his own ideas and they would collaborate and come up with the finished product. Albert's creative contribution to *The Avengers* was enormous. If I had to say one thing, I would say that he harnessed Brian's considerable talents.'

Although the Thorson series was well received in Britain, and international sales had grossed over £18,000,000 – with Paris awarding the Macnee/Thorson partnership *Le Prix Triomphe* in 1970, the show's success was still dependent on it being accepted in America.

For some inexplicable reason, the American Broadcasting Company decided to screen the series in direct opposition to the immensely popular *Rowan and Martin's Laugh-In* shows, and for the first time, *The Avengers* met an unbeatable opponent – the American television audience ratings. Faced with such opposition, the show only managed to reach 69th position in the top 100 ratings. Soon after, ABC telephoned Clemens to say that they wouldn't require any further episodes of *The Avengers* after the 33 Thorson shows.

I asked Linda Thorson why *she* thought the show had failed. 'That's it exactly' she replied. 'We found ourselves in a no-win situation. The *Laugh-In* series was the biggest thing on American television at the time and we just didn't get the ratings. The spy thing was on the wane by then – although I believe that we could have gone on for say, another year, but the money wasn't there.' Would she have stayed on if the series had continued? 'Well, yes. I'd made 33 episodes and I would have been very happy to have done it for another year. I think Patrick was glad that it was all over, but I was in the swing of it. I was very sad that we went up in a rocketship in *Bizarre* and never came back.' (Steed came back of course. But what of Tara? As Linda told me recently: 'She's now a Space Cadet!')

Although *The Avengers* went on to become the single biggest foreign currency earner of any television series (a record it still

Opposite: Tara defends Steed's right to pursue his convalescence without interruption.
A scene from *Noon Doomsday*, filmed at Brian Clemen's Bedfordshire home.

holds today), Thames Television couldn't afford the cost of producing the show alone. The final story went before the cameras
on 16 February 1969. The studio lights were switched off and
The Avengers came to an (abrupt) end.

However, though the series was gone, it was never forgotten.
Thanks to syndication, cable and satellite television, the re-runs
just keep coming, and *The Avengers* is still playing on TV screens
throughout the world. As we shall see, interest in reviving the
series continues unabated.

SEASON SIX CHRONOLOGY

Episode	Title
1	Invasion of the Earthmen
2	The Curious Case of the Countless Clues (aka The Murderous Connection)
3	The Forget-Me-Knot
4	Split
5	Get-A-Way!
6	Have Guns – Will Haggle (aka Invitation to a Killing)
7	Look – (stop me if you've heard this one) But There Were These Two Fellers..
8	My Wildest Dream
9	Whoever Shot Poor George Oblique Stroke XR40?
10	You'll Catch Your Death (aka Atishoo, Atishoo, All Fall Down)
11	All Done with Mirrors
12	Super-Secret Cypher Snatch (aka Whatever Happened to Yesterday?)
13	Game
14	False Witness (aka Lies)
15	Noon Doomsday
16	Legacy of Death (aka Falcon)
17	They Keep Killing Steed
18	Wish You Were Here (aka The Prisoner)
19	Killer
20	The Rotters
21	The Interrogators
22	The Morning After
23	Love All
24	Take Me to Your Leader
25	Stay Tuned
26	Fog (aka The Gaslight Ghoul)
27	Who Was That Man I Saw You With?
28	Pandora
29	Thingumajig (aka It)
30	Homicide and Old Lace (aka The Great Great Britain Crime/Tall Story)
31	Requiem
32	Take-Over
33	Bizarre

Producers: Albert Fennell & Brian Clemens
Executive in Charge of Production: Gordon LT Scott
Consultant to the series: Julian Wintle (Episodes 129-138)
Production Controller: Jack Greenwood
Story Consultant:: Philip Levene (Episodes 129-140)
Script Editor: Terry Nation (Episodes 142-161)

Production Designer: Robert Jones
Music by: Laurie Johnson
Music Supervision by: Laurie Johnson
Score: Howard Blake
Music Editors: Karen Hewerd and Paul Clay

Invasion of the Earthmen:

a) *The cosmetic gun, with the lipstick in its barrel and compact in its butt, was originally mooted for Emma Peel, by Marie Donaldson, circa June 1965.*

b) *John Bryce had intended that Steed would forsake his beloved vintage modes of transport in favour of the AC Cobra he drives in this story. Stuntman Rocky Taylor road-tested the car, registered as LPH 800D by AC Cars on 20 November 1967. Immediately afterwards, one of the technicians discovered that someone had left a spare battery in the AC's boot. Acid had leaked from it, damaging the car's bodywork. Steed would never drive the car again – much to the relief of Patrick Macnee, who felt uncomfortable behind the wheel.*

c) *As filmed by Bryce and his time, the total running time of this episode (before editing) was 59.31!*

d) *Stunt co-ordinator Joe Dunne dislocated his shoulder in a mistimed fall.*

e) *Don Sharp directed both the original episode (and the additional filmed scenes required by Brian Clemens) with second unit director Johnny Hough as his assistant.*

Have Guns – Will Haggle:

a) *The Bryce-produced version commenced filming on 23 October 1967, under the direction of Robert Asher. The first day of production was delayed for 78 minutes when Steed's car failed to arrive at the location on time, Then numerous other delays plagued the production. Day four saw another delay when the Add-a-Vision camera broke down. The weather was so bad on day nine that the crew had managed to clock in just .39 seconds of usuable film! (A portent of what was to come.)*

b) *Cyd Child worked on all four Bryce episodes. She remembers those first few weeks as 'Awful! I came back and Joe Dunne asked me to visit the studio to see if I was a suitable double for Linda. I was. Those episodes looked terrible and they were never actually screened. I couldn't wait to get home at nights. They were horrible, so horrible that I just couldn't believe that it was going to last.'*

c) *Director Harry Booth filmed additional material for the remake on 6/7/8 February 1968 (including the scenes at the Ballistics Centre, the interiors of Tara's flat, the interior lift scenes, the phone box and exteriors of the open road), before Ray Austin took over the directorial chores on 14 February 1968.*

Look – (stop me if you've heard this one) But There Were These Two Fellers.....:

a) *Actor Bill Shine (playing Cleghorn) was struck on the head by a SFX club which was thicker than intended. He sustained a slight injury, but continued working.*

b) *Patrick Macnee was sent home unwell at 9.30am on day 14 of filming. He returned to the studio two days later.*

c) *A representative of British Oxygen was required on the set for the Oxyacetalyne Torch sequence.*

d) *Julian Chagrin is a famous mime artist. Linda Thorson later became his assistant during his stage show.* *

The Curious Case of the Countless Clues:

a) Fourth under the Bryce-production banner, this had been in production for two days when Clemens/Fennell returned to the fold – but the script was far removed from the episode as transmitted. Brian Clemens and Phil Levene expanded the idea and filming continued throughout December (back-to-back with The-Forget-Me-Knot*) with director James Hill and second unit director Johnny Hough, adding further footage at a location in Essendon, on 17 January 1968.*

b) This episode marked up the highest total in the running-stakes, with a staggering 75 minutes: 9 seconds pre-editing total in the can!

c) Linda Thorson recalls that when a rough cut of this episode was screened by ABC in America, they sent it back. 'They said that I had to re-dub the sound-track because I was breathing too heavily in the fight scenes and it sounded slightly orgasmic...'

SEASON SIX EPISODES

129 INVASION OF THE EARTHMEN

by Terry Nation

John Steed (Patrick Macnee) Tara King (Linda Thorson) Brett (William Lucas) Huxton (Christian Roberts) Emily Wade (Lucy Fleming) Bassin (Christopher Chittell) Rodney Trump (Warren Clarke) Sarah (Wendy Allnutt) Bernard Grant (George Roubicek)

Designed by Robert Jones
Directed by Don Sharp

Students at the Alpha Academy run by Commander Brett engage in mortal combat, and each winner is then kept in a cocoon, ready for when they can be re-activated to invade other planets. Steed and Tara stumble upon Brett's scheme, while searching for agent Bernard Grant who has gone missing. The Avengers gain entrance to the training college... however, getting out again proves to be a far greater problem. Returning to Tara's flat, Steed comes down to earth with a bump!

Filming completed: 21 November 1967
TX: 27 April 1969

130 THE CURIOUS CASE OF THE COUNTLESS CLUES

by Philip Levene

John Steed (Patrick Macnee) Tara King (Linda Thorson) Earle (Anthony Bate) Gardiner (Kenneth Cope) Stanley (Tony Selby) Sir Arthur Doyle (Peter Jones) Janice (Tracy Reed) Robert Flanders (Edward de Souza) Sir William Burgess (George A Cooper) Herbert Dawson (Reginald Jessup)

Designed by Robert Jones
Directed by Don Sharp

When Steed and Tara probe a death in Dulwich, they find that there are just too many clues. Earle and Gardiner specialize in frame-ups and murder, planned in minute detail. Disturbed by Steed's ability to detect the red herrings they have set up, Earle plans to frame Steed for the murder of Tara King. Steed tries to warn her, but Tara cartwheels to victory. Hurt in the melee, Steed ponders Tara's extensive gift – a yard of champagne in a special elongated glass.

Filming completed: 19 January 1968   TX: 18 May 1969

131 THE FORGET-ME-KNOT

by Brian Clemens

John Steed (Patrick Macnee) Emma Peel (Diana Rigg) Tara King (Linda Thorson) Sean Mortimer (Patrick Kavanagh) George Burton (Jeremy Young) Mother (Patrick Newell) Karl (Alan Lake) Simon Filson (Jeremy Burnham) Brad (Douglas Sheldon) Dr Soames (John Lee) Sally (Beth Owen) Taxi Driver (Leon Lissek) Jenkins (Tony Thawnton) The Gardener (Edward Higgins)

A shot taken during the filming of the first Thorson title credits.

The-Forget-Me-Knot:

a) Cyd Child scored a double in this episode. She doubled for both Diana Rigg and Linda Thorson in the glass factory fight sequences (and stood in for both women on the staircase cross-over scene, while director James Hill lined up his shot).

b) Diana Rigg worked a total of four days on the production. The scenes with Emma Peel were filmed on 14/15/18 December, her schedule ending at 5.10pm on 19 December, with the cross-over scene safely in the can.

c) Adverse weather conditions (snow) affected the filming and Patrick Macnee arrived almost two hours late on the location when his chauffeur-driven car was delayed.

*d) The brief meeting on the stairs was all we had time to shoot – and all we needed. *

e) The strap-hanging stuff for Mother was, in fact, my little homage to Michael Powell (a director who made many movies with an Avengers *touch to them) and his film* The Queen's Guards, *where a similar device was used. **

Designed by Robert Jones
Directed by James Hill

There seems to be a curious kind of amnesia about. Mortimer tells Steed that there is a traitor in Mother's organisation, but he cannot remember who it is. Mrs Peel also forgets what she learns and is then kidnapped. When Steed awakes, he has no memory of events either. He seeks the help of a new recruit, trainee agent 69, Tara King, and together they trace Karl and Brad to their hideout – the Glasshouse. The real traitor is George Burton who has developed memory-killing darts. With the help of Mrs Peel and Tara King, Steed overpowers the gang, though no one is quite sure why. Mrs Peel is still needed – by her husband – so she leaves Steed in the capable hands of Tara King.

The newspaper headline reads 'Peter Peel Alive. Air ace found in Amazonian jungle... Wife Emma waits.' With a peck on the cheek and the half-whispered words 'always keep your bowler on in times of stress – and a watchful eye open for diabolical masterminds', Emma walks out of Steed's life forever. Enter Tara King, who learns that Steed likes his tea stirred anti-clockwise. Tara enters Steed's apartment. 'Mother sent me,' she begins. 'Tara...'. 'Ra-boom-di-ay,' grins Steed.

Filming completed: 19 January 1968
TX: 12 January 1969

132 SPLIT

by Brian Clemens

John Steed (Patrick Macnee) Tara King (Linda Thorson) Lord Barnes (Nigel Davenport) Major Peter Rooke (Julian Glover) Dr Constantine (Bernard Archard) Hinnell (John G Heller) Petra (Jayne Sofiano) Boris Kartovski (Steven Scott) Frank Compton (Iain Anders) Swindlin (Christopher Benjamin) The Butler (John Kidd) Harry Mercer (Maurice Good)

Designed by Robert Jones
Directed by Roy Baker

Berlin, 1963. Steed shoots top enemy agent Boris Kartovski. Now, Steed finds that his own friends are killing each other – every man seems to exhibit the traits of the dead Kartovski. Dr Constantine saved Kartovski from dying and has now developed a method to transfer his evil thoughts into other people's minds. Steed's arrival at the Nullington Hospital ensures that Tara does not become the final victim of the evil doctor – but has Steed already been given the Kartovski treatment?

Filming completed: 1 February 1968
TX: 9 February 1969

133 GET-A-WAY!

by Philip Levene

John Steed (Patrick Macnee) Tara King (Linda Thorson) Colonel James (Andrew Keir) Rostov (Vincent Harding) Major Baxter (William Wilde) George Neville (Terence Longdon) Paul Ryder (Neil Hallett) Lubin (Robert Russell) Ezdorf (Peter Bowles) Professor Dodge (Peter Bayliss) Peters (John Hussey) Bryant (James Bellchamber) Magnus (Barry Linehan) Price (Michael Culver) Lt Edwards (Michael Elwyn)

> **Designed by Robert Jones**
> **Directed by Don Sharp**

Russian agents appear and disappear at will, causing Steed to consider whether they have perfected a new type of weapon. When a teetotaller sips vodka, Steed realises that the Lizard Brand contains exclusive ingredients – the power to make things invisible. Threatened with extinction by an unseen enemy, Steed gives himself a tonic and becomes a shadow of his former self. Becoming invisible, he trusses up the enemy and makes the problem disappear. Case concluded, it's curtains for Tara, while an invisible Steed plays havoc with her plans.

Filming completed: 15 February 1968   TX: 27 July 1969

134 HAVE GUNS – WILL HAGGLE

by Donald James

John Steed (Patrick Macnee) Tara King (Linda Thorson) Colonel Nsonga (Johnny Sekka) Adriana (Nicola Pagett) Conrad (Jonathan Burn) Spencer (Timothy Bateson) Crayford (Michael Turner) Lift Attendant (Robert Gillespie) Giles (Roy Stewart) Brad (Peter J Elliott)

> **Designed by Robert Jones**
> **Directed by Ray Austin**

Three thousand FF70 rifles have been stolen and their new owner, Adriana, plans to auction them off to the

Split:
a) Seven days into the production, Linda Thorson and stunt double Cyd Child's wigs mysteriously disappeared. No report was logged as to when/if these were returned. Replacement wigs were hastily refashioned by the Make-up Department. b) Once again the team filmed more material than required for a final cut. This time 57.02.

A rare production still showing director Ray Austin (pictured extreme left) lining-up the dueling sequence from *Have Guns – Will Haggle.*

highest bidder. Steed finds himself bidding against Colonel Nsonga; if he loses, the Colonel will get the guns and a target: Tara. Nsonga wins, so Steed and Tara take to their heels. In the grounds of Stokely House, they find the guns and seek an explosive solution to their dilemma. The ensuing bang disables their pursuers and Steed expects a gift from a grateful president. He receives it – but it is hardly a roaring success!

Filming completed: 29 February 1968
TX: 30 March 1969

135 LOOK – (STOP ME IF YOU'VE HEARD THIS ONE) BUT THERE WERE THESE TWO FELLERS...

by Dennis Spooner

John Steed (Patrick Macnee) Tara King (Linda Thorson) Maxie Martin (Jimmy Jewel) Jennings (Julian Chagrin) Bradley Marler (Bernard Cribbins) Marcus Pugman (John Cleese) Lord Bessington (William Kendall) Seagrave (John Woodvine) Brigadier Wiltshire (Garry Marsh) Miss Charles (Gaby Vergas) Cleghorn (Bill Shine) Sir Jeremy Broadfoot (Richard Young) Merlin (Robert James) Fiery Frederick (Talfryn Thomas) Tenor (Jay Denver) Escapologist (Johnny Vyvyan) Ventriloquist (Len Belmont)

Designed by Robert Jones
Directed by James Hill

Comic killings leave the Avengers unamused and searching for a clown that kills. At Greasepaint Grange, Mr Punch gives orders to murder each Director of the Capital Land and Development Company. Posing as Gentleman Jack, 'a smile, a song and an umbrella', Steed enters the variety artistes' rest home. He attends a briefing session and unmasks the puppet – it is Seagrave, one of the directors. That's all folks – unless you count Steed's this one, that one, change of evening attire.

Filming completed: 19 March 1968
TX: 23 March 1969

Steed gives killer clown Maxie Martin a red nose in this quick-change scene from Look - (stop me if you've heard this one) *...*

136 MY WILDEST DREAM

by Philip Levene

John Steed (Patrick Macnee) Tara King (Linda Thorson) Jaeger (Peter Vaughan) Tobias (Derek Godfrey) Lord Teddy Chilcott (Edward Fox) Nurse Owen (Susan Travers) Slater (Philip Madoc) Reece (Michael David) Paul Gibbons (Murray Hayne) Dyson (Tom Kempinski) Winthrop (John Savident) Aloysius Peregrine (Hugh Moxey)

Designed by Robert Jones
Directed by Robert Fuest

Frustrated executives vent their anger in the safety of Dr Jaeger's clinic, but the psychiatrist ensures that each dream becomes a reality. The real villain is Tobias, who has used the doctor to kill off the other directors of the Acme Precision Combine Limited, leaving him in total control of the Board. Steed is the only remaining obstacle and Jaeger brainwashes a jealous suitor of Tara – Chilcott – into killing her partner. Tara ensures that the villains are carpeted for their actions. In thanks, Steed explains his uncontrollable craving for champagne. He likes it!

Filming completed: 1 April 1968   TX: 7 September 1969

137 WHOEVER SHOT POOR GEORGE OBLIQUE STROKE XR40?

by Tony Williamson

John Steed (Patrick Macnee) Tara King (Linda Thorson) Jason (Dennis Price) Sir Wilfred Pelley (Clifford Evans) Loris (Judy Parfitt) Ardmore (Anthony Nicholls) Tobin (Frank Windsor) Baines (Adrian Ropes) Anaesthetist (Arthur Cox) Keller (Tony Wright) Jacobs (John Porter-Davison) Jill (Jacky Allouis) Betty (Valerie Leon)

Designed by Robert Jones
Directed by Cyril Frankel

Dr Ardmore attempts to save the memory banks of 'George', the super computer, after several attempts are made to destroy it. George's creator, Pelley, refuses to help and Tara infiltrates his household to discover whether he is a traitor. George recovers enough to reveal that Pelley is being interrogated to reveal military secrets and Steed rushes in to save Tara from a fiery fate. Steed is delighted with the result – until the recipe supplied by George for a new cocktail explodes in his face!

Filming completed: 17 April 1968   TX: 16 February 1969

My Wildest Dream:
a) The driver's door of the Volvo was scratched and became displaced from its hinges, and the wiring under the dashboard of the Rolls-Royce (KK 4976) caught fire. Two days later, the off-side bumper of a car hired from AC Cars was damaged during a location shoot in London's W9 district.
b) Concerned about the 'violence' in this episode, most ITV regions screened the episode late in the evening.

Whoever Shot Poor George Oblique Stroke XR40?:
a) Stuntwoman Lynn Marshall (hired as stand-in for actress Judy Parfitt) doubled for Linda Thorson in Tara's fight with Jason (Dennis Price) in the study and balcony of Pelley's home.
b) Harry Booth acted as supervizing director for the Computer Laboratory scenes.
c) Director Cyril Frankel is one of the world's leading experts on modern ceramics/pottery – and is employed by Sotherby's as a consultant. *

You'll Catch Your Death:
Stuntman Frank Maher doubled for Dudley Sutton (as Dexter) in the exterior of Mother's head-quarters scenes and the interior fight in Steed's apartment.

138 YOU'LL CATCH YOUR DEATH

by Jeremy Burnham

John Steed (Patrick Macnee) Tara King (Linda Thorson) Colonel Timothy (Ronald Culver) Butler (Valentine Dyall) Dr Glover (Fulton Mackay) Matron (Sylvia Kay) Mother (Patrick Newell) Dexter (Dudley Sutton) Preece (Peter Bourne) Dr Fawcett (Charles Lloyd Pack) Maidwell (Henry McGee) Ralph Camrose, FRCS (Hamilton Dyce) Farrar (Bruno Barnabe) Janice (Fiona Hartford) Seaton (Geoffrey Chater) Georgina (Jennifer Clulow) Melanie (Emma Cochrane) Padley (Willoughby Gray) Herrick (Andrew Laurence) Postman (Douglas Blackwell)

Designed by Robert Jones
Directed by Paul Dickson

Steed keeps Mother posted about events, as he dons a gas mask to discover what lethal weapon lies within an ordinary evelope. Each victim was an anti-allergy expert who could have found a cure for Dr Glover's new killer virus. When Tara is chosen as the guinea-pig for the final test, Steed gives the baddies a cold reception. Then he too catches a cold. Nurse Tara to the rescue!

Filming completed: 24 May 1968   TX: 2 February 1969

139 ALL DONE WITH MIRRORS

by Leigh Vance

John Steed (Patrick Macnee) Tara King (Linda Thorson) Watney (Dinsdale Landen) Major Sparshott (Peter Copley) Barlow (Edwin Richfield) Colonel Withers (Michael Trubshawe) Mother (Patrick Newell) Pandora Marshall (Joanna Jones) Miss Emily (Nora Nicholson) Carswell (Tenniel Evans) Miss Tiddiman (Liane Aukin) Seligman (Anthony Dutton) Kottridge (Peter Thomas) Markin (Graham Ashley) The Real Colonel (Michael Nightingale) The Real Barlow (Robert Sidaway) Guthrie (Desmond Jordan) Williams (David Grey) Arkin (Peter Elliott) Roger (John Bown)

Designed by Robert Jones
Directed by Ray Austin

Tara sheds some light on how secrets have been leaking from the Carmadoc Research Establishment, when she finds a retro-meter stashed in a lighthouse. Conversations are being carried along radio waves until they are recorded elsewhere. Certain key personnel have been kidnapped and replaced by impostors. Before Steed can answer her call for help, Tara takes steps to deal with the gang herself. Her reward is dinner with a difference – in the middle of a field of buttercups. Well, 'the simplest pleasures in life are the most enjoyable!'

Filming completed: 13 June 1968   TX: 2 March 1969

140 SUPER SECRET CYPHER SNATCH

by Tony Williamson

John Steed (Patrick Macnee) Tara King (Linda Thorson) Peters (John Carlisle) Maskin (Simon Oates) First Guard (Alec Ross) Jarret (Clifford Earl) Vickers (Donald Gee) Ferret (Ivor Dean) Betty (Anne Rutter) Myra (Angela Scoular) Second Guard (Lionel Wheeler) Davis (Anthony Blackshaw) Charles Lather (Nicholas Smith) Webster (Allan Cuthbertson) Wilson (David Quilter)

Designed by Robert Jones
Directed by John Hough

Mother gets in a lather when cypher codes are stolen from HQ, particularly since nothing unusual ever happens at the establishment. Classy Glass Cleaners specialize in government contracts and make it a habit to clean out their secrets under the very noses of the security guards and the people who work there, all of whom are conditioned to believe that it is just another working day. The Avengers prevail and ensure that nothing will go wrong in the future. If only the same could be said for Steed – who is hypnotized by Tara into taking her for an expensive dinner.

Filming completed: 14 June 1968   TX: 26 January 1969

141 GAME

by Richard Harris

John Steed (Patrick Macnee) Tara King (Linda Thorson) Bristow (Peter Jeffrey) Manservant (Garfield Morgan) Professor Witney (Aubrey Richards) Brigadier Wishforth-Brown (Anthony Newlands) Henry Averman (Alex Scott) Dexter (Geoffrey Russell) Student (Archillies Georgiou) Manager (Desmond Walter-Ellis) Cooty Gibson (Brian Badcoe)

Designed by Robert Jones
Directed by Robert Fuest

In 1946, five men court martialled Sergeant Daniel Edmund for black market activities. Now the disgraced soldier has returned with a new

All Done with Mirrors:
a) Linda Thorson lost her voice during the making of this episode. She continued filming under the supervision of the studio doctor.
b) Stuntman Jack Silk doubled for Ketteridge (Peter Thomas) in the cliff-top motorbike sequence. Stuntwoman Liz Mitchell doubled for Linda Thorson in some of the cliff-top scenes.
c) Patrick Macnee was on holiday for most of the filming.
d) This was the first time Linda Thorson didn't wear a wig.
e) Rhonda Parker's first (uncredited) appearance as 'Rhonda'.
f) This episode was Ray Austin's directing debut. In his youth, Ray was Cary Grant's chauffeur and bodyguard. As a stuntman, it is he who gets his head dunked into the stew in Spartacus; *he is one of the pilots in the plane that crashes in the famous cornfield sequence in* Hitchcock's North by Northwest. *He also choreographed musical spectaculars for ATV and is a knowledgable antiques dealer.* *

Noon Doomsday:

a) Actor TP McKenna fell from his horse. Brian Clemens drove him to the doctor. McKenna had slight concussion and two cracked ribs; but he returned to work that afternoon!

b) Linda Thorson burnt her hand when pulling a stuntman from the well. A nurse drove her to the doctor's surgery. Linda returned to the set.

c) The episode was shot at Brian Clemens' farm in Bedfordshire – where he still lives, and some of the barns still survive. *

e) There is a scene where TP McKenna and Ray Brooks cut some telephone wires – then drop down into the wheatfield below. The wheat was not high enough – so when they drop down they go to their knees to simulate the height of the wheat – and then exit the shot still on their knees. *

face for vengeance. Each tribunal member is now forced to play a macabre game where death is the only winner. When Tara is captured by the madman, Steed, one of the men who sentenced Edmund, discovers the killer's hideaway and is forced to play 'Super Agent' before he can rescue her. Luckily Steed has the edge. Later he stacks the odds in his favour when he tackles Tara in a game that he has invented, called 'Steedopoly'!

Filming complete: 25 June 1968   TX: 19 January 1969

142 FALSE WITNESS

by Jeremy Burnham

John Steed (Patrick Macnee) Tara King (Linda Thorson) Lane (Rio Fanning) Melville (Barry Warren) Brayshaw (John Atkinson) Penman (Peter Jesson) Lord Edgefield (William Job) Mother (Patrick Newell) Rhonda (Rhonda Parker) Dr Grant (Arthur Pentelow) Gould (Larry Burns) Little Man (Jimmy Gardner) Sloman (Dan Meaden) Sykes (John Bennett) Plummer (Michael Lees) Sir Joseph (Tony Steedman) Amanda (Terry Eliot) Nesbitt (Simon Lack)

Designed by Robert Jones
Directed by Charles Crichton

Steed discovers that two wrongs do make a right when Mother's department attempts to prosecute Lord Edgefield. Dreemy Kreem Dairies have ensured that no one can tell the truth – each bottle of milk they deliver contains a lying drug. Tara succumbs and is unable to pass her information to Steed, before being kidnapped and forced into a butter-making machine. Steed, however, drinks his coffee without milk, so he sees through the ruse and rounds up the dairymen. Free to try on her new dress, a bemused Tara is nonplussed when Steed is rude – but is that an half-empty glass of milk by his side?

Filming completed: 11 July 1968
TX: 23 February 1969

143 NOON DOOMSDAY

by Terry Nation

John Steed (Patrick Macnee) Tara King (Linda Thorson) Kyle Farrington (Ray Brookes) Norman Grant (TP McKenna) Sir Rodney Woodham-Baines (Griffith Jones) Roger Lyall (Lyndon Brook) Gerald Kafta (Peter Bromilow) Mother (Patrick Newell) Rhonda (Rhonda Parker) Perrier (Peter Halliday) Sunley (Anthony Ainley) Dr Hyde (John Glyn-Jones) Carson (David Glover) Cornwall (Lawrence James) Taxi Driver (Alfred Maron)

Designed by Robert Jones
Directed by Peter Sykes

An old enemy of Steed's drops in on the Avenger, while he is recovering in a rest-home for agents. As the clock ticks away, Tara finds that she is the only obstacle stopping Kafta, a man Steed sent to prison, from killing Steed. Using her gun to deadly effect, Tara mops up the would-be killers employed by Kafta to help him dispose of his enemy. Then Steed spearheads his own defence and despatches Kafta in a shoot-out at high noon. Steed's thanks to his partner for saving his life? His plaster leg cast – brimful of presents.

Filmed completed: 30 July 1968   TX: 16 March 1969

144 LEGACY OF DEATH

by Terry Nation

John Steed (Patrick Macnee) Tara King (Linda Thorson) Sidney Street (Stratford Johns) Humbert Green (Ronald Lacey) Baron Von Orlak (Ferdy Mayne) Dickens (Kynaston Reeves) Henley Farrer (Richard Hurndall) Zoltan (John Hollis) Ho Lung (Leon Thau) Gorky (Tutte Lemkow) Oppenheimer (Peter Swanwick) Slattery (Vic Wise) Winkler (Teddy Kiss) Dr Winter (Michael Bilton)

Designed by Robert Jones
Directed by Don Chaffey

Steed is puzzled to receive an ornate dagger and Tara tries to locate its origins. Numerous bounty hunters pursue the dagger, but every one dies as they attempt to retrieve the object. The Avengers solve the riddle – the dagger is the key to Henley Farrer's treasure, a fabulous black pearl. But Farrer is still alive, the legacy being but a trick by Farrer to get his enemies all under one roof. With the pearl up for grabs, the villains come out fighting. Steed and Tara dissolve their ambitions, then drink a toast with the world's most expensive glass of wine.

Filming complete: 9 August 1968   TX: 9 March 1969

145 THEY KEEP KILLING STEED

by Brian Clemens

John Steed (Patrick Macnee) Tara King (Linda Thorson) Baron Von Curt (Ian Ogilvy) Arcos (Ray McAnally) Zerson (Norman Jones) Captain Smythe (Bernard Horsfall) Mother (Patrick Newell) Verno (Arthur Howell) Golda (Bill Cummings) Smanoff (Frank Barringer) Bruno (William Ellis) with Hal Galili, Nicole Shelby, Rosemary Donnelly, Gloria Connell,

Legacy of Death:
a) The location schedule had to be revised when Tara's Lotus developed mechanical trouble, and refused to budge, losing the second-unit team two-hours of shooting.
b) This episode is, of course, a spoof on The Maltese Falcon. *Author Terry Nation – creator of the Daleks for* Doctor Who *– once wrote for Tony Hancock.* *

They Keep Killing Steed
a) Linda Thorson fell ill and was sent home. Away for five days, she returned to the studio before she was fit enough to continue filming. As a result she did post-synching on Noon Doomsday
b) Stuntman Paul Weston doubled for Steed 4... and Steed (the real one)... and 'Victim' Steed. Stuntman Cliff Diggins doubled for Steed 3... Steed (the real one) and Ray McAnally.
c) Actor Richard Bebb (the narrator's voice in Who's Who?*) supplied the (post-synced) voice for 'Victim' Steed. Actor Ronald Baddley supplied the voice for Mintoff Steed.*

Jennifer Croxton played Lady Diana Forbes-Blakeney in *Killer*. She had previously appeared as a photographer in the unseen Thorson story, *Invitation to a Killing*.

Michael Corcoran, Ross Hutchinson, Reg Whitehead, Anthony Sheppard, Angharad Rees, George Ghent

Designed by Robert Jones
Directed by Robert Fuest

Two Steeds threaten to cause explosive trouble at a peace conference, but which one is the real Avenger? The ploy backfires when Arcos and Zerson cannot distinguish between the real Steed and his duplicate. Only Tara seems able to spot the difference – the Avengers share a mutual taste for strawberry shortcake! It's time to sunbathe. Not on holiday – but in Tara's apartment!

Filming completed: 29 August 1968   TX: 6 April 1969

146 WISH YOU WERE HERE

by Tony Williamson

John Steed (Patrick Macnee) Tara King (Linda Thorson) Charles Merrydale (Liam Redmond) Maxwell Greene (Robert Urquhart) Basil Crighton-Latimer (Brook Williams) Parker (Dudley Foster) Mother (Patrick Newell) Stephen Kendrick (Gary Watson) Mellor (Richard Caldicot) Vickers (Derek Newark) James Brevitt (David Garth) Miss Craven (Louise Pajo) Mr

Maple (John Cazabon) Attractive Girl (Sandra Fehr) Rhonda (Rhonda Parker)

Designed by Robert Jones
Directed by Don Chaffey

A postcard from her uncle finds Tara visiting an unusual hotel – once they take up residence, the guests never leave. Mother sends his nephew, Basil, to assist, but he also succumbs and ends up red-faced when he fails to make good his escape. He nevertheless helps Tara to pan the opposition and Steed arrives to find that hotel manager Maxwell's plans have slipped-up. Tara slips up too when she is left holding the baby!

Filming completed: 12 September 1968
TX: 25 May 1969

147 KILLER

by Tony Williamson

John Steed (Patrick Macnee) Tara King (Linda Thorson) Lady Diana Forbes-Blakeney (Jennifer Croxton) Merridon (Grant Taylor) Brinstead (William Franklyn) Clarke (Richard Wattis) Mother (Patrick Newell) with Harry Towb, John Bailey, Michael Ward, James Bree, Michael McStay, Anthony Valentine, Charles Houston, Jonathan Elsom, Clive Graham, Oliver Macgreevy

Designed by Robert Jones
Directed by Cliff Owen

Agents from Mother's office are being tricked into a deadly rendezvous with a professional killer named Remak, a computer programmed for murder. Each body is carefully left in a graveyard, wrapped in plastic. With Tara away on holiday, Mother assigns Lady Diana, from Special Forces, to help Steed. Tracing Remak to Lower Storpington, Steed runs the gauntlet of the murder rooms and, together with Lady Diana, pulls the plug on the automated killer and its operator, Merridon. Back at his apartment, Steed finds Tara waiting for him with a big surprise, concealed in a small box...

Filming completed: 27 September 1968   TX: 4 May 1969

Killer:
a) Jennifer Croxton did the majority of her own stuntwork, with Cyd Child doubling for her in two sequences only: the fight in Wilkington's study and the sequences filmed on the village set. Croxton sprained her ankle doing the stunts. b) Michel Proudfoot holds the record for being the unluckiest man on the production team. Hospitalized for one night when stung by a wasp, he returned to the location shoot two days later and was this time hit by a car and hospitalized for eight days!

148 THE ROTTERS

by Dave Freeman

John Steed (Patrick Macnee) Tara King (Linda Thorson) Kenneth (Gerald Sim) George (Jerome Willis) Reginald Pym (Eric Barker) Palmer (John Nettleton) Mother (Patrick Newell) Rhonda (Rhonda Parker) with Frank Middlemass, Dervis Ward, Harold Innocent, Tony Gilpin, Amy Dalby, John Stone, Charles Morgan, Harry Hutchinson, Noel Davis, John Scott

Designed by Robert Jones
Directed by Robert Fuest

Tara finds that rotten deeds are rife in the Department of Forestry Research. Wainwright has turned against his old colleagues and perfected a fungi that turns wood into sawdust. Steed's investigations hit a low key when Kenneth and George dissolve a piano which falls on the Avenger, while the men escape. The roof caves in on Tara while she is hiding in a hut. Tracking the rotters to Wainwright's headquarters, armed with a captured spray gun, Steed brings the plans of the villains crashing down around their feet. Back at home, Tara confesses that she has forgotten to buy the mushrooms for Steed's gourmet meal. He grins and produces a giant fungi grown by Professor Palmer.

Filming completed: 8 October 1968   TX: 20 April 1969

149 THE INTERROGATORS

by Richard Harris and Brian Clemens

John Steed (Patrick Macnee) Tara King (Linda Thorson) Colonel Mannering (Christopher Lee) Minnow (David Sumner) Lieutenant Roy Caspar (Philip Bond) Mother (Patrick Newell) Blackie (Glynn Edwards) Rasker (Neil McCarthy) Mullard (Neil Stacy) Norton (Neil Wilson) Mr Puffin (Cardew Robinson) Captain Soo (Cecil Cheng) Naval Officer (Mark Elwes) RAF Officer (David Richards)

Designed by Robert Jones
Directed by Charles Crichton

Tara becomes the latest victim of a clever scheme to extract secret information from agents. Believing they are on a training course, the agents are interrogated by the opposition. Steed follows Tara to the interrogation establishment, but is astounded to find that the duped agents have orders to eliminate him; merit points will be awarded to the agent who shoots him with pistols, which they believe are loaded with blanks. Tara leapfrogs to his rescue and Colonel Mannering is exposed. Steed now interrogates Tara, for the vital ingredient of her home-made soup.

Filming completed: 22 October 1968   TX: 13 April 1969

150 THE MORNING AFTER

by Brian Clemens

John Steed (Patrick Macnee) Tara King (Linda Thorson) Merlin (Peter Barkworth) Jenny Firston (Penelope Horner) Brigadier Hansing (Joss Ackland) Sergeant Hearn (Brian Blessed) Major Parsons (Donald Douglas) Yates (Philip Dunbar) Cartney (Jonathan Scott)

Designed by Robert Jones
Directed by John Hough

Steed plans to take the charming spy, Merlin, into custody, but events backfire when Merlin uses a sleep capsule as a method of escape. Steed and Merlin awake to find a day has passed and a state of martial law has been declared. The population must be evacuated because of the threat of a nuclear bomb. Brigadier Hansing has created the ruse to overthrow the government, using troops loyal to him. Steed and Merlin mount a combined attack and put the opposition to sleep and order is restored. Tara awakes and asks if anything exciting has happened. It has and will do so again – when Steed opens the gift left on his doorstep by Merlin.

In *The Morning After* Steed and super-spy Merlin wake to find London deserted and under martial law.

Filming completed: 5 November 1968 TX: 11 May 1969

Love All:
a) Director Peter Sykes accidentally damaged Steed's Rolls-Royce when demonstrating how he wanted Patrick Macnee to play the scene.

151 LOVE ALL

by Jeremy Burnham

John Steed (Patrick Macnee) Tara King (Linda Thorson) Martha (Veronica Strong) Nigel Bromfield (Terence Alexander) Sir Rodney Kellogg (Robert Harris) Mother (Patrick Newell) Thelma (Patsy Rowlands) with Brian Oulton, Frank Gatliff, Ann Rye, Zulema Dene, Peter Stephens, Norman Pitt, John Cobner, Robin Tolhurst, Larry Taylor, David Baron.

Designed by Robert Jones
Directed by Peter Sykes

Lovestruck public servants pose a security risk for the Avengers, so Steed visits the Casanova Ink Company to meet Rosemary Z Glade. The romantic novelist is a computer, but the novels she writes contain a hypnotic pattern of microdots – the reader falls in love with the first person they meet. With Tara under their spell and heading for a fall, Steed sees to it that love conquers all and affectionately takes the love merchants into custody. Seeing Steed when she awakens from her hypnotic trance, Tara takes a back seat for his affections – Steed's Rolls is full of female admirers!

Filming completed: 18 November 1968
TX: 13 July 1969

152 TAKE ME TO YOUR LEADER

by Terry Nation

John Steed (Patrick Macnee) Tara King (Linda Thorson) Colonel Stonehouse (Patrick Barr) Mother (Patrick Newell) Captain Tim (John Ronane) Cavell (Michel Robbins) Major Glasgow (Henry Stamper) with Penelope Keith, Hugh Cross, Elisabeth Robillard, Michael Hawkins, Sheila Hammond, Bryan Kendrick, Raymond Adamson, Mathew Long, Cliff Diggins, Wilfred Boyle.

Designed by Robert Jones
Directed by Robert Fuest

The Avengers' next case proves difficult to penetrate. A briefcase full of secrets and money can only be opened by its intended owner, so Steed and Tara must follow the container until contact is made. Tara follows a false trail and almost pays with her life and Steed is surprised when the case is returned to Mother: there must be a traitor within his own team. With Stonehouse identified, Tara ensures that the traitor wins the booby prize. Enter a dog, Fang, with a talking briefcase – which appears to be unable to stop rattling!

Filming completed: 29 November 1968
TX: 15 June 1969

153 STAY TUNED

by Tony Williamson

John Steed (Patrick Macnee) Tara King (Linda Thorson) Proctor (Gary Bond) Lisa (Kate O'Mara) Mother (Patrick Newell) Father (Iris Russell) Wilks (Duncan Lamont) Collins (Howard Marion-Crawford) Sally (Denise Buckley) Kreer (Roger Delgado) Dr Meitner (Harold Kasket) Travers (Ewan Roberts) Taxi Driver (Patrick Westwood)

Designed by Robert Jones
Directed by Don Chaffey

Has Steed returned from a holiday he can never forget or has he never left? A strong sense of déjà-vu takes Steed to Kreer's house, where he has indeed been kept in captivity and brainwashed over the previous three weeks. To allay Father's worries, Tara has also been keeping an eye on Steed, and she foils Kreer's plan to trick Steed into killing Mother. Safe at last, Steed is no longer a shadow of his former self. When Tara performs the holiday ritual previously enacted by her partner, Steed offers her a holiday in the sunshine. Tara turns it down...!

Filming completed: 13 December 1968   TX: 8 June 1969

Take Me to Your Leader:
a) *The motorbike driven by the character called Trent; and the bubble car driven by the stuntman doubling for Steed, were badly hit in the stunt driving sequence. The studio picked up the tab for repairs.*
b) *The judo men in the Judo Room sequence were played by: Alf Joint, Joe Cornelius, Nosher Powell and Terry Plummer, stuntmen all.*
c) *The dog in the episode was named Toby*
d) *The voice of the briefcase was that of actor Harvey Hall*

Stay Tuned:
Stuntwoman Dorothy Ford doubled for Kate O'Mara

Opposite: All this hanging around is killing me. A scene taken on the set of *Love All.* The man with his arms around Linda Thorson is stunt double Paul Weston.

Fog:
a) The horse pulling the hansome cab was named Planet. The mare was paid £41 for its services, the handler £30.
b) Damage was caused to the Ridge Village green by the unit transport. The studio picked up the tab for the landscaper's fee.

154 FOG

by Jeremy Burnham

John Steed (Patrick Macnee) Tara King (Linda Thorson) Sir Geoffrey Armstrong (Nigel Green) Mark Travers (Guy Rolfe) Mother (Patrick Newell) Carstairs (Terence Brady) Sanders (Paul Whitsun-Jones) Maskell (David Lodge) Fowler (Norman Chappell) with David Bird, Frank Sieman, Patsy Smart, Virginia Clay, John Garrie, Bernard Severn, Frederick Peisley, Stan Jay, Arnold Diamond, William Lyon Brown, John Barrard

Designed by Robert Jones
Directed by John Hough

Murders in the mist alert Steed to the possibility that the Gaslight Ghoul has returned and is killing anew. Two foreign delegates in London for a disarmament conference have already got the point. Steed visits the Gaslight Ghoul Club and finds that Travers, the club secretary, is an arms dealer who would benefit from the conference being wrecked. Travers' attempts to deflect him from the truth have failed. But what of Mother? He's not too far away – as Steed and Tara soon discover!

Filming completed: 31 December 1968   TX: 23 June 1969

Roger Moore (ITC's *The Saint*) was a frequent visitor to *The Avengers*.

155 WHO WAS THAT MAN I SAW YOU WITH?

by Jeremy Burnham

John Steed (Patrick Macnee) Tara King (Linda Thorson) Fairfax (William Marlowe) General Hesketh (Ralph Michael) Gregor Zaroff (Alan Browning) Gilpin (Alan MacNaughtan) Mother (Patrick Newell) Dangerfield (Alan Wheatley) Phillipson (Bryan Marshall) Miss Culpepper (Aimee Delamain) Perowne (Richard Owens) Kate (Nita Lorraine) Hamilton (Ralph Ball) Powell (Ken Haward) Pye (Neville Marten)

Designed by Robert Jones
Directed by Don Chaffey

Dangerfield and Zaroff manufacture enough circumstantial evi-

dence to cast doubts on Tara's loyalty. She is suspended from her current assignment – to check the security arrangements guarding The Field Marshall, a vital piece of military equipment. Steed boxes clever to expose the real villains and Tara is reinstated. Dangerfield's ploy to force Mother into de-activating The Field Marshall has failed. Back home, Steed assembles a tower of champagne glasses then proposes a toast to his colleague, whom he never, ever, suspected of funny business – well, almost never!

Filming completed: 10 January 1968
TX: 31 August 1969

156 PANDORA

by Brian Clemens

John Steed (Patrick Macnee) Tara King (Linda Thorson) Mother (Patrick Newell) Rupert Lasindall (Julian Glover) Henry Lasindall (James Cossins) Murray (Reginald Barrett) Juniper (John Laurie) Miss Faversham (Kathleen Bryon) Hubert Pettigrew (Anthony Roye) Uncle Gregory (Peter Madden) Carter (Geoffrey Whitehead) Xavier Smith (Reginald Barrett) Young Gregory (Raymond Burke)

Designed by Robert Jones
Directed by Robert Fuest

The Lasindall brothers plot to defraud their senile uncle of his hidden treasure. To convince him that his bride, Pandora, is still alive, they kidnap Tara and force her to play the role. Overwhelmed with joy, Gregory points to the treasure, but the Lasindalls destroy the priceless Rembrandt while searching for the wealthy stache. Enter Steed to save Tara from playing the dummy. Tara's headache might be over, Steed's is just about to begin – when he clocks the present Tara has left for him....!

Filming completed: 17 January 1969
TX: 10 August 1969

157 THINGUMAJIG

by Terry Nation

John Steed (Patrick Macnee) Tara King (Linda Thorson) Inge Tilson (Dora Reisser) Teddy (Jeremy Lloyd) Kruger (Iain Cuthbertson) Professor Truman (Willoughby Goddard) Major Star (Hugh Manning) Dr Grant (John Horsley) Brett (Edward Burnham) Stenson (Vernon Dobtcheff) Pike (Russell Waters) Phillips (Michael McKevitt) Williams (Neville Hughes) Greer (John Moore) Bill (Harry Shacklock)

Who Was That Man I Saw You With?:
a) Because her limousine broke down, Linda Thorson arrived at the studio three hours late. The day's schedule was re-arranged, with three cast members, William Marlowe, Alan Wheatley and Nita Lorraine and their stand-ins called, but not used. This meant an additional day's shooting at extra cost.
b) Holding the record as the 'fittest man' on the production team: Production Manager, Ron Fry, who lost not one day's absence due to illness!
c) Second fittest man (and proud of it): Assistant Director Ron Purdie, with just one day's absence due to a tummy bug.
d) Fairfax's car (an Austin 3 litre) hit the MG being used on a location shoot, then was itself damaged when the camera team marked the car's roof during the setting up of the camera inside the Austin.

Pandora
*This is one of Linda Thorson and Brian Clemens' favourite episodes. *

Thingumajig:

a) Whatever they contained, the 'boxes' certainly cast a spell on Linda Thorson. She caught a heavy cold while on location and was absent from the production for five days. She returned to the studio during the production of Requiem, *and was required to work overtime filming her role in that episode and doubling-up on* Thingumajig.

b) Actor Jeremy Lloyd was briefly married to Jo Lumley. He went on to write Are You Being Served? *and* 'Allo, 'Allo, *and then to appear in* The Avengers *stage play. In between he wrote for* Rowan and Martin's Laugh-In, *which eventually caused* The Avengers *to be cancelled!* *

Homicide and Old Lace:

'It just didn't make any sense,' says Brian Clemens, talking about the original episode, produced by John Bryce under the direction of Vernon Sewell. 'When we cut this together, it just didn't work. If this one had been submitted to me, I wouldn't have accepted it – it was science fiction, without

Designed by Robert Jones
Directed by Leslie Norman

In the catacombs of an ancient church, something stirs and it kills.... The Avengers get a shock when two electrical killers begin to exterminate an archaeological team. The boxes, invented by Kruger, release a deadly discharge of electrical energy. One of them has been received by Tara, the other is tracked by Steed to the catacombs. The Avengers box clever and throw some water in the works. Well, champagne actually! Later electrical fuzz affects Steed's TV set and Tara is given a precarious mission.

Filming completed: 21 January 1969   TX: 1 August 1969

158 HOMICIDE AND OLD LACE

by Malcolm Hulke and Terence Dicks

John Steed (Patrick Macnee) Tara King (Linda Thorson) Mother (Patrick Newell) Harriet (Joyce Carey) Georgina (Mary Merrall) Colonel Corf (Gerald Harper) Dunbar (Keith Baxter) Fuller (Edward Brayshaw) Rhonda (Rhonda Parker) with Donald Pickering, Mark Landan, Kristopher Kum, Bari Jonson, Stephen Hubay, Bryan Mosley, Gertan Klauber, Kevark Malikyan, John Rapley, Anne Rutter

Designed by Robert Jones
Directed by John Hough

Mother celebrates his birthday by sharing 'five fingers of old red eye' with his aunts, Harriet and Georgina. He relates the story of the Great Great Britain Crime: Steed was pitted against Intercrime once again as they plotted to steal every art treasure in the UK. Colonel Corf, head of security is fooled into helping the gang collect the booty, but the Avengers triumph after a game of hide-and-seek. Afterwards, Steed and Tara join Mother and Rhonda for a celebratory toast. But who puts the words into Rhonda's mouth?

Filming completed: 21 January 1969   TX: 6 July 1969

159 REQUIEM

by Brian Clemens

John Steed (Patrick Macnee) Tara King (Linda Thorson) Miranda (Angela Douglas) Firth (John Cairney) Wells (John Paul) Mother (Patrick Newell) Murray (Denis Shaw) Rista (Terence Sewards) Barrett (Mike Lewin) Jill (Kathja Wyeth) Bobby (Harvey Ashby) Vicar (John Baker) Rhonda (Rhonda Parker)

Designed by Robert Jones
Directed by Don Chaffey

Steed babysits Miranda, a star witness in an on-going trial. Meanwhile, Tara, recovering from multiple injuries, mourns the passing of Mother. Major Firth appeals to Tara to tell him how to contact Steed. It is vital that he be informed. He too is in danger: his gold pencil contains a bomb. But Tara cannot remember. When her memory is jogged, she discovers that her injuries are a trick. Firth and his medical team are impostors intent on tracking down Steed in order to dispose of him. But Rhonda turns heroine and ensures that Steed and Miranda survive. A good job too. Otherwise Steed would never have discovered that he has royal blood coursing through his veins!

Filming completed: 13 February 1969
TX: 17 August 1969

160 TAKE-OVER

by Terry Nation

John Steed (Patrick Macnee) Tara King (Linda Thorson) Grenville (Tom Adams) Laura (Elizabeth Sellars) Bill Bassett (Michael Gwynn) Circe (Hilary Pritchard) Sexton (Garfield Morgan) Lomax (Keith Buckley) Groom (John Comer) Clifford (Anthony Sagar)

Designed by Robert Jones
Directed by Robert Fuest

Steed arrives at Bill Bassett's house to wish him a February Christmas, but finds him held captive by Grenville and his gang. With tiny phosphor-bombs implanted in their throats, the Bassetts cannot prevent a rocket gun being trained on Critchley Manor. Grenville attempts to kill Steed, and the Avenger tricks them into thinking that he is dead. Unable to warn Tara that she is walking into a trap, Steed catapults himself into a full recovery and becomes a pain in Grenville's neck. Back in his apartment, Steed plays invisible golf and Tara has a smashing time convincing him that she knows how to swing a club.

Filming completed: 21 February 1969
TX: 24 August 1969

161 BIZARRE

by Brian Clemens

John Steed (Patrick Macnee) Tara King (Linda Thorson) Helen Pritchard (Sally Nesbitt) Captain Cordell (James Kerry) Jonathan Jupp (John Sharp)

an redeeming spookiness to carry it off. There had to be a "twist" in our endings, this episode didn't have one.' So he invented the framing device, and Johnny Hough, second unit director on the original version, was handed the task of knocking this one into a usable format. The director had plenty to work with, the original episode was 63 minutes, 43 seconds in duration!

Requiem:
Actor John Cairney's voice was indistinguishable from that of James Mason. Some say he dubbed the famous actor on occasion. *

Bizarre
a) Helen Pritchard (played by Sally Nesbitt) was doubled in the fall from the train by stuntman Roy Scammell.
b) Director Leslie Norman was the father of Barry Norman. He directed and produced films: The Cruel Sea, Mandy, *etc. And, as an editor, was the first British person to cut sound film, for Hitchcock's* Blackmail. *

Bagpipes Honeychap (Roy Kinnear) Mother (Patrick Newell)   Tom (Michael Balfour) Bob (Patrick Connor) Mrs Jupp (Sheila Burrell) Shaw (Georg Innes) Charley (Ron Pember) The Master (Fulton Mackay)

Designed by Robert Jones
Directed by Leslie Norman

'A dead man who isn't dead.' An unlikely case of reincarnation leads Steed to a cemetery where people are dying to get into Happy Meadows. A fake fakir offers a package holiday straight to the Paradise Plot in Happy Meadows, for a price. Steed arranges his burial and awakens to the sound of music and dancing. When a distraught Tara has his coffin exhumed and finds the box empty, paradise turns sour for the grave tricksters. Their mission complete, Steed and Tara find themselves unwitting passengers on a rocket voyage.

Filming completed: 3 March 1969   TX: 14 September 1969

How *Bizarre*. A rare production still show-ing Tara escorting the 'dead' from a grave in Happy Meadows Cemetry.

Watching the rocket beginning its ascent, Mother turns to the camera and addresses the viewers:
'They'll be back .... you can depend on it!'

THE END?

THE NEW AVENGERS

Twenty-six colour filmed episodes starring

PATRICK MACNEE, GARETH HUNT, JOANNA LUMLEY   **1976/77**

PRODUCTION HISTORY

A FTER THE FAILURE of the stage production (it closed after only six weeks), *The Avengers* went into television limbo – at least as far as the British television channels were concerned, with only Channel 4 giving the filmed series an airing in 1983-84. It did, however, continue to appear on American television screens at regular intervals. Some stations even showed all the eighty-three filmed episodes on eighty-three consecutive nights, while others screened four episodes a day!

Six years passed, then, in 1975, Albert Fennell and Brian Clemens received a call from a French television and film executive, Rudolph Roffi, asking if Patrick Macnee and Linda Thorson were available to do a television commercial for

A memo pinned to the wall in the Toronto studio said: 'Fake champagne should be carried at all times for Steed.'

The New Avengers came about after Frenchman, Rudolph Roffi, engaged Patrick Macnee and Linda Thorson to do a television commercial for Perrier Jouet champagne.

Casting for the roles of Gambit and Purdey took place on 20 January 1976, at Pinewood Studios. Courtesy of Brian Clemens, this is the list of names, some famous, of people who were interviewed / auditioned on that date, and made the shortlist for the second day, on 27 January. In no particular order of merit, they were: The Ladies: Jan Harvey, Carolyn Seymour, Jan Francis, Barbara Kellerman, Prunella Gee, Geraldine Moffatt, Sara Douglas, Trudie van Doorn, Louise Jameson, Joanna Lumley, Lisa Harrow, Cassandra Harris, Diane Weston, Rula Lenska, Diana Quick, Gabrielle Drake, Ann Zelda, among others. The Men: David Rintoul, Malcolm Stoddard, John Nettles, Gareth Hunt, Lewis Collins, Harry Meacher, Tommy Boyle, Ian Charleson, Michael Elphick. The following did film tests: Ann Zelda, Joanna Lumley, Cassandra Harris, Diana Quick, Gabrielle Drake, Lewis Collins, Gareth Hunt, Harry Meacher.

Perrier Jouet champagne, to be shown on French television (Linda Thorson was a big name in France at the time).

Linda was contacted, as was Patrick Macnee, as a sort of tribute to *The Avengers*, and the commercial was made at Elstree Studios during the summer of 1975.

Six months after the commercial played on French television, Roffi, having discovered that *The Avengers* was no longer in production, rang Clemens to ask why. Explaining that, although he and Albert Fennell had always believed that the show would one day reappear (the reason Clemens had kept their options open by having Steed and Tara shot into space: 'What goes up, must come down – eventually'), Clemens told the Frenchman that they had been unable to interest any British company in financing a new production, which would cost over £2,000,000 to produce. In the event, it would cost at least double that sum.

A few weeks later, Clemens received a second call from France. It was Roffi, saying: 'I have the money. When can we start production?' Within three hectic months, Clemens, Fennell and ex-*Avengers* music arranger, Laurie Johnson, had formed The Avengers (Film & TV) Enterprises Ltd. – at the time the only truly independent TV company in the UK – in association with IDTV Paris. Plans were formulated to produce a new series of twenty-six films under the name of *The New Avengers* (they couldn't use the original series title because it was copyrighted to that series.)

Aware that it would be difficult to mount any new *Avengers* series without the presence of the stalwart Avenger, Patrick Macnee (as Clemens told the press at the time, 'Avenger girls can come and go, but if Patrick Macnee fell down a manhole tomorrow, it would be the end of *The Avengers* for good'), Clemens rang the ex-Avenger at his Hollywood home. At first, Macnee was hesitant to accept. He thought it was some gigantic joke and asked for more time to consider the offer.

Macnee asked them to send a script. They never did. But, believing that he was still young enough and energetic enough to play a recognizable Steed, and convinced that he had something more to contribute to the role, he had decided within two weeks to face the challenge. (When he was first cast in the role in 1960, he was a swashbuckling 38. Now he was 54.)

Finding a new *Avengers* girl to step into the boots vacated by Honor Blackman, Diana Rigg and Linda Thorson was to prove as daunting as any of the cases investigated by Steed. Brian Clemens has vivid memories of the time. 'We interviewed something like 300 girls. From that original list, I produced a shortlist of about 20 names. We tested about 10.' (His original handwritten and typed casting sheets show that 19 actresses made the shortlist for the role of the *Avengers* girl, and eight actors were considered for Gambit. See margin notes.)

One of the hopefuls was Joanna Lumley, who had previously been turned down for the part of Hannah Wild, in the stage

play. 'It was difficult getting to meet them,' she told me, 'because they apparently didn't want me. It took forever just getting into the audition. I tried very, very hard for it because I wanted to do it. I couldn't believe it when I heard I had landed the part.'

Brian Clemens remembers things differently. 'About a year before this, Jo had been in one of the *Doctor Phibes* movies, a tiny part, playing a nurse. I'd got to know her on the set and thought that she was a very entertaining lady – brilliantly funny, with a male sense of humour. When we started auditioning the girls for *The New Avengers*, I told Albert that I would like Jo Lumley, but we agreed to test all the girls just in case...' He recalls that his agent sent a girl along to the auditions. She was very good and looked a likely candidate to land the part – until they discovered that she had the most terrible laugh. 'So in the end we settled for the person I'd wanted right at the beginning: Jo Lumley. The interesting thing about the auditions is that we put a girl and a boy opposite each other and it was purely coincidental that Gareth Hunt tested opposite Jo. We took both of them.'

Steed and his new partners pose for photographers at the press reception to launch *The New Avengers*.

Gareth Hunt told me that he played a scene written by Clemens. 'It was really like an excerpt from one of the shows. I recall a funny moment when Joanna and I sat on one of the ornate tables they were using in the test, and broke it – but that wasn't in the script. Luckily we were both chosen for the series.'

At the time the media were reporting that one of the original *Avengers* ladies was being courted to return to the series. Brian Clemens made light of the fact that they encouraged this sort of thing. 'The thing about *The Avengers* was that our publicity machine was ever so good. We always had a huge launch when looking for the girl. A launch when we had found the girl, then, after letting a little bit of time go by, dressing the girl. So *The*

Avengers – at least in this country, before it came on screen – was always in the ether; it was always in everybody's mind; they were all waiting to see that first episode. We handled that very well.' (As we'll learn later, this time around the cogs of the publicity machine had lost some of their bite.)

On 8 March 1976, Nigel Dempster's Diary page in the *Daily Mail* carried this:

JOANNA SCOOPS THAT SUPER-ROLE AS STEED'S AVENGERS SUPER GIRL....
'With aspiring hopefuls still clamouring for the female lead in the new *Avengers* series, which starts production next month, I can reveal that the role has now been filled. The debby-voiced Miss Joanna Lumley, 29, has been chosen to take over the part pioneered by Honor Blackman and subsequently inherited by Diana Rigg and Linda Thorson.'

Originally, the new *Avengers* girl was to have been called Charly, but before filming, Clemens discovered that there was a perfume of that name on the market. Not wishing to spend lavish amounts of money endorsing another company's product, the name was changed. Joanna is credited with suggesting the name Purdey – after the most revered and expensive gun in the world.

Before filming started, Clemens told the media: 'Purdey will be a stockings and suspenders girl – giving lots of glimpses of thigh. She will be tough, yet vulnerable, with a huge sense of humour. The *Avengers* girls will have gone full circle with Joanna. So much so that she won't have to burn her bra – she can put it back on.'

It's not too surprising, then, that male viewers waited with bated breath (and eager anticipation) for their first glimpse of Steed's new Girl Friday. Reality, however, isn't always that simple or – in the case of television hype – is seldom what we'd been led to believe. Although it soon became obvious to the more discerning viewer that Miss Lumley was indeed wearing 'single hose', regular views of stocking-tops and suspender tabs were all too conspicuous by their absence – with only the rooftop-climbing scenes in *Target*, and the titillating close-up of Purdey's black stocking-tops in *To Catch a Rat*; allowing the onlooker a clear (though all too brief) glimpse of thigh. Mind you, in fairness to Joanna Lumley, neither she nor her clothes designer, Catherine Buckley, were happy about this before filming started. As Joanna told me: '*They* said she was going to be a stockings and suspenders girl. I said that if she was *the* most effective sleuth in the world, or part of some enormous Secret Service, then she would *have* to wear efficient and sportsman-like clothes. So it was filtered out, because when climbing over a barbed-wire fence or shimmying up a drainpipe and scaling a roof while wearing high heels and suspenders... well, *I* had to do it and it was lucky I didn't break my ankle.'

Purdey as she might have been – before Joanna Lumley visited John Frieda's hair salon and emerged with her world famous Purdey bob.

At the time, Joanna was sporting a mane of long blonde hair. Before filming began, however – and apparently against studio wishes – she had it cropped into the now familiar Purdey bob.

'It's fine,' said Joanna at the time, 'if you have long, healthy, shining hair like Diana Rigg, but look at mine – it's really quite tatty. As I'm going to be leaping about the place and working outside a lot, it's bound to go frizzy. So I thought I'd have it shortened.' (A glimpse of Purdey as she might have been, with Joanna sporting shoulder-length auburn hair, can be seen in the alternate live-action title montage, filmed before the actress decided to cut her hair.)

Such action might have sent the producers into fits of hysterical outrage. Clemens and Fennell knew better. They accepted this as a fait accompli and took full advantage of the million pounds worth of free publicity Joanna's lead had given them. Clemens accepts this, but maintains that it wasn't the look he was after. 'I think that if she had kept her hair as it was, she would have been even more attractive. It was the Farrah Fawcett-Majors look that I was after.'

Purdey was a girl of the Eighties. Sexy, for a TV heroine, very sexy. Not promiscuous, but not a virgin either. An ex-ballerina, she made use of her high-kicking legs to dispatch her opponents in a series of athletic manoeuvres that relied as much on speed and surprise as on power and flexibility. She could use her hands, too, and shoot the pips out of an apple at 20 paces. And she could run like an Olympic athlete, drive anything from her orange drop-head sports car to a motorbike, and acquit herself favourably on a paratrooper's assault course.

Purdey was tough. She dressed in frills and soft, flowing materials. As you would expect from her unique personality, her permanent pad was different, too. She lived in the biggest, most sensuously decorated bedsitter in the world. A gutted basement flat in London, refurbished in feminine Art Deco style and colours which accurately reflect its occupant. Right down to the fact that her bedroom door was little more than a hanging curtain of beads.

Mike Gambit was different, too. A man of the next decade, there hadn't been a hero like Gambit before. He was hip, yet dressed quietly to merge easily with the high-power world of espionage and corruption in which he worked. He could be quiet and deceptively still, until he flared into action, when he would strike as fast as a cobra, using his lethally effective hands. He drove a car with consummate skill – experience of Formula One racing put to good use – and he could turn his Jaguar XJS on a sixpence. He could move faster than the eye could follow and shoot any firearm fast and straight. Rumour had it that Gambit was once an Army man (a major in the Paras), and before that a mercenary, once wrestling crocodiles, until he decided to take up more exciting work!

Like Purdey, he lived in London, in a super modern apartment, for which he'd chosen ultra-modern decor and every conceivable electronic device, right down to an automated bed!

Bowler hat, umbrella, buttonhole, immaculate dress, an appreciation of the better things in life – John Steed was still the suave, elegant man who knew that Britannia ruled and was still sworn to defend her from her enemies. But his circumstances had changed. He still had his mews flat in London, but now preferred to spend most of his time in a big house in the country, 'Steed's Stud' as it was called, where, when not engaged in more dangerous tasks like saving the world from destruction, he bred beautiful horses and entertained beautiful women.

Clemens drummed up a classic confrontation between master and pupil in Hostage. *Assigned to bring Steed in for questioning (when Steed is suspected of being a traitor), Gambit, catching his colleague red-handed with the evidence, draws a gun and threatens to take Steed into custody. 'Then you'll have to kill me...,' says Steed. 'Once you start you'll have to kill me.' Gambit knows better: a leg shot will do. He cocks the gun. 'Don't make me do it!' Steed sighs. 'All right – it's Purdey. They've got her!' Gambit is unmoved. Steed implores. 'Those papers are the price!' Gambit sneers. 'Yes, that would be your last card – use Purdey against me.' He moves towards his colleague. Steed pleads with him to give him a chance to run. Gambit remains unmoved. 'Please?' begs Steed, kneeing his colleague in the privates. Down goes Gambit. Taking the evidence, Steed prepares to leave, then, an afterthought. 'I did warn you – I never fight fair!' Gambit isn't listening; he's out cold!*

He hadn't mellowed – just grown perkier.

He'd got a new car, too. The Bentley was still there, lovingly garaged for the occasional recreational spin (or so the publicity handout led us to believe – it was seen once only, in flashback, from an earlier episode), but Steed had seen the light. Villains had little respect for such splendid machinery and with each outing, the risk of a scratch – or worse, a bullet hole – increased. His current mode of transport blended the practical with the beautiful. The practical was a Range Rover, suitably converted for a man of Steed's impeccable style. The beautiful was the Big Cat, a wide-wheeled, highly polished road version of the Jaguar Racing Coupé; a docile monster capable of 200mph, hand-made and tailored, and a worthy stablemate for the Bentley.

I asked Brian Clemens why the need for a change? His reply is quoted in full: 'We (Albert Fennell and I), decided to be relentlessly British to make the series stand out in foreign countries (especially the USA); hence the red white and blue motif. Anyway, we felt the old country needed a boost around then, which is why we went to British Leyland.

'Previously we had excellent relations with Lotus, who were anxious to provide the cars for *The New Avengers.* They openly admitted that the use of the Lotus Elan as Emma Peel's transport was largely the reason why the marque became known and successful in the USA. They said it had given them millions of pounds worth of free publicity – all in return for the loan of a car.

'However, this time we needed a volume manufacturer who could provide not only the snazzy transport for the stars on screen, but also provide us with unit cars, pickups, etc. Lotus did not have anything in this range – so we went to BL – and so entered a time of trial and cock-ups.

'The Rover was still under wraps at that time, literally; it was transported from place to place under disguising covers. It was not reliable – and BL were slow in making repairs, or providing an alternative car.

'Amazingly, when the Jag went wrong we actually had to go elsewhere and hire one, BL being unable to fill the gap! The Jag saloon that Pat occasionally drove was a special suspension model intended for circuit racing. Everyone hated it because it was such a handful to drive under normal conditions. The stuntmen particularly, because it was difficult to skid or do hand brake turns. The Jag sports on the other hand was excellent for stunt work.

'BL sent us an MGB. I borrowed it one evening and sat in the car park for nearly an hour trying to engage reverse. Eventually I had to have it pushed out – and drove home knowing I could not select reverse. Later I found out that the gear knob – on which the gear patterns was etched – was actually from an Austin Princess (or similar car) on which the reverse is in exactly the opposite direction to the MG! I never thought to question the gear knob and spent all that time trying to get a gear where there was none.

'BL invited us to the Motor Show – but we had to be at the 'reception' desk by 5.30, which meant us stopping shooting an hour early (very expensive). We drove to Earls Court – and spent quite a while trying to find somewhere to park – no parking space having been reserved for us.

'We got into the main hall and arrived at the BL stand, which was empty. Yes, empty. All the reps had pissed off at near the end of the day for a pint.

'Freelance photographers took photographs of the stars against the Mercedes stand (thus giving the Germans some free publicity). Eventually, the Merc people took pity on us and offered us a drink from their well-stocked hospitality stand. Eventually the BL rep arrived – showed us the new cars in a cursory manner – and never offered us a drink. He pissed off, we left abruptly.

'Later, when I remonstrated with the rep, mentioning that his company would be getting millions of free publicity in return for the loan of a few vehicles, he replied: "Oh, yes, you are showing the Rover on screen a lot, but how will 'they' know it is a Rover?" The mind boggled. We would have gladly swapped for another manufacturer, but we were too deeply entrenched now to back out.

'In contrast, when we needed a motorbike for Jo, we went to a *Japanese* manufacturer – and, within hours they replied: How many bikes did we want? What colours? Did we need them sprayed in special colours? If we gave them a little time they would be pleased to produce a special 'Purdey' bike for our use! In that one incident I realised why the Japanese industry was growing so rapidly – and the British one was doomed for oblivion.

'Later, on *The Professionals*, we involved Ford – a US company – and again received excellent and professional treatment.'

In a footnote, Brian added: 'Later, the Steed Rover was returned to BL, and they decided to raffle it off amongst the staff. The unions objected because it was elitist – it would only be fair if *everyone* could win a car! I think it was then just sold off.

'The only good thing that came out of the BL association was that they paid a lot of money to make a PR film on their cars, the footage of a hair-raising ride through the ravines, etc., which was taken by us and seamlessly inserted into an an episode [*The Lion & The Unicorn*].

'I have never bought a British car since, and I doubt that anyone associated with the *New Avengers* drove a BL car for a long time after that. My first cars were MGs, Sunbeams, a Daimler Dart – a series of Jaguar E-types – then nine Ferraris in a row. Today I drive a Merc (perhaps recalling that day at the Motor Show?). I still retain my numberplate 140 MPH – if an *Avengers* fan sees me, give me a toot!'

Patrick Macnee, to a Canadian reporter: 'As Steed I try to illuminate an aspect of British life that is horrendous and terrible – the Black Hole of Calcutta, the Heights of Quebec, the loss of our colonies – but in spite of it all, like the Scarlet Pimpernel and the Little Brown Jug, one keeps smiling.'

The relationship between the new team was that of partners, equals, good friends. Though they were poles apart – Steed in a locked cell would 'con' the jailer into opening the door, Gambit would kick it down – one factor welded them together as a team, mutual respect. And a shared sense of humour.

The annoucement that Steed was to have a new sidekick in the series left me with a feeling of unease. How, I wondered, would this association affect what had previously been seen as a winning format? I had reservations that the introduction of a third member to the team (particularly that of a male) would relegate Steed's character to that of a Mother figure – a kind of Mr Waverly to Gambit and Purdey's Solo and Kuryakin – and leave Steed delegating the action to his younger protégés.

Indeed, why change the format at all? Brian Clemens supplied the answer. Asked why he thought it necessary to introduce the character of Gambit, he told me: 'Because *The Avengers* has *always* changed, moved forward. Because also, Patrick Macnee was that much older, we needed a younger man to handle at least some of the action. Don't forget, this was called *The NEW Avengers*, so we had to stay true to that, otherwise the critics would have hammered us for just serving up a new batch of the old *Avengers*.'

Certainly, considering that Patrick Macnee was forty-seven when the original *Avengers* series ceased production in 1969, and a seven-year gap separated the new series from its predecessor, it is hardly surprising that *Sunday Mirror* columnist Pat Boxall asked on 11 January 1976: 'Can Steed make it again?'. Boxall went on to say that, as a one-time *Avengers* fan, she was alarmed that Patrick Macnee (at 53, and having seen off three glamorous sidekicks) was still being asked to play the sophisticated Steed. She added that he was 'pushing his luck to put a fourth on his arm and did someone in those ivory television towers believe that time doesn't tick-tock for men?' Considering the facts, an understandable question.

Surprisingly, however, it appeared that time had indeed stood still for the ever ebullient Mr Macnee and, although the media led us to believe that 'Steed has mellowed', in fact he'd hardly changed at all. True, he was slightly heavier – though only in the first few stories; by the time that the second 13 episodes began production, Patrick had slimmed down and looked every bit as suave as the 'slimline' Thorson series model. True, the much-loved four-and-a-half litre 1929 vintage Bentley – loaned to *The Avengers* production by a Huddersfield garage owner for the duration of the series – and Rolls-Royce trademarks were no longer in evidence, though a 'reference' to the former does appear in part one of the two-part episode *K is for Kill*. The vehicle seen in the background as Steed telephones Mrs Peel – who has since changed her name – was courtesy of some unused film footage, while the vehicle seen in the opening moments of this story was hired for one day's filming.

Convinced that he still had something to contribute to the role, Patrick Macnee returned as the suave, elegant Steed.

But Steed's character had hardly changed at all. Still as immaculate as ever, bowler-hatted, he continued to spread British good manners. In short, Patrick Macnee was back as Steed. Avenging, though it was certainly not better than before, was nevertheless well worth waiting for.

The New Avengers as a show differed little from the previous *Avengers* stories. The bizarre qualities were still there to delight the viewer. These included a man whose mere touch could spell death; Nazis alive and well, and living as monks on a remote Scottish island; a sophisticated device that transferred people's thoughts by scrambling their brain; a 'monster' rat; and even Steed's old enemy, the dreaded Cybernauts.

Brian Clemens explained: 'The situations are just as fantastic, but, this time, we carefully framed our stories so that, no matter how mind-blowing the plot, we made it believable. And that is the big change, if you want to point out the difference!

Asked why he had missed a golden opportunity to go full circle and name original Avenger, Ian Hendry, 'Keel' in To Catch a Rat, *Brian Clemens cleared up the mystery once and for all: 'What happens is that the scripts are written a long time before you cast. So that character was written as "Gunner" and it was locked into the script – there was no way to change it. It wasn't written for Ian Hendry. But once I knew that we had got Ian, I thought, well, there must be some people who will recognize him as the old Doctor Keel, so we might as well have a little fun (by adding the dialogue, "I know that I'm 17 years late, but welcome back".) Like a lot of things in* The Avengers, *it was very subtle, you had to look for it.'*

The old Avengers were brilliant cardboard characters. In *The New Avengers* I used thicker cardboard. I tried to involve our viewers a little more in the personal side of the leads. Though he is denying this now, and has probably forgotten that he ever said it, Patrick was all for this new approach. The previous series had a very loyal following, but we never got Middle America (or its equivalent across the world) – the sort of viewer who took a quick look then changed channels because they found the stories "silly". This time I added more depth – annoyed the true *Avengers* fans – but picked up a few million others along the way.'

Asked to pinpoint the format difference between *The Avengers* and *The New Avengers*, director Johnny Hough said: 'The difference for me was that there was a certain kind of magic that bounced between two people and, when directing three people, that magic was triangulated. It came in three parts; it wasn't a one on one situation. So the relationship between Purdey and Gambit wasn't the relationship between Steed and his earlier partners. You now had this relationship between Gambit and Purdey, the relationship between Purdey and Steed, and the relationship between Steed and Gambit. One had all these different relationships to consider, so that was the main difference, it was no longer a one on one situation – and it's debatable whether that diluted the action of the series or whether it enhanced it.'

Clemens put the *Avengers'* amazing track record down to a 'happy knack right from the start'. He said at the time: 'We were always at least two or three years in advance of our time. It was costume, without being period costume. We even upstaged James Bond, with karate, kung fu, mini-skirts and women's lib, and we managed to stay ahead. This time we mean to top all that has gone before. Audiences have grown more sophisticated, and the successful show must get ahead of them. This is what we've tried to do – to produce a show that is in the Eighties. A show that will seem as fresh as ever, but still stay ahead of its nearest emulators. The production values of the new series are higher than any other television series in the world. The use of location exteriors is a 100 percent improvement. You are going to be seeing a lot of Britain in the new series, but *Avengers*-style, weird, bizarre, unusual locations.'

Changes in fashion were not as predominant as in the earlier *Avengers* series. No black leather for Purdey. Instead she wore a wardrobe designed by London-born Catherine Buckley. These included silk dresses, gathered at the waist and tied at the shoulder, with skirts in pleated chiffon; a kimono in orange, black, green, red and yellow flower-print silk, with long sleeves and side slits; black cotton jump suits, with an *Avengers* lion motif and the name Purdey trimmed in white and red (worn only once in the series); a luxurious evening dress in red, green and blue latex, with velvet top and lurex – and Purdey's olive-green fighting suit, worn just the once in the first episode (and referred to by Joanna Lumley as The Green Slime!). Clemens confirmed that they never used this again because it looked appalling. Cyd Child recalls that the costumes Buckley sent to the studio were fabulous, but totally impracticable. 'I remember Wardrobe saying one day: "What am I supposed to do with these things? We've got a scene to do with Joanna scrambling through the woods and what not, and look at what she's sent me." There was this skirt which had a label on it saying: Not to be washed. Not to be dry cleaned. There wasn't even a double costume for it! It was absolutely ridiculous.'

The original intention was to make Gambit a swinger – complete with jeans and bomber jackets. (Gareth Hunt had expressed a preference for these). The end product, however, was a very up-to-the-minute man who wore expensive, well-cut, three-piece suits in a traditional business dark blue pin-stripe, and moth-head checks and plain gaberdine, worn with smart ties.

Not even the producers dared to play around with Steed's attire. As ever, his wardrobe retained a wide selection of colourful bowler hats, some of which were as useful as they were decorative. One, for instance, had a steel crown, which was ideal for protecting his head from attack and handy for knocking out the opposition. Another had a steel brim, which served as a deadly missile when thrown like a Frisbee. A third bowler had a miniature receiver built into the crown, leading Purdey to remark "I wouldn't let too many people see you doing that – they might think you were talking through your hat!" The tightly-furled brolly was also still in evidence – a weapon in itself when used to hook an opponent's arm, or for fending off attacks. The umbrella also doubled as a swordstick, with a thin rapier blade hidden inside its shaft. This, coupled with Steed's knowledge of fencing, was, like everything else about him, impeccable.

For the new series, Steed would be seen wearing – along with the familiar Edwardian suits – riding breeches, shooting jackets, blazers and sportswear.

Martial arts had long been the hallmark of *The Avengers* ethos, so Clemens and Fennell were determined to get the very best people to teach Joanna and Gareth how to create their own brand of havoc. Prior to filming, Cyd Child and Ray Austin (who had shared a long association with *The Avengers* series), were brought in as fight arrangers. They rigged up a gymnasium in the studio, and the two stars were subjected to a vigorous fitness training programme. Cyd, who would stunt-double Joanna in the series, recalls the training session. 'I was given the band room at Pinewood Studios to use. We equipped this with some weights for Gareth – somebody else advised him about his weight training and I got both of them doing a fitness training routine. They did about an hour with me, Jo doing lots of training to improve her muscles and make her more supple, and

Gareth Hunt was filming a scene for Target *which required a police box to be blown up. Told that the amount of explosive required to acheive this had been carefully worked out, the actor rehearsed the stunt. 'The explosives man had been a little over-enthusiastic,' said Gareth. 'The police box went up with a great roar and smoke covered everything. I was blown of my feet by the blast!' When he got up again everyone was laughing. He borrowed a mirror from a make-up girl, 'and saw that I had a blackened face and my hair was full of tiny bits of blue paint, which had previously been on the police box!'*

while she was doing that, Gareth was doing weights. Then they both did lots of shuttle runs and various other fitness things. When they'd done that, Jo would put in an hour of ballet training – a ballet teacher came along for this – and we'd round off the day doing other things. They really did some hard training, some *very* hard training. I told them "You're going to hate me. You're really going to hate me." But Jo was pleased, despite the fact that she'd cried, "Enough! I hate it. I hate it!" towards the end. She telephoned me afterwards, when she had some filming to do, to say that the cameramen couldn't keep up with her when she was running.'

Jo Lumley remembers: 'I did an assault course for paratroopers that was a beast – really frightening. I never fall; I'm like a cat – but I had to leap off ropes and swings and things. It was a bit hairy because you have to do it with this extreme look of nonchalance on your face. You get black shins from bruises and great ripped bits on your thighs. I never got hurt in fights because we fight with stuntmen; I kick them and they go "eeurgh" and crash over backwards. It's climbing over walls that does it.'

Cyd told me an amusing story about how Joannna Lumley was directly responsible for getting her the job as Purdey's stunt double on the series. 'They'd tried several different doubles for her, none of whom was ideal. Jo kept insisting that she wanted me to double for her. I spoke to Ray Austin who said, "Can you lose three stone?", because Jo was another skinny one. He was joking, of course, but I went on a diet and lots a lot of weight and still they weren't convinced. Jo and I thought that it was possible, but no one was taking us seriously. So Jo arranged for me to go and see her hairdresser and we had a wig cut the same as the Purdey bob. Then she took me to her dress designer and got her to lend me an outfit identical to hers. I donned the wig, changed my clothes and we presented ourselves on the sound stage, side by side, and they shot a short test. Jo had to run past the camera and I had to follow her in the same shot. They viewed this and agreed that I could double for her.'

Asked if they did their own stunts, Joanna told me: 'I steeled myself to do them because it is so much more interesting if you are getting involved with all the filming, rather than sitting back and watching someone else do all the juicy bits. The stunts I didn't do were those with the motorbikes, because I can't ride a motorbike, and they wouldn't cover me for insurance.' The motorbike sequences were done by stuntman Colin Skeaping, dressed as Purdey and sporting a wig. Joanna could certainly handle herself, as one of the stuntmen found out. He was playing a Russian agent in a fight scene. He turned his body a second too late and received Joanna's foot in the solar plexus. The toughie collapsed like a deflated balloon.

Fight perfection in front of the camera was achieved and arranged by Ray Austin. Every movement was carefully plotted, checked and rehearsed in slow motion – but the close-ups of Purdey's high kicks, at least in the early days of production, was achieved by the actress having her leg propped-up on a tripod! Gareth said: 'Joanna and I became very involved in it. One didn't feel that you were playing a character totally unless one did actually do a lot of the stunts yourself – and we were very fit. We were obviously not allowed to do the really dangerous stunts, like turning cars over. But we did do certain things which we possibly shouldn't have done – like diving through windows. Even when one realises that "sugar glass" was used, it could still cut your head – as it did mine.' (Gareth *did* ride the motorcycle – and almost badly injured himself when he went out of control and ended up in a row of bushes.) His most bruising moment came in Paris, before the series started. A master of martial arts, dressed in a red leotard and black swimming trunks and carrying a cane, had set up a publicity stunt. The man told Gareth to hold a gun. The Avenger did so. Swish went the cane and the gun went flying. 'Then he whacked me round the ear,' said Gareth, 'It really hurt. Then he did it again, for the photographers and he hit me behind the other ear.' To prove his point, the man then kicked the gun out of Gareth's hand and booted him in the crotch!

Gareth Hunt starred as Mike Gambit, a hero for the Seventies.

As written by Clemens, the original script for The Last of the Cybernauts..?? *had the Avenging trio luring Cybernaut-Kane into a patch of wet tar at the rear of Purdey's flat.*

One other major change was *The New Avengers* theme music. The opening bars remained the same, with a large percussion section playing a syncopated rhythm against strict reiterated semi-quavers in 4/4 time on a small bongo, and a counter melody played on the tom-tom, followed by the familiar strains of the original *Avengers* theme. But this soon gave way to a faster, punchier theme tune to signal that this was *The NEW Avengers*. Brian Clemens explained the need for the change: 'Laurie couldn't use the original theme because that was copyrighted to that series. So there were problems there. It is very difficult to control Laurie anyway because, for one thing, he's not a man who rewrites. He comes in and spends weeks or months doing this and it's a fait accompli. It's very difficult to change him because he doesn't charge – he only takes the PRS (Performing Rights Society) fees. The new theme was composed after discussion between all three of us.'

Before filming began, the producers issued a production brief to writers and directors:

THE NEW AVENGERS
Some notes on style

Times have changed, and *The Avengers* must not only change with them but – hopefully – keep ahead of the game. Pace is the thing; exposition, in the main, will be kept down to a minimum and, although the *Avengers*, the *NEW Avengers*, will never be hidebound by the strict format of self-imposed restrictions, there are certain guidelines we want to abide by... unless a particular episode demands a different treatment:

1) Wherever possible we will not see characters coming through doors; we will pick up the scene after the normal how-do-you-do's are over. Cut – and we will be there... unless of course the whole sequence is built around what actually lies behind the door, or in any other way makes a virtue of seeing someone come through a door.
2) Establishing shots per se – are out. For instance, an exterior shot of a house is not desirable if the only thing it is saying is: 'Here is the house the next scene should take place in.' However, it says, 'Here is the house, and here is the villain creeping towards it...' that's OK. The shot must say something.
3) Inserts are not desirable. Not *isolated* inserts. If it is necessary to see the headline of the paper Steed holds, then see it with him – incorporate him with a pan or a tilt or even an over-the-shoulder with the insert. If we *have* to pick up an isolated insert later in the schedule, then the visual story-telling of the initial scene has gone awry.
4) The fights should be as indicated in the scripts – the new girl will be shot so as to capitalize on her grace and sexuality coming in, of course, for close moments of impact.

The new man should be shot – from great stillness – into a blur of close shots – a blur of fast movement – and out again to the stillness we will come to associate with him before and after vigorous action.

Steed, of course, will continue as before – often resorting to sheer guile and the use of props to achieve his purpose.

5) Steed is the one, vital element from the old *Avengers* to be regarded as *untouchable*. He will remain much as before – save that there are now scenes in which to externalize a hitherto unexplored dimension to his character.

6) As before – and again, where possible – *The Avengers* will create its own world – so that the normal day-to-day traffic should be ignored. Shooting, say, in London Airport, may give us problems – but in a case like that, then one should stay very firmly involved and shooting on our protagonists.

7) In conclusion, *The NEW Avengers* look will stem from a number of subtly different elements. One will certainly be the increased use of location exteriors. Two must be an increased pace in the narrative. Pace is paramount. Given the choice between the fight that – no matter how much fun it provides – goes on too long – and the crisp action that leads to maximum impact – we must lean towards the latter.

And one word of caution – we are aiming at a worldwide sale. This means walking a not too difficult tightrope of varying censorship restrictions. Generally speaking most of these problems have been ironed out at the script stage, but there must arise occasions when on the spot decisions have to be made... and shot. When in doubt – the ultimate yardstick must be is it in good taste? Never forgetting an equally important question... is it ENTERTAINING?

> *Brian Clemens & Albert Fennell*
> *January 1976*

Another noteworthy entry in the same document details the draft scenario for what was intended to be the series' *original* title sequence. This is far removed from the one to which we are accustomed:

Through the middle of a frozen frame bursts the original title logo of *The Avengers*, coinciding with the familiar first few bars of Laurie Johnson's earlier *Avengers* theme. The logo grows larger until it fills the screen and an inverted 'V' and the word 'new' is inserted – both scrawled like graffiti – an afterthought. It now reads *The New Avengers*. With the addendum 'new' comes the music, the new music, acknowledging the novelty.

The picture dissolves to a long shot of an empty horizon, where, striding briskly into shot, is the tall, immaculate, bowler-hatted figure of John Steed. Without slackening the pace, he adjusts his bowler to a jaunty angle and smiles:

STARRING PATRICK MACNEE AS JOHN STEED

As he exits past the camera, we return to the horizon, where, hurrying into shot come Gambit and Charly; she, a step or two behind him, hurrying to close the gap between them:

Cut to a close-up of Gambit, striding purposefully along:

?????? AS MIKE GAMBIT

Pausing, he looks back to where Charly has stopped to lift her skirt and adjust her stocking-top to its suspender belt an intimate moment which ends as she glances up and catches Gambit's eye, at which point she drops her skirt back into place:

AND ?????? AS CHARLY

Hurrying over to where Gambit waits, they both look ahead to Steed, still striding briskly along. Glancing knowingly at her companion, the new girl, unexpectedly, puts both fingers to her lips and whistles!

Steed stops in mid-step and turns to face them, then, casually placing his umbrella to his shoulder, he waits while his companions hurry to his side:

PRODUCED BY ALBERT FENNELL & BRIAN CLEMENS

Together, they exchange smiles before – a team now – they turn in unison and stride away as one:

SUPERIMPOSE DIRECTOR AND EPISODE TITLE

A slight variation of this was used in the closing scene of *The Eagle's Nest*, where, mission complete, the trio link arms and stride briskly away to the *Colonel Bogey March*.

As we know, this sequence was abandoned in favour of the 'silhouette' version. When asked why Brian Clemens replied: 'Because by that time the age of computer-graphics had arrived and we decided that as our product was a child of the Eighties, we would take advantage of the available technology.' The red-white-and-blue lion motif was designed by Clemens after he had produced a 'flick' book showing how the titles should appear – computer animators did the rest.

The production went before the cameras in April 1976, at Pinewood Studios. Any initial success *The New Avengers* might have had was sabotaged before it ever reached the screen. The ITV network failed to reach agreement on when the programme should be shown.

Some channels opted for Sunday evenings, others for Tuesdays, and the remainder screened the show on Friday nights. (Quite a contrast to the prime-time Saturday evening spot which the original *Avengers* had always been allocated.)

This understandably infuriated the producers. As Clemens told me: 'It was thrown away! Having built the publicity thing into a volcano, it erupted at different times in different places! We should have been networked from day one. It was total madness. With a proper network showing we could have emptied the streets on our opening night. It is tragic because *The Avengers* was the best adventure series British television ever made. But isn't that just typical of Britain, to sabotage and to underrate that which we do best?'

It seems that the original plan was to film 26 episodes, with a short break following the completion of the 13th story, before continuing to film the final block of 13. This was not to be. During the recess, Clemens was contacted by Roffi, who told him that the series would have to go back to the drawing board. Largely because the series was being financed by French and Canadian money, both countries were demanding changes in the second block of films. The French backers in particular felt that Purdey wasn't sexy enough. They wanted Joanna Lumley to put on a sexier act and dress in more sultry creations. 'Purdey is short of lip gloss, and her wardrobe is dull and drab,' said Roffi. Though they'd liked what they'd seen, the French had certain reservations and wished to see Purdey dressed in top French designs, like those of Yves St Laurent. 'In general terms,'

The New Avengers. One fact welded them together as a team. They were partners, equals, good friends, each as important as the other.

Roffi told the British press, 'I think the stories could be sexier, more violent also, but still remain sophisticated.'

Joanna Lumley, angered by the critcism, blasted back: 'We don't want to see bottoms and breasts, do we? I think the public have had quite enough of that on TV and everywhere else. Aren't people bored with actresses who lick their lips trying to be sexy? It will be a pity if *The New Avengers* has to jump on the bandwagon because of the influences from other programmes. As an actress, I believe improvements can be made. But I've never thought I looked dowdy.

'My own dress designer is considered to be sexy and sophisticated by the French. But we did have some problems with the earlier shows because, after the first three or four, it was a rush

Purdey how she might have been, had the French backers got their way with her fashion designs.

to get the right clothes. This time, more thought has gone into it. The French certainly have a way with women's fashions, so there will be a French selection when the series comes back.'

Patrick Macnee agreed that more sex and violence could signal the death of the show. 'Ours is a surrealistic Grimm's fairy tale, sort of terror,' he said. 'If we start pumping bullets into people's stomachs, we're done for. And it's a joke that the French should ask for more violence when the Americans are so interested in buying the show. They've got the biggest no-no against violence – viewers are even striking against *Starsky and Hutch*.' As things turned out, when the show eventually reached America, long after it had stopped production, CBS saw it as far too violent and screened it at 11.30pm, or later.

Changes were made, and as promised, about half of Joanna's new wardrobe for the 'second season' was of French origin. The rest, however, was chosen by Joanna herself. She visited Betty Jackson, at Quorum, and selected a string of dresses and skirts, including an assortment of mini-skirts, that she wore on and off the screen.

Then came the news that the backers were demanding that several episodes of the second 13 stories should be made overseas. Brian Clemens picks up the story: 'The input of Roffi and the French was largely ignored. By this time they owed, and continue to owe, us money. So they were in no position to dictate terms.' He recalled that, on at least three occasions, Albert Fennell and he personally paid the crew and actors, a statement confirmed by Jo and Gareth. 'It was always "the cheque is in the post" sort of thing.' They nevertheless acceded to Roffi's request to keep the show on the road. (He says that Mr Roffi was later arrested in France for fraud.)

In the event, said Brian Clemens, 'three episodes were filmed in France and four in Canada – although one of the Canadian syndicate of backers wanted twice as many. 'We made the episodes there for the same reasons,' he continued, 'because both countries had invested money in the series. And, this may have been a political decision, I'm not sure – they had to be seen to be employing some nationals, hence we found ourselves there – to, I think, the series' detriment.' Interestingly, had six episodes been filmed in Canada as requested by the Canadian backers, *The New Avengers* would have visited Niagara Falls. A suggested storyline said that Gambit and Purdey would be floated over the Falls in a barrel!

However, changes were in store. Purdey's smooth-as-glass mushroom bob gave way to a shaggy but controllable hairstyle. John Frieda was the man responsible for both the original bob and the new cut. Other changes were made, to give the second 13 stories their fair share of sexy moments. Purdey's role was made sexier. In one episode, *Obsession*, she met and fell in love with an old flame (who turned out to be a bad lot.) We even got to see her in bed! Gambit's character was broadened and developed. He was given a succession of dolly-birds and other female admirers.

Even the formerly untouchable John Steed was revealed as a man with a past – and a romantic interest!

Clemens told me: 'It becomes clear that Purdey is carrying on with somebody. And Purdey's guardian angel, Mike Gambit, will receive more attention. We're strengthening his character, and giving him a collection of girls all to himself. He still fancies Purdey, of course. And she isn't exactly adverse to him either! But as they work together, face death together, if they slipped between the sheets, might that not take the fine edge off their relationship? And as Purdey has pointed out, they just don't have the time. Mind you... one day! Steed and Purdey are something again. After all, Steed is a handsome, virile, experienced man – and Purdey can't help but know that. Especially the "experience". That intrigues her. And Steed, undeniably, finds her very attractive. So give them the right set of circumstances

Gambit fancied Purdey – and she wasn't exactly adverse to him either. But as they worked together, faced death together, they simply didn't find the time to pop between the sheets.

and something could happen. Although those circumstances haven't arisen yet, it's always there.' On-screen romance, or love-making, between Gambit and Purdey remained taboo.

However, the modern-day knight in shining armour, who wore a bowler for a visor and carried an umbrella for a lance, Patrick Macnee, was unsure about Steed's new, romantic role. 'When you're in your fifties, however good you look or feel, you've got to act your age,' he said. 'You're not really supposed to start leaping into bed with young ladies on the television screen. It would look ludicrous.' In fact, he wasn't too happy with Steed's new role at all. As he told me: 'I believed that I still had something more to contribute to the part. In fact it wasn't until the second 13 stories that my voice was heard and I became more in keeping with the original Steed. I confess that I didn't like being "retired" to Steed's Stud – nice house and all that, but rather boring.' Clemens placated him and promised that Steed's women would be of the more mature variety and Steed's character took on more of his old style.

Once again (possibly due to the programme being made by an independent company), Steed and his colleagues lost the battle of the ratings. The second 13 stories suffered the same fate as the first batch – no network showing by the ITV network.

This time around, *The New Avengers* did not even dent the viewing charts, nor gain an early sale in the financially essential USA market. That came sometime later.

Brian Clemens believes that this was the most reprehensible thing of all. Suddenly, sometime around the end of production, the big news broke that we had sold to the American network and Albert, who knew that everybody would now want a piece of the action, set up a meeting between TF1 (the French), Film Finance and EMI – because they owned the original *Avengers* and had subsidized some of the studio costs – and Pinewood, who had given us free studio space against a percentage of the profits. The meeting was set up for 12 o'clock and he got there and found that they had already held the meeting one hour earlier and they'd all left!'

The producers immediately began negotiations to get financial backing for a further series. They failed to do so.

And if they had found backers? Would Clemens have done things the same way? 'Once I was in it I would. Now I wouldn't. But once you're in it, you've got to run with it. I really do think that if the last eight episodes or so of *The New Avengers* hadn't been made outside our jurisdiction, it might well have run longer. Unfortunately, in terms of production, the worst episodes came at the end.'

I gave him the last word. What, in his opinion, is the secret of the show's longevity? 'It's that timeless quality – a mixture of an anachronistic, stylized world, plus a science fiction look. It's still very fresh. I hope the final reason is because they were very well made.'

dowsill of Steed's lounge. 'Who are these?' she asks. 'Oh, just some of the fillies I've toyed with,' Steed replies, his back turned towards her as he selects a decanter. 'She's magnificent,' says the woman, picking up a photo of Cathy Gale. 'Yes, beautiful. We went through some tricky situations together. Faithful. Reliable.' comes the reply. 'And this one?' (Emma Peel) 'Oh, very spirited – and very special. Fantastic creature... had to take the whip to her though, sometimes.' The woman turns to stare at him, then looks at a picture of Tara King. 'Excellent. Great action, but liked her oates too much...' says Steed. Turning to face her, he adds, '... I sold her to an Arab prince. I think he eventually had to shoot her.' 'Shoot her!' exclaims the guest, turning to look at the photos again. 'Oh...' grins Steed, realization dawning as he walks to her and crosses to a second set of framed photographs on the opposite side of the room: pictures of his race horses, '...I thought you were referring to these.' Priceless!

NEW AVENGERS CHRONOLOGY

Episode	Title
1	The Eagle's Nest
2	The Midas Touch
3	House of Cards
4	The Last of the Cybernauts...?
5	To Catch a Rat
6	Cat Amongst the Pigeons
7	Target!
8	Faces
9	The Tale of the Big Why
10	Three Handed Game
11	Sleeper
12	Gnaws
13	Dirtier by the Dozen

End of the first filming block

14	Hostage
15	Trap
16	Dead Men are Dangerous
17	Medium Rare
18	Angels of Death
19	Obsession (aka Missile)
20	The Lion and the Unicorn
21	K is for Kill – The Tiger Awakes, Part One (aka The Long Sleep)
22	K is for Kill – Tiger by the Tail, part two
23	Complex
24	The Gladiators
25	Forward Base
26	Emily

Producers: Albert Fennell and Brian Clemens
(Episodes One to Twenty-Five)
Music Composed by: Laurie Johnson
Production Supervisor: Ron Fry (Episodes One to Fifteen)
Associate Producer: Ron Fry
(Episodes Sixteen to Nineteen, Twenty-One to Twenty-Six)
Production Designer: Syd Cain
Coordinating Producer: Ray Austin
(Episodes Twenty-Three to Twenty-Six)
Avengers (Film & TV) Enterprises Ltd
&
IDTV TV Productions, Paris
(Episodes One to Twenty-Two) and Nielsen-Ferns Inc, Toronto
(Episodes Twenty-Three to Twenty-Six)

(The four Canadian episodes carried an additional opening credit)
Albert Fennell and Brian Clemens present
The New Avengers in Canada

('Emily' carried an additional credit)
Produced in Canada by: Hugh Marlow and Jim Handley

THE NEW AVENGERS EPISODES

The Eagle's Nest: *Actress Trudi Van Dorne later killed herself (by hypothermia) on a deserted beach.*

1 THE EAGLE'S NEST

by Brian Clemens

John Steed (Patrick Macnee) Mike Gambit (Gareth Hunt) Purdey (Joanna Lumley) Von Claus (Peter Cushing) Father Trasker (Derek Farr) Karl (Frank Gatliff) Hara (Sydney Bromley) Brown-Fitch (Trevor Baxter) Lady with Dog (Joyce Carey) Main (Neil Phillips) Stannard (Brian Anthony) Barker (Jerold Wells) Gerda (Trudi van Doorne) Nazi Corporal (Peter Porteous) Ralph (Charles Bolton) Jud (Ronald Forfar)

Clemens confirms that the castle used as the monastery in The Eagle's Nest, *was that also used in* Highlander.

Directed by Desmond Davis

The eminent surgeon, Von Claus, is abducted and taken to St Dorca, a retreat for monks. Steed and fellow Avengers follow to find him treating 'Germany's greatest treasure': Adolph Hitler is still alive! The monks are actually Nazi troops planning a new Third Reich. The Avengers close down the unholy monastery and exit whistling.

TX: 22 October 1976

The Midas Touch: *Actor Ronny Lacey, heavily disguised and padded for the role, was shooting at Heathrow when the crew wrapped up and left for home – without him. He was left in his bizarre outfit, trying to find someone to help him get home. Most bystanders shied away from him.*

2 THE MIDAS TOUCH

by Brian Clemens

John Steed (Patrick Macnee) Mike Gambit (Gareth Hunt) Purdey (Joanna Lumley) Freddy (John Carson) Vann (Ed Devereaux) Hong Kong Harry (Ronald Lacey) Turner (David Swift) Lieutenant (Jeremy Child) Curator (Robert Mill) Garvin (Ray Edwards) Midas (Gilles Millinare) Sing (Pik-Sen Lim) Doctor (Charles Tranchell) Tayman (Lionel Guyett) Simpson (Geoffrey Bateman) Boz (Tim Condren) Morgan (Peter Winter) Froggatt (Bruce Bould) Choy (Bruno Elrington)

Directed by Robert Fuest

Professor Turner has created Midas – a young man who carries every disease in the world. Vann, a foreign diplomat, pays Turner to unleash Midas on a visiting princess. Alerted by an old friend, Steed pursues Turner. Purdey infiltrates Turner's office and, overpowered, is promised to Midas upon completion of his mission. The female Avenger slams the lid on Turner's creation, whilst Gambit gives Vann the chop.

TX: 12 November 1976

3 HOUSE OF CARDS

by Brian Clemens

John Steed (Patrick Macnee) Mike Gambit (Gareth Hunt) Purdey (Joanna Lumley) Perov (Peter Jeffrey) Roland (Frank Thornton) Cartney (Lyndon Brook) The Bishop (Derek Francis) Spence (Mark Burns) Jo (Geraldine Moffatt) Suzy (Annette Andre) Olga (Ina Skriver) David (Murray Brown) Professor Vasil (Gordon Sterne) Boris (Dan Meaden) Tulliver (Jeremy Wilkin) Frederick (Anthony Bailey)

Directed by Ray Austin

Master spy Perov is prevented by the Avengers from taking the defector, Vasil, back to Russia. Now in disgrace, he feigns death and activates the House of Cards. Upon receipt of half a card, sleeper agents are reactivated and try to kill designated targets. The scheme works and brings Steed out into the open when he goes to protect Vasil. Perov follows to kill them, but Purdey punches him out.

TX: 29 October 1976

4 THE LAST OF THE CYBERNAUTS...?

by Brian Clemens

John Steed (Patrick Macnee) Mike Gambit (Gareth Hunt) Purdey (Joanna Lumley) Felix Kane (Robert Lang) Malov (Oscar Quitak) Dr Marlow (Gwen Taylor) Professor Mason (Basil Hoskins) Frank Goff (Robert Gillespie) Fitzroy (David Horovitch) Laura (Sally Bazely) Mrs Weir (Pearl Hackney) Second Guard (Martin Fisk) Terry (Eric Carte) First Guard (Ray Armstrong) Cybernaut (Rocky Taylor) Tricia (Davina Taylor)

Directed by Sidney Hayers

While being pursued by the Avengers, Felix Kane nearly died in an intense fire. Determined to take revenge, he enlists the help of Frank Goff to reactivate the Cybernauts. Goff worked on the original design. Crippled by severe burns, Kane

House of Cards:
Actor Jeremy Wilkin later refused to allow this episode to be repeated.

A rare publicity still of Joanna Lumley and Gareth Hunt, taking a break during a location shoot for *The Last of the Cybernauts.*

Last of the Cybernauts..?:
Directed by Sidney Hayers, who had shot the first of the Cybernauts episodes. A brilliant editor, Sid made a number of movies, and later directed all the action stuff on A Bridge Too Far.

To Catch a Rat:
This featured original Avenger Ian Hendry. Also in the cast was Edward Judd. They had something in common: both had high profile starring roles in movies, but finally failed to live up to their early promise and were reduced to character roles.

Cat Amongst the Pigeons:
Directed by John Hough, who started on the second unit for The Saint, *got his first episode director break with* The Avengers, *and went on to direct Peter Fonda, Orson Welles, etc, in Hollywood. John is currently an executive in The Grade Organisation.*

uses cybernetics to replace his useless limbs and sets out to kill Purdey. Luckily, Steed is on hand with a thousand and two ways to reap the benefits of spray-on plastic skin.

TX: 5 November 1976

5 TO CATCH A RAT

by Terence Feely

John Steed (Patrick Macnee) Mike Gambit (Gareth Hunt) Purdey (Joanna Lumley) Irwin Gunner (Ian Hendry) Cromwell (Edward Judd) Quaintance (Robert Flemyng) Cledge (Barry Jackson) Grant (Anthony Sharp) Finder (Jeremy Hawk) Operator (Bernice Stegers) Nurse (Jo Kendall) Farmer (Dallas Cavell) Mother (Sally-Jane Spencer)

Directed by James Hill

When Irwin Gunner regains his memory, he attempts to complete his mission – to trap the White Rat, a double agent. Steed's only clue is that Gunner shot his opponent in the leg 17 years earlier. But finding Gunner is proving difficult because he makes contact through an obsolete code. When the agent's whereabouts are pinpointed, Steed races to the scene, but the White Rat is on his trail. Steed and Gambit arrive too late to prevent Gunner dying at the hands of the traitor, but Gunner nevertheless has the last word.

TX: 3 December 1976

6 CAT AMONGST THE PIGEONS

by Dennis Spooner

John Steed (Patrick Macnee) Mike Gambit (Gareth Hunt) Purdey (Joanna Lumley) Zarcardi (Vladek Sheybal) Turner (Matthew Long) Rydercroft (Basil Dignam) Professor Waterlow (Peter Copley) Lewington (Hugh Walters) Bridlington (Gordon Rollings) Hudson (Joe Black) Foster (Patrick Connor) Tomkins (Kevin Stoney) Merton (Andrew Bradford) Controller (Brian Jackson)

Directed by John Hough

The Avengers flock to investigate mysterious deaths of ecologists. Thousands of feathers found at the scene of the crime suggest that wild birds are the culprits. Purdey seeks answers by visiting the Sanctuary of Wings, but the warden, Zarcardi, serenades his feathered friends and the bird on Purdey's hand draws blood. The Avenger is now prisoner in a locked room, surrounded by thousands of screeching, feathered assassins. Her colleagues pussyfoot in with feline help and pluck Purdey to safety.

TX: 19 November 1976

7 TARGET!

by Dennis Spooner

John Steed (Patrick Macnee) Mike Gambit (Gareth Hunt) Purdey (Joanna Lumley) Draker (Keith Barron) Henko (Robert Beatty) Bradshaw (Roy Boyd) Jones (Frederick Jaeger) Myers (Malcolm Stoddard) Klokoe (Deep Roy) Dr Kendrick (John Paul) Lopez (Bruce Purchase) Talmadge (Dennis Blanch) Palmer (Robert Tayman)

Directed by Ray Austin

Natural causes or foul play? When five agents die after completing their target practice, it seems that someone has tampered with the targets. Instead of being duds, the bullets filled with poison are firing back. Now Purdey has set off down the course and received a 'hit' – one that marks her for death. When Steed is the next to succumb, Gambit must find the antidote and stop a killer before he wipes out the entire department.

TX: 26 November 1976

Target:
This was the episode Brian Clemens took to America to try to interest people in the work of Ray Austin.

8 FACES

by Brian Clemens and Dennis Spooner

John Steed (Patrick Macnee) Mike Gambit (Gareth Hunt) Purdey (Joanna Lumley) Dr Prator (David De Keyser) Mullins (Edward Petherbridge) Mark Clifford (Neil Hallett) Wendy (Annabel Leventon) Bilston (David Webb) Sheila (Jill Medford) Craig/Terrison (Richard Leech) Torrance (Donald Hewlett) Attendant (Robert Putt) Tramp (JG Devlin) Peters (Michael Sheard)

Directed by James Hill

The brilliant plastic surgeon, Dr Prator, recruits drifters from the Mission for the Distressed and Needy, and uses them as doubles to replace government officials. Gambit and Purdey infiltrate the Mission and are chosen by Prator as his next doppelgangers. Prator, meanwhile, has been ordered to find a suitable double for John Steed – allowing Steed to play a double game of his own and extricate his colleagues from a face worse than death!

TX: 17 December 1976

9 THE TALE OF THE BIG WHY

by Brian Clemens

John Steed (Patrick Macnee) Mike Gambit (Gareth Hunt) Purdey (Joanna Lumley) Harmer (Derek Waring) Irene Brandon (Jenny Runacre) Bert Brandon (George Cooper) Turner (Roy Marsden) Roach (Gary Waldhorn) Poole (Rowland Davis) Minister (Geoffrey Toone) Mrs Turner (Maeve Alexander)

Directed by Robert Fuest

Released from prison, Bert Brandon plans to recover a secret document that he hid many years before. It contains information that would rock Whitehall to its foundations, but the government hasn't taken the bait. Brandon is pursued by Poole and Roach and Purdey and Gambit, but dies at the hands of hoodlums searching for his secret. Purdey finds a clue – Brandon's boots. The trail leads to Surrey, and Purdey eventually finds the papers, after some funny business, which reveals the traitor.

TX: 10 December 1976

10 THREE HANDED GAME

by Dennis Spooner and Brian Clemens

John Steed (Patrick Macnee) Mike Gambit (Gareth Hunt) Purdey (Joanna Lumley) Ranson (David Wood) Juventor (Stephen Grief) Ivan (Tony Vogel) Larry (Michael Petrovitch) Professor Meroff (Terry Wood) Masgard (Gary Raymond) Tony Field (Noel Trevarthen) Helen McKay (Annie Lambert) General (Ronald Leigh-Hunt) Doctor (John Paul) Professor (Hugh Morton) Gary (Bill Bailey)

Directed by Ray Austin

Steed entrusts Masgard, McKay and Field to each memorize a third of the Three-Handed Game: a vital secret document in code, designed by Steed. Master spy Juventor wants it and he has a thought-transference machine at his command. Steed gets word of Juventor's plans and decides to guard Fields. His colleagues will protect the two other agents. The Avengers fail and Juventor steals the code. However, Purdey leads him a merry dance before she and her colleagues bring down the curtain on Juventor's plans.

TX: 21 January 1977

The producers saw Purdey as a stockings and suspenders girl – giving lots of glimpses of thigh, but the idea was dropped.

11 SLEEPER

by Brian Clemens

John Steed (Patrick Macnee) Mike Gambit (Gareth Hunt) Purdey (Joanna Lumley) Brady (Keith Buckley) Tina (Sara Kestelman) Chuck (Mark Jones) Bart (Prentis Hancock) Bill (Leo Dolan) Ben (David Schofield) Fred (Gavin Campbell) Pilot (Peter Godfrey) Hardy (Joe Dunne) Policemen (Jason White and Tony McHale) Dr Graham (Arthur Dignam) Phil (George Sweeney)

Directed by Graeme Clifford

Brady steals several canisters of S95, a new sleeping gas, and proceeds to place parts of London in slumber. With the population snoozing, Brady and his gang can steal everything. The Avengers find that they are the only active citizens left in their area and, tired of rounding-up the criminals on their own, they radio for help before sleeping off their previous efforts.

TX: 14 January 1977

Sleeper:
Directorial debut of Australian editor, Graeme Clifford. He went on to marry Laurie Johnson's secretary Patricia (now a TV producer in Hollywood). He then directed Frances *– which garnered Oscar nominations for Jessica Lange and Kim Stanley.*

12 GNAWS

by Dennis Spooner

John Steed (Patrick Macnee) Mike Gambit (Gareth Hunt) (Joanna Lumley) Charles Thornton (Julian Holloway) Walters (Morgan Shepherd) Carter (Peter Cellier) Harlow (John Watts) Girl (Anulka Dubinska) Motor Mechanic (Ronnie Laughlin) Ivan Chislenko (Jeremy Young) George Ratcliffle (Patrick Malahide) Tramp Joe (Keith Marsh) Tramp Arthur (Ken Wynne) Malloy (Keith Alexander) Couple in Car (Denise Reynolds and Peter Richardson)

Directed by Ray Austin

When Thornton and Carter begin their own research at the Ministry of Agriculture, they use radioactivity to increase the growth rate of plants. Unfortunately, they also wash radioactive liquids down the sink and create a monster in the sewers – a beast that grows to enormous proportions and starts to feed on human flesh. The Avengers go underground and Purdey is used as live bait, so that Thornton can kill the rat, but it is Gambit who stops the carnivore dead in its tracks.

TX: 21 December 1976

13 DIRTIER BY THE DOZEN

by Brian Clemens

John Steed (Patrick Macnee) Mike Gambit (Gareth Hunt) Purdey (Joanna Lumley) Colonel Miller (John Castle) Sergeant Bowden (Shaun Curry) Travis (Colin Skeaping) General Stevens (Michael Barrington) Captain Tony Noble (Michael Howarth) Terry (Brian Croucher) Major Prentice (Stephen Moore) Harris (Alun Armstrong) Colonel Foster (Ballard Berkeley) Doctor (John Forbes-Robertson) Keller (John Labanowski) Orderly (David Purcell) Freddy (Francis Mugham)

Directed by Sidney Hayers

Colonel 'Mad Jack' Miller has formed a special 19th Commando Unit, which can be hired by the highest bidder. Steed becomes concerned when General Stevens fails to return from a camp inspection. His being found dead in the Middle East could start a Cold War, so Gambit joins Miller's commandos and Purdey tags (unofficially) along. Both are exposed and taken prisoner, before Gambit kicks his way to freedom. Miller chooses death over dishonour before Gambit can arrest him, leaving Purdey stranded in a minefield.

TX: 7 January 1977

14 HOSTAGE

by Brian Clemens

John Steed (Patrick Macnee) Mike Gambit (Gareth Hunt) Purdey (Joanna Lumley) McKay (William Franklyn) Spelman (Simon Oates) Walters (Michael Culver) Suzy (Anna Palk) Packer (Barry Stanton) Vernon (Richard Ireson) Marvin (George Lane-Cooper)

Directed by Sidney Hayers

Spelman, a double agent, arranges to have Purdey kidnapped and then blackmails Steed into stealing the Full Allied Attack plans. When Steed is implicated in murder, McKay orders Gambit to follow him since it appears that Steed has turned traitor. Gambit's showdown with Steed leaves the younger man smarting, but Steed has all the fun of the fair when he rescues Purdey from a hail of bullets. Gambit arrives in style, on a Ghost Train, and the Avengers mop up the opposition.

TX: 21 October 1977

In *Hostage* Purdey is kidnapped and used as the pawn to get Steed to steel top secret defense plans.

Trap:
*Yasuko Naggazumi
was the wife of Ray
Austin. She also
played Robert
Vaughan's secretary in
The Protectors.
Yasuko plays concert
piano, and speaks
Hungarian, French
and English perfectly.
Her father is a distin-
guished surgeon in
Tokyo. Her daughter,
Mikki, plays with pop
group 'Lush'.*

15 TRAP

by Brian Clemens

John Steed (Patrick Macnee) Mike Gambit (Gareth Hunt) Purdey (Joanna Lumley) Soo Choy (Terry Wood) Arcarti (Ferdy Mayne) Dom Carlos (Robert Rietty) Tansing (Kristopher Kum) Yasko (Yasuko Nagazumi) Marty Brine (Stuart Damon) Murford (Barry Lowe) Miranda (Annegret Easterman) Mahon (Bruce Boa) Williams (Larry Lamb) Girlfriend (Maj Britt)

Directed by Ray Austin

The Avengers team up with the CIA to investigate Soo Choy, a Chinese overlord joining the drugs trade. Choy tricks the Avengers onto a flight into his territory and lays plans to behead his opponents and hand them over to the syndicate. Gambit will be the first to suffer a painful death. But the Chinese soldier who brings Purdey in has a familiar bowler hat, allowing Gambit the opportunity to break free of his bonds. The Avengers arrange a Chinese take-away.

TX: 14 October 1977

16 DEAD MEN ARE DANGEROUS

by Brian Clemens

John Steed (Patrick Macnee) Mike Gambit (Gareth Hunt) Purdey (Joanna Lumley) Mark Crayford (Clive Revill) Perry (Richard Murdoch) Penny (Gabrielle Drake) Hara (Terry Taplin) Dr Culver (Michael Turner) Sandy (Trevor Adams) Headmaster (Roger Avon) Russian Doctor (Gabor Vernon)

Directed by Sidney Hayers

Rest in Peace John Steed! Ten years earlier, Crayford was shot by Steed when trying to defect. Now the traitor has returned to kill the Avenger, before he himself succumbs to the bullet lodged in his heart. Before taking Purdey as hostage, Crayford torments Steed by destroying the agent's valuable art and porcelain collection. The showdown is set at a Victorian folly and Steed is in Crayford's gunsights. But when Gambit races in he finds the traitor dead. Steed's ten-year-old bullet has finally found its target.

TX: 9 September 1977

17 MEDIUM RARE

by Dennis Spooner

John Steed (Patrick Macnee) Mike Gambit (Gareth Hunt) Purdey (Joanna Lumley) Wallace (Jon Finch) Elderly Man (Mervyn Johns) Richards (Jeremy Wilkin) Victoria Stanton (Sue Holderness) Roberts (Neil Hallett) McBain (Maurice O'Connell) Dowager Lady (Diana Churchill) Model Girl (Celia Foxe) Young Man At Seance (Steve Ubels) Freddy Mason (Allen Weston)

Directed by Ray Austin

Wallace uses his team of informers for personal profit, but when he has to kill Mason, he realizes that Steed will now investigate his department. He hires Richards to kill the Avenger, but Stanton, a 'fake' medium discovers that her powers are real and warns Steed. She helps Steed keep ahead of the assassination attempt and the profiteer is arrested. But Stanton is unable to foresee the length of Wallace's sentence.

TX: 23 September 1977

Dead Men Are Dangerous: *In the opinion of Brian Clemens, this is perhaps one of the best episodes ever. It was seldom repeated because an artiste objected to the re-run.*

Medium Rare: *Jon Finch turned down the role of Doyle in* The Professionals. *Mervyn Johns was retired and living in Granville Hall, a home for retired actors – but was persuaded out of retirement to do this part.*

Opposite: Brought down in enemy territory, the Avengers find themselves pursued by Soo Choy's soldiers, in *Trap.*

Angels of Death:
Caroline Munro was famous as the The Lamb's Navy Rum Girl – she also starred in the only movie Brian Clemens directed, Captain Chronos, Vampire Hunter

18 ANGELS OF DEATH

by Terence Feely and Brian Clemens

John Steed (Patrick Macnee) Mike Gambit (Gareth Hunt) Purdey (Joanna Lumley) Manderson (Terence Alexander) Tammy (Caroline Munro) Reresby (Michael Latimer) Pelbright (Richard Gale) Jane (Lindsay Duncan) Wendy (Pamela Stephenson) Coldstream (Dinsdale Landen) Sally Manderson (Melissa Stribling) Simon Carter (Anthony Bailey) Colonel Thompson (Hedger Wallace) Pam (Annette Lynton) Cindy (Moira Foot) Martin (Christopher Driscoll) Mrs Pelbright (Jennie Goossens)

Directed by Ernest Day

A complex case finds Steed visiting a health farm to see if the clinic's prospectus contains all of its advertized services. Forty-seven deaths from natural causes have one common factor – the clinic. Soon Steed finds himself trapped in a maze where agents are interrogated until they die or go mad. Purdey is also a victim. Gambit arrives to play Angel of Mercy, and rescue Steed and Purdey as the walls close in.

TX: 16 September 1977

19 OBSESSION

by Brian Clemens

Obsession:
Quite coincidentally, says Brian Clemens, Martin Shaw and Lewis Collins appear together in this episode. They were later to acquire fame as The Professionals

John Steed (Patrick Macnee) Mike Gambit (Gareth Hunt) Purdey (Joanna Lumley) Larry Doomer (Martin Shaw) General Canvey (Mark Kingston) Commander East (Terence Longdon) Kilner (Lewis Collins) Morgan (Anthony Heaton) Wolach (Tommy Boyle) Controller (Roy Purcell)

Directed by Ernest Day

Purdey believes that she has come to terms with her former relationship with Larry Doomer. Now she meets Doomer again at an aerial display for visiting Arab leaders, and she has second thoughts. Doomer's father was killed by some of the visiting delegation, and he plots revenge. Helped by Kilner and Morgan, he intends to fire a missile at the Houses of Parliament during the Arabs' visit. Purdey tracks down the missile site, but it is a bullet shot by Gambit which finally ends their affair.

TX: 7 October 1977

20 THE LION AND THE UNICORN

by John Goldsmith

John Steed (Patrick Macnee) Mike Gambit (Gareth Hunt) Purdey (Joanna Lumley) Unicorn (Jean Claudio) Leparge (Maurice Marsac) Henri (Raymond Bussieres) Ritter (Jacques Maury) Marco (Raoul Delfosse) Minister (Gerald Sim) Grima (Henri Czarniak) First Bodyguard (Jean-Pierre Bernard) Second Bodyguard (Ludwig Gaum)

Directed by Ray Austin

The Avengers head for France to arrest the Unicorn, a brilliant killer. However, the Unicorn is accidentally killed by his own men threatening a gang war. To prevent trouble, Steed pretends that he has the Unicorn in custody, but the gang retaliates by kidnapping a prince. A swap is arranged, but Steed gets to hear that the prince has been made into a booby trap. Purdey's knowledge of football saves the day.

TX: 30 September 1977

21 K IS FOR KILL – The Tiger Awakes, Part One

by Brian Clemens

John Steed (Patrick Macnee) Mike Gambit (Gareth Hunt) Purdey (Joanna Lumley) Colonel Martin (Pierre Vernier) General Gaspard (Maurice Marsac) Stanislav (Charles Millot) Toy (Paul Emile Deiber) Jeanine Leparge (Christine Delaroche) Kerov (Sacha Pitoeff) Turkov (Maxence Mailfort) Minsky (Frank Oliver) Guard (Guy Mairesse) Secretary (Cyrille Besnard) Soldier (Krishna Clough) Salvation Army Major (Kenneth Watson) Monk (Tony Then) Penrose (Eric Allan) Ivan (Eric Desmaretz) Vassili (Sylvain Clement)

Directed by Yvon Marie Coulais

Back in France once more, Steed becomes involved when young Russian soldiers begin to attack civilian targets that were used in the last war as military locations. As each young soldier dies, he ages. General Gaspard believes that he even recognizes one of the dead soldiers from the Second World War. Mortar shell fire on a chateau would seem to confirm that someone is still fighting the war...

TX: 28 October 1977

Lion & the Unicorn: *Most of the interiors were shot in what had been the home of Monsieur Eiffel, who built the famous tower. Naturally many of the rooms afforded a terrific view of that edifice. Lunch was taken nearby in what had been the home of Sarah Bernhardt.*

22 K IS FOR KILL – Tiger By the Tail, Part Two

by Brian Clemens

John Steed (Patrick Macnee) Mike Gambit (Gareth Hunt) Purdey (Joanna Lumley) Colonel Martin (Pierre Vernier) General Gaspard (Maurice Marsac) Stanislav (Charles Millot) Toy (Paul Emile Deiber) Jeanine Leparge (Christine Delaroche) Kerov (Sacha Pitoeff) Turkov (Maxence Mailfort) Minister (Alberto Simono) Waiter (Jacques Monnet) Minsky (Frank Olivier) Guard (Guy Mairesse) Secretary (Cyrille Besnard)

Directed by Yvon Marie Coulais

Guns and umbrella at the ready, the Avengers prepare to defend Britain from her enemies.

Two hundred and two 'K' agents have been accidentally reactivated by a rogue satellite, and of them one hundred have been taken prisoner or died. Now Steed, Gambit and Purdey must race against time to find the two remaining men. Colonel Stanislav is aware of the two 'K' agents and their missions, but he wants them to succeed in killing the French President and General Gaspard. Their deaths will plunge the world into war, unless the Avengers can stop them.

TX: 4 November 1977

23 COMPLEX

by Dennis Spooner

John Steed (Patrick Macnee) Mike Gambit (Gareth Hunt) Purdey (Joanna Lumley) Baker (Cec Linder) Talbot (Harvey Atkin) Karavitch (Vlasta Vrana) Koschev (Rudy Lipp) Patlenko (Jan Rubes) Cope (Michael Ball) Greenwood (David Nicholls) Miss Cummings (Suzette Couture) Berisford Holt (Gerald Crack)

Directed by Richard Gilbert

The Avengers visit Toronto to discover the identity of X41, codenamed Scapina, a deadly agent. Their contact is killed and then the killer himself commits suicide. Believing that the key to Scapina's identity is locked in the files of a new security building, Purdey enters the establishment's basement control room – a fortress which can only be entered via a bulletproof glass box, controlled by a computer. Too late she realizes that the building itself is Scapina. Faced with extinction, Purdey fires herself up for a downpour. Enter Steed – with umbrella raised!

TX: 11 November 1977

24 THE GLADIATORS

by Brian Clemens

John Steed (Patrick Macnee) Mike Gambit (Gareth Hunt) Purdey (Joanna Lumley) Karl Sminsky (Louis Zorich) Chuck Peters (Neil Vipond) O'Hara (Bill Starr) Tarnokoff (Peter Boretski) Barnoff (Yanci Bukovec) Cresta (Jan Muzynski) Hartley (Michael Donaghue) Huge Man (George Chuvalo) Rogers (Dwayne McLean) Ivan (Patrick Sinclair) Nada (Doug Lennox)

Directed by Claude Fournier

Sminsky uses his KGB skills to form an elite training organization, which threatens to unleash hundreds of skilful killers onto Canadian territory. Steed discovers that Sminsky is in Canada to destroy their computer files on enemy agents, effectively putting back the Canadian security system by twenty years. A trail of dead security men leads the Avengers to their prey and, after closing ranks and closing down the Russian's training camp, Steed and Gambit bowl the gladiators over.

TX: 25 November 1977

25 FORWARD BASE

by Dennis Spooner

John Steed (Patrick Macnee) Mike Gambit (Gareth Hunt) Purdey (Joanna Lumley) Hosking (Jack Creley) Bailey (August Schellenberg) Ranoff (Marilyn Lightstone) Malachev (Nick Nicholls) Halfhide (David Calderisi) Milroy (Maurice Good) Doctor (John Bethune) Glover (Antony Parr) Harper (Les Rubie) Clive (Toivo Pyyko) Czibor (Ara Hovanessiaan) Radio Operator (Richard Moffat)

Directed by Don Thompson

Steed goes fishing on Lake Ontario for a legacy bequeathed by Typhoon Agatha in 1969. A Russian agent dies carrying a MK VI controlboard and his destination appears to have been the lake. Investigating the lake, Purdey is abducted by a group of divers. Beneath the surface, she finds an aquatic community of enemy agents on constant alert for the Third World War. Meanwhile, Steed's fishing expedition nets him the location of the enemy and he tries to bluff them to the surface by bombing them with depth charges. Steed is as surprised as anyone when Purdey rises from the depths – her automatic trained on the enemy.

TX: 18 November 1977

26 EMILY

by Dennis Spooner

John Steed (Patrick Macnee) Mike Gambit (Gareth Hunt) Purdey (Joanna Lumley) Douglas Collings (Les Carlson) Phillips (Richard Davidson) Miss Daly (Jane Mallett) Kalenkov (Peter Torokvei) Mirschtia (Peter Ackroyd) Reddington (Brian Petchey) Arkoff (Don Corbett) First Policeman (Sandy Crawley) Second Policeman (John Kerr) Mechanic (Don Legros) Radio Operator (Jack Duffy) Chicken Farmer (Ed McNamara) Third Policeman (Pat Patterson) Fourth Policeman (Bill Ballentine)

Directed by Don Thompson

The Fox eludes Steed once again, and he has only one clue – the Fox's palmprint on the roof of a car. The car, Emily, is owned by Miss Daly who agrees to let the Avengers take it for forensic examination. The Fox follows them, determined to eradicate the print and his henchmen succeed in destroying the car, but not the evidence. With Collings exposed as a double agent, Steed presents Miss Daly with a new car.

TX: 17 December 1977

Emily had a habit of disappearing from the schedules, more often than not in favour of the replacement *The Gladiators*.

In Memoriam:
The following will be sadly missed –
Albert Fennell
Gordon L.T.Scott
James Hill
Howard Thomas
Malcolm Hulke
Eric Paice
Ian Hendry
Don Chaffey
Dennis Vance
Tony Williamson
Dennis Spooner
Philip Levene
Bill Bain
John Lucarotti
Leslie Norman
Patrick Newell
Quentin Lawrence
Robert Jones
Julian Wintle
Robert Asher
Marie Donaldson
Cliff Owen
Peter Cushing
Robert Fennell

THE MAN WHO KNEW TOO MUCH –
BRIAN CLEMENS NOTES:

• The Rose in the Gun motif was 'inspired' by the late James Hill. He went to Cuba to shoot a documentary and was looking for a title shot. Eventually he found it – a Cuban guard, was happily taking a siesta outside Castro's palace, cradling his rifle. Someone had popped a flower into its muzzle. Irresistible!

• Brian Clemens is distantly related to Samuel Langhorne Clemens – otherwise known as Mark Twain.

• Laurie Johnson had a hit show in the West End: *The Three Musketeers*, with Harry Secombe. He was never able to see the show because he is claustrophobic!

• In his youth, Albert Fennell was a soccer player of professional standard.

• Albert Fennell was one of a long line of Fennells in the British film industry. Dad ran a studio – as did Albert later. Brother Jack was the studio manager at Pinewood. Sister Elsa won Oscars for her dress design and wardrobe. Son Robert was an assistant director and production manager. Various nephews and nieces are still working in the business.
As producer, Albert seldom took credit. He was associated with *Tunes of Glory*, *This Sporting Life* etc.

• In Hollywood, Ray Austin became an expert 'wrangler'. He could, by lengthy training and kindness, make a horse fall in a predetermined spot. He first met Brian Clemens when both were working on ATV's *Ghost Squad*.

• Brian Clemens is reputedly the fastest two-fingered typist in the world. Patrick Macnee used to call him 'the mad typewriter'. Brian still works on a series of old, portable, manual typewriters.

• The late James Hill won the DFC and was shot down twice during the Second World War. The second time he was put into the famous Great Escape Stalag, where he became The Forger (later played in the movie by Donald Pleasance). James was a jazz pianist to Oscar Peterson standards, and composed scores for several of his movies. He won an Oscar for his documentary Guessipina and later directed *Born Free*.

• Robert Fuest is a painter who has had several exhibitions.

• Sidney Hayers was a fighter pilot with a distinguished war record.

• Patrick Macnee now lives in Palm Springs – his neighbours are Bob Hope, Frank Sinatra and ex-President, Gerald Ford. His daughter Jenny was once personal cook to The Rolling Stones.

Patrick was once refused entrance to the famous Raffles Hotel because, although wearing a collar and tie, his immaculate jacket did not quite match his slacks, and so was not a suit. Patrick was in Singapore to collect an award for Best Dressed Man!

Patrick spent almost as much time in Canada as he did in the UK during the Fifties and Sixties. He is now an American citizen. During the war he commanded an MTB and was detailed as part of the search to find the Bismark. Happily he didn't get within sight of it!

His son, Rupert, is a TV producer.

• Ray Austin is now an American citizen too – as well as being an Irish baron! Ray served in the Korean war and was a PT instructor. He directed and produced the latest *Zorro* TV series and many others on US TV.

• *The Avengers* won several awards, amongst them Best Family Show on TV. It won many European awards, and was twice nominated for an Emmy.

• Since 1965 *The Avengers* has been running on TV somewhere in the world every week.

• It is the only British TV series ever to be shown on American network TV at prime time.

• Gareth Hunt is related to actress Martita Hunt. He plays guitar and sings.

SPIN OFFS

SIMON OATES and SUE LLOYD   **1971**

STAGE

IN APRIL 1971, almost two years after *The Avengers* faded from British television screens, the media began carrying reports of a new *Avengers* production – a stage show! John Mather, former head of the William Morris Agency in Europe, had negotiated with ABC/EMI to obtain the rights to transfer the popular television series to the British stage and, to quote Mather's words, 'blast the British theatre into the Seventies'.

Mather acquired the services of one-time *Avengers* writer, Terence Feely, and producer/writer of the television series, Brian Clemens, to produce the script for the show. As Clemens told me; 'I actually wrote the story and Terence did the script... a very funny script. It was a very funny show.'

Speaking to *TV Zone* magazine (Issue 47), Terence Feely said that when they came to write the play, they let their imaginations run free. 'We had a wild story, far wilder than anything that appeared on television, because we said that if we were going to do it for the theatre we had to be further out than anything the audience had seen on television – otherwise why would they come to the theatre?'

'The script is read,' said Mather. 'I now have the difficult task of finding the stage equivalents of the Patrick Macnees, the Honor Blackmans and the Diana Riggs of this world.'

Patrick Macnee *was* approached but, he says: 'I told them that I considered that *The Avengers* was a *television* product – not even a film product, and was essentially for the small screen which was, of course, one of its unique qualities. Slightly slapdash and casual, it wasn't crafted in the way that the Bond films are crafted. Bond films are really the ultimate in that form of mad, slightly callous, superficial, forceful, crazy, wild and funfilled extravaganzas. The stage is a place that should look dazzling and beautiful, but basically remain a place for the exchange of ideas, dialogue and characters – and not whiz, bang, wallop.' None of Macnee's original co-stars was approached.

By early May, Mather announced that Simon Oates (who had previously played a trendy, well-dressed scientist in BBC's *Doomwatch* production, and had appeared in several episodes of *The Avengers*) had been signed to play John Steed.

'I was very dubious about the bowler,' Oates said at the time. 'I had the distinct feeling that if I wore the thing in public, a chap might rush up and kiss me.' (No one did – which isn't sur-

With the Avengers – anything can happen. But not, it seems, a long West End run! Standing: Sue Lloyd and Simon Oates. Seated: Kate O'Mara

prising when you consider that Mr Oates is 6ft 4in and a former Army heavyweight boxing champion.) Brian Clemens told me that he believed that Simon Oates was perfectly cast in the role and injected it with the bonhomie associated with Macnee's performance.

Kate O'Mara (who Clemens suggested for the role of Madame Gerda, the villainess of the piece, after she had been in a play he had written), complained that the vinyl suit she had to wear for the role stopped her from sitting down, and creaked when she walked.

The part of Steed's new female partner in the show, Hannah Wild, took slightly longer to fill. It eventually went to blonde actress, Sue Lloyd.

When told that Hannah would have to fight 10 girls while Simon Oates threw a villain into the orchestra pit, Oates said to the producer: 'Tell you what, why don't I fight the girls and Hannah can have the bloke!'

The following is a slightly edited version of an article printed in the *London Evening News*, 2 July 1971, written by James Green:

NOW THE AVENGERS GO WEST

That sopisticated hokum series, *The Avengers*, which had the right chemistry of in-jokes and send-ups to become a TV cult, is all set to become a stage show. Directed by Leslie Phillips, using a helicopter, a Bentley, and back-projection on stage, it opens in Birmingham shortly and arrives in the West End on 2 August.

Not, however, with Patrick Macnee as agent John Steed. When the TV series ended, unflappable Macnee took his bowler and carnation off to Los Angeles. In his place, Simon Oates, debonair and handsome, will bring his own kind of stiff upper lip to the role of Steed.

They have found him a new girl assistant, Sue Lloyd. Her job is to knock 'em out with looks or hooks. To date, four actresses have enrolled as Steed's Girl Friday. I have been interrogating them all...

Honor Blackman, alias Mrs Cathy Gale, Avenger girl MK1. A 5ft 6in ash-blonde, noted for kinky black leather gear, she says: 'I played Cathy for two years, and the kinky leather thing was an accident. At first I wore culottes but they looked awful. So I changed to tight pants. But when I threw a man over my shoulder they split up the middle, and there I was in front of the camera with my knickers hanging out. So we had another think. I already had leather trousers. Boots to match seemed a good idea, and it all happened from there. As it turned out we were way ahead of fashion. Cathy Gale was super for me and I enjoyed my time tremendously. She was an anthropologist originally, you know, and was brilliant at everything. Judo, guns, fencing... she could do the lot. We made her a widow because the producers didn't want a love interest with Steed, but as a widow she could flirt and there was always a feeling that someday romance might happen.

'I received some very strange fan mail as Cathy, some of it so weird they wouldn't let me see it. Some people seeing me thumping around in black boots with no man in my life, and practically carrying a whip, decided that I must be a lesbian, and I had some extraordinary offers.'

Diana Rigg, alias Mrs Emma Peel, Avenger girl MK2. Chestnut-haired, single, 5ft 9in and statuesque, she specialised in sci-fi space clothes and sexy second-skin catsuits. 'I had two years as the widowed Emma and I've little idea how she differed from Cathy because I never saw Honor in the part and only saw a few of my own shows. My girl was a great character, who used judo, among other things, to look after herself. She was also financially free.

'Escapist stuff, of course, but really pointing towards the future, because women today have become more realistic and self-sufficient. They are moving in the direction of Emma Peel.'

Linda Thorson, alias Miss Tara King, Avenger girl MK3. Canadian, another five-foot-niner, unmarried, brown-haired, her trademark was fluffy, pink feminine dresses.

'I had eighteen months as Tara and she was the only one of Steed's girls to be single. I used a lot of wigs and changed from blonde to brunette and redhead. I decided that she was in love with Steed. Any girl who would risk her life and spend that much time with a man must be in love. I think my interpretation influenced the producers and they let me play it that way. Viewers noticed that she was in love with him and, judging by the letters received, Steed's image changed as a result. He seemed to care, too.

'One problem was that fashions were changing and they didn't know whether to put me in minis or maxis. Usually they settled for midis. Another difference was that Tara didn't go in for karate; but fought more as a girl – scratching, kicking and lashing out with her handbag.

'The part came early in my career, right after drama school. I'm glad I did it.'

Sue Lloyd, alias Hannah Wild, Avenger girl MK4.

Unmarried, 5ft 8in, reddish-gold hair.

'When I walk out as Hannah Wild, it will be my first time on the London stage. I see Hannah as a highly intelligent girl with a certain hardness. Practical, yet with a lot of warmth. She's fond of Steed, but otherwise there is no man in her life. On the action front, her accomplishments will include shootings, half-nelsons, and the occasional karate chop.

'Since Kate O'Mara as the villainess is in black shiny leather, they've given me a crimson leather fighting outfit. I also wear a golden leather suit and dusty pink costume.

'Obviously, having had so little stage experience, the first night will be doubly tense for me. What must help is that I did face a studio audience while making *His and Hers*.

'Some people think I'm a toughie – rather like Hannah Wild – but I don't agree. If I seem hard that's a cover. Because, actually, I'm a big softie. What I've discovered is that the really dangerous girls who need watching are the wide-eyed innocents!'

THE AVENGERS ON STAGE
Reprinted from the official theatre programme

'Is there anyone, watching television over the last 10 years, who has not tuned in and listened to that familiar theme music without a thrill of anticipation? For John Steed is the modern Robin Hood, and we know in advance that he will not come to harm, even though he never made Marion. Every week we have switched on to Steed and his faithful girlfriends – Cathy Gale, Emma Peel, Tara King – those cynical, leather-clad females who could kiss or chop you according to their moods.

Now Steed and his latest Avenger girl – Hannah Wild – are presented on stage in a fast-moving ourageous comedy, with all the panache and gloss of the imperturbable Avengers, but with the sinister and exotic Madame Gerda, leader of the Forces of Evil, and her incredibly wicked gang of beautiful girls.

With the Avengers – anything can happen!'

I count myself fortunate to have been present at the premiere at the Birmingham Theatre, 20 July 1971. For those who missed seeing the show – or those who may have seen it, and would like a memory-jogger – here's a personal review of that first night performance.

John Mather's promise that the production would have 'a very special look' was not just idle boasting. Nothing was overlooked in an effort to provide the audience with 'something different' in British theatre production and, as Mather had promised, to 'blast the theatre into the Seventies'.

The show itself had all the offbeat appeal of the successful

Poster outside The Prince of Wales Theatre.

television series: imaginative sets, 16 in all; colourful trendy costumes; more than 30 dolly birds. It all helped to give the production an up-to-the-minute look.

The ambitious sets, designed by Michael Young, included a full-scale replica of Steed's vintage Bentley (a 10-ply, cardboard cutout, pushed onto the revolving stage by stagehands, who skipped off the platform just before the car came into view – or were supposed to!); Steed's luxurious penthouse apartment; the top secret Operations Room of MI5; the Brain Room of the Master Computer; Madame Gerda's Academy for Young Girls (complete with scantily-clad nymphets); even a helicopter landing!

Simon Oates, immaculate in his trendy suits, shooting jackets and Cuban heel shoes, made an excellent Steed.

Sue Lloyd, in her red, fawn and off-white trouser suits, made a luscious Hannah Wild, and Kate O'Mara, in her black shiny PVC suit and thigh-length boots, completed the trio as the evil (though rather too attractive) Madame Gerda.

The plot concerned the efforts of Madame Gerda, and her gang of young students, to overthrow the governments of the world and infiltrate their spy networks. By using the Giant Computer Brain, Gerda has developed a method of making herself and her girls invisible. Only Steed is immune to her plot and is able to see the girls. This leads Mother to suspect that his prize agent has gone mad, and he has Steed committed to hospital!

Needless to say, Steed escapes, only to find that Gerda and her gang have all the world's security ministers in their power.

After numerous battles with the enemy (the scenes in which Simon Oates ad-libbed his fights with his unseen assailants were hilarious), Steed finally convinces his chief that he is sane, and thwarts Gerda's evil plot. But not before he has been court-martialled (and we learn that his licence to kill has two endorsements on it), stripped of his rank of Major (and stripped of his fountain pen camera – for photographing fountain pens), and undergone various forms of torture (being whipped by a half-naked girl while tied to the Giant Computer Brain, which was a giant phallic symbol).

Yes, the accent *was* on comedy, and Simon Oates and Sue Lloyd shared further funny moments. Steed and Hannah are set upon by three girl robots, and while Hannah tackles two of them, Steed and his assailant fall backwards over a sofa. A few minutes pass, during which time various articles of ladies' underclothing are thrown out, followed by a leg, an arm, etc. Finally, Steed emerges, saying: 'That's the first time I've ever *un*screwed a girl. Still, she's (h)armless now!' Plus Simon Oates telling a dying robot to 'get on with it, man, robots don't have death scenes', and then turning to Sue Lloyd to tell her that 'he died babbling of Green Shields!'

There were also many unscripted funny moments. In one, Miss Lloyd hit her opponent over the head with a plastic bottle, and had to stand and watch while it slipped from her hands and bounced across the stage. And Kate O'Mara fell flat on her bottom when the rope ladder she was climbing collapsed.

However, it was the first night (when things are expected to go wrong), and no one seemed to mind, least of all Simon Oates himself, who finished the show with the lines: 'Why not come back tomorrow night and see how the show really ends?'

The show ran its scheduled two-week trial run in Birmingham, then transferred to the stage of London's Prince of Wales Theatre, for a limited engagement. Very limited, unfortunately, since it only ran for a few weeks. As Sue Lloyd recalled during an appearance in the BBC2 TV programme *On Stage* (15 August 1987), the 'prop' problems continued to plague the production. She told viewers of an amusing incident during that run: 'It was a very ambitious show – perhaps too ambitious. Kate O'Mara was supposed to be invisible at certain times and special effects allowed her to vanish into special props which would part to allow her to step inside. There was this trick sofa, which had been designed to open and swallow her up. Unfortunately, what happened one night was that she pressed the button and nothing happened. After several uneasy moments she gave up trying and tiptoed off the stage. In the next scene, Jeremy Lloyd came on and was supposed to be sitting down for a straightforward tea scene. He no sooner sat down when, wham, the sofa opened up like giant jaws and poor Jeremy disappeared into it. The problem was that he was too big to go all the way inside, and his head and shoulders were left sticking out at a ridiculous angle. Watching this, I couldn't keep my face straight any longer. Everyone was hysterical – none more so than the audience.' (Perhaps the Prince of Wails would have been more appropriate?)

Brian Clemens holds the opinion that the play floundered on money. 'If it had been done like *Phantom of the Opera*, it would have run for ever. It was too ambitious for the time. The critics liked the idea, but not the execution. It should have played out of town for about six months to get it right, iron out the difficulties with the props. There were no difficulties when writing the show. It was just the way they did it. It was some years ago and people didn't do things like that on stage; now they do it all the time. The sets move and things go up and down; it's a whole new art form. It really wasn't the play and it wasn't the cast.'

A couple of interesting 'facts' emerged from the show. Steed was the youngest of a family of eight – the other seven being girls. And he was christened John Wickham Gascoyne Berresford Steed!

Cast

(in order of appearance)

James – Steed's new butler (Julie Neubert) John Steed (Simon Oates) Hannah Wild (Sue Lloyd) Melanie (Wendy Hall) Carruthers – an MI5 agent (Jeremy Lloyd) Parsons – an MI5 agent (Kenton Moore) Chummers – an MI5 agent (Paul McDowell) Maitland – an MI5 agent (John S.Landry) Walters –

the Minister for Internal Security (Anthony Sharp) Madame
Gerda (Kate O'Mara) Victoria – one of Gerda's gang (Lisa
Collings) Prunella – one of Gerda's gang (Gail Grainger)
Wanda – one of Gerda's gang (Gypsie Kemp) Air Marshall
Striker (Derek Tansley) General Bull (John S Landry) Admiral
Drake (Tim Buckland) A Psychiatrist (Derek Tansley) Military
Police Sergeant (Tim Buckland) Military Policeman (Paul
McDowell) Mother, chief of MI5 (John S Landry) Miss Lacey,
his secretary (Mary Llewellin) Nicola – one of Gerda's gang
(Joanna Ross) Jasmine – one of Gerda's gang (Kubi Chaza)
Emma – one of Gerda's gang (Helen Gill) Miranda – one of
Gerda's gang (Heather Kydd) A Nurse (Gail Grainger)
Scarman – Gerda's bodyguard (Kenton Moore) A fantasy maid
(Gail Grainger) A fantasy masochist (Joanna Ross) A fantasy
cricketer (Kubi Chaza) and various dignitaries and wives,
guards, secretaries, passers-by, etc.

The Action of the Play

Act I

Scene I	John Steed's Penthouse Apartment, morning
Scene II	A helicopter, somewhere in Scotland that night
Scene III	Steed's Bentley, that night
Scene IV	Top Secret Operations Room somewhere in Scotland, that night
Scene V	Whitehall Communication Centre, the next day
Scene VI	Steed's apartment, later

Interval

Act II

Scene I	An office at the Ministry of Internal Security, next day
Scene II	Steed's apartment, later that day
Scene III	Conversation à deux
Scene IV	Madame Gerda's Academy for Young Ladies, late afternoon
Scene V	Ministry of Internal Security, that evening
Scene VI	Steed's apartment, minutes later
Scene VII	Ministry of Internal Security, that night
Scene VIII	Brain Room of the Master Computer

PRODUCTION CREDITS

Director: Leslie Phillips
Producer: John Mather
Writers: Terence Feely and Brian Clemens
Designer: Michael Young
Fight Sequences: Tim Condron
Mr Oates Suits by: Bentley, Perry and Whitley
Miss Lloyd's costumes by: Berkely Sutcliffe
Publicity: Fred Hift Associates

RADIO

STEED MK 2

If the idea of *The Avengers* on stage strikes you as somewhat bizarre, what could be more strange than our bowler-hatted hero and his female aide appearing on radio? That is exactly what happened next in *The Avengers'* saga.

A series of *Avengers* radio plays was produced for the South African Broadcasting Company by Sonovision Ltd. The first episode was broadcast in January 1972. Starring Donald Monat as John Steed, and Diane Appleby as Mrs Emma Peel, the stories were freely adapted from the original Patrick Macnee/Diana Rigg television scripts, plus one or two Macnee/Thorson stories (though the characters were always portrayed as Steed and Emma).

Broadcast on Springbok Radio, the episodes provided a nightly cliff-hanging situation for listeners. Each fifteen-minute episode contained one complete story, or a serialised adventure lasting from five to eight episodes.

The tongue-in-cheek feel of the original television series was achieved by the use of a narrator (Hugh Rouse), whose interjections supplied most of the humerous aspects to each story.

The stories were adapted by Tony Jay and Dennis Folbigge, who also directed the series. The show was dreamed up by Johannesburg freelance radio producer David Gooden, who pursued the idea after seeing the series during a visit to Britain. He applied for and bought the radio rights. Oddly enough, the producers of *The Avengers* knew absolutely nothing about this. As Brian Clemens confirms: 'Neither Albert or myself – nor Laurie Johnson (whose title theme music, and several cuts from his *Synthesis* jazz suite, were played during the broadcasts) knew anything about this ,until someone sent us a recording of the show. EMI licenced the radio thing themselves.'

Episodes known to have been broadcast are: *From Venus with Love, The Joker* (complete with a totally new version of the song *Mein Liebling, My Rose*), *Dial a Deadly Number, The Quick, Quick Slow Death, A Sense of History, The Fantasy Game* (Honey For the Prince), *The Super-Secret Cypher Snatch, The Morning After, Who's Who?* and *A Deadly Gift* (The Cybernauts).

Four other scripts were sent to the company, but it is not known if these were ever used. These were: *The Correct Way to Kill, The £50,000 Breakfast, Wish You Were Here* and *Killer.*

'En Garde, Steed': Donald Monat and Dianne Appleby, Steed and Emma in the South African Radio series.

SCREEN

As previously mentioned, the idea to do a big screen cinema version of *The Avengers* was mooted in 1963, when Head of ABC, Howard Thomas, was approached by Louis de Rochemont with the idea of doing a Dimension-150, 70mm film. What hasn't been made clear until now, is why the movie never got made. Brian Clemens supplied the answer. (Incidentally, you'll be reading an awful lot of comments from Brian in this chapter. With the exception of two of the titles discussed here, he has been involved with all of them.) 'The original idea was to take the series onto film – but a one-off film sounded good. The problem was that Howard Thomas never understood what made *The Avengers* tick. Before entering the television business he had been a sports reporter and he was always asking for *The Avengers* to be involved at the Wembley Cup Final – because ABC had lots of footage taken there in their archives. So when I started saying that we ought to put *The Avengers* on film – or make it into a movie – and got Howard Thomas involved and interested, typically he brought in Louis de Rochemont, whose main claim to fame was that he had made the movie *The House on Thirty-Second Street*, a marvellous movie, shot just like a newsreel. I met de Rochemont and he had no idea at all about *The Avengers*! In the past he'd made stuff like *The Naked City* television series, so I thought that he must surely be capable of making *The Avengers* – so I went along with them. I even produced a storyline.'

Despite the fact that discussions were held to mount a film with Patrick Macnee and Diana Rigg, nothing happened on the 'movie' front for several years. Then, in 1978, sometime after completing *The New Avengers*, Brian was approached to write the script for *The Avengers USA*, filmed in 1978. Produced by CBS. TV in America, he wrote two scripts for the projected series, *Escapade* and *Illusion*. Only the former, the pilot story, was filmed. Starring Joanna Lumley lookalike Morgan Fairchild as Suzy, an American-based version of Purdey, and Granville Van Dusen as Joshua, a US-government equivalent of Steed, in between bouts of 'bed-hopping', the agents were selected by 'Oz', a computer, to undertake a case involving security secrets being sold to the highest bidder by a freelance agent. Produced by Quinn Martin/Woodruff Productions, a series failed to materialise – despite the fact that Morgan Fairchild was enamoured by 'Clemens British accent' and was 'looking for an opportunity to work with that other "top English voice", Patrick Macnee!' Clemens told me how this came about. 'Quinn Martin wanted an American-type *Avengers* show. We did the pilot and it just stopped there. Quinn Martin was like Lew Grade. He said "Let's do it!" and it was done.'

One year later, on 2 September 1979, the *Sunday People* newspaper carried the following (edited) article by Tony Purnell:

STEED RIDES AGAIN – THANKS TO YANKS

John Steed, television's most successful secret agent, is all set to make a comeback.

Actor Patrick Macnee has his brolly, bowler and buttonhole booked to make another series of *The New Avengers* early in the New Year.

It looked liked the end for the Old Etonian hero 18 months ago when no one would put up the cash to make more of the costly adventures.

But now the Americans have come to Steed's rescue.

Producer Brian Clemens explained: 'The show is a big hit in the States and the Americans have agreed to provide most of the finance for another 26 episodes. Other companies over here are also interested and it is now just a case of sorting out who puts in what.'

Patrick Macnee, 57, said, 'I have told Brian I will defintely be available. I have a great affection for *The Avengers*.'

In the last series, Patrick and Joanna Lumley were joined by dashing Gareth Hunt as Mike Gambit and it put Steed's nose out of joint. Patrick confessed, 'I was pushed rather into the background and complained. Gambit was taking over a lot of the stuff that Steed would have done. Changes were made and I was quite happy in the end. The three of us are great friends and there is a wonderful bond between us.'

Both Joanna and Gareth said they would be interested in making more New Avengers.

Brian Clemens said: 'It would be nice to have the three together again, but not essential. Avengers girls can come and go, but if Patrick Macnee decided to drop out of the picture, it would signal the end of *The Avengers* for good.'

CBS in America wanted to inject $140,000, and London Weekend TV (influenced no doubt, by the success of their joint venture with Fennell and Clemens' Avengers MK1 Productions – *The Professionals* series) agreed to put up the remaining cash, but that still left about £25,000 short for each episode.

Almost five months to the day of the announcement in the *Sunday People*, the following appeared in the *Daily Mail* of 9 February 1980, written by Paul Donovan:

STEED'S A WANTED MAN

The giant American network CBS, which is showing ITV's *The Avengers* coast-to-coast every Friday night, wants to turn the legendary series into a two-hour feature film.

And the bowler-hatted star Patrick Macnee – who made his first appearance as John Steed 20 years ago – said this week: 'I would be absolutely delighted to do it again.'

Mr Macnee, who spent his 58th birthday on Wednesday flying home to Britain from Bombay after completing a movie, added that he was keeping himself free of commitments after mid-May.

As he spoke, Mr John Redway, the West End agent for both him and Brian Clemens – as well as ex-*Avengers* star Diana Rigg – was in New York discussing the project.

Said Mr Clemens: 'CBS are showing 13 episodes featuring Diana Rigg which were made around 15 years ago. It was way ahead of its time – and still stands up well today.'

Asked whom he would like as his leading lady in a possible film, Patrick Macnee replied, 'I love Diana Rigg, adore Honor Blackman and Linda Thorson and have the greatest admiration for Joanna Lumley. It's a profusion of riches, isn't it?'

The idea never got past the starting gate – although a script was commissioned and written. 'That was written for Gerry Parencio,' Brian Clemens told me. 'It wasn't made because that's the nature of the film business. He ran a cable network and he hired us [Clemens and Dennis Spooner] to write a script.' Called *The First Avengers Movie*, the late Dennis Spooner told my colleague John Peel [co-author of the *Avengers* novel *Too Many Targets*], 'We called it that in the hope that it would then lead to a second movie and so forth.' Joking that the movie had a cast of millions, he added: 'It's the New, New Avengers, because Pat Macnee is in it and Gareth Hunt and there will be two new women.' The script for the movie says it all.

THE FIRST AVENGERS MOVIE

Screenplay by Brian Clemens
Story by Brian Clemens and Dennis Spooner

The action is set firmly on the road to Avengerland in a pre-title teaser that staggers the imagination. A small plane carrying half a dozen passengers, a large white box bearing the legend 'Cream Cakes. Do Not Refrigerate Or Crush', makes a perfect landing at a small airfield runway. Trouble is, when the airfield control men open the planes' door, they are staggered to find that the pilot and his crew, though still dressed, have been picked clean. Each man is now a skeleton!

Cut to titles (written exactly as they appear in the script.) The first bars of the familiar *Avengers*' music bring us through to:

THE MAIN TITLES
Which, for the benefit of the uninitiated, tells us:
(Each title accompanied by a visual of the star in
question)

The FIRST *Avengers* MOVIE
With a cast of thousands!

Headed by PATRICK MACNEE *as* John Steed -
Super-Secret-Security-Agent-Extraordinary
More than ably assisted by GARETH HUNT *as* Gambit
Introducing (Sexy new girl) ..... *as* Carruthers
And starring (American girl) ..... *as* Suzy Stride
With (star cameo role) ..... *as* General Cavalo

The FIRST *Avengers* MOVIE
With a cast of thousands!
FINISH MAIN TITLES *and:*

20. EXT. CARRUTHERS' PLACE. DAY.
As we shall see, it is a tall apartment block, with an
alley at one side, down which we can
see the fire escape.

OPEN ON THE WHEELS OF A CAR *as they skid to a*
stop and INTO CLOSE SHOT. *(The car is an open top*
Morgan.)
PAN *as the door opens, and feet race from the car, up*
some steps – then stop.
WHIP PAN UP TO FIND & HOLD *ON GAMBIT'S*
craggy, handsome features as he pushes
the button of the intercom by front door.

GAMBIT
Carruthers! We're needed!

The intercom crackles with a vague girl's voice – then:
CUT TO:

21. INT. CARRUTHERS' APARTMENT. DAY.
NOTE: We do not have to see anything of the
apartment at this stage. What follows is a carefully
conceived montage to give the new Avengers girl an
entrance. It must be shot as scripted.

ALL SHOTS ARE IN TIGHT CLOSE SHOT, EDITED
TO BECOME ALMOST SUBLIMINAL IMAGES AS:

GIRL'S TORSO. *We arrive a beat after it has been*
discreetly covered by a bra. But then the bra

*disappears around the other side of the torso!
We are left looking at the strap at the back – and
realise we have been looking at a girl's BACK! (Many
women put their bra on back to front, do up the tricky
fastening, then turn it right round).*
CUT TO:

GIRL'S LOINS. *Panty clad – but even as we see this,
so trousers are pulled up to cover panties from sight.*
CUT TO:

GIRL'S HEAD. *A turtle neck sweater envelops it and
is just being pulled down over her head. Her
luxuriant, glossy hair emerges – but before we see the
face that follows:*
CUT TO:

GIRL'S FOOT. *Small and elegant, and just being
thrust into a soft leather pump.*
CUT TO:

CLOSE UP. MOP OF GLOSSY HAIR – *as a brush
pulls it into shape.
Off, we hear buzz of intercom and:*

GAMBIT'S VOICE
Carruthers!

CUT TO:
22. EXT. CARRUTHERS' PLACE. DAY
GAMBIT *leans on buzzer as:*

GAMBIT
It's supposed to be urgent!

CUT TO:
23. INT. CARRUTHERS' PLACE. DAY.
FAVOUR A DRESSING TABLE *(artiste's style with
light bulbs all around the rim).
Reflected in the mirror we see* CARRUTHERS' *slim
and sexy shape, clad in trousers and sweater – but we
do* NOT SEE HER FACE!
*This is because a poster has been stuck on the mirror
at just this position.
It is quite old and tatty – and is a circus poster –
featuring a famous trapeze team:* 'THE INCREDIBLE
CARRUTHERS'. *There is Dad – a strong and
handsome man – Mum – a head shorter, very slim
and beautiful. And Baby (who has grown up into* OUR
Carruthers) – about seven years old, looking as pretty

*and intelligent as the young woman she has grown
into.*

GAMBIT'S VOICE
Carruthers!

Buzzer sounds again.
CARRUTHERS' HANDS *pick up a long, gold neck
chain with a pendant attached. They pause – then the
pendant is juxtaposed to the poster and we see that the
photos either side of the pendant are of her Mother
and Father.*
CUT TO:

24. EXT. CARRUTHERS' PLACE. DAY.
GAMBIT *leans on buzzer again.*

GAMBIT
*Listen – if you're not down
here in 30 seconds ....*

CARRUTHERS' VOICE
(vague – off)
Coming......!

GAMBIT *reacts – steps back – then looks in horror at:*
CUT TO:

ANGLE ONTO FIRE ESCAPE *at side of building.*
LONG SHOT TO CARRUTHERS -
*she is descending the fire escape like the trapeze
artiste she once was – swinging down from one
platform to the next.*
GAMBIT *all but covers his eyes as:*

GAMBIT
(whispers)
I could have made it 50 seconds.

24. *At the last section of the fire escape –*
CARRUTHERS *starts to swing to and fro, preparing
for a last, spectacular leap.*
*Then she swings out – lets go – and as she performs a
somersault in mid-air:*
CUT TO:

GAMBIT: *this time he does close his eyes – we hear
the sound of a squashy landing.*
GAMBIT *opens one eye and looks to where:*
CARRUTHERS *has landed in the passenger seat of*

his open top car.
HOLD ON CARRUTHERS IN CLOSE SHOT. *She smiles.*

Several scenes later, we are presented to the American girl, Suzy Stride.

29. INT. MILLER'S PLACE. DAY.
TIGHT ON STEED *as he enters, pauses for a moment to look at:*
The small and pleasant place – empty.
RESUME STEED – *he starts to move into the body of the place then senses something – suddenly he spins round and:*
CUT TO:

STEED'S EYELINE:
CLOSE SHOT: MUZZLE OF A GUN *pointed at him –*
PAN UP FROM THE GUN
FAIRLY SLOWLY – *across a beautiful bosom – onto the even more beautiful face of* SUZY STRIDE.
She is about 38, American, and quite stunning.
STEED *is quite unfazed – he smiles, doffs his bowler and:*

STEED
How do you do?

But, like lightning, he completes the movement and brings the bowler hand down on the gun, knocking it from SUZY'S *hand!*
SUZY *reacts – half makes a movement to dive for the fallen gun but:*
The tip of STEED'S *umbrella neatly flicks it away across the room.*
SUZY *stares at him – then suddenly crouches in a rather unorthordox karate stance.*
STEED *regards her.*

STEED
Do you know the counter to that?
(she stares)
I do – and it usually ends in tears.

Then, to her amazement, he turns his back on her and strolls away across the room, to lightly bend to pick up the gun and hold it in his hand.

STEED
I sometimes think you Americans

place too much emphasis on
firearms.

SUZY
How did you know I was....?

STEED
(interjects)
Suzy Stride? CIA operative
I've seen your photograph in the files.

SUZY
(stares at him)
The derby – the umbrella....
You must be John Steed.

STEED
Since I sprang from a union between my father,
Joshua Steed, and his wife Araminta – I think I must
be.
(he tosses her gun back, turns to survey the place)
Find anything yet?

SUZY
(defensive)
Who said I was looking?

STEED
You didn't. But we both of us know that Frank Miller
was one of your top agents – now dead, and leaving
a lot of questions ...
(smiles)
which might be more quickly answered if we pooled
our resources...

SUZY
Frank was OUR agent ....

STEED
.... who died in MY country ....

SUZY
We take care of our own.

STEED
I think Frank, wherever he is, might dispute that.

SUZY
(defensive)
He was undercover – out of touch...

STEED
Working on what?

Frank was working on a tip-off of a takeover – perhaps a military coup – but you will have to wait until the movie is made to find out what happens next.

As for the cast of thousands, the clue is in the last card in the final credits: it reads: The Ants .... played by themselves.

Incidentally, Clemens and Spooner had John Cleese in mind for the role of George, a man who lives in an hot-air balloon so that the 'invisible enemy' can't get at him!

And that is where the story ended, until, on 15 March 1985, the *Broadcast* magazine, a weekly media journal, announced that Sarah Lawson, head of the newly formed Taft Entertainment Group, was considering the development of a pilot film for a new series of *The Avengers*, together with Brian Clemens, who would be writing the screenplay. Clemens confirmed that Patrick Macnee would once again be heading the team as John Steed, but the new Mrs Peel was yet uncast. 'We are going back to grass roots, and it will be far more like the old *Avengers* rather than *The New Avengers*,' revealed Clemens. 'Patrick Macnee would like to re-create John Steed as a more avuncular figure,' said Sarah Lawson. 'He will have two younger operatives working for him, one English, one American, partly to provide a hook for viewers, partly to give it a more international flavour.'

As before, however, the project was dependant on a US network pick-up and, though both Lawson and Clemens were optimistic of its chances, the project was given the cold shoulder once again.

Clemens wrote the script. Called *Reincarnation*, the following extracts have been selected to introduce the new characters for, as the series was to be known, *The Avengers – International*.

(Note: asterisks mark the points in the script where I have jumped to another scene)

REINCARNATION

by Brian Clemens

ACT ONE

EXT. ROAD. DAY.
As a Lotus Elan (same colour and model as that once driven by Emma Peel) comes screaming around a bend.

NOTE: *At this stage we do not identify the driver – what we see is an exciting montage as:*

Gloved hand shifts gears.
Feet hit brakes and throttle.
The car wheels bite the tarmac.
The car executes a perfectly controlled slide around a
corner.

WE NOW REVEAL *that the Lotus is racing an*
express train – travelling a parallel road to the rail
road track.
We 'build' this visually exciting sequence – and then
the parallel road turns away from the railroad track
– enters a road running through a pine forest, so that
the train is lost from sight.

EXT. FOREST. DAY.
As the Lotus zooms right up at camera.

EXT. RAILROAD STATION. DAY.
The train slows to a stop – PASSENGERS *alight and*
embark.

EXT. ROAD. DAY.
The Lotus swerves through several other cars as it
speeds along.

EXT. RAILROAD STATION. DAY.
CLOSE ON GUARD *as he blows his whistle and:*
The train starts to move away again.

EXTERIOR. OUTSIDE STATION. DAY.
As the Lotus skids to a stop and:
ANOTHER, LOWER ANGLE *as feet vault out of the*
car and run towards the station.

EXT. RAILROAD STATION. DAY.
The train is really rolling now.
The GUARD *turns and reacts as he sees the tall, slim*
figure of a WOMAN *sprinting the length of the*
platform after the fast receding train. The WOMAN
wears figure-hugging pants and top, and a close
fitting cap. The GUARD *tries to intervene, but she*
evades him and JUST *manages to grab at the last*
carriage of the train, JUST *as it leaves the platform,*
and, as she swings herself aboard, the GUARD *stares*
after her.
INT. TRAIN. DAY.
The WOMAN *stands, her back to us, getting back her*
breath and then tugging off her cap and shaking loose
a long mane of gorgeous hair. THEN *she turns into*
camera and, FOR THE FIRST TIME, *we clearly see*

MRS. PEEL.
SAMANTHA *to her friends, 'SAM' to her intimates,
she is young, beautiful and very sexy in a cool
'Hitchcockian' mould. Her figure is superb, long and
leggy – and her IQ matches up. One of the several
daughters of an English Lord, she is titled in her own
right, but prefers to be plain 'Mrs'. Her mode of dress
can range from the kind of 'fighting/action' outfit she
wears now – through the current mode of mannish
suits, etc., – but when* SHE *wears them you would
never, ever mistake her for a man! The other end of
the scale are the wild, almost punkish clothes that
the young covet, and can identify with. We will come
to know that even if she slipped into an old flour bag,
she would look terrific. She is a natural 'clothes
horse'.
Now, recovered from her drive and sprint, she sets
off along the swaying corridor of the train.*
CUT TO:

ELSEWHERE ON THE TRAIN. *As* MRS PEEL
*comes hurrying along – moving past the doors of
several 'sleepers' now – reaching the right one – she
opens the door and looks in at:*

INT. SLEEPER. DAY.
MRS PEEL'S RESTRICTED EYELINE IN TO
WHERE:
STEED, *wearing the kind of well-cut tweeds a gentle
man takes to a country party, is sitting, looking at the
barrels of a shotgun!*
MRS PEEL *reacts and instantly plunges into the
small confines of the sleeper – she grabs the gun
barrels – pushes them up – and at the same time
slugs a terrific blow at the man holding them. The
man brilliantly fends off the blow – changes it into a
handlock. Which* MRS PEEL *changes into her hand
lock – it is stalemate, and she finds herself looking
into the face of* CHRISTOPHER CAMBRIDGE.

STEED
*That's it! That's enough!
(he insinutes between them – pushing them apart
about six inches)
It's a draw.
He takes the shotgun from both their hands, and then
introduces:*

STEED
Mrs Peel – she's part of our mob.

Christopher Cambridge – he's part of theirs.
From across the Atlantic.

MRS PEEL & CHRIS *regard each other*
appraisingly – she with some caution, he with a
frankness we shall come to know well.

CHRISTOPHER CAMBRIDGE *is a young, tall,*
handsome American. Edgar J would have been proud
of him, because everything about him is discreet for-
mal. With his height and physique, he could hardly
disappear into a crowd, but with his mode of dress,
always a suit or a jacket of expensive but discreet cut
and colour, and almost always a collar and tie – and
his deceptively quiet and self-effacing manner and
most of all, the eye glasses he wears from time to
time - glasses, that, like Clark Kent, seem to heighten
his attraction rather than conceal it – he does man-
age not to be a sore thumb. Which is a distinct advan-
tage if you happen to be the ruthless, efficient, highly-
trained agent that Chris actually is. In a funny sort of
way, he is the American alter ego of the equally
urbane and immaculate John Steed.

MRS PEEL
I'm sorry – when I saw the gun – I thought ....

CHRIS
(interjects)
I thought the same – when you burst in here ....

STEED
I was merely showing him my Purdey

MRS PEEL *reacts to this name!*

STEED
My shotgun. *I'm going on a shoot – grouse, pheasant*
and, I'm assured, a Burgundy of unrivalled
excellence.

(**Author's note:** We skip several pages of the script to learn
more about the new characters.)

INT. RESTAURANT CAR. NIGHT.
CLOSE ON CHAMPAGNE *as it pops – and we* PULL
OUT TO REVEAL STEED *pouring*
wine for MRS PEEL & CHRIS.
THEY *drink, then* CHRIS *studies* MRS PEEL.

CHRIS
'Mrs Peel'? I seem to recall that name......

MRS PEEL
The other *Mrs Peel.*

STEED
My partner – Emma Peel.

MRS PEEL
My mother-in-law.

CHRIS
Mother-in-law?

STEED
*Samantha – or 'Sam', as only I and three other
people are allowed to call her....*

MRS PEEL
Two.

*Steed smiles at her and it is evident there is a special
bond between them.*

STEED
*Two. Sam married Peter Peel – Emma's son –
hence.....*

MRS PEEL
I'm Mrs Peel, the second.

STEED
*Not a blood relative – but in the same unique,
delightful mould.*

CHRIS
*I've never had the pleasure of meeting the
original – but I'll certainly drink to
the second Mrs Peel.*

*(And – later in the script – we find the three characters
installed at 'The Prince of Wales Hotel', with Steed seemingly unconcerned that someone maybe trying to kill
him.)*

MRS PEEL
Steed. John. Please take this seriously.

STEED
No. You can if you wish, but I intend having a good night's sleep – and being out on the moors early tomorrow.

CHRIS
At least let us check it out.

STEED
That's your prerogative.

DURING *this the* DESK CLERK *has handed* STEED *a key, then banging the desk bell.*

DESK CLERK
Where IS that porter? Alfred!?
(He hurries away to look for him)

MRS PEEL
You're a stubborn man

STEED
(shakes head)
Wise. Long in the tooth. Experienced.

MRS PEEL
Stubborn. Pig-headed. And carefree, courageous. And not a bit long in the tooth!

She kisses him lightly on the cheek – and STEED *smiles, moves to ascend the stairs.* MRS PEEL *remains, gazing after him – then* CHRIS *enters shot.*

CHRIS
You like him a lot, eh?
(SHE nods)
Care about him?
(SHE nods)
What will you wear at his funeral?
(That brings her down to earth)

MRS PEEL
Check the place out?
 CHRIS
(Nods)
Check the place out.

MRS PEEL
Someone grey, old and sneezing!

THEY *move away.*

INT. HOTEL. NIGHT,
MRS PEEL & CHRIS *come back from seperate ways
and meet near the desk.*

CHRIS
Anything?

MRS PEEL
(Shakes head)
You?

CHRIS
No.

MRS PEEL
Better check the grounds.

CHRIS
Yes.

MRS PEEL
Don't pull your gun until we get outside.

CHRIS
I don't carry a gun.

MRS PEEL
You don't!?

CHRIS
(Shakes head)
If I get into trouble, I fight with my feet.

MRS PEEL
Karate?

CHRIS
I run!

EXT. ROAD. NIGHT.
As the Lotus comes speeding around a curve.
INT. LOTUS. NIGHT.
MRS PEEL *drives expertly and very fast.* CHRIS
alongside. He pats the car.

CHRIS
For an old one – she really moves fast.

MRS PEEL
It belonged to my mother-in-law.

CHRIS
Emma Peel? I hear she was some lady.

MRS PEEL
Some dame.

(**CHRIS** *reacts*):
That's what she is now: 'Dame Emma Peel'
'For services rendered' It's like a knighthood ...

Now wherever did Brian Clemens get that idea!?

Clemens confirmed that the script was written as a pilot, his intention being to film 13 episodes and, perhaps, introduce further characters as the series progressed. 'It was for Sarah Lawson and Michael Grade, who was then her husband – and a short time before he became first controller at the BBC, then Head of Channel Four. That wasn't made because it all comes down to money. People say "That's a good idea. Let's do it." They scrape together enough money to pay me to write it – then nothing!'

Jerry Weintraub was the next mogul to enter the picture, with his idea to produce 'a multi-million dollar, big-screen version of *The Avengers*, with Mel Gibson as John Steed' – at least, that's what he told me when I was asked to visit his London office on 9 June 1987, a few days after his company had taken control of the original EMI film library from the bankrupt Cannon Group. Adamant that the film would go into production 'within the year, just as soon as I have a script', I took up his offer of working as a consultant on the movie. I was to proof read the draft script, and confirm that it remained faithful to the ethos established by 'the television people' (or not as the case may be). For this I'd receive of course, pro rata payment for my services, together with a credit. 'I trust that your passport is valid, Dave? You'll be needing it. Expect a call when I have a script.' I returned home to give my wife the good news. I received word sometime later that Sam Hamm, of *Batman: The Movie* fame, had prepared a script. I heard nothing from Jerry Weintraub. The movie wasn't made.

Meantime, American television producer, Michael Sloane, had set in motion plans to reuinte Patrick Macnee, Honor Blackman and Linda Thorson, in an Eighties TV version of the show. To be written by Sloane, this would have been called *The Avenging Angel*. (Like everyone else, Sloane couldn't use the original *The Avengers* motif. That was held copyright by, at that time, The Weintraub Entertainment Group.) This time around, the production looked an odds on certainly to go ahead. As Linda Thorson told me at the time: 'It's an episode where Linda

Thorson (Tara King) and Honor Blackman (Cathy Gale) meet at Steed's funeral. They've obviously never met before. They meet and commiserate, and then go off to do something and then.... well, I don't want to tell you the outcome. In fact Michael Sloane would love to do a brand new series of *The Avengers*. He's going to see the people who own the copyright and ask for the rights.' The producer failed to get them. The project died.

Weintraub entered the picture again five years later, when he announced that *The Avengers*' movie would go ahead with a 'new and exciting story from scriptwriter Don McPherson.' Mel Gibson was still being touted for the role of John Steed – despite the fact that the superstar had told his friend Michael Sloane: 'Why would I ever play John Steed? I would never dream of playing him. Patrick Macnee would play him!'

In that same year, David Fincher, director of *Aliens 3*, went on record as saying that he would like to do an *Avengers* movie, in black and white, with actor Charles Dance as the bowler-hatted hero.

Neither project progressed beyond the talking stage.

Things remained quiet for some time. Then, on 21 June 1994, the *New York Daily News* carried the hot newsflash:

AVENGERS' FEATURE HAS STRONG AP-PEEL

While producer Cubby Broccoli is gearing up to start his latest 007 epic with Pierce Brosnan as star, film maker Jerry Weintraub is prepping up his big screen version of *The Avengers* and says,

'It's the woman's role that's the choice role. She'll be the James Bond of the movie.'

Weintraub has sought for 10 years to find a winning way to translate the vintage series, in which Patrick Macnee played Mr Steed and Diana Rigg served as Emma Peel, into a feature film, 'and it's finally worked – it's happening,' says the producer.

'Sure there will be a Mr Steed, but it's the Emma Peel role that will be the standout. It's the best woman's role to come along in 25 years.'

Weintraub says he expects to start his *Avengers* in February – unless he makes a Sylvester Stallone movie first.

He did so, producing the Sylvester Stallone/Sharon Stone movie *The Specialist*.

While promoting the film in Paris, Jerry Weintraub confirmed to the media that *The Avengers* would be his next production. 'The screenplay is written, and it is very, very good. It's *The Avengers*, but younger than you remember them. It is set today, in the Nineties.'

Writing in the *Daily Express*, 13 December 1994, showbiz columnist Jason Solomons reported that: 'Hollywood moguls were given a swift karate kick in the ribs last night over plans to make a film of the cult TV series *The Avengers*.

'The Americans want Sharon Stone to play the leather-clad Emma Peel, with Mel Gibson as suave John Steed.

'But the British team behind the Sixties show think that glamour couple Elizabeth Hurley and Hugh Grant should take the lead roles.

'Brian Clemens, who wrote the original series starring Patrick Macnee and Honor Blackman, threw the first punch last night, 'Americans making *The Avengers* is like making *The Godfather* in Watford,' he said.

'American producer Jerry Weintraub insists that the script retains a uniquely British flavour.'

The script? Somewhere down the line wasn't yours truly offered the opportunity to 'endorse or pan' the screenplay? Yes, I was – so I faxed Jerry Weintraub, not with the intention of reminding him of this (or that I had documentary proof to substantiate his offer), but to ask him to confirm that the movie was – finally – going ahead. If so, might I possibly have a short synposis of the storyline for inclusion in this chapter: this would, after all, give the movie some free advance publicity. No reply was received.

The idea of casting Liz Hurley as Emma Peel was no doubt influenced by the fact that the actress had landed the starring role as a character named Circe in *The Resurrectors* – promoted as being an updated version of *The Avengers* by Fox TV in America, who received worldwide press coverage (including a mention of the prestigous *Entertainment This Week* USA TV show) in 1993.

Miss Hurley, pictured in a black-leather bomber jacket, black velvet hose and black knee-length boots, went on record as saying: 'I'm one of the biggest fans of *The Avengers* and I loved all the female characters they have had over the years. I loved Emma Peel in particular and always wanted to play that kind of role. I'm delighted to have the chance.

'When they asked me what Circe should wear, I knew that it just had to be something sexy. That kind of stuff is just perfect for all the action scenes.' Liz was confident that the new show would be a hit with both American and British viewers.

Fox TV maintained that it was Hurley's dark-haired good looks, in the Emma Peel mould, which clinched her the role in *The Resurrectors*. The company had reworked the old *Avengers'* formula with a hard-edged, modern feel.

'Liz and her two co-stars make up a glamorous trio who kidnap people, fake their deaths, and then force them to carry out missions.'

'It's a pretty wild idea,' said Liz. 'We just grab these people and use them for our own ends.

'The point is that if people think our hostages are dead then nobody can suspect them, which makes them a great cover for our escapades.'

Some months after the news was carried by British newspapers, I spoke to a representitive of Fox TV. Had the movie been made? Yes it had. When could I expect to see it? Soon. Two years later and the movie still hasn't played on TV, in America or anywhere else. Does *The Resurrectors* exist? Your guess is as good as mine. That said, I think Liz Hurley is a far better choice for the role of the new *Avengers* girl than, say, Sharon Stone, or any number of the Hollywood bimbos casually dropped into conversation as possibles for the Weintraub production.

Will *The Avengers* return? To reiterate Mother's last words from *Bizarre*: 'They'll be back ... you can depend on it!' – in which case the producers, be it Brian Clemens or anyone else, will have to deal with Jerry Weintraub, who (somehow or other) walked away with the copyright ownership of the title for all movie rights!

The last word I leave to Patrick Macnee. Asked by Paul Madden if he thought that he would be the last person to play John Steed, he replied: 'I haven't the remotest idea. I understand that someone has written an *Avengers* film, so there will certainly be another Steed. But then you can't have a 70-year old Steed can you? So I probably won't be the last.'

Before anyone accuses me of not doing my homework (particularly readers living overseas, who have already taken me to task for omitting these from my previous books), it is well that I make reference to several *Avengers* 'films' – two of which played on the cinema screen in foreign territories, four of which played – well, therein lies a surprise.

Apparently a company called Insel released a theatrical cinema presentation of *The Avengers* in West Germany. Entitled *Emma Peel: Meiner Tolleste Abenteuer Mit John Steed*, and released on 30 September 1968, this was in fact *The £50,000 Breakfast* and *Murdersville*, edited together, without any linking scenes to make sense of the plot.

One year later, on 1 October 1969, the Odeon Cinema in Lisbon played *Os Vingadores (Adventuras de Steed e Peel)*. This, too, was an unauthorised compilation of the Rigg colour season episodes, *Never, Never Say Die* and *The Superlative Seven*, cleverly put together with a short ' introduction' by Steed (courtesy of a sequence from a short promo film produced by the *Avengers* team for foreign markets). Too compound the crime – and con the cinemagoers – the distribution company, Filmitalus, had the termerity to add an 'intermission' break to the 'movie', and issued front-of-house movie posters which jumbled up the cast – and writing – credits, giving the impression that all the participants were appearing in the same movie – hence the billing: Com. Patrick McGnee, Diana Rigg, Christopher Lee, Jeremy Young, Charlotte Rampling, Donald Sutherland, Philip Levene, Brian

Clemens, c Laur E Johnson (their spelling mistakes). Neither release was authorised by the *Avengers* production company.

Nor was the series of mini-movies filmed in the Sixties starring Diana Rigg as a lady troubleshooter, whose looks and demeanour are not a million miles away from the character she played in *The Avengers*. Indeed, anyone viewing these might be forgiven for believing that the character *is* Emma Peel in all but name.

Produced in Super 8mm film, two titles were filmed: *The Diadem* and *The Minikillers*. Distributed in Germany and France and (unofficially) released in Britain and the USA, both titles were withdrawn shortly afterwards.

The Diadem: This short black and white adventure scores a resounding zero in the entertainment stakes, the film being little more than a series of loosely edited sequences showing Diana (dressed throughout in Emma Peel outfits akin to those worn by her in the black and white series) racing about in search of a package which has been stolen from her home. In the space of 20 minutes, she swims with dolphins (sans any explanation as to why she is doing so), chases the thief through an underground vault (a sequence which occurs in the film *before* she has actually caught the thief stealing the package from her home – the editing is that lax), tangles with a snake, and fights several villains before taking possession of the Diadem, a jewelled tiara.

Filmed in Germany, by someone named Gerard M (no surname or other production credits appear on the film) the movie has a musical theme similar to the tag theme composed by Laurie Johnson for the monochrome *Avengers* episodes, plus sound effects but no dialogue.

Filmed in colour, *The Minikillers* starts sprightly enough, with a *Minikilllers* vocal title theme sung over visuals of a distorted doll's face. Once again, no dialogue accompanies the action, but sound effects and music are dubbed throughout.

Promoted under the banner: 'Charm, humour, bikini, mini-skirt... the bad guys are dumb, but their weapons are sophisticated', the forty-five-minute story is serialised in four parts: *Operation Casta Brava, Heroin, Macabre, Flamenco*.

Part one begins with Diana enjoying a siesta beside the swimming pool of a luxury hotel where one of the guests is selected for death by a gang of killers. The method used is a self-propelled child's doll which, activated by a remote-control device (a gentleman's pocket watch), kills to order by squirting poison into the victim's face. Diana makes off with both the doll and control device, and the chase is on to find the killers.

The action (and clarity of storyline) goes downhill from here, parts two and three being little more than an excuse to place Diana in an exotic setting and have her race around in the briefest of mini-skirts and a bikini, zip around in a sports car (and take the reins of a horse-drawn hearse), but mainly to capitalize on the hand-to-hand fighting techniques she displayed as Emma Peel.

A further nod to *The Avengers* appears in part four. Strapped to a diabolical device which threatens to pulverize our heroine (a prop which wouldn't have been out of place in a grade 'B' episode of *Doctor Who*), Diana gums up the works and uses the remote control device to see off the gang leader.

Filmed in Spain by AccentFilm International Productions, this time the producers believed their product good enough to credit everyone concerned.

Produced by: H G Luckel and D Nettemann
Written by: W V Chmielewski and W W Chmielewski
Directed by: W W Chmielewski
Music Score: Jonny Teupen and H Rettenbacher
Edited by: Erika Vinter

They really shouldn't have bothered. While streets ahead of *The Diadem* in the action stakes, the movie is amateurish in the extreme.

The question remains: when exactly were the films made, and whatever possessed Diana Rigg to appear in this sort of nonsense in the first place? The fighting technique used by the actress in *The Diadem* suggests that this was made during (or shortly after) the production of the monochrome *Avengers* episodes, her hairstyle being another pointer to the period. Evidence suggests that *The Minikillers* was almost certainly made sometime in April 1967, during the two-week break of production on the colour *Avengers* season. The actress has never acknowledged her participation in either film. Indeed it is likely that she harbours the wish to forget that she ever took part in such drivel. But the these things have a habit of crawling out of the past to make you cringe!

FILMING TECHNIQUE

FROM SCRIPT TO SCREEN

MAKING MOVIES is a strange old business. The techniques involved in providing the viewer with an action-packed 50-plus minutes of lucid television entertainment require the specialized talents of a great many people. Nothing could be more specialized than the skill of the scriptwriter, whose flair for putting down the words is restricted by the confines of the shooting schedule, and by the order in which scenes must be filmed to make best advantage of the budget. Then there is the film editor, who has to cut the exposed film into the story that unfolds on screen. The situations, dialogue and on-screen action in a typical *Avengers* episode are plainly visible to see each time we tune in, or watch an episode on video. But the actual order of the *scripting* and *filming* of each episode is light years away from the action as we see it.

Take for instance *Dead Man's Treasure* – which begins with the scene:

Danvers' car comes screeching down a country lane, followed by a second car, with Carl at the wheel. Alongside him sits Alex, gun in hand. Danvers is driving for his life.

We follow the car chase as the cars speed on through the night, shoot past the camera; Danvers glancing over his shoulder then up ahead, a look of terror on his face.

Danvers takes a bend fast, then reacts as he spots a house. There is a gateway – and the gates are open. Danvers swings the wheel, makes a turn, shoots through the open gates and skids to a stop on the driveway.

As Carl's car speeds on through the night, Danvers leans foward, panting heavily. We see that he is mortally wounded. He looks at the passenger seat. On it rests a small box. Danvers stares at it then looks at the house. It is large, silent and unlit. Making a decision, Danvers picks up the box and alights from the car. Carrying this with him, he stumbles towards the house.

Some distance down the road, Carl and Alex realize that their prey has given them the slip. Carl starts the car and makes a fast turn. We see that Danvers has gained access to the house. He moves further into the room, looking for a place to hide the box. His eye rests on a small, red treasure chest standing on a table, surrounded with pamphlets and invitation cards.

Moving closer, he rifles through the papers, opens the chest, places the box he has carried inside it, then picks up an invitation card and starts to write on it.

Carl and Alex, meanwhile, are moving back along the country lane.

Inside the house, Danvers has completed the invitation card and has slipped it into an envelope which he is now addressing. Slipping the envelope amongst the pile of already addressed envelopes on the table, he begins to move towards the exit.

Stumbling back to his car, he eases his way painfully into the driving seat, guns the car's engine, speeds out of the gateway and turns out onto the road – just passing Carl's car as it comes from the other direction.

Carl and Alex react, gaze after Danvers car and give chase.

We return to the house (an exterior view) then pan with the camera to the table on which rests the pile of invitation enelopes. The one addressed by Danvers is prominent. It reads: JOHN STEED ESQ."

Fade in episode title: **DEAD MAN'S TREASURE**

The sequences described cover scenes: 1 through 27 as defined in the script. The actual order of shooting these was:

Scenes 1, 3, 5, 7, 9, 11 to 16, 18, 20, 23, 26 were filmed (on location) on 9 June, 1967, DAY FIVE of the production. Scenes 2, 6, 8, 10, 19, 22, 25, 27 FIVE days later (inclusive of the weekend) on DAY EIGHT, with scenes 4, 17, 21, 24 shot on DAY TWENTY (of a 23-day shoot, the episode running five days over schedule.)

The next scene (as we view it on screen) is defined in the script as scene 28, the interior of Steed's flat, which comes immediately after the episode's title credit and two line teaser: 'Steed rallies round – Emma drives for her life'.

Steed is gazing anxiously out of the window. The door bell sounds, he pauses for a moment then crosses the floor and opens the door.

Emma is leaning against the door jamb, looking provocative, a mysterious glint in her eyes.

They speak and Emma produces two bottles of champagne (at 'three-thirty two in the morning!') Further dialogue passes beween them which tells us that Steed is waiting for Bobby Danvers, a courier, who was bringing top secret documents ('hot stuff') to Steed.

Danvers arrives. He appears normal, then he sways, attempts to grip the wall, falls and leaves a bloody hand-print.

Steed and Emma crouch over him and Danvers confirms that they didn't get the box. 'I hid it...confused the trail.' Danvers' eyes start to flicker. Steed bends closer. 'Hid it....treasure chest. Red treasure chest...' whispers Danvers. His head lolls. He dies.

Steed regards him grimly – then meets Emma's eye.

The sequence in Steed's flat account for scenes 28 through 31 in the script. Some of the action was filmed on DAY NINE (scenes 28, 31) with the remainder of scene 31 being filmed TEN DAYS later, on the studio set.

The on-screen scenes showing Carl and Alex chasing Danvers in their car, and overhearing Danvers' conversation with Steed and Emma (Scenes 29, 30 as scripted) were part-filmed, by the second unit, on DAY NINE and completed eleven days later, on DAY TWENTY.

It is interesting to note that many of the 'exterior' car rally scenes were filmed indoors, on the sound stage, using *front* projection, the first time that this had ever been used on any British television series. Of the 146 scripted rally-driving scenes, over 60 were filmed using this process – the actual exterior location scenes requiring 12 days to film.

Astonishingly enough, only one accident (involving a vehicle rented from Kingsbury Motors) blighted an otherwise clean slate. The E-type Jaguar (648 CYU) was badly damaged when stunt-man Romo Gorrara (doubling for actor Neil McCarthy), skidded on a wet surface and struck a gatepost. (It could have been worse. Director Sidney Hayers, pencilled in the following notation on the front cover of his script: 'Very difficult action scene.)

The stylized closer (Scene 222 in the script) showing Emma getting to grips with Steed's electric razor (and ending up 'droopy' in the process) was, as one might expect, filmed last, on 11 July – six days AFTER the episode had been completed – by director Robert Day, on the set of *The £50,000 Breakfast*. Amazingly, the scene took 87 minutes to get into the can!

Robert Day was also required to film two 'inserts' for the episode ONE MONTH LATER, on 9 and 16 August, whilst directing *The Positive-Negative Man*. That production ran four days over schedule.

It didn't end there. Before tunesmith, Laurie Johnson, could compose and add his music score, the episode had to be post-synched.

Post-synching is the art of replacing dialogue and sounds recorded on location, which might turn out to be unusable due to the extraneous sounds picked up by the soundmen. Indeed, some location scenes are shot mute: for instance the sounds of footsteps in an empty corridor, or someone walking up a gravel drive. These are added later, in the studio, by the sound effects team – more often than not with actors who played no part in the overall production 'doubling' for Macnee and Rigg, who were required to be on another set. (Post-synched footsteps during the Rigg colour season were provided by 'actors' Anne Selwyn and Barry Johnson. Both crossed over to the Thorson episodes.)

The sound of a car engine being started might not be audible in a sequence filmed outside the controlled environment of the studio. The sound of fist fights, gun shots, dialogue between actors recorded outdoors is liable to be wiped out by the tweeting of our feathered friends, or the sound of a jumbo jet flying overhead.

These and dozens more unwanted noises are removed from the soundtrack and re-recorded in crisp clarity by the sound effects team during post-synch recording sessions set aside for when the actors are free to attend.

LOCATIONS

As for the locations themselves, many of them still exist, changed little by the ravages of time. Here's a footprint sketch of some, though by no means all, used by the team during production.

Edgwarebury Hotel, Edgwarebury Lane, Elstree: *You Have Just Been Murdered, The Curious Case of the Countless Clues, Wish You Were Here.*

Caldecote Towers (Rosary Prior High School), Common Road, Elstree Road, Bushey: *The Master Minds, They Keep Killing Steed.*

Mill Hill Golf Club, Barnet Way/A1, nr. Highwood Hill: *The Thirteenth Hole*

Shenley Hall, Rectory Lane, Shenley: *The Bird Who Knew Too Much, Dead Man's Treasure, You'll Catch Your Death.*

Kendal's Hall (Radlett Prep School), Watling Street, Radlett: *What the Butler Saw, From Venus With Love, Stay Tuned, Take-Over.*

Haberdashers' Askes School, Aldenham Road, Elstree: *The Master Minds, The Cybernauts, The Grave-Diggers, Too Many Christmas Trees, Never, Never Say Die, Return of the Cybernauts, Split, Have Guns – Will Haggle, Dead Man's Treasure, Killer, Legacy of Death, Requiem.*

The International University, The Avenue, Bushey: *A Sense of History, Death's Door*

Starveacres, Watford Road, Radlett: *Small Game for Big Hunters, Something Nasty in the Nursery, Have Guns – Will Haggle, Escape In Time.*

Edge Grove School, Oakridge Lane, Aldenham: *Two's A Crowd, What the Butler Saw, The See-Through Man, You'll Catch Your Death.*

Tykes Water Lake, Bridge, Aldenham Park, Elstree: *Two's A Crowd, Silent Dust, Small Game for Big Hunters, The Hidden Tiger, The Hour That Never Was, Honey For the Prince, You Have Just Been Murdered, The Postive-Negative Man, Epic, Look – Stop Me...*, *They Keep Killing Steed*, and the Thorson titles.

Deeves Hall Cottage, Deeves Hall Lane, Near Ridge: *Silent Dust, A Touch of Brimstone, Escape In Time, Dead Man's Treasure, From Venus With Love, The See-Through Man*.

Aldbury Village: *Murdersville*. This is also seen in *Dead Man's Treasure* and *Homicide & Old Lace*

There are, of course, dozens of other locations, all within a short drive of Borehamwood and Pinewood film studios.

Please be advised that several of the places mentioned stand on private property. Discretion is advised when visiting these – unless you join the experts who organise annual Avengers Treasure Hunt outings. Location details taken from:
A Guide To Avengerland by Anthony McKay
Listing over 250 locations used in the filming of *The Avengers* and other classic television series. Copies may be obtained from:

Timescreen Publications
88 Edlington Lane
Warmsworth
Doncaster DN4 9LS
Send SAE for price and details of the Treasure Hunt

SEEING DOUBLE

Who's Who?
Exciting and realistic action sequences punctuated every episode of *The Avengers* and, on countless occasions, the stars would be asked to perform a death-defying leap from a tall building; cling precariously by their fingertips to the bonnet of a fast-moving car; or leap from an out-of-control vehicle. Or did they? Of course not. The production company obviously couldn't take the risk of having their most valuable assets injured by a mistimed stunt. Such an injury could have hospi-talized the star for weeks or – in the case of a broken limb – months, and added thousands of pounds to the production costs in delayed shooting time, not too mention the extremely high insurance premiums. The really dangerous sequences were handled by 'doubles', those unsung heroes of celluloid mayhem who ensure that the impossible appears believable – the stunt artists.

322 The Ultimate Avengers

Look again as Steed leaps to safety over the giant bulldozer blade in *The Fear Merchants*, or at Tara as she faces the motorcycle assailant, before plunging from the clifftop in *All Done With Mirrors*. Perhaps the sight of Mrs Peel diving from the springboard in *The Bird Who Knew Too Much* quickened your pulse? If so, you're in for a surprise. Steed was in fact Rocky Taylor, a professional stuntman who handled the majority of Patrick Macnee's stuntwork throughout all the Rigg episodes – a role he continued in *Invasion of the Earthmen* until the role of Macnee's double was handed over in the Thorson series to Paul Weston.

Cyd Child, a stuntwoman who specialized in 20ft leaps and falls from balconies, joined the series in 1966, when the colour series started (before that stuntman Billy Westley had doubled Diana Rigg). Cyd handled the 'rough stuff' for Diana Rigg, Linda Thorson and, later. Joanna Lumley. It is Cyd that we see doubling for Linda in the clifftop scene. Close scrutiny with your VCR pause button will reveal that it is Cyd who manhandles the prison guard in *The Living Dead*. Cyd was dunked in the water, on the ducking stool, in *Murdersville*, had her *derrière* singed in *From Venus With Love*, and had her head held (playfully) under water, in the river fight scene beneath the bridge, in *You Have Just Been Murdered*. Amazingly, the only injury she received during the entire run was a badly cut wrist during the filming of *Target*.

As for the diving stunt, it was performed by stuntman Peter Elliott! Peter also doubled for Linda Thorson in the trampoline sequence in *Have Guns – Will Haggle*. Wearing Tara's clothes, make-up and a wig, he springvaulted over the perimeter fence – and dislocated his shoulder blade. Oddly enough, two other stuntmen, Gerry Crampton and Frank Henson, doubled for Linda during this episode.

Even those breathtaking fight sequences were never quite what they seemed. These were meticulously planned by stunt arrangers Ray Austin (the Rigg stories and *The New Avengers*), and Joe Dunne (the Thorson stories), who led both the stars and their doubles through endless rehearsals until an on-screen punch-up could look convincing and a punch, supposedly 'connecting' with a villain's jaw, in reality stopped fractions of an inch from its target. Then, by clever camera angles and tight post-production editing, the blow would appear to land on the designated area of the actor's body.

Once again the stunt doubles stood in for the bouts of fisticuffs and rough-and-tumble action, while close-ups of the stars were later edited into the finished scene, leaving the viewer with the impression that they had just witnessed a full-blown encounter between star and on-screen villain. This, of course, is hardly 'cheating', for it is what appears on screen that counts. If a little bit of camera trickery adds extra sophistication to the proceedings, we should perhaps offer our thanks to those 'unseen' heroes who, by their expertise, add that touch of realism to the action.

This is not to say that the stars sat on the sidelines while the stunt people did everything. The principals could – and did – handle the weekly bouts of fisticuffs and less risky feats (thereby incurring, sometimes, minor scratches and injuries). Indeed, every single one of them wouldn't have had it any other way. The stars did as many of the stunts as they could, as they were allowed to do, but always within the confines of safety limits that avoided any undesired consequences.

DREAM MACHINES

Cars have always played a major part in *The Avengers*. It is difficult to conjure up a mental image of Steed and his colleagues, without recalling their personal mode of transport. Emma's powder blue Lotus, the red and maroon speedsters of Tara, the gleaming Vanden Plas lines of Steed's vintage machines or, indeed, the all-British roadsters of *The New Avengers*. All have become part of the *Avengers* folklore.

It was not always the case, however, and though Steed did drive a vintage car in the Blackman episode *Don't Look Behind You* (at the instigation of Brian Clemens, who thought it was time for a change), in the videotaped series he was more likely to be found behind the wheel of everyday saloon cars. His colleague, of course, professed a preference for two wheels (the powerful Triumph motorcycle of *Build a Better Mousetrap*), but she, too, could sometimes be viewed driving a sleek white MG sports. In each case, it is more likely that the cars had been driven into camera range by the sweat and muscle of studio technicians. The series was, after all, taped live in the studio, and exterior scenes were kept to the minimum.

The cars really came into their own when, with the advent of the first filmed series in 1964, the creative brains behind the show decided to develop the idea of the stars driving a mode of transport that would, to some degree, reflect their own character traits. The ploy worked, and the cars quickly became a trademark of the series.

The following guide provides a starting point for the car-conscious amongst you to define who drove what:

THE AVENGERS

Model	Reg. No:	
EMMA PEEL		
Powder blue Lotus Elan S2	HNK 999C	B/w episodes
Powder blue Lotus Elan S2	SJH 4999D	Colour episodes*1

Model	Reg. No:	
JOHN STEED		
Bugatti	GK3295	Blackman series
Vauxhall Saloon	XT 2273	Some Rigg b/w episodes
Bentley 1926 4 litre	UW 4887	Rigg b/w episodes/Rigg col episode
1928 Green Label Bentley	YK 6871	Rigg colour episodes *2
1926 Green Speed Six Bentley	RX 6180	Rigg colour episodes *3
1927 Green 4 litre Bentley	YT 3942	Rigg colour & Thorson episodes *4
1927 Yellow Rolls-Royce Silver Ghost	KK 4976	Thorson episodes
1928 Yellow Rolls-Royce Phantom One	UU 3864	Thorson episodes *5
Olive Green Land Rover	WX 887	Rigg colour episodes
Trojan Bubble Car	CMU 574A	Thorson episode
Maroon AC Cobra	LPH 800D	Thorson episode *6
TARA KING		
Maroon AC Cobra	LPH 800D	Thorson episodes *6
Red Lotus Europa	PPW999F	Thorson episodes
Mini Moke	LYP 794D	Thorson episode
MOTHER		
Silver grey Rolls-Royce	3KHM	Thorson episode
Brown Mini Moke	THX77F	Thorson episode
LADY DIANA FORBES-BLAKENEY		
White MGB	BMW 300G	Thorson

THE NEW AVENGERS

Model	Reg. No:	
JOHN STEED		
Olive green 5.3 litre Jaguar Coupé	NVK 60P	Season one episodes *7
Yellow Rover saloon	WOC 229P	Some Season two episodes
Green Range Rover	TXC 922J	Some episodes
MIKE GAMBIT		
Red Jaguar XJS	MLR 875P	Season one and two episodes
White Range Rover	LOK 537P	Some episodes
PURDEY		
Yellow MGB Drophead Sports	MOC 232P	Season one episodes
Yellow Triumph TR7	OGW 562R	Some Season two episodes
Yellow/Black Honda motorcycle	LLC 950P	One episode
Red Honda motorcycle	OLR 471P	One episode

The stars also drove various locally-hired vehicles in the episodes made on location in France and Canada.

* 1 The car has come up for auction several times, most recently in America. Reserve price $12,500.

* 2 This model was featured regularly in the 1967 situation comedy series *George and the Dragon*, starring Sid James and Peggy Mount.

* 3 In January 1984 this changed hands for £49,500

* 4 This machine made a 'guest' appearance in part one of *The New Avengers* story: *K is for Kill*

* 5 Familiar? It should be. This model frequently turned up in both *The Benny Hill Show* and *The Morecambe and Wise* programmes. The vehicle was bought in 1983 by Yorkshireman Peter Yates, for 'a few thousand'. Today it is maroon and white – and worth £100,000. (Peter won't part with it. It earns him £100 a time at weddings.)

* 6 Steed in a low-slung sports car?

* 7 Interlink new and used car specialists, based in West Bromwich, West Midlands, bought this model in 1985. (The car was offered for sale to the Avengers fan-club.) It is not known whether they still have it.

THE MERCHANDISE

A full guide to The Avengers and The New Avengers spin-offs

One aspect of promoting *The Avengers*/*The New Avengers* both here and abroad was merchandise. The copyright owners earned royalties from the sales of *Avenger* tie-ins, and during the Sixties and Seventies numerous items of related merchandise were licenced. Books, annuals, comic strips, toys, records were distributed. Aficionados of the series had a field day, and quickly found they needed bottomless pockets to keep in step with the items on sale.

The following pages include items of merchandise known to have been issued, and others that, though licences were issued, never appeared on the retailers' shelves. The most comprehensive guide ever published, it will prove invaluable to the serious collector.

Obviously, with the passage of time, many of the items listed have disappeared or lie dormant and forgotten in someone's attic. However, many items do still exist, and a morning spent searching the shelves of your local junk shop or a visit to a nearby jumble or car boot sale can unearth many a priceless item. Happy hunting.

THE AVENGERS

Toys and Related Items

The Corgi Gift Set, No 40 is perhaps the best known – and certainly the most collectable. Issued in 1966 at a list price of 16/9d (86p), this contained replicas of Steed's 1929 Bentley and Emma's Lotus Elan.

The Corgi catalogue (complete with reproductions of the two cars plus two small photographs of Steed and Emma) described the package in this way: 'Steed's Bentley has been impeccably reproduced right down to the bonnet strap, spiked wheels and detailed interior, with a figure of John Steed at the wheel. Emma's Lotus Elan, complete with standing figure of Emma, is fitted with opening bonnet, plated engine and detailed interior with tip-up seat and suspension.' The company actually went so far as to include three (some say seven) moulded plastic umbrellas in the Bentley's boot. The complete set was offered in an attractive presentation box which had artwork of Steed and Emma on both top and sides, and when opened it revealed a display unit with further artwork.

For some inexplicable reason, Corgi insisted on issuing the set with a red (not racing green) Bentley and a white (not powder blue) Lotus, so a word of caution to anyone being offered a set containing a green Bentley: Corgi issued a further Bentley model in 1967, and though this contained a bowler-hatted figure behind the wheel, it is in fact based on another television series, *The World of Bertie Wooster*, and has no connection with *The Avengers*. Corgi never issued Gift Set number 40 with a green Bentley (despite what that dealer tells you!)

Incidentally, though Corgi re-licensed the *Avengers* set in 1969 and planned to issue a further model, no further set was issued, because the dies for the model were destroyed in a fire at the factory. The *TV Times*, 11-17 June 1994, ran a readers' competition to win Genuine Sixties Avengers Memorabilia. Pick of the prizes on offer was the Corgi Gift Set, No 40, valued (said the magazine) at around £1,500! Someone goofed. The current dealer price for this, in very good, to better condition, wavers at £320-£350. A mint set would cost you £400.

The Avengers Jigsaw Puzzles, a set of four, was manufactured by Thomas, Hope and Sankey exclusively for Woolworths in 1966. Each puzzle consisted of 340 pieces and was 11in x 17in in size.

The pictures for this highly prized and much sought-after set were based on episodes from the Rigg b/w filmed series. Each contained an artist-depicted scene on both puzzle and box.

The first in the series, No Escape, shows Steed and a rather obese gentleman fighting as they hang precariously out of an open railway carriage door. Mrs Peel, viewed in the next compartment, holds her assailant in an armlock. Although we're given to believe that this is based on *The Grave-Diggers* episode, Mrs Peel's attire (a white beret, complete with 'target' motif) points to it being based on *The Town of No Return* – though no such scene appeared in either story!

The second puzzle, Castle De'ath, features a scene from that episode, and depicts Steed, complete with kilt and sword, warding off an attack by a fearsome-looking bearded opponent, as he decends a stone staircase. Emma is featured in the background, pinning a second surly villain to the floor with her foot while threatening him with a gun.

Puzzle number three, In the Basement, contains a scene based on *Death at Bargain Prices*. It shows a leather-clad Mrs Peel throwing a villain down a flight of stairs in the basement sports department of a large store. Her colleague stands over a second prostrate figure, brolly at the ready.

The final puzzle, Archery Practice, depicts Steed pinned to a large outdoor archery target by an arrow, while a leather-clad Emma holds the archer at gunpoint. The scene is from *The Master Minds*.

The Avengers Steed Swordstick was issued in 1966, by Lone Star Products. Complete with a secret Aqua-Moisturiser, Patrick Macnee is pictured on the packaging in typical Steed fencing stance, this time with the swordstick superimposed over his usual umbrella. The stick consisted of a brown, tubular, plastic sheath and a grey plastic sword with a yellow handle. The stick squirted water by pushing the toy sword back into its sheath. Alternatively, the toy could be used to fire corks. This is extremely rare. The same company also issued a miniature Steed bowler hat to complement Swordstick.

The Avengers Shooting Game is high on collectors' wants lists. It is possibly the rarest item of all, so rare, in fact, that I've been unable to verify the date of manufacture, believed to be 1967 – or anything beyond the fact that the board game was manufactured by Merit Toys, had a splendid artwork cover showing Steed driving the Bentley towards a gang of villains who are attempting to make their getaway in a Jaguar saloon car, as a gun-tottin' Emma fires at them. Hit the Dynamite and 'Up' Goes the Car is the legend depicted on the packaging. The game came with a pistol, two safety darts and a stand-up target.

The Emma Peel Doll. Manufactured in Hong Kong, this was a 10in high plastic doll, dressed in black leather trousers, a short black woollen coat, white rollneck sweater and black plastic boots. The outfit was loosely based on the PVC airman's outfit worn by Diana Rigg in *A Surfeit of H$_2$0*, and came complete with a plastic base and a metal strut to support the doll when standing. The figure is shown holding a gun in her right hand.

Other outfits are contained in the package. These range from two further pairs of trousers, one of brown plastic, the second in dark grey wool; a white plastic tunic; a black plastic coat; a white plastic rainer (trimmed in black); and a pair of black mittens. The box has a clear plastic front and is yellow with the words, THE AVENGERS, in large print. When the doll is removed from the packaging, a black silhouette of Steed is depicted on the rear of the cardboard backing. Beware of imitations! You may be offered a 1993 rehash, the contents of which differ slightly from the one described. The giveaway signs are: Emma is dressed in a black mini-jacket and skirt (the sleeves, hem and pockets of which are trimmed in white) and the box packaging carries the words The AVENGERS 'NEW' EMMA PEEL DOLL, including 3 sets of new

clothes. Clever – but an unauthorized fake! Quite recently, a trader in a well-known London street market, had fifteen of these for sale – and unloaded the lot, at £300 each.

ABC TV licensed a range of **Avengers Wristwatches** (as worn by Diana Rigg in some episodes) to a company called Old England. Slightly smaller than a gentleman's fob watch, these are bulky but attractive. Several models in various colours and straps were manufactured: The Avenger (original selling price £4.19.6d (£4.95p) and The Great Avenger, at £5.10s (£5.50p). The latter is the more rare of the two. If you are tempted to buy one of these, ensure that it bears the maker's name – or has the words, *The Avengers*, on its dial.

Other items licensed, but never issued, were: **A Shooting Round Corners Gun** (Chad Valley 1965); **The Avengers Stationery Pad;** A set of **View Them Yourself** film slides; an **Avengers Bagatelle;** and an **Emma Peel Dress Cut-Out Book.**

Books

Between the years 1963 and 1969, twelve paperback books were issued to tie in with the television transmissions. Each of these contained an original story based upon the characters from the series, several of which are highly sought-after. The 12 titles are listed below in their chronological order of publication.

The Avengers, by Douglas Enefer (Consul Books 1963).

This features the only story to star Steed and Mrs Catherine Gale.

Deadline, by Patrick Macnee & Peter Leslie (Hodder and Stoughton, 1965). **Dead Duck,** by Patrick Macnee & Peter Leslie (Hodder and Stoughton, 1965). Both these titles, starring Steed and Mrs Peel, are regarded as the best in the series. Both are rare. However, both titles were repackaged in 1994, by Titan Books. Complete with terrific new photo covers of Macnee and Rigg, these are a must for your collection.

Nine other paperbacks, officially listed as The Avengers Series, were issued between 1967 and 1969. The first four titles were published jointly in both the UK and USA, while the remaing five titles were distributed in the American market only.

Avengers 1: The Floating Game
Avengers 2: The Laugh Was On Lazarus
Avengers 3: The Passing of Gloria Munday
Avengers 4: Heil Harris

All four titles by John Garforth (UK: Panther Books. USA: Berkley Medallion Books, 1967). Stories feature Steed and Mrs Peel. Book 4 is the rarest.

Avengers 5: The Afrit Affair
Avengers 6: The Drowned Queen
Avengers 7: The Gold Bomb

All three titles by Keith Laumer (Berkley Medallion Books, 1968). Book 5 features Steed and Mrs Peel; books 6 and 7, Steed and Tara King. Book 7 is the one sought-after.

Avengers 8: The Magnetic Man
Avengers 9: Moon Express

Both titles by Norman Daniels (Berkley Medallion Books, 1968 & 1969). Book 8 features Steed and Tara King, book 9 Steed and Emma Peel. Both titles are rare.

An interesting point is that, although Berkley Medallion

Books issued only nine titles, they did in fact license twelve.

Four titles were issued in France, and four in Germany (**Der Wreckers**). These are the same as the UK Panther Book titles.

The Television Crimebusters Omnibus (edited by Peter Haining, Orion Books, 1994), contains the short story, What's A Ghoul Like You Doing In A Place Like This?, by Peter Leslie. Featuring Steed and Tara King, the origin is credited to Atlas Publications, and is believed to have been written for one of the company's Avengers annuals.

An oddity in the book line was a short (112-page) novel, **The Saga of Happy Valley**, that appeared in Australia in 1980. Written and published privately by down under Avengers' buff, Geoff Barlow, this featured a brand new adventure for Steed and Emma – or Steade and Peale, as the author dubbed them, for obvious reasons. A cracking good read, this is infinitely better than most of the previous titles. (Incidentally, EMI, then *The Avengers* copyright owner, graciously allowed this book to continue to be sold privately – provided no further copies were published after the initial print run. Anyone thinking of publishing, or using in any way, the characters or situations from the series is well advised to think again!) This is obviously much sought-after by Avengers aficionados. Count yourself lucky if you own a copy.

An interesting read is **John Steed – An Authorised Biography: Volume One: 'Jealous in Honour'**, by Tim Heald. Published in the UK in 1977 by Weidenfield and Nicolson, this is the fictional biography of Steed's early years up to his first encounter with Mrs Catherine Gale. Intended as the first in a series, no further books were published.

Too Many Targets, by John Peel and Dave Rogers (St Martin's Press, 1993) captures the atmosphere and timelessness of the TV series in a well-crafted all-new adventure featuring Steed, Mrs Gale, Emma Peel, Tara King – and Dr David Keel, in a multi-layered, fantasy story, interwoven with fast action and witty dialogue. The book is out of print and a must-have on collectors' lists.

Recognized as the best pictorial book to be published, is **Chapeau Melon et Bottes de Cuir** (Huitiéme 8 Art, France, 1990), by Alain Carrazé and Jen-Luc Putheaud. This 208-page, coffee-table book is crammed full of b/w and colour pictures and is simply stunning to look at (and read – provided you can understand the French text). A British edition was mooted, but failed to appear.

Finally, though not really an *Avengers* item, worthy of note is **Honor Blackman's Book of Self Defence** (Andre Deutsch, 1965). The introduction is written by Honor herself and contains references to *The Avengers* and the 'Cathy Gale' connection. The book contains over 130 b/w photographs of Honor Blackman being put through a catalogue of judo routines by Black Belt judo experts, Joe and Doug Robinson.

Comic Annuals/ Comics

The first comic annual to feature *The Avengers* was published in 1962. Entitled **TV Crimebusters** (TV Productions), this is of particular interest to aficionados of the series as it is the only publication to feature a story starring the original team of John Steed and Dr David Keel. The 7-page story, in comic-strip format, with additional picture stills from the 1961 series, is called The Drug Peddler.

The first (of three) official *Avengers* annuals was published in 1967. Titled **The Avengers** (Souvenir Press/Atlas Publications), this contains 92 pages of picture strips and text stories plus various features on the series starring Steed with Mrs Peel. The cover depicts Steed and Emma battling it out with two uniformed (Russian?) soldiers on a castle staircase. Also included are 40 b/w and colour photographs. Incidentally, I have come across references to a second Steed and Emma Peel annual. However, this was not a commercial (officially authorized) publication and was 'bootlegged' by a group of American fans and circulated from their homes in 1966. Oddly enough, correspondence points to several copies of the book being offered for sale in South Africa!

A second annual, and the first to feature Steed and Tara King, was published by Souvenir Press/Atlas in 1968. This continues the format of the first annual and runs to 80 pages. The cover features a head-and-shoulders shot of Steed wearing a dark suit, while sporting the proverbial bowler, brolly and red carnation, plus two inset drawings of Tara. The annual includes 25 b/w and colour photographs.

A third (and final) annual was distributed in 1969, again featuring Steed and Tara, and contains the same number of pages as the previous year's annual. The cover depicts a full-face shot of Steed while Tara, gun at the ready, peers over his left shoulder, with 25 b/w and colour pictures accompanying the text.

Various TV-related annuals carry features on the series. The best of these are: **Television Show Book** (Purnell, 1965), with a four-page feature on the Macnee/Blackman series; **Television Stars** (Purnell, 1965), containing four pages of text and pictures from the Macnee/Rigg series; **Girl Television & Film Annual** (Odhams Press, 1964), with features on Patrick Macnee and Honor Blackman, and the following year's annual which contained a feature on Diana Rigg.

The Avengers also featured in numerous comic strip publications. The most notable of these were the stories printed in full colour in **Diana – The Popular Paper For Girls** (DC Thompson, 1966/67). Beginning with number 198 (3 December, 1966), and lasting for 26 weeks (the duration of a full-blown *Avengers* TV transmission run?) each edition contained a two-page strip which pitted Steed and Mrs Peel against such unlikely adversaries. These included: Madame Zingara, a woman with a method of weaving trance-inducing material

which, when woven into a dress for Mrs Peel, turns Steed's colleague into a Zombie; modern-day Vikings loose on the streets of London; Black Heart and her deadly band of midgets; a power-crazed scientist bent on destroying England by the use of 'brainwashed' pet animals; The Mad Hatter, where Steed's bowler becomes a deadly weapon; and the Sinister Six, a group of six notorious criminals who band together to destroy the Avengers.

The artwork on this strip was of the highest quality throughout and is a pure delight, making the complete set a highly and eagerly sought-after item.

The Avengers No 1 (Thorpe & Porter, 1966). Published in the UK, this 68-page, all b/w comic contained four picture strips: The Mohocks, The K Stands for Killers, No Jury – No Justice and Deadly Efficient. All four stories featured Steed and Mrs Peel. While the artwork leaves a lot to be desired, this is nevertheless a highly collectable item.

John Steed – Emma Peel (Gold Key Comics, 1968). This one-shot, 32-page, all-colour comic was published in the USA and contained two picture stories, The Roman Invasion and The Mirage Maker. The artwork was appalling, but the comic is now a collector's piece. Although the cover title is as above, the comic was actually registered as **The Avengers No 1,** but this was changed to avoid conflict with the Marvel Comics Group superhero title of that name.

TV Comic (Polystyle) regularly featured an *Avengers* comic strip between 1965 and 1971. The first *Avengers* story appeared in issue number 720 (2 October 1965), and strips featuring Steed and Mrs Peel (and later Tara King) continued to appear on a semi-regular basis until the early Seventies. Avengers strips and text stories also appeared in the company's TV Comic annuals.

Further adventures of *The Avengers* (Steed, Emma and Tara) could also be found in the London Express Features syndicated comic strip (reprinted in colour as *Mit Schirm, Charme und Melone*, in Germany). Scandinavia and Germany also had its own comic strip, *Der Wreckers*. Strangely, a 34-page b/w comic of this name, containing the last two stories from the Thorpe & Porter, *The Avengers* No 1 title, turned up as issue number 2106 of the Scandinavian **TV Classics** comic!

In 1990, British publisher, Acme Press, joined forces with the American-based Eclipse Comic Group to publish **Steed and Mrs Peel,** a three-part, prestige mini-series comic based upon the series. Issue One featured part one of The Golden Game, by writer Grant Morrison. Illustrated by Ian Gibson, this featured Steed, Mrs Peel and Tara King. Two further issues went on sale, with books two and three carrying a second story, Deadly Rainbow, by Anne Caulfield, a TV script-writer. A solo adventure for Emma Peel (though Steed did put in an appearance), this kicked-off where the events that unfolded in the TV episode *The Forget-Me-Knot* left off. Incidentally, collectors should watch the page numbering on these – the Morrison story spans three issues, with the page-numbering of each comic picking up where it left off in the previous issue.

Magazines

Meet The Avengers Star Special No 15 (World Distributors, 1963) is notable for being one of two official TV tie-ins published to promote the series, the other being the *TV Times* Souvenir Extra. (See *The New Avengers* merchandise listing.) Advertised as 'an exciting behind-the-scenes visit with the stars of ABC's Top TV Show', this contains 44 pages of text features on the Patrick Macnee/Honor Blackman series. Also included are interviews with both the stars and production staff, and the publication is rounded off with over 30 b/w photographs. Rare, this now appears on dealers' lists at an incredible £35!

   The TV Times Diana Rigg Spectacular, an 8-page all-colour magazine supplement, was published by the UK television journal *TV Times* in 1969. The supplement, devoted entirely to the *Avengers* star, contained features including 'Diana Rigg on Stage', and the centre-page spread pulled out into a giant size 'bioscope' of Diana's career, with 18 b/w and colour photographs. Note: This was a supplement, stapled into the centre pages of the programme magazine. It could not be purchased on its own.

   Probably the rarest (and most certainly the oddest) magazine supplement was the 12-page **Man's Journal** dossier, which told the story of Steed's search for Miss Chlorophyll Jade! Presented free with the April 1966 edition of *Woman's Journal*, and issued as a promotional gimmick to promote the new Terylene gentleman's fashion line being sold by the Austin Reed high street chain of gentle-man's outfitters, this b/w and colour rarity gave us The Strange Case of the Green Girl, an opus from the pen of Brian Clemens, in which Steed, played in pictures throughout by Patrick Macnee, found himself hot on the trail of Mr X, an Arch-Fiend and Diabolical Mastermind, to boot, who had captured the delectable Miss Jade (played in pictures by actress Jane Birkin).

   Well worth looking for is **Tele Seriés.** Published in France, this 80-page full colour magazine, devoted entirely to coverage of popular television, is the best of its kind. Issues 11 and 12 (January and February 1988) carried 14 pages on *Chapeau Melon et Bottes de Cuir*.

   Recently arrived from France, is the 'Special Tribute to The Avengers' edition of *Generation Séries* magazine (January 1995), the first of a two-issue overview of *The Avengers*' history. Its publisher/editor, Christophe Petit, has a long association with the series and it is seldom that the magazine does not contain a feature on *The Avengers*. This edition is stunning, with 26 of its 54 pages being given over to Chapeau Melon et Bottes de Cuir (both *The Avengers* and *The New Avengers*). The magazine (written in French, of course) is well worth tracking down. A masterpiece!

Records / Compact Discs

High on the aficionados 'most wanted' memorabilia list are records containing the original (or cover) versions of The Avengers' Theme, or incidental music pertaining to the programme. The majority of these have long since been deleted, but some can still be found in specialist record shops (if you have the money) or car boot sales (if you wish to keep control of your purse strings). Known to have been issued are:

Singles / Extended-Play

The Avengers Theme by Johnny Dankworth & His Orchestra (Columbia DB 4695, 1961). The original theme from the Hendry/Macnee series.

The Avengers by Johnny Dankworth & His Orchestra (Fontana TF 442, 1963). A revised arrangement of the above, used for the Macnee/Blackman series.

The Avengers Theme by The Laurie Johnson Orchestra (Pye 7N 17015, 1965). Theme to the Macnee/Rigg series.

TV Themes (Pye NEP 24244 – Extended Play – 1966). Featuring Laurie Johnson's original *Avengers* Theme.

The Avengers Theme by The Joe Loss Orchestra (HMV/POP 1500, 1966). A cover version of Laurie Johnson's Theme.

TV Themes – A Gift from Pascall Murray (MCPS ATV 1 (B) – Extended Play, 1969). A special 'give-away' containing Laurie Johnson's original Avengers theme.

Kinky Boots by Patrick Macnee /Honor Blackman (Decca F11843, 1964).

Kinky Boots by Patrick Macnee/Honor Blackman (Cherry Red, Cherry 62, 1983). A re-issue of the above.

Kinky Boots by Patrick Macnee/Honor Blackman (Cherry Red, 12 Cherry 62, 1963). A 'Maxi-single' extended-play version of the above, in picture sleeve. This also contains a cover version of Laurie Johnson's Avengers Theme by The Roland Shaw Orchestra.

TV Thriller Themes (Fontana TFE 17389 – Extended Play). Contains a cover version of Johnny Dankworth's Avengers theme, played by Johnny Gregory and His Orchestra.

TV Themes 1966 (PYE NEP 24244 – Extended Play, 1966). Contains Laurie Johnson's original Avengers theme.

Albums / CD's

Channel Thrill: The ITV Thriller Themes (Fontana TFL 5170, 1961). Contains cover version of Johnny Dankworth's Avengers theme.

The Avengers and Other TV Themes (Wing WL1087,

1961). Contains cover version of Johnny Dankworth's Avengers theme by the Johnny Gregory Orchestra.

The Big New Sound Strikes Back Again by The Laurie Johnson Orchestra (Pye 7N 17015, 1966).Contains The Shake.

Themes For Secret Agents by The Roland Shaw Orchestra (Decca PFS 4094, 1966). Contains cover version of Laurie Johnson's Avengers theme.

Underworld (Mercury MCL 20089, 1966). Contains cover version of the Laurie Johnson Avengers theme by The Reg Guest Syndicate.

The Avengers Theme & Other TV Music (Hanna Barbara, 1966). Contains Laurie Johnson's original Avengers theme.

The Avengers & Other Favourites by The Laurie Johnson Orchestra (Marble Arch. MAL 695, 1967). Contains Laurie Johnson's original Avengers theme.

Time For TV by the Brian Fahey Orchestra (Studio Two/EMI Two 175, 1969). Contains cover version of the Laurie Johnson Avengers theme.

Theme From The Avengers by Jerry Murats Harmonicats (Hallmark, CHM 269, 1969). Contains cover version of the Laurie Johnson Avengers theme.

Themes And... by The Laurie Johnson Orchestra (MGM/CS 8104, 1969). Contains the original 'Tara King' Avengers theme, plus the 'Tag Theme' music.

The Phase 4 World of Thrillers (Decca SPA 160, 1971). A compilation album containing a cover version of Laurie Johnson's Avengers theme, by Roland Shaw and His Orchestra.

50 Popular TV Themes by The Bruce Baxter Orchestra (Pickwick 50/DA 315, 1977). A double album containing a cover version of Laurie Johnson's Avengers theme.

Music From The Avengers/The New Avengers & The Professionals by The Laurie Johnson Orchestra (UK: Unicorn-Kanchana PRM 7009, USA: Starlog/Varese Sarabande ASV 95003, 1980). Contains the title theme music and selected incidental music from all three series. These are not the original dubs, but newly-recorded using the original orchestrations. Although the tracks were the same in both the UK and the USA, the packaging wasn't. The UK sleeve opened up into a double sleeve and contained numerous photographs from the series. The USA version was issued in a single sleeve which portrayed Steed and Emma framed by a pair of scales.

Original TV Hits of the Sixties (Filmtrax/Moment 105, 1986). Advertised as 'The Collectors Edition', this contained the Brian Fahey Orchestra cover version from the album 'Time For TV.'

Themes From the Sixties (Waterloo Sunset/Pinnacle WSR 002, 1988). Contains a cover version of the Laurie Johnson Avengers theme.

Television's Greatest Hits: Volume 1 (Silva Screen PRT

Film 034D, 1988). A compilation album featuring Laurie Johnson's Avengers theme.

ITV Themes (Pickwick International SHM 3248, 1988). Includes cover version medley of Laurie Johnson's The Avengers/The New Avengers themes.

Les Disques Des Seriés Americaines Volume 1 (Lai Loi. TV1 NR 30, 1988). A French compilation album, this includes a cover version of Laurie Johnson's Avengers theme, Chapeau Melon et Bottes de Cuir.

Curtain Up (Columbia 335X1572, 1989). Includes the original Johnny Dankworth Avengers theme.

Power Themes 90 (FAB/Telstar STAR 2430, 1990). Includes a 'rap' version of the Laurie Johnson Avengers theme.

The Rose & The Gun by The Laurie Johnson Orchestra (Fly CD 103, 1992). Contains newly-recorded versions of The Avengers theme/The Tag theme/The New Avengers theme.

An A to Z of British TV Themes from the Sixties to the Seventies (Castle Communications PLAY 004, 1992). Includes Laurie Johnson's original Avengers theme.

Top TV Themes (Castle Communications MACCD 152, 1993). Includes Avengers track from above CD.

Themes From the Sixties: Volume 1 (Future Legend FLEG 1T 1994). Includes cover version of Laurie Johnson's Avengers theme, played by pop group The Grave.

Miscellaneous

During the mid-Seventies, Derann Film Services, a Midland-based home movie supplier, issued four *Avengers* titles for the home movie market. The episodes were supplied on Super 8mm film and were: *From Venus With Love, The Living Dead, The Positive-Negative Man* and *Return of the Cybernauts*. Each was issued in two formats: a full version on 3x400ft reels, and a 15-minute 'condensed' version on 1x400ft reel. These prints were later discontinued, prior to which they were offered at a 'bargain' price of £54.95p per 45-minute episode! To achieve the 45 minute length, Derann edited out the opening and closing 'teaser' scenes, plus linking material (scenes showing the Avengers driving around in motor cars). The result was most acceptable, and copies of the Super 8mm titles are still being offered for sale at Movie/TV fairs.

A company called Centaur Films also produced a full-length print of *The £50,000 Breakfast* for the home movie market. The six-reel colour print was mastered in optical sound.

Another home movie company, Mountain/Fox Films, licensed six episodes from EMI, for distribution to world markets, on 16mm film. These were: *Epic, Mission – Highly Improbable, The Fear Merchants, The See-Through Man, Return of the Cybernauts* and *The Hidden Tiger*. Several of the films were hired by Film Society's.

Not so widely known is that the production company (EMI)

licensed six Super-8mm titles to an American company, Sunstand, which supplied many of the world's airlines with in-flight movies. The titles, issued between 1975 and 1978, were: *From Venus With Love*, *Escape In Time*, *The Bird Who Knew Too Much*, *Something Nasty in the Nursery*, *The Positive-Negative Man* and *The £50,000 Breakfast*. They were then supplied to the French airlines UTA and Air Afrique, and were issued in dual-language prints so that passengers could listen to the original soundtrack or a French overdub. The contract expired in 1980, and all six prints were returned to the EMI film library.

Special merchandising rights were given to various other outlets. In 1969, Spillers, the pet food producers, ran a con-sumer-orientated promotion campaign using *The Avengers* to promote their product. The campaign took the form of a detec-tive/spy story of approximately 1,000 words, and entrants were invited to select certain salient points in the story that related to the questions asked on the entry form. Over 6 million packs were distributed to major outlets throughout the UK.

In Germany, two major fashion houses joined forces to pro-mote a man-made fabric fashion tie-up. The companies, ICI and Povel, went on to issue both men's and women's wear in the 'new' material, with photographs and live-action film of *The Avengers* stars being used to promote the products. Also in Germany, an enterprising West German umbrella manufactur-er, Knirps, used Patrick Macnee's Steed character to promote his new line. Macnee filmed two commercials for the company and specially selected *Avengers* film clips were used to round of the campaign.

Never slow to realize that related merchandise was a money-earner (the production company earned royalties on all items sold), the copyright owners held their own fashion display in the Palm Beach Casino basement room of the Mayfair Hotel, London, in 1967. The event, devised and coordinated by Edser Southey Design Associates, and produced by Michael Edser, promoted over 54 'Avengers-wear '67' items. Among these were the entire range of 'Emmapeelers' (the catsuits worn by Diana Rigg), and a range of Pierre Cardin 'Steed' attire, plus shoes, hats, gloves, scarves and bags, etc. Of particular interest to *Avengers* buffs was the special entrance 'ticket' supplied for the occasion. This took the form of a standard-size playing card and featured a joint image of Mrs Peel and Steed as the Queen and Knave of Hearts. The guests were treated to a screening of a colour Rigg episode.

Diana Rigg promoted Lux Toilet Soap, and could be seen in a TV commercial promoting the *Daily Mail* Ideal Home Exhibition, and later, in magazines promoting SWAPL (South West African Persian Lamb). Linda Thorson did several TV and magazine promotions for Belle Color hair dye.

In 1987, Patrick Macnee and Linda Thorson could be seen on TV in two seperate 20-second commercials for Amplex Roll-on Deodorant and Fresh Breath Capsules (courtesy of film clips from the series).

An item that would have been high on the list of collectables was a set of two separate bubble-gum cards, containing over 144 colour pictures (one set each for Patrick/Diana, Patrick/Linda). These were licenced by a West German sweets and confectionery company in 1970 to tie-in with the German television screening. The cards were never issued. Aficionados would have to wait two decades before cards of any description were made available. In 1993, a company called Cornerstone Communications Inc., in Tucson, Arizona, negotiated an exclusive agreement with *The Avengers* copyright owner for the production of trading cards based upon the show. The first set (of three) were made up of 81 b/w images. Set number two, distributed some months later, provided the buyer with 99 colour images. Set three should be available by the autumn of 1995. Keep your eyes peeled for these. They are stunning!

Among the merchandise licences considered, but turned down were: a daily comic strip feature in the *Daily Mirror* or *The Sun* and the subsequent publication of the strip in paperback format; *Avengers* Painting Books; 'Emma Peel' shoes and boots; *Avengers* wallets, badges, a fob-watch; a line of *Avengers* men's toiletries; a toy replica of Emma's cosmetic gun with lipstick in barrel and compact in butt (never used in the series); and a mascot for Emma Peel! (The mind boggles at what this may have produced).

THE NEW AVENGERS

Toys and Related Items

Like its predecessor, The New Avengers production company cast its eyes towards the merchandise market and numerous items of interest were issued.

Dinky Toys issued two die-cast model cars in 1977. The first of these, Model Number 112 **Purdey's TR7,** was, according to The Dinky Toy Price Guide (Ernest Benn, 1982), issued in two different formats. One has silver flashes on its doors and sides, with black and silver trim and white interior. A black letter 'P' is on the bonnet and the model was designed with a double 'V' in silver in front of it. The second version is green, and has the word Purdey on the bonnet. The latter is the more valuable of the two.

The second model, Number 113 **Steed's Special Leyland Jaguar,** was advertised in the Dinky catalogue, but was never officially issued – though several prototype models were illegally 'spirited out' of the factory, and are therefore extremely rare and worth a great deal of money. In medium green (greenish blue or medium blue, dependent on which brochure one read), with gold stripes along each side, the model is also known to exist with a long orange flash, silver wheels and bumpers, with fawn or white interior and a figure of 'Steed' at the wheel.

A similiar fate – that of being stolen from the factory – befell Model Number 307 **The New Avengers Gift Set.** Never, officially, released, this contains Purdey's TR7 and Steed's Special Leyland Jaguar, plus a novel fly-off assailant.

Also highly collectable are two Revell Plastic Assembly Kits: **Purdey's TR7** and **Gambit's XJS** (1979) The first, issued in yellow and black plastic, and the second, in red and black, were both 1.25 scale models and came in easy-to-assemble kit form and nicely produced boxes with photos of Purdey and Gambit on each.

The New Avengers also spawned some children's board games. Of these, **The New Avengers Mission Kit** (Thomas Salter, 1976) is the most collectable. This was issued with a photograph of the trio on the packaging and contains a plastic gun and silencer, plastic gun holster, hand grenade, magnifying glass and an assortment of cardboard cutouts that in turn make up a 'code-breaker'. Also included are a paper passport and a plastic camera that actually works, or so the manufacturers would have us believe.

'An exciting game for 2-4 players' is the way **The New Avengers Board Game** (Denys Fisher, 1977) was described. The game came complete with a nicely-designed board, a bowler-hat and umbrella spinner, plus playing models. In fact the game is as 'exciting' as Ludo!

There was also **The New Avengers Shooting game** (Denys Fisher, 1976). Intended for 2-4 players, this came in an attractive presentation box and contained cardboard cutout figures, a clockwork-operated window set in a cardboard cutout house. The object of the game (no doubt inspired by the story, *Target*) was to shoot the cardboard silhouettes out of the window – provided the enclosed pellet-guns worked!

Arrow Games issued a set of four **New Avengers Jigsaw Puzzles** in 1976. Each measured 24x18 in and came complete with artiste-depicted box and puzzle designs. The first of these has Steed, Gambit and Purdey in the foreground against an action backcloth of a car, helicopter and burning buildings. The second puzzle portrays Purdey giving an action-packed, high-legged kick to Kane's half-man-half-Cybernaut, while Steed and Gambit race in through the door. Puzzle three displays a montage of the New Avengers and a Cybernaut, and the final puzzle depicts Steed leaving Number 10 Downing Street. The quality and artwork on these is superior in every way to *The Avengers* puzzles.

Female fans could also buy the official **Purdey Doll,** though I suspect that many males were also tempted to do so. Manufactured by Deny Fisher, the figure was dressed in the purple leotard worn by Purdey in *The Eagle's Nest* , and came complete with tights, shoes and a patterned skirt. Further out-

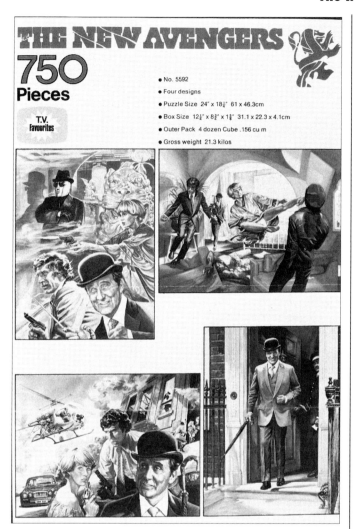

THE NEW AVENGERS
750 Pieces

T.V. Favourites

- No. 5592
- Four designs
- Puzzle Size 24″ x 18¼″ 61 x 46.3cm
- Box Size 12¼″ x 8¾″ x 1⅝″ 31.1 x 22.3 x 4.1cm
- Outer Pack 4 dozen Cube .156 cu m
- Gross weight 21.3 kilos

fits were advertised of the back of the packge. In the words of the manufacturer 'Purdey leads such an exciting life, she needs an outfit for every occasion' (including, it seems, two leotard fighting outfits: the one Joanna Lumley wore in Episode One being green, the one pictured on the packaging being lilac – which appears again on the picture sleeve of the record single). For special dates, there was a cream trouser suit with chiffon trimmings; for glamorous occasions, an elegant black dress with fur stole or a green halter-neck dress with long flowing scarf; for relaxing, a rust-coloured jump-suit or red catsuit; and for practical wear, a suede trouser suit with matching hat and scarf. The 10in doll was sealed in a plastic bubble on a cardboard display board, which had an artist-depicted drawing of Joanna Lumley on the cover. I can't resist saying it... Absolutely Fabulous!

Advertised in the Denys Fisher '77 catalogue but never shipped to the shops were the **Steed and Gambit Figurines.**

Described as 'Action Figures', the brochure described how the 'dolls' might have looked had they been produced. 'Dressed in his smart suit. bowler hat and carrying that famous umbrella, the John Steed 11in figure is ready for action-packed adventures! With a pull of the handle, Steed's umbrella converts amazingly to a sword stick and, by operating a button in his back, Steed's fencing arm lunges forward with a cut and thrust action! The features of the handsome Avenger, Gambit, are captured in this super 11in action figure! Ready for adventure, Gambit is dressed in his white karate suit, which displays his black belt to the full! By pressing a button in Gambit's back he will deliver a 'stunning' karate chop!'

Books

Six *New Avengers* paperbacks were issued during the course of the series and, unlike the *Avengers* books which contained original stories based on the characters, these were novelisations based on episodes from the series. All six titles were published by Futura Books and, in chronological order, were:

House of Cards by Peter Cave, 1976
The Eagle's Nest by John Carter, 1976
To Catch a Rat by Walter Harris, 1976
Fighting Men by Justin Cartwright, 1977
The Cybernauts by Peter Cave, 1977
Hostage by Peter Cave, 1977

The last three titles were not published in the USA, so these are marginally more valuable for collectors. All six titles were published in hardback as lending library editions.

Patrick Macnee's delightful and hilarious autobiography, **Blind in One Ear** (Harrap 1988), is well worth searching out. Written by Patrick himself (with the 'ghostly' hand of Marie Cameron) the *Avengers* star talks intimately about a life that has been every bit as extraordinary – if not more so – than any of his roles in the theatre, film or television. *The Avengers* is, of course, well-documented. A delight!

Comic annuals / Comics

In 1977, Brown and Watson published the first of two New Avengers annuals. This contained 64 pages of text and picture stories, and came complete with over 40 b/w and colour photographs. The second annual was issued the following year and followed the same format, but this time contained over 50 photographs.

For the completist, the same company produced a 1979 annual called **TV Detectives,** which contained two pages on Gambit and Purdey.

Only one *New Avengers* comic album was issued. Printed in France under the title **Chapeau Melon et Bottes de Cuir** (Collection TeleJunior Number 1, 1977) this contained six strips in full colour. The artwork was second to none, although, oddly,

Steed was shown throughout driving his Bentley! The strips were: La Malédiction de Falkenstein, Le Repairé de l'Aigle (two original stories, the latter 'lifting' an idea used in *The Eagle's Nest*), Le Secret de Midas *(The Midas Touch)* La Morte Avcutes Ailes (an original story, with 'guest star' Boris Karloff), Le Cybernauts *(The Last of the Cybernauts...?)*, and Le Mysterie de la Planéte 'Y' *(Tale of the Big Why)*.

Two stories from the above, Le Cybernauts and Le Secret de Midas, were reprinted in a bumper 164 comic published in Belgium as **Tele Junior, Almanach 1980.** The Le Repairé de

l'Aigle story was presented as a giveaway in the April (Number 14) edition of the French magazine **Tele Series**, mentioned earlier.

Records / Compact Discs

Only two official singles were released between 1976 and 1980. The first of these, **The New Avengers Theme** by The Laurie Johnson Orchestra (EMI 2562, 1976), was a faithful version of The New Avengers theme, and carried an extra bonus in the form of A Flavour of The New Avengers on side two. This gave dialogue extracts from a couple of the episodes, complete with car-chase in stereo. Another plus factor was that the single was issued in a full-colour picture sleeve.

It was 1980 before a second 'official' version of The New Avengers theme was issued. Once again in a picture sleeve, this contained **The New Avengers Main Title Theme,** played by the London Studio Orchestra, conducted by Laurie Johnson, and is a single version of the same track from The Avengers/The New Avengers/The Professionals Unicorn-Kanchana album mentioned earlier.

Albums / CD's

20 Great TV Themes (K-Tel NE972, 1977). Contains a cover version of The New Avengers theme by Sounds Orchestral.
TV Music Spectacular (Reader's Digest GTVS 8B, 1978). This 8-record boxed set contains a cover version of The New Avengers theme by Bert Rhodes and the London Festival Orchestra.
Out of the Box (Polydor POSP 356, 1981). Contains a cover version of The New Avengers Theme.
Screen Action (EMI/Music For Pleasure, MFP 6017, 1988). Contains a cover version of The New Avengers theme.

Miscellaneous

The New Avengers featured in a rub-down set of transfers issued by Letraset (1977), which depicts a scene from the episode *Last of the Cybernauts...?* and depicts Kane and his metal-headed sidekicks in pursuit of Steed, Gambit and Purdey.

Scandecor Posters issued a giant-size poster of the trio in 1976, but this quickly sold out and is now very rare.

Fashionwise, very little was offered during the series' lifespan, though Joanna Lumley did model for a window-display mannequin, and her face could be seen in dozens of women's fashion-house windows. Joanna also promoted Carlo Dini's Purdey Fragrance, 'a perfume in the timeless French tradition, made for the exciting woman of today! Purdey for the woman with style'. and Slumberland bed linen. Patrick Macnee endorsed Right Guard body deodorant (on the London Underground, with actor Ken Parry as a passenger), Colibri Lighter products, Timex Watches (for French TV), and could be seen in two tele-

vision commercials for Vauxhall motors, in which he was seen pushing two Vauxhall saloons into a garage forecourt (lifesize cardboard cutouts of Steed were pictured in the background). In America, he promoted the New Ford Granada ('My latest love is American, the new Ford Granada...') .

Fan Magazines

I have already covered commercial magazines, but one aspect of published merchandise that certainly warrants your attention is Fanzines – which perhaps I should define. As the name implies, the word was coined by collectors to describe a fan magazine – a publication produced privately by fans for fans. These can range from the raw quality of the 'homegrown' product (once produced on a duplicating machine – today, with computer technology and laser printers sometimes making them indistinguishable from quality magazines), to the professional (and expensive) typeset product. In some cases, the magazines are produced by over-zealous fans who, though their intentions are sincere, often cannot afford the finance needed and these magazines seldom survive beyond two or three editions – some also fail to take into account the fact that all television series are held in copyright, and the copyright ownership people should be contacted before taking steps to publish the mag.

Strange though it may appear, despite its enormous popularity, *The Avengers* never received as much fanzine coverage as other popular shows of the period. However, one or two magazines were issued during (and after) its lifespan. Of these a few are worthy of mention. Probably the best of those issued during the Sixties was one produced in the USA called **En Garde.** This was produced quarterly and ran to eight issues, with numbers 1 – 6 being of particular interest. A well-produced American magazine was **The Avengers/Patrick Macnee**

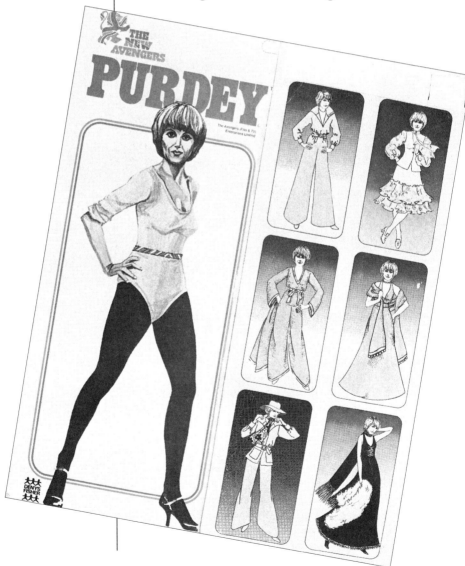

Fan Newsletter. Produced between 1978 and 1980 by young enthusiast Heather Firth, each issue came complete with rare photographs, excellent artwork, interviews and interesting text features on *The Avengers* stars.

A second fan-sheet appeared during that period, the **Gareth Hunt/Joanna Lumley Avengers Fan Club.** Published by US enthusiast Cindy Phares, this ran to over 14 editions and contained lots of interesting *Avengers* features, again with well-reproduced photos of the stars and first-class artwork.

Very collectable (provided you lay your hands on an original copy, this is extremely rare) is the **ACTA Official Dossier on The New Avengers.** Produced by a group of fans living in South Africa, who called themselves ACTA (Agents Countering The Avengers), fans of the show could be excused for believing that this was an 'authorised' magazine. Copyrighted to The Avengers (Film & TV) Enterprises Ltd. 1977, it had absolutely nothing to do with the production company. It was nevertheless beautifully turned out and contained dozens of previously unseen photographs from the series, the format being produced in the form of a 'Top Secret' spy dossier.

The first UK fan club, **The Avengers Appreciation Society,** produced two fanzines based on the show (June/Autumn 1981). The first was an 8-page introductory issue, while the second contained 20 pages of features and photographs. The society also issued a picture magazine which folded out into a poster.

In April 1982, David Caruba, hooked on the series when it first begin syndication in the USA during the early Seventies, issued the first photocopied edition of **With Umbrella, Charm and Bowler** (being the American translation of the German name for *The Avengers* – 'Mit Schirm, Charme und Melone.'), and this was followed four months later by issue number 2. By January 1983 the magazine had proved so popular that the publication was continued in a professionally printed newspaper format, and the fanzine increased in both circulation and page count. However, even quality fanzines reach a crisis point, and WUCB was soon to fold – to be replaced by David Caruba's commercially produced magazine for secret agent connoisseurs, **Top Secret.** Though not strictly an *Avengers* magazine, this nevertheless contained some of the best *Avengers* features ever published – with Issue number 1 carrying a stunning full-cover picture of Steed and Mrs Peel. Sadly both magazines are no longer in print.

Then came **On Target – The Avengers.** Making its debut in 1983, this rapidly progressed from an A5 duplicated fanzine, into a slicker, 28 (or more) page A4 format which ran to 10 issues, plus a 56-page Look Who's Talking: All-Interview Special, until, in 1987, the title was changed to **Stay Tuned.** Three issues later, this too ran into financial difficulties and bit the dust, the final edition being published in December that year – leaving the fan quarter sans any Avengers fanzine, until an enterprising group of fans based in Leeds produced **Bizarre** (The Avengers Mark One Appreciation Club) magazine. Containing an overview of *The Avengers/The New Avengers* and *The Professionals* (the series produced by the original *Avengers* team) the fanzine ran to three issues of well-researched features before closing its doors.

You can't keep a good thing down. **Stay Tuned** returned a few months later, in a new, spectacular, commercially-printed format. Six issues later the magazine is still going strong and the magazine's future appears to be assured, with fans from all over the world mailing in subscriptions. Edited and produced by yours truly, details of membership can be obtained from the following address. UK: please enclose a SAE envelope; overseas enquiries: send an International Reply Coupon.

Stay Tuned
PO Box 45
BILSTON
West Midlands
WV14 8DJ